D1552472

AMERICAN
TRADE
AND POWER
IN THE 1960s

AMERICAN TRADE AND POWER IN THE 1960s

Thomas W. Zeiler

Columbia University Press

New York

382.0973
Z46a

Columbia University Press
New York   Oxford

Copyright © 1992 Columbia University Press

All rights reserved

Library of Congress Cataloging-in-Publication Data

Zeiler, Thomas W.
American trade and power in the 1960's / Thomas W. Zeiler.
p.   cm.
Includes bibliographical references and index.
ISBN 0-231-07930-3 (alk. paper)
1. United States—Commercial policy—History—20th century.
2. United States—Commerce—History—20th century.   3. United
States—Economic conditions—1961–1971.   I. Title.
HF1455.Z45   1992
382'.0973'009046—dc20   92-15550
                                                                    CIP

Casebound editions of Columbia University Press books
are Smyth-sewn and printed on permanent and durable acid-free paper.

Printed in the United States of America
c 10 9 8 7 6 5 4 3 2 1

An earlier version of chapter 3, "The Politics of Protection in Textiles and Lumber,"
appeared as "Free-Trade Politics and Diplomacy: John F. Kennedy and Textiles,"
Diplomatic History 11 (1987):127–142. Reprinted by permission of Scholarly Resources, Inc. An earlier version of chapter 4, "Political Trade-Offs in Oil and Tariffs,"
appeared as "Kennedy, Oil Imports, and the Fair-Trade Doctrine," *Business History
Review* 64 (1990):286–310. Copyright (c) 1990 by the President and Fellows of
Harvard College.

To my parents

CONTENTS

NINE
American Trading Power in the 1960s and Beyond   246

PREFACE

In the late 1970s, when I began thinking about international affairs, United States power had acquired a much different status than in the decade before. Earlier, the country abounded with confident optimism about its role in the world, and, most important, exercised its authority among its allies as the uncontested leader, capable of solving domestic and overseas problems. By the Carter era, America was wracked by self-doubt, a sluggish economy, and seemingly waning strength relative to the vitality of its friends abroad. Despite the cheerful nationalism of the ensuing Reagan-Bush years, the United States, in my mind, had clearly not come back, at least in terms of its predominance of the first two decades of the postwar period. Just looking at the competitiveness of Japanese trade, the lack thereof of American exports, the vibrant economies of the European Community, and the booming U.S. debt attested to my pessimistic, but perhaps realistic, outlook.

Public and academic debate has developed over the past several years regarding the so-called decline of American hegemony, or outright dominance in the world economy; whether, in fact, it really has occurred, and if so, what were the reasons behind the deterioration of the Pax Americana. The Kennedy-Johnson years have also faced intense scrutiny, because it was in this epoch that American power supposedly reached its height, only to be dashed by exaggerated expectations, the weight of an expanded welfare state, and the divisive and burdensome war in Vietnam. I believe that at least in an economic sense, the United States began its decline as early as Kennedy's presidency—primarily because of the recovery and rise of Western Europe—and that the country has been fading ever since.

This study is an attempt to prove this assertion by exploring United States foreign trade policy, in addition to addressing a key debate among historians concerning the motives, aims, and outcome of U.S. foreign policy. Readers interested purely in the history of the era might wish to skip the introductory section. For those who remain, I have taken an approach to my subject that is based on models drawn from international relations scholarship and that thus pertains to ongoing theoretical arguments among historians. In doing so, I address the historiography of U.S. and foreign economic policy since World War II in general and, to a lesser extent, the Kennedy and Johnson administrations.

The theoretical, secondary, and primary sources used in this book reflect my efforts to probe the influences on policy-making from all levels in domestic and international society. It should be noted that understanding foreign inputs into American decisions suffers from a dearth of archival grounding, due to the still-classified nature of overseas materials for the period under study. American archives disclosed some of the policies of other nations, as did EEC press releases, GATT working minutes and publications, interviews, and correspondence. The end result, it is hoped, sheds more light on academic debate, as well as on the transformations in American trade and power over the past decades.

Several people and institutions assisted in the research and funding for this project. For sources and financial aid, I am indebted to the following: Ronald Whealen, Jim Cedrone, Michael Desmond, Maura Porter, Suzanne Forbes, and William Johnson at the John F. Kennedy Library, and the Kennedy Library Foundation for research grants; John Caldwell at the Carl Albert Center of the University of Oklahoma, and the Visiting Scholars Program; Linda Hansen and Regina Greenwell at the Lyndon B. Johnson Library, and a Moody grant from the Johnson Library Foundation; the Society for Historians of American Foreign Relations Bernath fund; and numerous other archives, libraries, and institutions that are listed in the bibiography. I wish also to thank George Ball and Howard Petersen for granting me interviews.

I am grateful to the following people for their teaching, guidance, encouragement, and, very often, willingness to read drafts or chapters of the manuscript: Susan Aaronson, Mark Cioc, J. Garry Clifford, Eric Einhorn, Vincent Ferraro, Robert Griffith, George Herring, Michael Hogan, the late Robert McNeal, Thomas Paterson, Ronald Story, Imanuel Wexler, the members of the Five-College International Relations Seminar, and particularly Robert Schulzinger. My special appreciation extends to Stephen Pelz, who, as my thesis adviser, provided advice and support, a model of scholarly excellence, and friendship throughout and beyond my graduate school career.

Friends who helped out in various ways on this project include Jim Cedrone, Jim Helwig, Catherine Prudhomme, and especially Halil Padir for providing accommodations and friendship. Thanks also are in order to Alice Zeiser of the University of Massachusetts and Pat Murphy of the University of Colorado for their mastery of word processing magic that got the manuscript into legible form. I would also like to thank my editors at Columbia University Press, Kate Wittenberg and Jonathan Director. I thank them all.

My deep obligation is to Rocio, who bore the brunt of my absences, anxieties, and ramblings about history, research, and writing, all of which went well beyond what could be expected of any spouse. I can express my gratitude to her only in part by acknowledging her contribution to this study.

ABBREVIATIONS

ACMI	American Cotton Manufacturers Institute
AFL-CIO	American Federation of Labor-Congress of Industrial Organizations
AOC	Associated Overseas Countries
ASP	American selling price
CAP	Common Agricultural Policy
CNTP	Committee for a National Trade Policy
ECSC	European Coal and Steel Community
EEC	European Economic Community
EFTA	European Free Trade Association
GATT	General Agreement on Tariffs and Trade
GNP	Gross national product
GSP	Generalized System of Preferences
IMF	International Monetary Fund
IPAA	Independent Petroleum Association of America
ITC	Interagency Textile Committee
ITO	International Trade Organization
LDCs	Less-developed countries
LTA	Long-Term Textile Arrangement
MCA	Manufacturing Chemists Association
MFN	Most-favored-nation status
NAM	National Association of Manufacturers
NATO	North Atlantic Treaty Organization
NLMA	National Lumber Manufacturing Association

NTBs   Non-tariff barriers
OECD   Organization for Economic Cooperation and Devel-
            opment
OEP   Office of Emergency Planning
OPEC   Organization of Petroleum Exporting Countries
RTA   Reciprocal Trade Act
SOCMA   Synthetic Organic Chemical Manufacturers Associa-
            tion
STR   Special Trade Representative
TEA   Trade Expansion Act
UMW   United Mine Workers
UNCTAD   United Nations Conference on Trade and Develop-
            ment
WCLA   West Coast Lumbermen's Association

AMERICAN
TRADE
AND POWER
IN THE 1960s

INTRODUCTION

In the mid-1960s, for the first time since the Second World War, the United States lost international trading strength relative to its major industrial allies. By no means temporary, this occurrence began a downward swing in America's world leadership that lasted into the ensuing decades. The impact of this misfortune was often hard to discern, although the mounting independence of Western Europe from U.S. diplomatic policies was but one indication of the retreat from outright global dominance. On the economic front, the descent was striking. A dwindling trade surplus, failed efforts to solve a chronic balance-of-payments deficit, and increasing monetary problems marked the initial dissipation of international commercial might. Persistent and enlarging trade deficits, coupled with inflation, oil shortages, defense spending and other foreign and domestic woes, maintained the trend. Although the United States was still the world's strongest power, the country no longer held its preeminent position of the immediate postwar years. The relative decline had complex political, economic, and strategic causes and results, and developed into an issue that not only worried contemporary policymakers but became a subject of academic and public debate.[1] This study uses foreign trade policy as a means to grapple with the sources and meaning of the decline—to discover why the United States lost power, how it dealt with its predicament, and what kind of global economic system leader America was, and became, during the period of its retraction.

A basic cause of the United States' relative loss of power was the rising potency of friends abroad. Predominant since World War II, America in the 1960s faced a potent trade rival, the six-nation European Economic Community (EEC), an emerging pan, and an increasingly assertive Third World. In the early postwar years, Western European particularly had accepted the guidance of the United States over economic recovery and security, although they did so largely without sacrificing their own national autonomy to the leader of the capitalist nations. Now the large market of the EEC—the Six or Common Market—not only fortified the Western alliance but also threatened U.S. trade by combining efficiently produced exports with protectionism against imports. In short, Europeans enjoyed more decisive leverage at international trade negotiations than ever before. In the meantime, other advanced and less-developed countries (LDCs, the South, or the periphery) challenged American trade and foreign policies. Presidents John F. Kennedy and Lyndon B. Johnson hoped that a refashioned liberal trade program would allow the United States to continue to lead, in the words of political scientist David Calleo, this "plural squirming world" that imperiled America's or preeminent position in the political economy of the "Free World."[2] But by the end of the Kennedy-Johnson years America's trade partners had eroded this prior "hegemonial" power, that is, the productive efficiencies and military strength that allowed the United States to control, set, and maintain the rules of behavior that governed the global capitalist order.[3]

Although the statistics showing a decline would not appear until 1965, signs of languishing American power were present to such an extent that Kennedy chose a foreign trade bill, the Trade Expansion Act, as the centerpiece of his legislative agenda of 1962. The bill would serve many purposes, among them fostering more efficient industries at home and furnishing the president with a needed victory on Capitol Hill. But the Trade Expansion Act aimed most directly at meeting the vigor of the Six by boosting U.S. exports, which, in turn, would help pay for North Atlantic Treaty Organization (NATO) and foreign-aid expenditures that had run America into the red since the late 1950s. The measure granted the president authority to lower trade barriers on a reciprocal basis with the Six and other countries at the so-called Ken-

nedy Round of the General Agreement on Tariffs and Trade
(GATT). The implication of these trade negotiations reached fur-
ther than the economic realm, however. Trade issues affected
United States–European diplomacy, development in the Third
World, and, most important, America's ability to exert influence
around the globe.

The focus by Kennedy and Johnson on exports and imports
indicated the historically critical role played by trade policy in
foreign affairs. President Herbert Hoover demonstrated this relationship by signing the Smoot-Hawley Tariff Act of 1930, which
raised tariffs to their highest levels in U.S. history and precipitated
a trade war that shut down two-thirds of the world's trade. The
outcome was devastating. Plummeting exports undermined national economies, worsened the global depression, and provided
an opportunity for fascism to take root in Germany. Unable to
confront Hitler, in part because of their weakened economies,
European democracies unsuccessfully appeased Germany, and the
second destructive war of the twentieth century ensued. Not surprisingly, the link between trade restrictions and the rise of fascism
weighed heavily on decisions made in Washington after the war.[4]

The Depression-era trade wars had a significant influence on
American leaders when they established the postwar liberal trade
order. But by Kennedy's presidency, the United States also sought
to bolster its economy for the sake of more profits for private
interests and Keynesian growth policies, and to correct its balance-
of-payments deficit (more international expenditures than earnings) in order to raise revenue for overseas military and economic
aid. As the 1960s began with U.S. economic power at its height,
these aims seemed within reach. But by the decade's end, Kennedy
and Johnson had failed to maintain a healthy trade surplus (more
exports than imports), and as a result an even greater pace in the
waning of American strength and capabilities confronted later U.S.
leaders.

Scholarly Debate and Methodology

Power, the motivations behind and the decision-making structure
of American foreign policy, and the role of the United States as the

leader of the capitalist world economy have long engaged scholars. Historians working on economic diplomacy have borrowed methodology and theories from political scientists and economists in order to integrate a more profound understanding of global relations into their narratives. Yet historiographical arguments persist and often either go round in circles or fizzle without resolution, as new archival materials that support or refute individual viewpoints become available. As historian Bruce Cumings has warned, "Sometimes the piling on of empirical evidence merely adds to our problems, rather than solving them; we need theory to sort it all out and make sense of it."[5] While this study indeed adds new data, it also attempts a reassessment of the historiography through an interdisciplinary theoretical approach to the Kennedy-Johnson trade program.

Because overseas trade touched not only foreign policy and power but national economies, American trade policy considered a host of external and internal elements. Inputs into decisions on trade policy derive from four sources—the international environment, the government, the socioeconomic realm, and individual decision makers. America's place in the GATT trade system, GATT rules and norms, issues concerning national security, global economic stability, and trade competition from abroad figured into decision making at the international level. At the governmental level, the impact of executive branch bureaucracies, Congress, and political parties were important. And since business, industry, labor, and agriculture had trade agendas, these socioeconomic, or societal, interests influenced Congress and the executive branch. Finally, the ideological orientations, political experiences, and values of decision makers at the individual level played key roles in determining trade policy.[6]

Because debate about American foreign economic policy has not only been the domain of historians, but also of political scientists and economists, it is instructive to synthesize the arguments of these disciplines into three theories—market, class conflict and statist, and that each explain, from unique perspectives, the impact of the four sources on trade policy.[7] The market and class conflict schools will be presented here and assessed in the final chapter. Yet it is the statist theory that most convincingly explains the motives, aims, decision making process, and results of U.S. trade policy during the Kennedy and Johnson years. Thus, the statist view forms the basic interpretive framework of this study.

The External Environment

The Market School

Although most remote from reality—even ahistorical—the market school interpretation is nevertheless popular with neoclassical economists, many of the major economics textbooks, and given lip service by such free-market advocates as President Ronald Reagan. The school posits that markets should be free from political interference in the interest of efficiency, growth, and consumer choice. This free-trade view, guided by the laissez-faire liberalism of Adam Smith and David Ricardo, prefers that a competitive marketplace allocate resources by a nation's comparative advantage in production. Under the theory of comparative advantage, each nation exports the goods that it makes more cheaply and efficiently relative to the production of other countries. Thus, nations benefit by selling what they make best and buying cheaper goods from others. As a result, efficiency rules the international economy, growth is maximized, and consumer costs are minimized.[8]

The free movement of goods across national borders, guided by governmental oversight, serves all traders, claims the market school. Capitalist governments manage the international economy much as they do their domestic systems, by establishing rules and regulations that ensure that no country (or interest group) procures an advantage that undermines production and global cooperation. But the separation of the political from the economic domain must govern trade. That is, supply and demand, rather than political dealing, set prices. Advanced countries export according to comparative advantage, while the LDCs, although lacking efficiency at first, achieve competitiveness over time and eventually profit. Free trade, devoid as much as possible from government intervention, thus helps the most productive exporters, but in the long run enriches all nations, profess market theorists.[9] A key to market school assumptions is the concept of productionism, which has been appropriated by class conflict scholars, but applies to the

statist view as well. This guiding ethic of Keynesian growth policies undergirded America's postwar liberal trade agenda. Productionism aimed to equalize production and consumption, while
increasing aggregate global output. Thus, regarding foreign affairs,
instead of reallocating resources and profits so that weaker countries could obtain a larger percentage of benefits, American policymakers sought to expand the "economic pie" in order to provide
all nations with a bigger slice. This approach was not a bad deal
for other countries; productionism promised a growing economy
once postwar recovery was complete, while the United States assumed the burdens of the Western alliance by financing military
and aid commitments. In essence, productionism avoided old conflicts, which had been caused in part by scarcity, writes historian
Charles Maier. It "de-ideologize[d] issues of political economy
into questions of output and efficiency," he explains, by placing
economics above politics.[10] Market scholars view productionism
as a means devised by American leaders to achieve capitalist growth
and abundance after World War II.

The American-sponsored trade order, based on productionism,
provided mutual trade profits for global capitalists, insists the
market school. Unfortunately, lament these scholars, politics usually took precedence over economics. GATT nations, the United
States included, all too often veered from the ideal of free trade in
order to accommodate powerful interest groups, or attain security
objectives abroad. Despite the divergences, the school generally
applauds American efforts to build and maintain an open, competitive world trade system within the confines of national political
restraints. Thus, market proponents agree that Kennedy and Johnson labored to ensure that all nations profited and grew in the
global system through trade based on comparative advantage.[11]

The Class Conflict School

The class conflict school directly confronts the market view. Although class conflict scholars allow that global economic relations,
and not politics, determine trade policy, they differ by claiming
that class struggles determine profits. At home, capitalists and
labor contest each other. Abroad, the battle transpires between the

world system hegemon's traders, bankers, and multinational corporations against other members of the industrial "core" centers (the North), or between the core and the Third World nations in the "periphery," or South. In effect, powerful economic interests with hegemony (comparative advantages) in key products unite into large-scale monopolies that control either weaker core nations or the periphery through "free-trade imperialism." The result is a system of exploitation that enriches and protects the hegemon of the core nations while it forces the LDCs and others into a state of dependency.[12]

Although class conflict scholars examine the intra-core economic exchanges, the main focus of their "world systems" approach is on North–South relations, which is, they maintain, an "unequal" trade relationship in the core's favor. In the postwar world, the LDCs, many just recently sprung from colonial status, possessed underdeveloped economic and political systems. In trade, they exchanged semiprocessed goods and mostly raw materials (usually one main crop) for finished manufactures from the advanced countries. In doing so, they suffered adverse "terms of trade," or a differential in export and import prices. In other words, they received less for their agricultural exports than they spent on imports from the North. Such losses prevented the use of export revenues for economic development and diversification, and the insistence of advanced nations, particularly America, on low tariffs, exacerbated these ruinous terms of trade. Freer trade served the North, which had most of the comparative advantages, leaving the markets of the South exposed to core penetration and dominance. Thus, the decline of American hegemony occurred mainly in intra-core relations; the United States maintained its superiority over the periphery.[13]

The United States, the capitalist world leader, garners the blame from class conflict scholars for such an unequal economic system in the postwar era. As the hegemon in the international economy, with comparative advantages in many products, America not only gained disproportionately from core–periphery trade, but also from inter-core commerce. Thus, the United States, hiding behind the facade of "free world" leader in the fight against global communism, perpetuated its superiority by forcing the door open abroad to its exports, and closing its doors to competitive imports. Some class conflict theorists avow that by exporting excess output abroad, the United States hoped to avoid depressions at home caused by greedy overproduction. Yet all advocates of the school underscore America's selfish, pernicious behavior at the expense of other nations.[14]

The viewpoint also attacks productionism, which functioned to strengthen America's lockhold on the global economy. Although growth was desirable, class conflict historian Thomas McCormick argues that the rising economic "tide" helped only the biggest, most efficient ship. In the postwar era, America was an ocean liner; other nations were just dinghies. Thus, free trade served the "hegemonic" United States because of its sheer size and comparative advantages. Meanwhile, the rules that governed the system were stacked against the ability of others to catch up to America, and in the case of the periphery, to develop.[15] Thus, concludes the class conflict school, the Kennedy-Johnson pursuit of an open, multilateral trade regime disguised America's intention of amassing mounting profits from exports, shutting out imports, and maintaining its dominance among rich and poor countries. The GATT trade system, under the thumb of the American hegemon, pursued and preserved the exploitative relationship between the United States and its industrial economic partners, and between the core and the periphery.

The Statist School

The statist interpretation varies from the two previous schools by claiming that free-market economic relations are often subordinated to the political aims of promoting national power and wealth. Thus, through trade policy, the state intervenes in the global marketplace in order to maximize a country's strength and status relative to others. Contrary to the market and class conflict views, the statist interpretation assumes a gap between liberal economic theory and actual practice in the trade order. Economically superior nations indeed voice support for trade based on comparative advantage, and powerful hegemons with productive efficiencies endeavor to exchange goods according to the principle. But the principle is often not put into practice; governments sacrifice economic gains for political or diplomatic objectives. Protectionism exemplifies this divergence from free trade, claim statist scholars. America permitted Western Europe and Japan to resort to restrictive trade measures after World War II in order to aid their recovery efforts. The United States also raised tariffs and other barriers, not only for the protection of weak industries, but to ensure that products deemed critical to the nation's security were made by Americans. Surely protectionism reduced aggregate national income, yet it also boosted defense and power. In other words, trade restrictions were necessary to build viable economies and stable political systems, attract large segments of the American population to internationalist goals, and promote Washington's leadership over the Western alliance.[16]

Explicit in the statist interpretation is the notion that "national interests" are critical to trade policy. These interests include enhancing national security (through both a powerful military and a prosperous economy), autonomy in policy making from other nations, and profits for private interests. Liberal trade is desirable, but not purely for economic accumulation, as market school adherents claim, or for dominance and exploitation, as the class conflict school argues. Rather, the government mobilizes producers to trade in order to guarantee, at the minimum, the nation's survival, or for national aggrandizement, at the maximum. Even as Christopher Chase-Dunn, one world system theorist admits, "The complicated game of competition in the capitalist world-economy is a combination of profitable commodity production with efficient use of geopolitical power."[17] The amalgam of political, security, and economic national interests adds up to a complex array of factors affecting decisions on trade policy that only the statist school satisfactorily explains. Thus, the quest for profits through export expansion, and the consequent pursuit of political and security objectives—in other words, neomercantilism—statists contend, reveals an intricate web of policy choices and decisions.

Statist scholars, in fact, applaud American "hegemony," but for various reasons related to narrow economic and general foreign policy goals. For one, America's comparative advantages and productionism helped build an open trade system that profited the

United States. With global economic and political superiority after the war, the United States recognized its self-interest in lowering tariffs, since it enjoyed comparative advantages in a wide array of lucrative trade goods. This neomercantilist objective of expanding exports guided the U.S. trade program, but commercial policy was not nearly that simple. America exercised its power in order to cut tariffs and prevent a recurrence of the trade wars that had wrecked the international economy of the 1930s. In addition, freer trade boosted productionism by increasing profits for all nations, which, in turn, helped national economies grow. And growth, American leaders believed, achieved political, diplomatic, and military objectives. Sustained growth would prevent political strife at home, accomplish the major United States postwar goal of Western European integration, and tighten the bonds of cooperation among alliance members in the dangerous cold war. In short, many statists argue that America adhered to the theory of "hegemonic stability," in which the United States asserted its power over the trade regime in order to keep the system open and expanding. By doing so, America would serve its own interests, and those of the alliance, of prosperity, integration, and security. The GATT regime under United States leadership therefore promoted American interests, but also maintained a liberal trade community.[18]

The statist view of American trade policy in the 1960s is most accurate because U.S. leadership improved most nations economically—although not necessarily America—while it promoted Western alliance security interests under the guidance of the United States. Surely, as class conflict adherent Thomas McCormick writes, the United States dominated the West militarily, diplomatically, and economically just after World War II. This strength, or hegemony, enabled America to exert its power, and for its own benefit. Many core nations, especially in Western Europe, viewed American productionism as self-serving, and feared, once they had recovered, that their home markets would be subject to uncontrollable U.S. export and investment penetration. Third World nations protested America's monolithic presence in their economies, which they claimed worsened their adverse terms of trade, dependency, and underdevelopment.[19] But the United States also acted on behalf of others as well as itself, and positive gains for advanced nations—although fewer for LDCs—were the result. And American dominance, albeit declining, protected the security of the capitalist allies.

Statists, however, argue that these very security imperatives doomed America to a steady erosion of power. Indeed, the school admires the intricacies of U.S. trade policy; the neomercantilist attempt to augment American power through higher exports coupled with the free-trade pursuit of providing benefits for all members of GATT. But, as the following narrative will show, for reasons of alliance strength and unity, America oftentimes subordinated its own parochial economic interests to the international economic well-being, thus helping its trade partners enlarge their market shares. By all means, trade helped the United States in the cold war by raising revenues for military and foreign-aid expenditures. But by the end of the 1960s, the capitalist hegemon found these costs to be intolerable. Unable to compete adequately with its allies and, at the same time, maintain its payments to the NATO alliance and Third World nations, the United States discovered a growing gap between objectives and capabilities. Failing to solve its international payments deficit, America could not adequately meet its commitments without serious economic repercussions at home and abroad. The end result was a quickening of the United States' relative decline in global power.[20]

The Internal Environment

GATT and the Politics of Trade

As in the external arena, U.S. trade policy followed the statist model in the internal environment. In fact, internal domestic sources played a key role in decisions. As three experts note, "Foreign policy became domestic politics" when applied to trade.[21] Guided by productionism, the president and Congress had a "domestic mandate" to run the economy equitably and profitably, and this duty carried over into the international economy. Thus, in formulating trade policy, leaders took into consideration both interest group desires in the internal political and economic scene and national goals as they applied to both the American economy as a whole and to the external world. In regard to the internal picture, as scholar Edward John Ray puts it, trade policy is the outcome of "macro" and "micro" approaches. The macro process relates to the government's ability to act autonomously—buffered from interest group pressure—on behalf of the collective, national interest of liberal trade. The micro approach reflects the preferences of particular constituents or lobbies, usually, but not exclusively, protectionist. A combination of the two, claim statists, explains the internal decision-making process.[22]

The international trade regime of the General Agreement on Tariffs and Trade mirrored the macro–micro structure. Although striving for unrestrictive trade, GATT was "open to manipulation and distortion" by governmental "interventionist practices" that had been legitimized in the domestic political economy, notes one critic of the trade order.[23] The market and class conflict schools naturally view this intervention as contradictory, inefficient, or exploitative. Yet the goal of high employment levels through Keynesian "demand management," or countercyclical spending and saving, was the aim of GATT. The statist school accepts such intervention as necessary to achieve national interests and maintain domestic support for liberal trade.

In other words, GATT's founders never designed the trade forum as a doctrinaire free-trade mechanism, since its "dirigiste" function permitted national governments to protect their home markets from harmful exposure to free trade. Included as a GATT norm was, for instance, a balance-of-payments clause that allowed nations to "escape" from or avoid tariff reductions in order to focus on expansionist domestic policies that would correct payments deficiencies. GATT also allowed for the regional discrimination inherent in the EEC customs union, permitted LDCs to protect infant industries, and exempted many U.S. farm goods from tariff cuts. Without such exceptions, in fact, few countries would have joined GATT in 1947. Thus, GATT required no commitment to free-trade orthodoxy; compromises between liberal trade and protectionism superseded the market school ideal of laissez-faire competition.[24] Such trade-offs in the trade system between governments, and among governments and societal interests, are implicit in the statist critique.

Not surprisingly, the priority of domestic interests in GATT gave political and economic groups influence in decision making. In the decentralized American political system, societal interests vie with semi-autonomous government officials to shape policy. Exerting pressure through the ballot and lobbying efforts in Congress, interest groups confront the president, who represents national (state) aims and holds extensive powers in trade. The president receives his authority from the Reciprocal Trade Act, which has been renewed ever since its passage in 1934, and he has the ultimate say in trade policy by representing the United States at GATT negotiations. But Congress and societal interests retain leverage because the president gets his trade authority for limited periods, after which he must submit a new trade bill to Congress for approval. Trade policy decision making thus entails a tug-of-war among societal and state interests.[25]

Debate over internal influences on decision making centers on the extent to which the state (executive branch) or societal interests (economic groups and voters working through Congress or government agencies) shape trade policy. The state, or "foreign policy executive," represents national and international concerns. Seeking to promote the overall interests of the country, the foreign policy executive—primarily the president, but also the State Department, Special Trade Representative, and other federal agencies—considers the effects of its decisions on other nations in GATT in making trade policy. In Bruce Cumings words, the president is not only the sole figure who is "responsible to the whole" nation and society, but he commands "the struggle within the state" over policy decisions. But since particular interests have considerable political power, the foreign policy executive is not free from societal restraints. The president faces reelection, for example, and also pressure from legislators to act on behalf of their constituents or risk rejection of key legislation. Thus, the foreign policy executive is, to an extent, circumscribed by the "representative" element in trade policy.[26]

The representative element—Congress and such "constituent" agencies in the executive branch as the departments of Commerce, Agriculture, and Labor—reflects the demands of politically mobilized groups in society. These groups are either "protection-biased" because they seek import barriers, or "trade-biased" exporters. On the whole, protectionists are the most powerful of the representative element. For most congressmen, endorsing free trade or consumer goals of low prices does not win elections. Instead, politicians champion protection for import-competing industries and for workers because the gains from protectionism are easily discernible at the voting booth. On the trade issue, constituents usually cast votes for politicians who urge higher tariffs.[27] The decentralized political structure, and the fact that presidents are obligated under the Constitution to seek legislative authority for their trade programs, also permits these groups access to policymakers at the very top.[28]

The campaign for protection from the representative element puts it on a collision course with the liberal trade foreign policy executive. Since 1934 the latter prevailed after tough fights because most societal interests understood the long-term implications of liberal trade to world peace and economic health. They also believed, until the late 1960s, that American hegemony boosted their prosperity because United States power, trade, and productionist programs were still unchallenged, and the country enjoyed sustained economic growth. Yet decision making involved an inevitable clash that forced both sides to compromise. A bargaining process balanced out the representative element's narrow priorities of profit and survival with the foreign policy executive's broad ambitions of maintaining an open GATT system, good relations with other nations, and national security. The president thus had to sell his trade policy, accounting for the needs of societal interests while pursuing national and international objectives.[29]

Yet disagreement exists over whether the export-oriented foreign policy executive or protection-biased representative element held sway over policy. Debate among the three schools revolves around pluralist and elitist interpretations of the internal decision making in United States foreign policy. Market scholars take a pluralist perspective, class conflict writers an elitist, neocorporatist view, and statists a combination that leans heavily to the pluralist side—a pluralist arrangement directed largely by elite members of the government.

Market School Pluralism

The pluralist model describes the competition among interest groups for trade benefits granted by politicians. In short, pluralism posits a causal link between interest group desires and eventual policy. Import-competing and export-oriented producers contend over trade policy in a process that lays bare the fragmented and competitive nature of the decision making process. The pluralist interpretation naturally focuses on Congress, since commerce is a "pocketbook" issue on which private groups spend millions of dollars lobbying on Capitol Hill. Because of its electoral accountability and role in passing or rejecting trade legislation, Congress provides the lever for interest groups to pressure the government.[30]

Trade policy essentially evolves from interest group pluralism, the market school argues, because the American political structure is so decentralized and open. Thus, various producers compete for influence in Congress. Ultimately, trade policy reflects their needs and goals; Congress and the president are captives of constituents at home. After the passage of the Reciprocal Trade Act in 1934, interests competed and pressured Congress for freer trade or protection (depending on their product) in a zero-sum battle that yielded winners and losers. This interaction, resulting in congressional logrolling, determined votes on trade bills. The foreign policy executive, therefore, ultimately bowed to the will of these interest groups in a pluralist, truly democratic, fashion in order to forge his trade policy.[31]

Class Conflict School Elitism

Again, just as in explaining the external environment, the market school view of internal decision making suffers from oversimplification. Interest group pluralism fails to explain, for instance, why trade policy remained liberal and tariffs came down even when many powerful interest groups campaigned for protectionism. Class conflict scholars respond to this puzzle by explaining that policy was really set according to the wishes of corporate America, or the trade-biased exporters, in alliance with elite decision makers in the government who pushed for liberal trade. In other words, elitism, not democratic pluralism, characterizes the U.S. political system. As Thomas McCormick argues, postwar American policy-making became more centralized under the executive branch, and increasingly bypassed Congress. The representative element developed into a "rubber stamp" for approving presidential executive orders, or such mandates as the Truman Doctrine.[32] Thus, contrary to the market view, elites guide and make decisions insulated from the democratic process.

Critical to the class conflict analysis is the notion that a consensus existed among government and societal elites. Massive propaganda, or cooptation of adversaries through the campaign for productionism by the foreign policy executive, endowed the elites' programs with a wide appeal and made support homogeneous. Yet persuasion was not always necessary. In trade policy, claims the school, a neocorporatist, privileged "aristocracy" of business, labor, industry, and agricultural groups joined with policymakers to formulate programs from which they won most of the economic rewards. To be sure, Congress was not irrelevant in the policy process. But neocorporatism assumes that the representative element acquiesced to the policies of the elitist "network" of government officials and corporate leaders.[33]

In other words, neocorporatism explains decision making as a cooperative process between the state and export-minded societal groups. The government tried to minimize interest group conflict by rationalizing the marketplace and tempering the vagaries of business cycles through productionism. Meanwhile, entrenched, efficient producers, by assuming influence over the trade policy process through informal alliances with state elites (and thus bypassing congressional logrolling), preserved their oligopolistic positions in the U.S. and international economies. Skewed in its representation of societal interests, maintains the class conflict school, trade policy channeled benefits into discrete sectors of the economy that ensured large profits for corporate America. Liberal trade policy thus achieved the interests of select, powerful societal elites outside of the democratic process. Congress was at best merely a willing cohort in the public–private, corporatist network.[34]

Statist School Inter-Branch Bargaining

The statist school disagrees with both neocorporatism and interest group pluralism in the foreign trade sphere. It views decisions instead as a product of confrontation and compromise between the nationally and internationally oriented foreign policy executive and the more parochial representative element. The school points to a state-centered structure, in which many international and domestic constraints are placed on an activist foreign policy executive. But policymakers are not passive in the face of interest group pressure, nor are they tools of class interests or the most powerful economic combines in society. Rather, decision making entails the White House coralling societal interests in order to achieve the nation's neomercantilist and internationalist objectives of increased wealth, political unity, and national security. Thus, a liberal trade policy emerges not from private sector pressure or corporate networks with elites, although both have inputs into decision making. Instead, policy evolves from pluralist bargaining between the foreign policy executive and the representative element *under* government direction, and *for* the national interest.[35]

In short, statists believe that through a process of inter-branch compromise between the executive and legislative branches, the state leads interest groups into accepting eventual policy decisions that sustain the drive toward liberal trade. That is, neither the state nor societal interests are autonomous actors; bargaining epitomizes the relationship between the foreign policy executive and the representative element. The Reciprocal Trade Act of 1934, by transferring authority for negotiating tariffs from Congress to the president, reduced the leverage of interest groups over policy, and therefore curtailed logrolling. But Congress still exerted influence because the president had to pass trade bills to get new negotiating authority. Thus, import competitors, as much as, or even more than, exporters, had leverage over policy. Although Congress represented groups seeking protection, and despite the fact that the president represented export competitors and broader strategic and economic interests, each accommodated the other. Only if he obliged important congressional blocs did this process yield the president ultimate direction over the trade program. Kennedy and Johnson did so, negotiating with Congress in order to use liberal trade policy to attain America's statist national interests of wealth, power, and security.[36]

The Statist Fair-Trade Doctrine

The statist inter-branch process allowed the president to address effectively the inherent clash between liberalism and protection—between the foreign policy executive and the representative element—in trade policy. This dualism undergirded the Kennedy–Johnson trade policy through a concept referred to as the "fair-trade" doctrine.[37] The tenet is drawn from the "managed trade" terminology of the 1970s (although in that period it applies to nontariff barriers), in which GATT permitted government intervention in domestic economies and international negotiations in order to decide trade barrier levels. The fair-trade doctrine equipped the foreign policy executive to promote tariff cuts for national and international interests while protecting, according to the wishes of the representative element, domestic sectors hurt by imports. The dualistic fair-trade approach also serves a methodological purpose of tying together the external and internal environments of trade policy decision making under one rubric, which meshes with the interpretive framework of the statist school.

The first part of the fair-trade doctrine concerned trade liberalization. Lowering trade barriers would boost exports, which would thereby spur national growth, help fund overseas military and economic aid commitments, and strengthen the West in the cold war. In short, American leaders could achieve their statist goals. Kennedy and Johnson hoped to use liberal trade, based on the theory of comparative advantage, for the profit of all traders. They even were willing, on occasion, to sacrifice protection from imports, or help for exporters through tariff negotiations, for the good of the global trade order. But the exchange of enhanced power for the nation and profits for strong producers would compensate any losses incurred by the United States. Through a process of hard bargaining with America's trade partners, beginning at the Kennedy Round of GATT, both presidents, wielding the fair-trade doctrine, sought mutually equitable and reciprocal trade agreements, closer bonds in the Western alliance, and greater power for their country.

Yet the other half of fair trade revealed that America would not abandon societal interests in the pursuit of a free-trade ideal. Thus, this part of the doctrine hinged on protectionism, since the United States embraced mercantilism as well as liberalism. Economic conditions and political realities in Massachusetts and Texas had taught Kennedy and Johnson, respectively, about the injurious effects of imports on society, and, most notably, the voting power at election time of producers hurt by imports. Therefore, as president, Kennedy tried various methods of protection and welfare state remedies in order to adjust inefficient producers to the effects of freer trade. But in order to assure acceptance of the bill by Congress, which was under pressure from protectionist constituents, he backed selective restrictions of imports, and also promised strict adherence to the rule of reciprocity at trade negotiations. Johnson was just as careful with congressmen from areas that were sensitive about imports. By this approach, both presidents sought to aid declining import interests and win meaningful concessions for exporters at the Kennedy Round. Fair trade thus required juggling local, national, and foreign imperatives in order to expand exports without causing undue harm to economically weak, but politically powerful, domestic interests.

In sum, the fair-trade doctrine based trade, as much as possible, on the principle of comparative advantage, from which the United States would gain as the capitalist system's economic leader, while reserving to each country a degree of autonomy to respond to domestic pressures in accord with GATT norms. In the case of the U.S. economy, some sectors might suffer, and, of course, Washington would continue to foot much of the bill for NATO and LDC aid programs. But Kennedy and Johnson hoped to guarantee that certain producers profited, that the trade surplus grew, and that the United States maintained its leadership over the global capitalist system and Western alliance. In the 1960s, fair trade evolved into a balancing act between, on the one hand, meeting the challenge of the Common Market, aiding the periphery, and assisting rising exporters, while on the other hand, cushioning certain inefficient American (and foreign) producers from the effects of higher imports. Unfortunately for the United States, however, the fair-trade doctrine, which allowed for the neomercantilistic pursuit of power and wealth in the international economy, could not stem America's relative decline in the world.

The crumbling of American hegemony during the Kennedy–Johnson years points to a major setback for the statist fair-trade policy, but there were certain successes, too. To note three examples, other allies became strong and prosperous, the alliance afforded effective security for its people, and the GATT trade system remained open. Indeed, the trade order was not self-regulating, according to market school precepts, nor was it inherently malignant for the weak so that the strong could easily prosper, as the class conflict school declares. Instead, as the statist view holds, U.S. trade policy operated in two mutually inclusive arenas—one political-military and the other political-economic. In the former, the cold war generated concerns about security, while competition and pluralism characterized the latter and had an impact on both American wealth and global leadership. The fair-trade approach was an attempt by the United States to resolve problems and challenges in both arenas by achieving national interests through a carefully conceived liberal trade program. The record shows the attainment of the military objective, but at the expense of American prosperity and most significant, international power.

As all schools recognize, U.S. potency declined particularly relative to the rising EEC, but also to Japan and others during the decade. Experiencing perhaps the shortest tenure as a hegemon in world history, America discovered that the costs of leadership were burdensome, in fact, too much so. This quandary, explains political scientist William Thompson, was part of the natural progression in "hegemonic maturity," in which other nations ride along in the system, strengthening themselves at the expense of the leader. Thus, periodic sags in the domestic economy, and increased rivalry from its trade partners, compelled the United States to work harder just to keep its superiority.[38] In the 1960s, America fought a losing battle on this score, and has fought one ever since. The following study examines the United States at its apex, and the initial period afterward, when the nation began its inexorable fall from hegemony.

CHAPTER ONE

Seeds of the Fair-Trade Doctrine, 1945–1960

The fair-trade doctrine emerged from the productionist, liberal trade program of the 1940s. But even then, with the lessons of the Depression-era trade wars well in mind, Americans did not universally embrace freer trade. Falling global tariffs in the early post–World War II years, which boosted exports but also increased imports, explained the reasons for this sentiment. By the late 1950s, protectionism heightened as foreign competition put added pressure on American producers. The dilemma was clear: liberal trade induced profitable and peaceful international relations yet played a part in economic woes at home. The period from 1945 to 1960 reveals the continuities and contrasts between John F. Kennedy's trade policy and that of his predecessors, and the international and domestic environments in which this policy evolved. Shaped by the ideological, political, economic, and diplomatic parameters of the international trade order, Kennedy's fair-trade doctrine, developed during this fifteen-year time span, would become the guide for trade policy in his New Frontier.

The International Sources: The Postwar Trade Regime

America's slipping power during the 1960s contrasted with the immediate post–World War II era. Despite spending large sums of money on aid to allies and its own arsenal during the war, the United States was wealthier relative to other nations than ever before once peace arrived. Because most other powers lay prostrate, America assumed the burden of economic reconstruction by attempting to stabilize exchange rates and rebuild trade by multilateralism, or the cooperative reduction of trade and payments barriers. Recovery was doubly important as the cold war required the recruitment of steadfast allies to fight international communism. Thus, America's responsibilities were enormous in the postwar years. Although its allies retained autonomy over much of their affairs, the United States became the capitalist world's banker, trader, planner, and military leader; the hegemon in the global political economy.

The trade order consequently reflected the American design of economic liberalism, of which three elements were prominent. First was the historic open-door policy, or an emphasis on equal access for all nations in world markets. Second, to ensure the open door, the United States insisted on multilateral trade agreements based on unconditional most-favored-nation (MFN) treatment; that is, a pledge of nondiscrimination that granted all traders the same concessions (or tariff and trade barrier reductions) agreed to by two countries in bilateral negotiations. The third element was trade based on the principle of comparative advantage, with the caveat that exemptions from tariff cuts were permissible as safeguards for domestic producers and as a fulfillment of obligations in imperial trade systems. Washington, with the acquiescence of its allies, integrated all three elements into both the ill-functioning Bretton Woods international monetary system, created to correct postwar national payments deficiencies, and the trade system under GATT.[1] They also provided the bases of the statist fair-trade doctrine.

Economics and politics undergirded these principles. Although its economy did not depend on foreign trade—combined exports and imports averaged about 8 percent of the gross national product (GNP) from 1945 to 1970—Americans still feared a recurrence of the trade wars that had worsened the Great Depression, led to economic autarky, and helped cause World War II. With some exaggeration, Americans, most notably Secretary of State Cordell

Hull, warned that "if goods can't cross borders, soldiers will."[2] Later, the cold war added to wariness over trade wars to spur the push for liberal trade. Presidents Harry S. Truman and Dwight D. Eisenhower (and their successors) believed that liberal trade fueled national economic growth, thereby stabilizing governments, furnishing funds for military and economic aid commitments, and bolstering Western security.[3]

By 1947, the creation of the General Agreement on Tariffs and Trade (GATT) gave American leaders a means with which to carry out their trade ideology and policies. Actually, GATT paralleled a larger effort under the International Trade Organization (ITO), envisioned to institutionalize comprehensive rules and principles on a wide range of issues that affected trade, such as cartels, commodity agreements, and employment. The ITO would function in the trade order much as the Bretton Woods system directed world finances. Deemed intrusive in the national economies of the participating countries, and overcommitting America to oversee various sweeping economic measures, the ITO was never ratified by Congress or other nations. Although initially a forum just for trade negotiations, GATT contained many of the principles and provisions of the ITO. But being provisional (hence easily terminated on short notice and not requiring permanent obligations), GATT was more acceptable, and thus replaced the ITO as the guiding force over the trade system. At its birth, GATT comprised twenty-three nations, or "contracting parties," which agreed to trade on a multilateral, nondiscriminatory basis, but also permitted exceptions to multilateralism by which they might "escape" from trade agreements to protect domestic producers. America hoped to limit these exceptions, but soon, ironically, invoked its own, especially against agricultural imports. Contracting parties discussed such behavior, as well as tariff levels, at successive bargaining "rounds" beginning in 1947.[4]

The first round of GATT in 1947 cut the inordinately high global tariffs then in existence. Stimulated by America's Reciprocal Trade Act of 1945, which lowered U.S. duties an average of 25 percent (the lowest in a century), the first GATT round started a boom in world trade. The nearly two dozen contracting parties cut half of their tariffs by at least one-quarter of their previous level, and slashed one-third of the duties by 35 percent. The next GATT rounds in 1949 and 1951, and meetings in 1955, reduced duties further but dealt primarily with the accession of new members such as West Germany and Japan. Yet the era of large tariff reductions ended in the early 1950s, primarily because more restrictive American trade acts permitted only modest decreases at the fourth (1956) and fifth (1962) rounds. By the mid-1950s, Congress sought a freeze on more reductions until GATT could address and control the burgeoning imports into the United States of the recovering allies.[5]

The Rise of Western Europe

With help from the United States, these allies had moved after the war to correct their balance-of-payments deficits and make their currencies convertible. That is, Western Europeans paid out more for goods and services than they sold, thus developing payments deficits that inhibited a free exchange of their currencies for trade purposes. The deficits also impeded a reduction of America's huge trade surplus because Western Europe (and Japan) could not afford to buy U.S. goods. Lacking adequate monetary reserves to reverse their payments deficits, America's allies relied on U.S. dollars in order to cover their currency shortfalls. Washington supplied dollars through aid and military payments, deliberately running a payments deficit itself from 1950 onward. Eventually, the allies collected enough dollars, which became the medium of exchange and reserve assets in the global economy, to bring their payments into balance and thus make possible the conversion of their currencies into dollars by 1958. The United States welcomed this development as a boost for its exports.[6]

Sluggish postwar trade, and its harmful effects on the allies' recovery, prompted the United States to push for liberalization of trade and payments. At first, America permitted its trade partners to restrict U.S. exports while absorbing large amounts of their goods in order to correct its allies' payments deficits. It backed the European Payments Union, a clearinghouse for financing trade, for instance, which discriminated against the dollar. But for long-term adjustments, the United States sought to stabilize European economies with the European Recovery Program, or Marshall Plan, from 1948 to 1952, and further stimulate trade competitiveness in Japan and Western Europe. In order to run the Marshall Plan and invigorate its allies, America helped institutionalize liberal trade through the Organization for European Economic Cooperation, which aspired to eliminate European bilateralism, remove import quotas, and enhance regional integration. The union of Belgium, the Netherlands, and Luxembourg (Benelux) in 1948, and the creation of the European Coal and Steel Community under the Schuman Plan of 1952, indicated progress toward these crucial goals; the European Economic Community, America hoped, marked their ultimate triumph.[7]

Established by the Treaty of Rome in March 1957, the Common Market was more than just a trade bloc. The treaty included the European Atomic Energy Committee (Euratom), a Council of Ministers of national representatives, and a supranational executive, the Commission. Comprising 168 million people in Europe and 63 million in associated areas, the EEC sought an intimate union among diverse European nations. To this end, it aimed to link the economies of Benelux, France, Italy, and West Germany by removing internal barriers to trade, investment, and mobility of capital and labor. Ambitious founders expected the Six, which within a decade became the world's largest trading unit, to "spill over" into a supranational political-economic federation that would henceforth discourage a renewal of Franco–German hostilities, build Western Europe into a potent adversary of Soviet expansionism, and compete against U.S. trade dominance in the region.[8] This more far-reaching integrationist dream would not be realized until the 1990s, but the Common Market quickly grew into an economic monolith in the 1960s.

For the sake of strengthening its economy, the EEC—as a customs union—premised its existence on trade discrimination against non-Community members. The Common Market installed a single external tariff under which each of the six nations averaged its tariffs into a unitary rate. High-tariff France and Italy and low-tariff Benelux and West Germany harmonized their duties, although reduction of quantitative barriers to imports progressed less rapidly. The Six also struggled to construct the Common

Agricultural Policy (CAP), a protectionist levy and quota system on food imports. Indeed, by protecting its markets, the EEC served notice that in the future, European trading rights would take precedence over the commercial objectives of all outsiders, including the trade system's hegemon, the United States.[9]

Backing up this determined policy was an emerging economy that augmented the EEC's global competitiveness. From 1938 to 1964, the aggregate gross national product of Western Europe as a whole increased by 85 percent, and industrial output alone increased two and one-half times. By itself, the Six generated $165 billion in goods and services, or about one-third of U.S. production. Yet in real purchasing power, the output of the Common Market was nearly one-half of America's, and the gap was closing rapidly. EEC steel production, for instance, rose from 36.6 to 62.9 million tons from 1952 to 1959, while American output stagnated at around 84.5 million tons. Also, in 1960, for the first time, industrial production in the Common Market bested that of the United States. And while America's share of the world GNP dropped throughout the 1960s, the EEC's rose. Western Europe's postwar recovery, helped by America's productionist ethic, was a success.

The European challenge to America in trade paralleled the impressive gains in production. The exports of Western Europe as a whole outpaced the region's production, and world trade, during 1938–1964. The United States remained the single largest trading nation, but the combined Six outstripped America in trade volume by 1960 (figures for Western Europe include external and intraregional trade). While the growth of EEC trade exceeded the rates recorded during the Golden Age of Europe from 1870 to 1913, moreover, U.S. commerce grew slower in the 1950s than during the pre-1914 period. Furthermore, as the American share of manufactured exports among industrial nations fell from the 1950s onward, the Common Market's percentage rose through the 1960s.

More telling, the United States' economic advantage over Western Europe waned. Washington's export edge was three times that of Europe's to America in the early postwar years, but as recovery concluded by 1960, this surplus was less than double. Also, the trade-diversionary effects of the EEC were beginning to take hold. That is, the share of exports from outsiders declined as the Six and

TABLE 1.1
U.S. and EEC Export Shares
(percentages)

Year	World exports		Exports of manufactures	
	U.S.	EEC	U.S.	EEC
1960	18.2	36.6	22.8	41.4
1966	16.8	38.5	20.1	43.2
1971	14.0	40.6	17.0	44.7

SOURCE: U.S. Department of Commerce, *International Economic Indicators and Competitive Trends* (September 1974):56–57.

the seven-nation European Free Trade Association (EFTA) increasingly dominated their own markets. The Common Market also enjoyed a steadily growing share of exports to the United States, while the percentage of EEC imports declined, and that of the EFTA barely rose, from across the Atlantic.[10] Western Europe had become America's trade rival, with the Common Market leading the way.

Washington regarded the EEC with both satisfaction and apprehension. America had encouraged regional integration as a means of speeding recovery, strengthening national economies, and increasing exports in order to reverse Western Europe's payments deficits and allow for currency convertibility. The Six also served to unify the region and integrate West Germany into the European order, thus providing a powerful NATO alliance partner in the cold war. The Common Market might not automatically seek liberal trade, however. It could raise protectionist barriers, shut out U.S. exports, and undermine the cohesion of the Western

TABLE 1.2
Origins of EEC and EFTA Imports
(percentage share of total)

Year	Intra-EEC	Intra-EFTA	EEC imports from U.S.	EFTA imports from U.S.
1958	34.7	16.4	12.2	9.3
1969	50.3	24.7	9.7	10.0

SOURCE: U.S. Senate Committee on Finance, Executive Branch Study No. 4, *Effect of Regional Trade Groups on U.S. Foreign Trade: The EC and EFTA Experiences*, 93d Cong., 1st sess., 1973, pp. 9–10, 20.

alliance. This possibility was disturbing, since the Soviet Union's economic challenge, impressive industrial and technological growth, and effective propaganda campaigns against Western capitalism had already placed pressure on NATO and American security efforts. In the meantime, relations among the Atlantic powers were oftentimes distressingly rocky. General Charles de Gaulle's return to power in France, in 1958, implied a more independent French stance from American designs in the alliance. Paris also simmered over America's rebuff of Anglo-Franco-Israeli actions against Egypt during the Suez crisis of 1956. Chancellor Konrad Adenauer of West Germany demanded a greater part in decisions on nuclear weapons, and joined France in seeking a more decisive role in global politics for Western Europe. Also, although Great Britain cherished its "special relationship" with the United States, the American slap on the wrist during the Suez crisis had been humiliating. And guardians of the British empire and other leaders across the political spectrum in London were not quick to forget their general frustration in having their country forced to its knees economically, with a consequent loss of world power, by its American cousin after World War II.[11]

In fact, Britain, America's closest ally in Europe, had posed a problem for the United States in the trade sphere. London had formed the EFTA in 1959 as a counter to the Six, and therefore in opposition to United States policy. Although smaller in population, export volume, and GNP than the EEC, the Free Trade Association, or "Outer Seven," imported as much as the Six and comprised a wealthier economy. Britain's proposal to fuse the EFTA and the Common Market under a consolidated Western European free-trade union drew American fire because such a bloc might gang up and discriminate against U.S. exports. But just as serious, because the Outer Seven resisted the political integration desired by the Six, and had no common tariff that linked members on an intimate economic basis like the EEC, it threatened America's paramount cold war desire of unifying the Western alliance. Britain neglected European political integration, thereby dividing the global trade regime and undermining allied cooperation.[12]

Thus, to some extent, both the Six and the Outer Seven vexed American policymakers. The United States sought politically intimate, outward-looking, "trade-creating" European partners instead of disparate, preferential, "trade-diverting" blocs. America acknowledged that as a rule, customs unions like the Six built up tariffs for the mutual protection of each member and that was worrisome. The EFTA was not a customs union but forsook the integrationist goal, and that irked America, too. And, while the EEC supported political integration and opposed trade restrictions, the Treaty of Rome did not ensure that such would be the case. As economist Bela Belassa told Congress in 1962, without global multilateral tariff cuts, the predicted elimination of internal tariffs in the Common Market would merely lead to discrimination against U.S. exports. Thus, Washington prodded Western Europeans to tailor their trade policies to the broad, cohesive political objectives of the alliance instead of resorting to protectionism.[13] As Kennedy and Johnson soon discovered, however, the allies did not always comply with this plea.

Trade with the Rest of the World

While European integration undercut American power, so did the trade and policies of other nations, particularly Japan. Scrapping reform of its former enemy's society for cold war strategic interests by 1948, the United States helped rebuild Japan's economy and transformed Tokyo into a close ally. By reorienting Japanese commerce away from the Western Pacific basin, granting its imports liberal tariff treatment, and fighting Western European opposition to Tokyo's accession to GATT, America stimulated a boom in Japanese trade that endured into the 1990s. While Washington enjoyed a 350 percent growth in exports to Japan during the 1950s, imports from Tokyo multiplied more than sixfold. Ranked thirteenth among exporters to the United States in 1952, Japan had climbed to second eight years later. Complaints from American producers about the Asian invasion of their markets, and continued Japanese trade discrimination, compelled Tokyo to adopt a comprehensive trade liberalization plan in 1960.[14] But trade patterns confirmed that Japan had developed into both America's commercial partner and rival.

Trade between Canada and America, each others' top export

TABLE 1.3

U.S. Merchandise Trade Balance with Major Industrial Trade Partners
(billions of dollars)

Year	U.S. overall trade balance	EEC	EFTA	Canada	Japan
1958	3.46	1.18	.10	.5	.3
1960	4.58	1.69	.67	.6	.4
1962	4.52	2.13	.23	.4	.2
1964	7.08	2.28	.56	.6	.2
1966	3.87	1.36	.06	.5	−.6
1968	.83	.41	.32	.1	−1.1
1971	−2.01	.76	−.07	−2.3	−3.2
1973	1.67	1.20	−.32	−2.6	−1.3

SOURCE: Werner J. Feld, *The European Community in World Affairs: Economic Power and Political Influence* (New York: Alfred, 1976), p. 186; U.S. Department of Commerce, *Statistical Abstracts of the United States, 1962*, pp. 885–886; *1963*, pp. 879–880; *1967*, p. 839; *1970*, p. 789; *1974*, p. 793; U.S. Senate Committee on Finance, *Staff Data and Materials on U.S. Trade and the Balance of Payments*, 93d Cong., 2d sess., 1974, pp. 4, 17–18.

markets, also unveiled looming challenges. The United States supplied nearly three-quarters of Canadian imports in the 1950s, and over half of all major product groups, except for textiles and petroleum. A trade deficit with America notwithstanding, Canada occupied roughly half of the U.S. market. America envisioned a free-trade zone of interdependent commerce and investment, a policy not accepted until 1988 and denounced as imperialism by many Canadians. Ottawa also protested injurious U.S. farm surplus disposal programs and oil import quotas, which limited Canadian exports. Prime Minister John Diefenbaker strained neighborly relations by the late 1950s by seeking closer, more preferential economic ties with Great Britain, at the expense of United States exports.[15]

Of all the issues in American trade policy, none were more contentious than those posed by the less-developed countries. Rebelling against the American-led GATT system, the South argued that the interests of rich and poor nations diverged, and that the core ignored the periphery's special problems. LDCs sought to aid their infant industries through protectionism, but despite GATT's development norm, which permitted deviations from liberal trade, they believed that existing trade mechanisms and rules were too limited in their effectiveness. The MFN principle was also meaningless for the South, which had few concessions to give in negotiations. Refusing to join GATT, many developing nations after the war tried to reform the system, or resorted to import substitution, an inward-looking plan that focused on cutting off imports as the route to industrialization.

By the late 1950s, this strategy had failed. Import substitution did not reduce foreign-made goods and few LDCs had transferred production over to manufactures. Most of them still relied on only one raw material commodity for export, making them vulnerable to world demand and price fluctuation. The South traded cheaper crops for the more expensive processed or semiprocessed items of the North, and these terms of trade failed to earn the LDCs enough hard currency to import capital goods and build an industrial base. As a result, industrialization stalled, core trade rules increasingly plagued the LDCs, and the Soviet Union proposed a new trade organization—separate from GATT—that would benefit the Third World. In response, a panel of GATT experts issued the Haberler report in 1958, which recommended that the North forgo reciprocity in negotiations with the periphery and pledge to augment Third World exports. Yet the LDCs remained skeptical about penetrating core markets and competing in world trade.[16]

Statistics explained the reasons behind their exasperation. To be sure, exports climbed from 1945 to 1960; Latin American exports rose by 22 percent, African by 42 percent, and Asian by a paltry 10 percent. Total Southern exports registered a 29 percent increase. But the more lucrative manufactured exports, limited to advanced LDCs (of which nearly two-thirds were Asian), were concentrated in a few products such as textiles, and accounted for merely 15 percent of the Third World export total. Furthermore, global trade patterns favored the North; the only sales that increased more than the exports of industrial nations came from the Middle East, where petroleum spurred exports. Most striking, between 1950 and 1960, the LDCs' share of world exports declined from 31.6 percent to 21.4 percent while the core's share climbed from 60.4 percent to 66.8 percent. Asia, Africa, and Latin America (excluding Venezuela's sizable oil exports) ran enlarging trade deficits from 1958 to 1961.[17] The postwar international trade order clearly failed to sustain the expanding exports needed by most of the Third World for development.

The Eisenhower administration did not help matters. Such aid programs as P.L. 480, or "Food for Peace," along with protective quotas on lead, zinc, oil, and textiles, retarded agricultural development and exports in the South, and helped U.S. exporters. Meanwhile, in the American market in these years, Africa was the sole gainer among the LDCs. In 1960, Kennedy indicted Eisenhower for not far surpassing Soviet investments in the South and for not helping the poor nations diversify their crops, form common markets, and stabilize their economies. As historian Burton Kaufman concludes, the periphery was economically worse off after Ike's eight years in office than before.[18] It remained for the Kennedy administration to correct this imbalance, if possible.

The Balance-of-Payments Deficit

By the end of the 1950s, the most ominous foreign economic legacy of Eisenhower's tenure—the balance-of-payments deficit—constrained America's ability to meet the challenges of foreign competitors and Third World development. The deficit caused a drain of U.S. gold stocks and, above all, threatened America's ability to meet overseas economic commitments.[19] The nation had run a payments deficit almost every year since 1950, but it had never reached more than $2.1 billion from 1950 to 1957. By 1958, Western Europeans had accumulated enough dollar reserves to allow for currency convertibility, but America continued to pour dollars into the region and elsewhere through military spending and aid programs. These expenditures caused a glut of dollars in European banks, which foreign financiers soon began cashing in for American gold, to the dismay of an anxious United States. The more America spent overseas, the more its gold reserves dropped, thus undermining confidence in the dollar, global economic recovery, and U.S. exports. By 1960, for the first time, foreign dollar holdings exceeded United States gold reserves, and by the November presidential election, America suffered its first run on the dollar when nations began to convert their dollars into gold at a rapid rate.

The ensuing "gold drain" was a product of American hegemony, because U.S. global leadership allowed for the seemingly uncontrollable deficit. But now, American power was on the decline, which heightened the strain on the country's international payments in various ways. For one, United States investment overseas spurred growing capital outflows. When added to American commitments to NATO and foreign aid, a run on the British pound, and currency convertibility, which allowed for speculation against the dollar, the payments deficit became a major burden. In 1958, the deficit caused gold holdings to fall by $2.3 billion, in contrast to the annual outflow of $200 million since 1950. Overseas spending, smaller trade surpluses, and a quick domestic recovery from recession in 1958, which raised the consumer demand for imports in America, caused the degenerating debit. The trade surplus dropped to $3.4 billion in 1958 and hit bottom at $1.1 billion in 1959, although it rose strongly in 1960. The payments deficit mimicked the trend of the trade balance, except for the surge in 1960. Thus, in 1959 the deficit amounted to $4.2 billion with only a slight improvement in 1960.[20] The plight of the payments deficit, with its resultant gold drain, depressed and alarmed American officials.

Taking the payments balance out of the red was Eisenhower's primary aim in foreign economic policy by the late 1950s, but his remedies foundered. He tied foreign loans to purchases of American goods, urged aid and military burden-sharing among the allies, and encouraged the disposal of surplus farm produce. He also began a program of export promotion and supported the formation of the Organization for Economic Cooperation and Development to facilitate allied cooperation on economic problems. Washington also looked to the Dillon Round of GATT in 1960 to lower tariffs and expand U.S. exports. But these efforts to reverse the deficit fell short and required the country to reassess, with an eye possibly toward curtailing, its foreign policy goals.[21] Foreign trade had become, even more than before, a key to America's international payments. Healthy overseas accounts, in turn, were critical to the nation's future security and economic aid capabilities. But the prognosis for the payments deficit was gloomy.

Governmental and Societal Sources of Trade

The payments deficit, the rise of the Common Market, and friction with trade partners pointed to the erosion of United States power. So did domestic economic problems, characterized by slower growth, outbursts of inflation, and more joblessness relative to the full employment levels in other nations. To be sure, the nation had enjoyed record levels of prosperity during the Eisenhower years, as corporate and manufacturing profits, individual incomes, and farm productivity soared. But major industrial areas of the United States, including Kennedy's own New England, had suffered from the loss of manufacturing as factories increasingly moved to the South in search of cheap labor. Farm incomes had also dropped throughout the 1950s due, in part, to the cuts in federal price supports of the Eisenhower administration. In order to highlight these and other Republican failings, Kennedy exaggerated these troubles, pledging to "get the country moving again" if elected president. But Eisenhower also wished to boost productionism, and the halting recovery in 1959 from recession frustrated him, too.[22] Clearly, the seeds of America's decline had been planted by the late 1950s, in both the international and domestic arenas.

The effects of foreign protectionism and competition on the American economy was one factor that impeded United States growth and power. As the merchandise trade surplus shrunk, so did exports of machinery, transportation equipment, chemicals, textiles, and steel. For instance, the United States became a net importer of steel by the late 1950s. In fact, overseas competition had such a large impact on the U.S. output that between 1950 and 1970, America's share of world steel production dropped from over 46 percent to approximately 20 percent. In addition, substantial farm exports would also soon confront the Common Market's restrictive farm system under the common agricultural policy. For example, the Six aimed to replace U.S. wheat in West Germany and Benelux with Italian and French grain. American producers' protests over these plans were somewhat disingenuous, since exporters enjoyed their own system of government subsidies that protected them from low world commodity prices. Along with other exporters of manufactures, however, farmers demanded more access to markets abroad.[23]

Imports took much of the blame from societal interests for domestic economic problems. Farmers lobbied for curbs on foreign goods despite a steady decline of agricultural imports throughout the Eisenhower years. Many manufacturers felt the impact of European and Japanese recovery and pressure from the periphery in the form of low-priced imports. Cotton textile imports, for example, more than tripled from 1950 to 1960. Import-competitors claimed such trends caused drops in production and employment. Nevertheless, although their own inefficiencies explained at least part of their problems, such stagnation further burdened struggling producers, and their grievances about imports received a hearing among the trade policy representative element on Capitol Hill.[24]

Congress, in essence, qualified the commitment to liberal trade by responding to the pleas of societal interests for protection. Legislators had learned the disastrous lessons of the onerous Smoot-Hawley tariff of 1930, and thus most endorsed liberal trade. Unlike Britain's unilateral trade liberalization in the 1860s, however, they made sure that the United States lowered tariffs solely on a reciprocal basis, starting in 1934. Furthermore, Congress took as its base point for duty reduction the high Smoot-Hawley tariff levels, and not a more reasonable reference, and also circumscribed the trade liberalism of the Reciprocal Trade Act (RTA) by attaching protective clauses to successive renewals from the late 1940s onward.[25]

These devices were ubiquitous. In 1947, Congress adopted the "escape clause" as a formal mechanism in trade negotiations, and along with the "peril point" provision in 1948 (repealed the next year but reinstated in 1951), it became a permanent part of the trade program. The escape clause, pursuant to investigations by the United States Tariff Commission, permitted a withdrawal of concessions from a trade agreement that might injure an industry. The peril point set a point at which such a concession, in the form of a tariff cut, threatened a producer. In addition, a waiver from GATT, written into the extension of Section 22 of the Agricultural Adjustment Act in 1948, imposed limits on commodity imports

regardless of prior agreements, in contradiction to GATT principles. In 1954, Congress also retained a weakened version of the
Buy American Act of 1933, which gave a preference to American
bidders for government orders. Furthermore, the national security
clause of 1955 permitted escape from a trade agreement if an
import reached such quantities that it impaired the country's defense effort.[26]

Loaded with these protectionist measures, the RTAs of the
1950s slowed, to an extent, the swing toward liberal trade. Eisenhower hailed his 1955 bill as a "tremendous victory" for liberal
trade, but it actually authorized tariff cuts of only 15 percent,
when earlier RTAs called for larger reductions. The RTA of 1958
was an even bigger retreat from liberal trade. The bill permitted
an industry, regardless of whether it was crucial to United States
defense, to seek protection under the national security provision,
and empowered Congress to override the president's refusal to
invoke the escape clause. This RTA granted authority to reduce
tariffs by only 20 percent. Liberal traders blasted the 1958 legislation, aimed at negotiating with the new Common Market over the
next four years, as "the most protectionist measure ever passed by
Congress in all the Reciprocal Trade renewals since 1934."[27] Such
statements divulged the ongoing clash between the foreign policy
executive and representative element. But in a narrower political
sense, the RTA of 1958 also brought criticism from congressmen
who sought to balance protectionism with liberal trade. Among
them was Senator John F. Kennedy, Democrat from Massachusetts.

Individual Sources: Kennedy's Fair-Trade Doctrine

Kennedy was the consummate fair-trader. He formulated his presidential trade policy while in Congress by reconciling the economic
and political realities of import-competing Massachusetts with the
national program of liberal trade. Foreign trade, wrote economic
adviser Paul Samuelson, was an issue of concern for Kennedy
because of his constituents' problems with imports. Yet he understood the essentials of liberal trade policy, noted economist Seymour E. Harris, convinced of its importance. Indeed, Kennedy

explained that choosing a position on trade in Massachusetts required a "split personality."[28] Some segments of the economy favored low duties in order to buy such raw materials as oil more cheaply, while others sought protection for such traditional, and increasingly inefficient, industries as textiles. Kennedy voted for the RTAs during his congressional career. Yet he qualified his support and urged protection for regional industries as a member of a special delegation of New England senators.[29]

On the protectionist side of fair trade, Kennedy blamed imports, in part, for the deteriorating sectors of New England's economy. For instance, he not only denounced government policies for ignoring the movement of textile factories to the southern United States, but also criticized the rising inflow of low-wage imports from abroad, which had diminished textile production. New England lost 150,000 textile-related jobs between 1929 and 1950 as hundreds of mills closed. In response, Kennedy denounced Eisenhower's inaction in limiting textile imports from Asia as a "lack of comprehension or misjudgment," or "indifference." The senator demanded quotas, and backed the "Geneva Reservation" of GATT, which permitted higher textile duties when GATT failed to provide sufficient protection for American industries.[30]

The fishing sector embodied the import problem. Kennedy cited lags in research and development and scarcity of some species as causes of industry stagnation. Yet after constituents informed him of the large yearly increases of fillet imports, he feared that without protection, this old Massachusetts industry would soon be extinct. He complained after Eisenhower refused to uphold a Tariff Commission report that recommended restraints on fish imports: the RTA was "not designed to crucify the ancient New England fishing industry," but it had permitted so much "cutthroat competition" from northern Europe that major ports were fast becoming "dead" cities.[31] Kennedy did not seek higher tariffs in such cases for the sake of "unjustifiable protection from foreign competition." Instead, he argued "that there are certain industries which by their nature are unable to compete with imports on a fair basis. In those situations, I feel that a tariff to equalize competition is necessary."[32]

This pragmatic view of trade, the basis of the fair-trade doctrine, enhanced Kennedy's image as a caring protectionist. The remedy was simple, he told a Massachusetts labor organization: "We know that our fisheries, our jewelry, and certain other industries need protection if they are not to be offered as a sacrifice to the theoretical principle of free trade."[33] He asserted in 1952 that liberal trade was "an ideal." The removal of trade barriers was possible only after U.S. industries were safe from injury; trade liberalization could not be a "one-way street" with America bearing the burden. Without import relief, the country would merely "be putting the cart of the ideal before the horse of our own bread and butter."[34]

In effect, Kennedy argued that theory did not mesh with the hard facts of regional depression in New England, or in global trends in trade. Contrary to popular belief, he noted (inaccurately) that the United States possessed low tariffs comparable to Scandinavia and Benelux. Consequently, American imports had more than quintupled over the past twenty-five years, while European protectionism endured. Kennedy complained that "a cardinal principle" of international trade had been violated; America was "being subjected to unfair and unequal discrimination" abroad.[35] When economist Charles P. Kindleberger called him a protectionist, Kennedy replied that his trade views were more complex than the label implied. He simply opposed unfair discriminatory trade practices against American goods that jeopardized the welfare of New England.[36]

Despite his tough statements against imports on behalf of constituents, Kennedy was not a protectionist. Although it might certainly be politically wise to voice support for protection, he grounded his trade policy on a New Deal faith that government must cure economic distress. Seeking a balance between national and local interests, the senator believed that the federal government had an obligation to modify U.S. trade policy when imports threatened entire industries. He sympathized with Eisenhower's dilemma of reconciling "the conflicting national interest" of freer trade with the "legitimate needs" of a few domestic interests. Just as President Franklin D. Roosevelt had overseen the transition to a war economy, however, Eisenhower must assist those hurt by the nation's trade policy.[37]

He found a means for national aid in a government-financed program of "adjustment assistance," borrowed from David McDonald of the United Steel Workers. The plan provided for compensation or retraining for workers, loans for businesses, and development aid to areas adversely affected by imports. Arguing that such assistance was not a subsidy, but consolidated existing federal aid programs into one act, Kennedy recognized that liberal trade was a permanent fixture of United States foreign policy. Thus, the plan would not result in the "mutilation" of the RTA. The escape clause had failed to protect producers, he claimed, since only three of forty-three applications for relief had been instituted. Instead of relegating industries to "suffer in silence" because of the national interest in lower tariffs, the president had a viable option. Adjustment assistance was a compromise, freeing "constantly increasing international trade so essential to the economic health of the United States without jeopardizing the welfare of affected industries and their employees."[38] The Eisenhower administration, and other anti–big government conservatives, rejected the relief program, and Kennedy fared no better when he tried to tie the plan to successive RTAs and the Area Redevelopment Act in the 1950s. Yet adjustment assistance, which he eventually attached to his own trade bill in 1962, allowed Kennedy to be a consistent fair-trader. He advocated protection for injured producers but stayed in the mainstream of New Deal ideology as a liberal trade adherent. By no means a doctrinaire free-trader, he told his constituents nonetheless to be realistic, for regardless of local attitudes, the postwar trend in foreign trade policy was toward less restrictions. Even for the fishing industry, he opposed excluding imports, arguing instead for a "fair and equitable" quota. "In all frankness," he wrote a voter, he approved of liberal trade.[39]

His father's profitable liquor importing business first taught him the financial benefits of lower tariffs. As ambassador to England, Joseph Kennedy had helped negotiate the Anglo–American trade agreement of 1938, which halved tariffs on a reciprocal basis between Britain and America. Spouting free-trade dogma, he claimed that liberalization would end economic conflict, increase the standard of living, and unify the democracies. Meanwhile, there was no doubt that tariffs cuts lowered prices, and thus enhanced the sales of imported liquor, of which the ambassador was a major concessionaire.[40]

Such personal gains aside, his son understood that the harmful effects of high tariffs damaged capitalist economies. Although cognizant of import injury, Senator Kennedy usually rejected low tariffs as the culprit. He argued instead that competition from the southern United States, and such factors of inefficiency as outmoded plants, expensive transportation and power, lack of diversification, and scarce capital investment caused economic difficulties in industries like textiles. When he backed a tariff hike, he preferred it to be a temporary measure, and adjusted downward once it fulfilled its need. High tariffs, he emphasized, provided only temporary answers to the competitive problems of American industry. While avoiding "indiscriminate competition" from others, the United States must encourage trade liberalization and enhance economic cooperation in the world. In sum, Kennedy supported the RTA because, as he explained, he was "a firm believer in subsequent international agreements by which other nations have been enabled to sell their products in the United States, as we sell our products abroad. World trade can never be a one-way street."[41]

Although sensitive to the potential political backlash from this liberal trade bent, he had no qualms in telling producers that they sometimes exaggerated the impact of import competition. Kennedy disputed protectionist contentions that imports worsened domestic employment, especially since nearly a third of New England's jobs relied on low-priced raw material imports, such as cotton, wool, and oil. Profits from exports of most firms overcame losses incurred from imports, he claimed. "If we depress imports," he said, "then there will also be reductions in exports. Foreign countries cannot buy our goods unless they have entry for theirs."[42] This push for reciprocity was the rationale behind the fair-trade doctrine.

His support of reciprocal trade attested to his interest in using trade as a tool in foreign policy. Profitable relations among allies outweighed protectionist benefits, a lesson garnered from the quarrels between America and Europe during the high-tariff 1930s. Like other postwar leaders, Kennedy advocated liberal trade to reduce economic nationalism and political conflict, and later viewed freer trade as a means to combat communist economic competition. Protectionism undermined America's ability to meet Soviet advances with attractive trade opportunities for the rich and poor nations alike. "It is a fact," he wrote a constituent as the EEC emerged in 1958, "that American rigidity would probably force European nations to seek trade outlets in Communist bloc countries with resulting adverse political consequences."[43] As the statist school claims, Kennedy, while anticipating higher profits for the United States, nonetheless recognized the need to subordinate the economics of trade to political and diplomatic objectives.

Friendly trade relations with Western Europe thus were important to Kennedy. In 1954, for instance, he opposed a strict adherence to the Buy American Act; U.S. employment had to be weighed against the economic needs of America's recovering allies. Furthermore, when the Common Market and the Outer Seven intended to raise trade barriers to outsiders as part of their unification process, Kennedy wished that they would "create an environment" in which all nations would willingly reduce restrictions in tandem. Bracing this belief in reciprocity with an institutional base, the senator backed the Organization for Trade Cooperation, a stillborn forum similar in design to the ITO, which would have granted the United States a "decisive voice" in a liberal trade order. Liberal trade was the "cement" of the alliance.[44]

The Third World was critical to Kennedy's liberal trade views. Visiting the Middle East and Asia in 1951, he witnessed the vulnerability of the periphery to Soviet influence, and thus, upon his return, he suggested a stepped-up aid program for the South. Kennedy noted the "economic gap" between the South and North because the periphery had not shared in the tremendous postwar growth in world trade. While he believed that recessions in the United States lowered the prices of LDC commodities, and thus worsened the South's deteriorating terms of trade with the core, he indicted Eisenhower for lacking imagination in dealing with poor nations. Kennedy recommended reducing tariffs and quotas, easing Export-Import Bank loan restrictions, and negotiating international commodity agreements in order to boost prices for the South. He also endorsed regional economic integration in the periphery as a means to enhance stability, self-sufficiency, and development efforts, and proposed ending unilateral farm surplus disposal schemes that disrupted commercial trade, to the detriment of the Third World.[45]

The unifying economic and political purposes of the fair-trade doctrine undergirded these modifications of LDC trade and aid programs. In the long run, stagnation in the South, due to decreased exports, would deleteriously affect the North by slowing down industrial expansion and, in turn, lead to self-defeating trade wars. Thus, Kennedy urged an increase in Third World income by ensuring that international trade channels remain open. By accelerating growth in the periphery through aid, more market access, and lessened import restraints, the North could show the South "that the democratic process is a persuasive method of creation, not frustration" in the cold war.[46]

By the late 1950s, Kennedy had developed his trade perspective into a coherent fair-trade doctrine. Recognizing that the expansion of world commerce was important, he nonetheless refused to give unqualified support to a trade policy that jeopardized the public welfare. His answer was a "double attack" of adjustment assistance coupled with the Area Redevelopment bill, which addressed inherent economic problems not caused by imports. And in 1959 he cosponsored labor legislation offering aid to producers hurt by low-wage imports, which protectionists argued placed high-wage industries in the United States at a competitive disadvantage. But he shied from protectionism, opposing versions of the bill that called for raising tariffs.[47]

When the last RTA of his Senate career exited the Senate Finance Committee in 1958, fair-trader Kennedy expressed his disappointment at its limited tariff bargaining authority, but was "pleased" that it strengthened the escape clause and peril point provisions. He voted for the bill, but noting the impending presence of the Common Market, he rejected the "sledgehammer approach" of protectionists in attaching "dubious" restraints on the president's power to lower tariffs a mere 20 percent for four, instead of five, years. Kennedy predicted that trade would remain a crucial element in U.S. foreign policy in the 1960s, especially in maintaining America's position in the international economy, domestic health, and cooperative relations with the allies. "I have long made my position clear," he told a voter. "We must have a reciprocal trade policy if we are to preserve our relationship to foreign governments and if we are to encourage our domestic industry to produce for foreign markets."[48]

But pragmatism and a good deal of self-interest should guide U.S. policy, he affirmed. In GATT negotiations, Kennedy candidly declared that Washington should not be "philanthropic." He expected Americans to be "hard bargainers" and demand equal concessions from other nations. But toughness must be mixed with the recognition that a healthy economy rested on the United States also giving concessions. Freer trade helped other nations earn dollars with which to purchase more goods, and thus led to a rising standard of living for all. In effect, the "great merit of the trade agreements system is that it permits all parties to the agreements to benefit."[49] Such was the ultimate purpose of the fair-trade doctrine.

On the presidential campaign trail in 1960, Democratic party candidate Kennedy tried to avoid the protectionist pitfall. He planned to stimulate the economy by boosting output among producers at an annual rate of 5 percent, because productionism was the "best protection" against displacement from imports. Noting America's lagging growth among industrialized nations, he warned against "economic slackness," since competition would be "keener" in the future. Witnesses at a hearing on United States–EEC relations echoed him. Congressman Mike Monroney (D-Okla.) said that the United States had become "overly fat and a little self-satisfied" in the 1950s, unconcerned about foreign competition. A failure to modernize, provide good service, or gear products to European demand had lost America its preeminence in the typewriter and small automobile markets, for instance, to a more "lean, thin, and hungry" Common Market.[50]

Yet debate during the campaign, not surprisingly, gravitated toward protectionism, since Kennedy, and Republican candidate Richard M. Nixon, knew that liberal trade had no voter appeal in economically distressed areas. Kennedy spoke with caution, particularly in the South, not only because textile firms there had suffered during the 1950s, but because he expected electoral difficulties over the Catholic and civil rights issues. Textile people groaned that both candidates were "free traders," but singled out Kennedy for criticism. He had denounced Eisenhower for increasing imports, they commented, but his record showed that he would "broadly boost, not restrict, imports."[51]

The Democratic platform, however, offered more protection than it was given credit for, although less than the Republican plank. The Democrats resoundingly endorsed the RTA as the means to meet the challenge of the Six, help the Third World, correct the payments deficit, and unite the West against communism. They adopted adjustment assistance to protect domestic industries. The Republicans, although pressing for liberal trade, supported more protectionist devices for aiding injured producers, including increased use of the escape clause, national security provision, and voluntary import quotas. This platform perhaps made Kennedy appear less willing to act for import-competitors, although aides also worried that his isolated protectionist remarks, such as requests for voluntary textile quotas, might be construed as inconsistent with liberal trade.[52] Yet Kennedy knew that his seemingly contradictory stance signified the tricky balancing act of fair trade, a doctrine that he now readied for the White House.

The campaign culminated Kennedy's congressional career of juggling liberal trade with a sensitivity to declining, but vocal, domestic interests. Many national leaders had done the same, for the postwar trade regime under GATT permitted protectionism at the same time that negotiations to lower barriers were under way. Coming from a state that epitomized the troubles brought on by imports, Kennedy accepted trade restrictions as a political fact of life. He clashed with Eisenhower on this score, since the president, as the foreign policy executive, naturally fostered national over regional solutions to the import problem. But Kennedy and Eisenhower agreed on the merits of liberal trade for national and international reasons.

Differences between Kennedy and the administration existed, however. As a New Deal adherent, the senator accepted the notion of wholesale government intervention in the economy. Thus, while the Eisenhower administration relied on such traditional devices as the escape clause and peril point to help import-competitors, Kennedy proposed the social security safety net of adjustment assistance. Although this measure changed the concept of import injury, exposing domestic interests to the full force of liberal trade, it provided more protection than the escape clause, which Eisenhower had invoked only rarely, and with little effect. In essence, Eisenhower remained entrenched in increasingly obsolete, ineffective, and at times, insensitive methods of dealing with imports. Ironically, by the end of his tenure, he had merely managed to feed protectionists, who weakened his authority to lower tariffs in 1958. Meanwhile, Kennedy, and the vanguard of the Democratic party, initiated an imaginative program that addressed current and future conditions in the domestic economy and the international trade regime. Their willingness to apply even doses of government aid and trade competition predicted a flexible and workable policy for the years ahead.

Such trade management underscored Kennedy's forward-looking vision in foreign affairs, which confronted America's declining predominance across the globe. While Eisenhower fostered liberal trade with Western Europe, an intimate Atlantic community, and Third World development, his actions seemed tired and flat. Kennedy, while seeking the same goals, hoped to adopt more forceful, dramatic ways of meeting the challenges to United States power by overhauling aid, trade, and general foreign policies. In trade, he planned to meet competition from the Six, the EFTA, Japan, and Canada, and attack flaws in the North–South trade system, seeking to stop the American decline in the world economy through energetic measures.

As statist scholars claim, Kennedy sought to use U.S. leadership in GATT in order to reassert American power over the global trade order, and thereby enhance the nation's power and wealth. Indeed, Kennedy and his predecessors placed security, political, and domestic economic objectives above the sole aim of economic profit through trade based on comparative advantage. As the cold war persisted and the Soviet specter steered U.S. calculations, American leaders expected to use trade for diplomatic and political ends. Thus, Washington hoped to further EEC integration, keep the Common Market open for the benefit of all members of a cooperative Western alliance, and expand U.S. exports in order to reverse America's payments deficit. Above all, the latter goal would ease the U.S. economic burden of free world leadership, and, Kennedy hoped, stem America's sliding power.

Kennedy thus took to the presidency a firsthand expertise in foreign trade and a recognition of the economic, political, and overarching national security considerations embedded in America's commercial policy. His familiarity with the liberal trade–protectionist dualism proved useful as he moved from the representative element to the sphere of foreign policy executive. In international commercial policy, the purpose of his administration, he announced, would be "to make effective the concept of responsible trade among free nations by means which will promote the economic prosperity of all peoples while ensuring equitable conditions of competition for our own industries."[53] The victory secured in November 1960, President-elect Kennedy set out to achieve this fair-trade objective.

capital account, causing an average deficit of $2.9 billion between 1960 and 1963, and a subsequent, dreaded gold drain. Pervading White House discussions, the deficit purportedly scared Kennedy as much as nuclear war because it threatened not only U.S. prestige and commitments abroad but gave such gold-horders as France leverage over America's global designs. That is, in order to balance international accounts, Charles de Gaulle could greatly influence Kennedy's foreign policy by threatening to cash in French dollar assets for American gold, thus further depleting U.S. bullion stocks. Also, the payments problem had a major impact on the entire Western capitalist system, for, as Kennedy explained, "we are the principal banker of the free world and any potential weakness in our dollar spells trouble, not only for us but also for our friends and allies who rely on the dollar to finance a substantial portion of their trade."[3]

The deficit also posed a paradoxical dilemma for New Frontier programs. Simply put, America's industrial growth, aggregate expansion, and recovery from recession, spurred by Keynesian growth polices, were good for the economy but not for the deficit, because such developments raised imports and thereby worsened the trade balance. But hiking tariffs, in order to slow imports, would also hamper the economy by jacking the prices of raw materials, capital goods, and consumer products, and thus undermine the president's productionist plans. Kennedy opted instead for wage and price guideposts in order to prevent inflation and keep U.S. export costs competitive. But most significant, the deficit demonstrated that America was not immune from economic distress, and could no longer shape its domestic stabilization policies without considering the international repercussions.[4] The payments imbalance thus forced Kennedy to frame trade policy in the context of global and domestic priorities, both of which had become harder to manage because of the relative weakening of America's world economic power.

The options available to the administration to eliminate the deficit included reform of the international monetary order, but Kennedy effectively blocked this viable alternative. The president asked the allies to share more of the burden for financing NATO, discouraged U.S. capital outflows, and encouraged foreign capital

TABLE 2.1
Breakdown of U.S. Balance of Payments
(billions of dollars)

Year	Balance of payments	Military spending	Foreign aid	Private** investments
1960	−3.7*	−2.8	−2.6	−1.7
1962	−2.9	−2.4	−2.8	−1.7
1964	−2.7	−2.1	−3.2	−2.3
1966	−2.2	−2.9	−3.4	−3.7
1968	−1.6	−3.1	−3.9	−3.2
1970	−4.7	−3.4	−3.8	−4.4
1972	−14.7	−3.6	−3.5	−3.4

* Minus signs signify net deficit spending.
** Long-term direct investments abroad of private capital.
SOURCE: U.S. Senate Finance Committee, *Staff Data and Materials on U.S. Trade and the Balance of Payments*, 93d Cong., 2d sess., 1974, pp. 1, 26–27.

inflows by keeping short-term interest rates high and long-term rates low. But significantly, he refused to devalue the dollar as a means to boost exports and curb European conversion of dollar holdings into gold. He wished instead to maintain the dollar's value and, in essence, have America's trade partners support his domestic productionist policies. By doing so, the artificially high price of the dollar could not withstand later pressure from speculators, and eventually, the overvalued currency helped undermine the Bretton Woods financial system.

Not surprisingly, the status of the dollar and the gold outflow provoked a call from other alliance members for a more pluralistic power-sharing arrangement in the global monetary regime. Most everyone agreed that a reform of the system was in order because of the United States' payments deficit and due to the recent ability of the Europeans to convert their currencies in financial markets. American Robert Roosa, undersecretary of the treasury, devised a plan for central banks to support the dollar's value by buying dollars, or dollar-denominated securities called Roosa bonds, when they were sold by speculators. But again, this created an artificial price for the dollar, and particularly angered the French, who believed that the United States got special treatment because the dollar remained the capitalist system's reserve currency. In short, the deficit allowed Washington to enjoy special privileges and dictate policy to the allies. Disgusted by this arrangement, de

Gaulle protested that America could run a deficit while other nations had to balance their payments or suffer controls imposed by the International Monetary Fund (IMF), the institutional regulator of the Bretton Woods system. This deficit permitted the dollar to dominate European economies, while the American government and business could continue their unlimited foreign expenditures, overseas investments at cheap exchange rates, and large-scale spending on New Frontier domestic programs. France wanted the United States to discipline itself under IMF rules by balancing its payments, and urged a return to a true gold standard instead of maintaining the dollar standard. Kennedy refused, but debate now developed within his administration.

Two views in Washington reflected the conflict over the dollar. First, Robert Triffin, an economics professor, worried about global liquidity and the gold drain. Since foreigners held more dollars than America had gold for redemption by 1960, the United States could no longer honor its gold-conversion pledge. But, because America provided two-thirds of the world's monetary reserves, an end to its payments deficit would mean a serious shortage of liquidity. Triffin's "paradox" thus placed the United States in a seemingly no-win situation; continuing the deficit would further erode U.S. power and economic growth, but terminating it might bring trade to a halt for lack of dollars. He had an answer to this dilemma, and it called for the multilateralization of IMF reserves now that European currencies were convertible and the American payments deficit persisted. That is, recognizing that European power had reached a rough equilibrium with American, Triffin suggested making the dollar just one of several reserve currencies in a re-formed IMF, which would act as a huge superbank. This sharing of reserve status, heeding European demands for more pluralism, eventually took place by the late 1960s in the form of Special Drawing Rights. But in the Kennedy years, the United States opted to retain the present dollar standard, and thus its dominance over the international monetary order.

Instead of following Triffin's advice of allowing the dollar to take its place among other currencies, the president sought to maintain U.S. hegemony by protecting the dominating position of the dollar. Pushed by C. Douglas Dillon, secretary of the treasury,

and Undersecretary Roosa, Kennedy chose this option by opposing
Triffin's reform, which had the endorsement of the State Department but which he viewed as premature. Kennedy preferred to
defend the established financial regime. His decision, like that
against devaluation, placed a growing strain on the dollar. Although enjoying temporary success, Kennedy's traditional approach failed in the long run. Improvement in the payments balance during the Kennedy and Johnson years was deceptive, as
higher military and foreign aid expenditures and an overvalued
dollar eventually exacerbated the deficit. Within a decade, after
enormous spending on domestic programs and the Vietnam War
added to the shaky American hold on its monetary status, the
entire Bretton Woods order collapsed.[5]

Kennedy, in fact, preferred to confront the deficit with new
foreign trade tools. While the president admitted that higher tariffs
might alleviate the payments crisis, he had long opposed protectionism. Reporting on the payments problem, Ball argued that
trade restrictions delivered only "ephemeral" gains. Protectionism
impeded long-term adjustments to global commercial patterns,
instigating a chain reaction of tariff hikes abroad and spurring
American investments overseas in order to circumvent these duties.
The resulting scenario of capital and job flight, Kennedy warned,
would worsen the deficit. Although scholars have since argued
that overseas investments do not necessarily reduce home country
exports, the surge in multinational activity worried a president
who understood mainly traditional economic theory. Attractive
opportunities abroad and the threat of high tariffs in Western
Europe had doubled United States investments in the Common
Market between 1959 and 1961, to nearly $1 billion.[6] Kennedy
feared that a rising tide of jobs would transfer overseas with these
investments, and as a consequence, a reduction in the trade surplus
as foreigners bought more from multinational subsidiaries producing in their countries. If this course persisted, a falling trade surplus, coupled with higher overseas investments, would mean an
ever-increasing payments deficit.

In order to thwart this trend, Kennedy turned to Ball to work
out the mechanics of a new trade policy. Ball offered several
measures that centered on freeing trade. "Competitive coopera-

tion" with Europe lay at the heart of his proposals. Now only the "strongest of the strong," America could no longer expect "an unquestioning response to our demands for a common policy" from the allies. Thus, an overhaul of the obsolete RTA would help the United States compete with the Six, prevent the Atlantic community from dissolving into separate trade systems, and lure Britain and the rest of the Outer Seven into the Common Market. The alliance would then spread around the financial burden of defense and aid programs that Washington had borne for so long, and which adversely affected the deficit.

Ball's recommendations also addressed the disappointing trade performance of the Third World. He urged low-income nations to make a serious commitment to accelerate growth by responsible development programs, but he directed his prescriptions to the core powers. He suggested that the North remove duties, taxes, and quotas on raw materials made primarily in the South, without requiring reciprocal tariff concessions. He also proposed phasing out the preferential trade systems of both the United Kingdom Commonwealth and the association that many African countries had with the Common Market. Preferences, often in the form of free access into markets, discriminated against LDCs that lacked such arrangements, particularly Latin America. Ball sought to maximize access to industrial markets for the periphery by championing the traditional MFN principle. These measures would help increase Third World export earnings and enhance development, he assumed.[7]

Kennedy endorsed Ball's overall trade plan, knowing that America's power would slip further if exports did not help right the payments imbalance. He agreed that protectionism provoked foreign retaliation and could turn the trade surplus into a deficit, thus adding to the dollar's woes and jeopardizing national security. Quite simply, he warned after his inauguration, "If we're not able to export substantially more than we import we're going to either cut all assistance to countries abroad or begin to draw our troops home."[8] Kennedy, as statists argue, drew a direct link between economics, politics, and defense.

But urging domestic listeners to support his trade policy was only part of the battle against the deficit. A major obstacle to a solution lay abroad, in Western Europe. The deficit displayed the Common Market's mounting ability to compel adjustments in America's trade and financial dealings, in a sense reversing the adage that when the United States sneezed, Europe caught a cold. While America suffered from periodic recessions, a growth rate that was one-third of the EEC's, and 7 percent unemployment, the economy of Western Europe (including Britain) performed better. West Germany claimed that there were five job openings for every one of its citizens unemployed. Italian and French chemical, steel, and appliance manufacturers reported such booming sales that they had to turn away orders. Western Europe was by no means immune to U.S. economic problems; the present American recession, for instance, had slowed the Common Market's export growth.[9] That a solution to the U.S. balance-of-payments crisis demanded that the international trade order remain open, however, was obvious, and that meant persuading a more independent and powerful Western Europe to cooperate with the plans and goals of the New Frontier.

The Protectionist Specter: The OECD and the Trade Bill

First, though, Kennedy needed the cooperation of American producers and Congress, which were pessimistic about the U.S. economy in part because of changes in the international trade order. The global trade regime had indeed reached a crossroads, wrote Professor Jacob Viner after Kennedy's first one hundred days, and this was due mainly to the Common Market. The Six planned to reduce their common external tariff by 20 percent by January 1, 1962, a year ahead of schedule. Washington had to offer comparable cuts at the Dillon Round of GATT, or risk witnessing the barricading of the Six behind a wall of tariffs. But Kennedy had not yet indicated which concessions he would grant to meet European offers. Even more serious, a rise in protectionism might tie his hands in promoting freer trade. As Viner cautioned, "the tide is running in a protectionist direction" in Congress and most of the nation because of a sluggish domestic economy and the balance-of-payments problems.[10]

Societal protectionists and their representative element in Con-

gress indicated this course in March 1961, during Senate ratification of the Convention of the Organization for Economic Cooperation and Development (OECD), a body of eighteen industrial
nations formed to enhance cooperation on trade, aid, and monetary issues. Small nations hoped to gain greater access into the
markets of larger countries by passing a Code of Liberalization.
The code would establish new trade policies through mutual
agreement, thereby evading restrictive clauses in such laws as the
RTA, and forcing large countries to open their economies. American protectionists opposed this "constitutional encroachment."
They believed, as they had years earlier during debate over the
ITO, that it would take trade policy out of the hands of Congress
and place it in the hands of the free-trading State Department,
which always seemed to acquiesce to foreign demands for lowering U.S. tariffs. Eisenhower had bowed to this sentiment, refusing
to attach the code to the completed OECD Convention in December 1960. Kennedy followed suit, and focused instead on the
forum as a way to facilitate solutions to the deficit, boost productionism, and encourage Western unity.[11]

Despite Senate approval of the OECD, however, protectionists
sent Kennedy a distinct message. J. William Fulbright (D-Ark.),
chairman of the Senate Foreign Relations Committee, received ten
times more letters opposing than backing membership in the organization. Many interests endorsed the OECD, but import-competitors, ranging from piano manufacturers to milk producers, did
not, fearing it would precipitate large-scale tariff cuts. They repeatedly asserted that the "shadow of the State Department hovers
over every domestic interest" hit hard by imports. With the State
Department running U.S. trade policy in the OECD, instead of
Congress, the protection-biased sector was left "voiceless."[12] In
the end, a congressional "interpretation" discarded the Code of
Liberalization, relieving America from its obligation to obey the
OECD. Yet protectionists still vowed to corral the president's
liberal trade designs, and more specifically, any trade bill that
came before Congress.[13]

Responding to these warnings, Kennedy decided to direct the
campaign for new trade legislation through a special White House
task force in order to create the impression that Ball's influence

would be limited. The task force would be headed by someone well-versed in trade politics, respected by Congress, and preferably Republican to assure a nonpartisan approach. The president settled on Howard C. Petersen, a former undersecretary of war and now a Republican banker from Philadelphia. Petersen criticized American and European protectionism, but chafed particularly at the potential trade-diversion effects of Common Market tariffs. Promoting the principles of just compensation, comparative advantage, and realistic access to markets, Petersen, a fair-trader, declared that "we shall have to create the fact and appearance of fairness" in trade.[14] In practice, the task force chairman worked with Ball and the State Department in order to formulate the trade bill.

Petersen clashed with Ball on the substance and timing of the trade legislation. Both desired authority to halve tariffs over five years, but differed on the extent of safeguards from imports. Ball sought to eliminate the peril point—the import level that permitted escape from a tariff agreement—while Petersen wished only to revise it to avoid a protectionist backlash. Their major disagreement concerned when to present the bill to Congress. Ball believed Petersen's suggestion of 1962 was too early to offer a radical liberalization of the RTA. Although arguing that an election year was not a good time to offer a tariff bill, and that Kennedy needed more time to educate the public on the benefits of freer trade, Ball worried less about Congress than about upsetting Great Britain's bid to leave the Outer Seven and finally join the Six.[15]

Britain's Application to the EEC

Britain announced this course in August 1961 in order to reverse its stagnating economy and trade with the rest of Western Europe. Many British opposed accession because of the possibility of losing sovereignty to the Six, farm subsidies that kept prices high for farmers, and the Commonwealth preferential trade system, whose members depended on duty-free access of their agricultural exports to Britain. Prime Minister Harold Macmillan pledged to protect these interests, but knew that future economic health rested not with the British-led EFTA but with the blossoming Common

Market, which had begun to drain U.S. investment capital from England. He also hoped Britain could reassume its position of political leadership in Europe. In short, England faced, as the prime minister acknowledged, a "grim choice" of being caught between "a hostile (or at least less and less friendly) America" and the imperious yet powerful Charles de Gaulle, or abandoning the Outer Seven, British agriculture, and the Commonwealth. For economic, political, and security reasons, he picked the latter option, worried about increasing EEC trade discrimination against his country and "Britain remaining outside a community which controlled a central position in what was left of free Europe."[16]

Except for de Gaulle, the Six in general encouraged Britain. Common Market farmers would gain from the accession, since Britain was the largest European importer of foodstuffs. And by the unification of EEC members' grain prices, scheduled to take place soon under the common agricultural policy, the Common Market would do away with the subsidies enjoyed by British farmers. Despite being the main exporter of agriculture in the EEC, and thus a prime beneficiary of British membership, France frowned on Britain because political history made the application suspect. England had not only stayed aloof from the Six but had been decidedly hostile in forming the rival Outer Seven. London's commercial and political ties to America also raised doubts about its commitment to a European bloc, which de Gaulle hoped would seek greater independence from U.S. policies. The British might favor Atlanticism instead of European power, thereby boosting U.S. influence in the region, undercutting the movement toward integration in the Common Market, and subverting French leadership on the continent. Macmillan responded by turning up the heat, reminding the French president that Europe was "menaced from all quarters, Africans, Asians, and Communists, and, in a quite different way, even from our Atlantic friends." He warned that a rejection of the membership application might force Britain "to set out on another course, which meant turning away from Europe" and halting the large sums of money London paid to maintain troops on the Continent.[17]

Kennedy recognized Gaullist suspicions, although he underestimated the French president's ability to influence EEC policy. London spoke of a "special relationship" between the United States and Britain, founded on political, cultural, and economic affinities. Although soured over the Suez incident, Britain hoped that relations would grow closer under the Anglophile Kennedy in order to prop up British influence in the world. This wish was part illusion, however. Kennedy and Macmillan were friendly, but the appointment of "Europe-first" proponent Ball implied a loosening of Anglo–American binds. The president, for instance, reportedly pleaded ignorant when the prime minister referred to the special relationship during a visit. In effect, the United States sought a special relationship not with the UK, but with all of Western Europe in a united Atlantic community.[18]

On these terms, Kennedy endorsed the application. Sounding a purely mercantilist warning, economist John K. Galbraith, the American ambassador to India, pointed out that adding Britain to the Six was foolish because the EEC would then be more competitive, hurt U.S. trade, and hence worsen the payments deficit. The president acknowledged this danger, yet believed that as America's "lieutenant" in the Common Market, London could prevent the Six from turning inward, counter Gaullist nationalism, and promote liberal trade. Although "in every case" it might not be in U.S. economic interests to back the entry, Kennedy added, "we believe [the UK] builds a stronger Europe."[19] As statist scholars argue, Kennedy considered U.S. political interests in tandem with aggregate economic gains.

British wavering troubled the accession, however. When sounded out by Britain concerning the application in March 1961, Ball applauded the entry on the condition that London promoted Common Market political integration. Nevertheless, before Macmillan visited Washington in early April, Ball cautioned Kennedy that the prime minister might seek the "best of both worlds"—trade advantages without a full commitment to Europe. The warning was timely; after his visit with Kennedy in which Macmillan backed EEC integration, the prime minister retreated. Under pressure at home, he asked the president to press for transitional arrangements for the benefit of UK agriculture, the Commonwealth, and the EFTA during Kennedy's meeting with de Gaulle in June 1961. De Gaulle rebuffed these representations, claiming that they confirmed British hedging on full support for the Six. Yet the request just as equally irked the administration. The United States opposed letting the Commonwealth have the same preferential access in the Common Market as French overseas territories enjoyed, while other LDCs suffered discrimination from the Six. Britain hoped to "slide sideways into the Common Market," argued Ball, by emphasizing economic, not political, imperatives. In sum, Macmillan seemed reluctant to sacrifice for the overall good of the Western alliance, contrary to American plans.[20]

British policy led Ball to anticipate problems at the UK–Common Market talks, begun in October 1961, and thus he wanted to delay Kennedy's trade bill until 1963. He reasoned that new trade legislation, by opening the way for reciprocal cuts in EEC barriers, might give British opponents of accession grounds to declare that membership was unnecessary once greater access to the Continent was a reality. Also, the Six might feel pressured by a new RTA forged on the hopes of enlarging the Common Market, and balk at the negotiations. Petersen and the president disagreed. Ball, countered Petersen, exaggerated the fragility of the UK–EEC talks, which might be pushed along if America had new authority over trade negotiations. Kennedy needed this power immediately, he argued, as the ongoing Dillon Round of GATT soon revealed.[21]

The Dillon Round of GATT

The Dillon Round tested the cooperative labors of America and the Common Market to refashion the trade regime. U.S. negotiators had the authority to reduce American tariffs by 20 percent, but because of peril point restrictions, most observers predicted that this goal was unattainable. Thus, since the Six would not trim their tariffs without reciprocal concessions from Washington, Sir Eric Wyndham White, GATT's secretary-general, pronounced that the Dillon Round would at best serve as a launching point for future progress in trade liberalization. This appeal was an attempt to relieve pressure from GATT contracting parties, who had never dealt with a customs union of such magnitude as the Common Market, and offset unrealistic ambitions among the Dillon Round participants.[22]

The talks focused on the EEC's offer to match the American 20 percent duty reductions with equal cuts in its common external tariff. Ball viewed the offer as a sign of Western Europe's determination to pursue liberal trade, but protectionists feared that U.S. concessions would expose import-sensitive industries at home. Adviser Seymour Harris also thought Kennedy too eager to accommodate the Six without criticizing their selfish policies, and naive in hoping that the EEC would consider U.S. export interests when deciding its import policy. Before multilateral reductions could begin, moreover, GATT rules obliged the Common Market to compensate exporters who were faced with higher duties after the Six had adjusted their individual rates to the common external tariff on January 1, 1962.[23] These broken "bindings," or previously agreed upon tariff levels, proved to be one in a line of disputes between all of the contracting parties—but primarily America and the Common Market—at the Dillon Round.

The Six had broken bindings on prior tariff commitments, which amounted to 1,100 rates valued at $2 billion worth of imports, after its members had averaged their tariffs together. GATT obligated compensatory concessions by EEC duty reductions on other products, but the Six resisted. In setting their external tariff, these nations averaged the high French and Italian rates with the lower German and Benelux duties. This procedure, they declared, lowered the overall aggregate tariff level of the Common Market and thus compensated outside exporters. After much haggling, America pried concessions on bound duties in the EEC totaling $1.6 billion on 991 rates, less than Washington had first sought. But the Six refused further cuts, and this phase of the talks, extended four months past its initial deadline, ended in the fall of 1961 with America's grudging acquiescence.[24]

Agriculture was another major point of contention at this time, and, in fact, plagued United States–Common Market trade relations throughout the 1960s, and well beyond. The protectionist common agricultural policy penalized efficient exporters; in essence, the CAP aimed to facilitate intra-EEC trade but curb imports from outsiders as part of a deal between France and West Germany. Paris accepted the primacy of Bonn's industrial exports in the Common Market, while West Germany agreed to lower its farm protection and permit France, which possessed almost half of the EEC's arable land, to dominate agricultural markets. Although the CAP was still in its formative stages in determining price levels and funding subsidies, its potential effects on U.S. exports were clear. It subjected food imports to a "variable levy," supplemented in some cases by tariffs, which relegated these imports to a marginal role of filling the decreasing gap between Common Market production and consumption. Simply put, food exporters, of which the United States was the world's giant, would soon find the door to EEC markets closed in many sectors. Wyndham White blamed the "inward-looking" CAP for the "bleak" outlook of the Dillon Round.[25]

By no means was the Common Market the only agricultural protectionist, but it was the major one regarding American interests. Indeed, the Outer Seven excluded farm and fish products from tariff reductions and, contrary to GATT rules, bargained solely on a bilateral basis, while the United States, suffering from a historically chronic production–consumption imbalance, also had a large government subsidy for farm goods. By the 1960s, however, Congress grew more reluctant to allocate funds for subsidies, and a comparative advantage in agricultural trade lent greater importance to export expansion as an outlet for production.[26] Thus, Washington viewed international trade barriers to agricultural exports, especially those under the emerging CAP, with growing consternation.

The payments deficit aroused this uneasiness. Kennedy, normally bored with farm topics, took an interest in agricultural exports as a response to the deficit (and also as a means to raise farm income and meet the reduced production goals of his supply management program), and thus set out immediately to assault protectionism overseas. He instructed Orville Freeman, the secretary of agriculture, to initiate an export drive to reverse the "marked lag" in trade barrier reductions abroad. The president urged curbs on these restrictions "to keep the door of the Common Market open to American agriculture, and open it wider still."[27] His attention to farm production can be partly explained in terms of the international political economy. America's comparative advantage in farm exports provided one answer to its balance-of-payments crisis.

Although the CAP was a prerequisite for Common Market integration, Kennedy hoped to guarantee access for U.S. farmers during the compensatory phase of the Dillon Round talks. Since the Six bought nearly one-third of United States agricultural exports (the variable levy penalized 40 percent of these), he asked Walter Hallstein, president of the EEC Commission, to consider outsiders' interests before putting the CAP in place in early 1962. Yet America would be lucky to hang on to its existing markets, much less increase access, since Common Market farmers sought a greater share of regional European trade. The Six, on the grounds that the unfinished CAP excused them from setting tariffs on key crops, began to flex their new trade muscle by resisting pressure from the alliance leader.[28] Again, signs of the imminent decline in American power were prevalent.

Kennedy labored with the politics of farm trade, too. Freeman warned him about the difficulty of selling the tough controls envisioned for the domestic farm program if it appeared that the United States had traded agricultural for industrial concessions at the Dillon Round. Southern peanut, rice, tobacco, poultry, soybean oil, and cotton producers were upset by the CAP, as were midwestern feed grains, wheat, and dairy exporters. Such bad feeling could spill onto Capitol Hill, where powerful legislators championed not only the cause of their constituents but expected the administration to fight Common Market farm protectionism against Latin American exports to Europe. "The politics that flows from the potential loss of significant agricultural markets, especially in the light of the need to sell the Congress a Trade Expansion Act and a long-term supply management farm program," noted Freeman, "is obvious."[29]

His hands tied by the CAP, however, Kennedy could do little else but try to maintain America's present level of access to Western Europe. He sent Charles Murphy of the USDA and TEA task force chief Petersen to make "a strong representation" to the Common Market on behalf of American farmers. They received assurances of access under "standstill" agreements, which froze existing tariff levels, but the Six refused to compensate the United States for bindings broken on one-third of American farm exports. The USDA suggested suspending the trade talks to signal American displeasure, but Kennedy abandoned the issue for the time being, especially since the Common Market's pledge on access met one U.S. demand. Western Europe's neomercantilist farm policy had won this round, but in any event, he expected to fight the EEC another day once his new trade bill gave him more bargaining authority.[30]

Besides, if he had pressed the Six too hard, he risked a collapse of the Dillon Round in the more promising industrial sector. In manufactures, remarked a U.S. official, "We're getting a damn sight more than we're giving away."[31] Washington welcomed the EEC's offer to cut tariffs by 20 percent in broad, "linear" sectors. Used internally by the Six in reaching their common tariff, this approach of across-the-board tariff cuts on all products in major categories of goods replaced the cumbersome method of negotiating on each item. Unfortunately, the United States lacked authority under the RTA to proceed with linear reductions. Thus, the Six attached exceptions to the linear provision because America could grant concessions on only one-fifth of the Common Market's requests on manufactured goods.[32] Not only had the EEC held its own in agriculture, but it appeared more generous than the United States in the industrial sector.

Since the Six recognized the limited authority of the RTA, yet expected some show of reciprocity, Kennedy proposed more concessions to forestall a collapse of the Round. A comparison of tariff rates on seven types of nonagricultural products showed that most Common Market duties ranged between 25 and 40 percent, while many American rates were either lower or higher. Although peril points legally emasculated his authority to reduce tariffs by more than 20 percent, Kennedy permitted negotiators to ignore the limits and grant concessions on $76 million worth of nonsensitive imports. Since the United States still gave substantially less than the EEC had conceded, the Six withdrew over 100 items from the bargaining table. The Dillon Round ended on March 7, 1962 with duty cuts averaging a rather feeble 10 percent for all contracting parties.[33]

Although disappointing, the results were not wholly fruitless. The talks on agriculture had won a promise from the Common Market to maintain the status quo on farm imports and stimulated efforts to reach agreement in the future. Both sides made concessions on manufactures; Western Europe on transportation equipment, electrical and industrial machinery, and chemicals, and the United States on machinery, electrical apparatus, steel, and automobiles. The participants also proposed a "Program for the Expansion of Trade" for the Third World. The plan suggested that the North forsake reciprocity from the South in order to permit the LDCs to protect their infant industries.[34] In short, the Dillon Round paved the way for more substantial reductions in trade barriers at the next round of GATT negotiations.

Most important, the talks allowed Kennedy, as the foreign policy executive, to assert national interests over the parochial concerns of protectionists. The Dillon Round publicized the need for new U.S. trade legislation. That is, by revealing his inadequate tariff authority and the anachronistic nature of the item-by-item negotiating approach, Kennedy focused on the "hampering features" of the RTA, which undermined the U.S. position at the Round. "Our negotiators were grievously short of bargaining power," he said, and although the Common Market had understood this fact, "we cannot be expected to bargain effectively in the future under the limitation of the present law."[35] In order to correct this deficiency, he offered his own trade bill to replace the outworn, now nearly thirty-year-old RTA.

Launching the Trade Expansion Act

Public feelers signaled this move. Returning from a trip to Western Europe, Congressman Hale Boggs (D-La.), a liberal trade advocate, asserted that a mere extension of the RTA would be "grossly ineffective" in future negotiations with the Common Market. He later held hearings on trade in November 1961, in which Christian A. Herter, the prior secretary of state, and William L. Clayton, a former undersecretary of state who had also headed the world's biggest cotton export firm, agreed with Boggs' viewpoint. While Western Europe moved forward, claimed Herter and Clayton,

America "drifted backwards" into protectionism, raising the specter of allied friction, disarray in the Third World, and ultimately, Western defeat to "relentless, irreconcilable, [and] merciless" communist expansion. Only a liberal trade policy, and even more progressive, a formal link to the EEC, perhaps through American membership in the Common Market, could avert these grave threats to Western security.[36]

The administration agreed with all of these opinions except the suggestion to join the Six, because other nations left outside of such an enlarged Common Market might fear that it would betray GATT principles and evolve into a closed, monolithic, discriminatory trade bloc. But in its descriptive qualities, the Boggs-Herter report mimicked the administration's stance. No longer could American economic health alone determine foreign trade policy, explained George Ball to the National Foreign Trade Council, in November 1961. Moscow hoped to win the cold war through economic competition, he said, and rising Soviet–Common Market trade was one indication of its mission. Western European business, moreover, had now recognized the EEC as an "inescapable fact." Thus, America was on "the threshold of a new trading world" that had no place for economic nationalism. Ball urged that Congress give the president the tools with which to bargain with the Six and maintain U.S. leadership in international commerce, the capitalist world economy, and the Western alliance.[37]

Third World development also figured into these efforts. Faced with an outcry against unequal terms of trade from many LDCs that were emerging from colonial status, the administration responded by joining the United Nations' call for a "Decade of Development." Kennedy initiated the Alliance for Progress as one major effort to achieve this goal, and sought to join trade with aid as a means to stave off communism in the periphery. As Ball wrote, Atlantic trade expansion directly affected the South. More trade would increase consumption in the North, thereby raising Third World exports and ultimately ensuring that the LDCs remain "closer to Lincoln than Lenin."[38] The ultimate purpose of Ball's prescriptions, as statists conclude, lay in a cold war context.

The momentum generated by the Boggs, Herter-Clayton, and Ball sorties, in addition to a meeting at Hyannisport on November

24, 1961 with Ball, Petersen, Hodges, White House aide Theodore Sorensen, and trade task force member Peter Jones, convinced Kennedy to back Ball's "bold" trade bill but send it to Congress in 1962, heeding Petersen's advice. Naturally, the central concern was Congress. Petersen admitted that since 1962 was an election year, legislators would be sensitive to constituents who had been hurt by imports, and thus most likely steer away from supporting a liberal trade bill. Seymour Harris had earlier warned Kennedy about listening to the doctrinaire free-traders, because if the president overstated the case for liberal trade, he would be "taking a large political gamble and probably a losing one" with his bill.[39]

Regarding the politics of trade, however, Kennedy did not need coaching. Contrary to some interpretations, the president had a keen sense of legislative politics and was an adept strategist. He appointed the respected Hodges to shepherd the bill through Congress, and retained the peril point because of its importance to protectionists. Lawrence O'Brien, his liaison with Congress, suggested a departure from the old RTA after encouraging talks with Congressman Wilbur Mills (D-Ark.), chairman of the House Ways and Means Committee, where the bill would be referred. Blaming much of the New Frontier's stalled legislation in 1961 on the president's delaying tactics, O'Brien pressed Kennedy to make the trade bill his top priority in Congress. Seizing the chance for a major legislative victory, Kennedy agreed, believing the weak RTA of 1958 had resulted from Eisenhower's timidity in the face of protectionists. Kennedy, whom advisers acknowledged understood Congress as well as anyone, thus took the offensive for "a big one."[40]

The president announced in early December 1961 his intention to send a trade bill to Congress. Speaking before the National Association of Manufacturers (NAM) and the American Federation of Labor-Congress of Industrial Organizations (AFL-CIO), he noted that the payments deficit, the Common Market, aid to poor nations, and the cold war provided the impetus for a new trade policy. America had no choice but freer trade, for protectionism would chase capital and jobs from the country and, above all, "diminish our stature in the Free World." Americans must accept that U.S. economic supremacy was over; no "part of the world market is any longer ours by default," because "the competition grows keener." Reciprocal trade was the only alternative, since no country would lower trade barriers unless offered adequate concessions in return. Drawing the battlelines, Kennedy promised that imports would rise because exports *must* rise. Inefficient industries were simply "standing in the way" of progress, and therefore stymied U.S. policies.[41] Members of the AFL-CIO and NAM might grumble, and advisers wince, at this unabashed declaration of liberal trade, but Kennedy had made his position abundantly clear well before on protection and tariff cuts, imports and exports, and inefficient and rising industries. Now he was merely spelling out his hard-headed fair-trade doctrine.

The Trade Expansion Act

On January 25, 1962, the president sent Congress his trade bill with a flourish of rhetoric. In order to detach the legislation from the almost obsolete Eisenhower RTAs, and to stress the productionist ethic, the administration christened the bill the "Trade Expansion Act." It aimed to afford "mutual benefits" to all of America's trade partners, boost Third World exports, and assist import-competing industries. A "wholly new approach," the TEA "could well affect the unity of the West, the course of the Cold War, and the economic growth of our nation for a generation to come," Kennedy proclaimed.[42] He could not have placed trade at the service of statist objectives any less forcefully.

For international trade negotiations, the TEA provided the president with four kinds of authority to be used over a five-year period ending June 30, 1967. In all four, the linear tariff-cutting procedure replaced the burdensome item-by-item method. The basic authority enabled the president to reduce tariffs by 50 percent of the rates existing on July 1, 1962, on a nondiscriminatory and reciprocal basis. Such a drastic cut, it was hoped, would induce the Six to grant wider access to outsiders' exports. Second, the TEA provided for the elimination of tariffs of 5 percent or less.

The third authority was the "dominant supplier" provision. On products in which the Six and the United States combined for at least 80 percent of world exports, the president could eliminate all tariffs. This zero-duty clause addressed the "commonality" between the EEC and America, in that together they dominated trade on goods in which both sought greater access. The dominant supplier applied to all nations under the MFN rule, but showed Kennedy's concern with the Common Market. The clause was also bait to lure the Six to accept British entry into the customs union. Without UK exports, only U.S.–Common Market trade in aircraft and margarine and shortenings amounted to 80 percent of global sales. The measure bothered de Gaulle, who viewed it as another attempt by Washington to force Britain on the Six. But now he was prepared to exercise his leverage in the EEC in order to upset American plans; by vetoing Britain's application, he could both abort the broad powers of the dominant supplier and gut a major aspect of Kennedy's Atlanticist design. This he would do in early 1963, a year after the announcement of the TEA.

The fourth authority promoted Third World exports. The TEA included sweeping powers to eliminate restrictions on tropical agricultural commodities supplied by the periphery, and not produced in large quantities in America. Seeking to curb the preferential tariff treatment accorded associated territories of the Common Market and the British Commonwealth, Kennedy wished to encourage Latin American exports to the EEC, which discriminated against these goods while many of them entered duty-free into the United States. There was self-interest in the clause; more EEC imports from Latin America would reduce U.S. imports from the hemisphere. Nonetheless, the tropical zero-duty provision was innovative and potentially far-reaching as a development measure for the South.[43]

In order to meet the goals of the four authorities, and promote trade based on comparative advantage, the TEA restricted the use of domestic safeguard provisions. The bill introduced new criteria that changed the "no-injury" philosophy of the RTA, deviating from the previous definition that permitted the escape clause even if imports were only partly responsible for injury of any segment of an industry. The TEA required proof that imports *directly* caused, and were the *main* factor in, persistent idling of a firm or unemployment. And, although the Tariff Commission would still conduct peril point hearings, it would only recommend, and no longer make, peril point determinations to the president. The TEA thus made resort to the escape clause more difficult.[44]

By no means did the TEA abandon all protectionist safeguards; Kennedy had an obligation to domestic producers as the foreign policy executive. The national security clause, which permitted a defense-related industry to withdraw from a trade agreement deemed harmful to the country's security, remained intact. The TEA also allowed escape when "indirect" competitive products, or import substitutes, displaced domestic production. For instance, imports of glace cherries were competitive with U.S. raw cherries, and therefore could be restricted. Non-tariff barriers, including foreign "voluntary" export restraints, were also options open to the president. Finally, he could also raise tariffs up to 50 percent of the rate existing on July 1, 1934 on dutiable or duty-free goods.[45] Ample devices for protection remained in the Trade Expansion Act so that societal interests would not be exposed to the full brunt of foreign competition.

But the mainstay of protection under the TEA was adjustment assistance. Advised by the Tariff Commission, the president determined eligibility for assistance, which was available to workers through unemployment compensation, retraining, early retirement benefits, and relocation aid. Farmers, manufacturers, and firms received technical advice on planning and implementing adjustments to imports, tax benefits and loans with liberal depreciation and amortization allowances, and aid to modernize and diversify plant facilities. Adjustment assistance eased the injury from duty reductions and provided an option to the seldom-invoked escape clause. It also promoted the principle of comparative advantage. The trend toward freer global trade forced American producers to be more competitive instead of hiding behind short-term protectionism. The "accent" of the TEA was on "adjustment" more than "assistance," noted Kennedy, in order to "strengthen the efficiency of our economy, not to protect its inefficiencies."[46] Adjustment assistance, the four tariff-cutting provisions, and the revised escape clause and peril point procedures aptly demonstrated that the TEA adhered to a statist compromise between protectionism and liberal trade, with an emphasis on the latter. That is, Kennedy's bill epitomized the fair-trade doctrine.

The most revolutionary reciprocal trade legislation since 1934, the TEA was a departure in tactics from prior U.S. trade policy. As the statist view contends, Kennedy appraised the global transformations affecting American commerce and the political limits of pressing the principle of comparative advantage in Congress. The TEA reflected a fair-trade balance of federal aid to cushion the effects of lower tariffs. It furnished the United States with the tools to adjust to a world in which it was no longer the sole leader, but enabled the country to achieve its neomercantilist aims of boosting exports, correcting its payments deficit, and meeting security obligations.

Like most observers, Kennedy predicted a long slide for the United States without a vigorous response in trade to transformations in the international political economy. America faced a choice between a stronger domestic and global economy, or endless recessions, deteriorating growth, and a fractured alliance. Columnist Joseph Kraft wrote that economic dilemmas at home, rising Third World demands for aid, and European drift toward a more independent course in economic and nuclear policy awaited America if Congress rejected the TEA. The United States would simply "default on power," Kraft warned, and "resign from history."[47] Although hyperbolic, this view was held in varying degrees by the members of the Kennedy administration.

Surely Kraft noticed that Kennedy had not made much progress in injecting U.S. power throughout the globe during his first year. The president suffered setbacks in his Western European policy, exhibited most noticeably by a troubled relationship with de Gaulle and Adenauer during Kennedy's visit with these leaders in June, and by the seemingly permanent division of the two Germanies, symbolized by the Berlin Wall in August. He also feared that France, especially, might block his design for an open and united Atlantic community by continuing America's gold drain and rejecting UK membership in the Common Market. Yet Britain further undermined his alliance policy by attaching conditions to its entry. Above all, Kennedy recognized that the payments deficit, the need for the OECD, and the results of the Dillon Round were all manifestations of Western European gains in trade power relative to the United States.

Conflicts at the Dillon Round particularly revealed this fact. By dropping below the peril points, Kennedy tried to forge a make-shift agreement with the Six. He abandoned hope of prying open the EEC's agricultural market, because the Common Market was not yet ready to give more, while he took what he could in the industrial sector. The president understood that the stalemate over farm exports, as well as America's inadequate offers on industrial tariffs, implied that Western Europe had bargained with the United States on an equitable basis. A realistic trade policy was in order, both to adjust America to its fading hegemony in the global political economy and to help the United States achieve its national security aims in the cold war.

The TEA was a logical outgrowth of the postwar foreign policy aim of the United States to build a concert of Western nations. Kennedy sought to use the promise of liberalized access to the American market to help the whole capitalist trade system. In effect, a global commercial coalition of rich and poor nations comprised a group that would be strong enough to defeat communism, poverty, and the potential for war. This approach was not exploitative or necessarily selfish, although it was an attempt to maintain American hegemony over the global political economy. And it was not predicated entirely on allowing market forces to determine the distribution of trade benefits, although trade based on comparative advantage was a goal. Instead, as statist theory makes clear, Kennedy sought a neomercantilist, fair-trade balance of protection and liberalism to provide funds for, and cooperative links within, the Western alliance. In defense policy, Kennedy tried to use U.S. military aid and other carrots to foster good relations in the alliance. In foreign economic policy, he hoped to employ the Trade Expansion Act to achieve these ends.

The primacy of the TEA propelled it to the top of the administration's legislative agenda of 1962. Adviser Arthur Schlesinger, Jr. argued that Kennedy's focus on foreign trade as a way to stimulate the U.S. economy, instead of domestic programs, was a "misdirection of the administration's limited political resources."[48] Critical of Kraft's "evangelical mood," Schlesinger nevertheless missed the intention of the Trade Expansion Act. It was a hallmark of the New Frontier's foreign policy; a panacea for present problems and future circumstances. The bill addressed a fundamental change in the international economic order and global power structure wrought by the Common Market and, to a lesser extent, other industrial powers and Third World nations. For the moment, the TEA warranted Kennedy's missionary zeal, although the optimism of accomplishing its goals would not be borne out by concrete results in years to come. Yet considering its sweeping provisions and intentions, there was much truth in the president's statement that as "NATO was unprecedented in military history, this measure is unprecedented in economic history."[49]

Without a doubt, moreover, Kennedy's political fortunes greatly influenced his fervor for his trade legislation. His need for a victory in Congress partly explained the TEA's top billing in 1962. The first year of the New Frontier had yielded him few major wins. His narrow electoral victory in 1960 did not allow him to ease legislation through Congress, an advantage his successor enjoyed in 1964. Kennedy believed that the issue of trade, if advertised as a crucial part of economic health and international unity, might present him with a much-needed win on Capitol Hill.

The TEA was a calculated risk, however. Much of Congress might accept liberal trade, but protectionists were making noise, as the OECD debate showed. The TEA's gutting of traditional safeguards aggravated them, and even those private interests amenable to freer trade opposed opening the U.S. market "willy-nilly" to imports. Democratic and Republican legislators alike now considered the ill effects of trade on particular producers and workers, rather than voting a straight party line on trade bills, as had been the case on earlier RTAs. In November 1961 the *Wall Street Journal* reported that protectionist sentiment in Congress had never been stronger. Other business experts predicted that protectionism "on Capitol Hill will clash head-on with the Administration," making the TEA campaign the "biggest" and "bitterest" battle over trade since the Smoot-Hawley high tariff debacle of 1930.[50] Because victory was not a sure thing, Kennedy sought to remove the most vocal protectionists from the path of his trade bill, in some cases working at conciliation well before he even announced the Trade Expansion Act.

CHAPTER THREE

The Politics of Protection in Textiles and Lumber

Mustering votes for the TEA promised to be a delicate task. Kennedy counted on support from midwestern farmers and industrial states in the east, midwest, and far west, all of which desired more exports. Yet in 1958 Eisenhower, too, had relied on these states but protectionists had compromised his bill by vitiating the tariff-cutting authority. In 1962 these same forces intended to mount an intense campaign against the TEA. Many protectionists did not oppose liberal trade on principle, but sought aid for industries suffering from imports. Realizing that his bill negated much of the RTA's protection, Kennedy still hoped to use the fair-trade doctrine to neutralize powerful congressional blocs, which represented the import-sensitive industries of textiles, lumber, oil and coal, and glass, before the Trade Expansion Act came to a vote.

TEA Prospects in Congress

The administration confidently predicted victory for the TEA, but off the record worried about its prospects. One senator estimated only forty votes for it in the Senate, while support in the House was also lacking. The president's congressional liaison office reported that even supporters of the 1958 RTA had turned luke-warm in recent years. Polling Congress, Theodore Sorensen told Kennedy that the TEA required bipartisan support, or would fail to pass. But Congress had stalled the New Frontier in 1961, prompting the *Congressional Quarterly* to warn of an "uphill struggle" for Kennedy legislation in 1962.[1]

The power structure on Capitol Hill attested to this opinion. The 87th Congress was the most conservative since 1954 because of a coalition of Republicans and southern Democrats that had existed since the late 1930s and that dominated both houses. Chairman Wilbur Mills of the House Ways and Means Committee supported Kennedy but was tough on imports. Senator Harry F. Byrd (D-W.Va.), whose Finance Committee (like the Ways and Means) would hear the bill, was a protectionist, and disliked the new president anyway. Kennedy sorely missed the leadership of liberal traders Lyndon Johnson in the Senate and House Speaker Sam Rayburn (D-Tex.), who had died in 1961. Adding to his problems was the fact that he got on badly with the new House Speaker, John W. McCormack (D-Mass.), while Senate majority leader Mike Mansfield (D-Mont.) lacked Johnson's power. Parti-san politics, moreover, inspired Republicans to oppose legislation on which the president had risked much of his prestige. By doing so, the opposition party, which gained twenty-one seats in the House and two in the Senate in 1960, hoped to derail Kennedy's reelection bid in 1964.[2]

Kennedy also faced resurgent protectionists. Many no longer contested liberal trade ideology but opposed the "mechanics" of the TEA; that is, the reform of the "no-injury" concept that emas-culated the escape clause and peril point process. Congressman John H. Dent (D-Pa.), who claimed that Kennedy ignored the effects of imports, led House protectionists. His Senate counter-part, Prescott S. Bush (R-Conn.), said that the TEA permitted a "reckless destruction of jobs," with little insurance except for the "untested" and "dubious" adjustment assistance measure.[3] Since 1962 was an election year, even congressmen who backed liberal trade might join the protectionists in order to ensure votes back home.

Cotton Textile Protectionism

Cotton textile interests, which had suffered recently from imports, were the largest protectionist group standing in the way of the TEA. Kennedy was familiar with textile problems, and at least a bit sympathetic to the plight of the industry, due to his Massachusetts constituents and the 1960 campaign. As a senator, he had spoken of Eisenhower's "shabby" textile import policy, but the presidential politics of trade in 1960 required a bit more balance toward liberal trade. Nevertheless, he based his campaign strategy on winning the South, New England, and big northern industrial states, and a protectionist textile policy would appeal in the former two regions, where the industry was strongest. Thus, during the campaign he pledged to Governor Ernest Hollings of South Carolina that a solution to the cotton textile problem would be a "top priority objective" of his Democratic administration. Hollings reciprocated by delivering votes for the Kennedy cause.[4] Now Kennedy had to make good on his promise.

Clearly, Kennedy's commitment to help the textile industry was sincere, because he sympathized with its employment crisis. From 1958 to 1960, imports of cotton goods increased nearly two and one-half times, a jump of over 76 percent, or $119 million. Since exports climbed very slightly, the cotton textile trade surplus, which had been $125 million in 1958, shrank to $19 million two years later. The effects were serious, especially on workers. For instance, in 1960 alone, 128 mills closed across the nation, forcing employment to drop to an all-time low. Higher imports and sluggish exports did not appear, however, to be the sole causes of industry problems, since production also rose, and would drop sharply starting no earlier than the late 1960s. Rather, recession and inefficient production were responsible for the stagnation. Nonetheless, a major manufacturing employer, the cotton textile industry amassed approximately 94 percent of its workers in sixteen states. Over half of these employees hailed from four deep south states—Alabama, Georgia, and North and South Carolina—and a substantial portion also came from Virginia and Tennessee. Due to 140 mill closings since 1951, these six states had suffered

TABLE 3.1
United States Cotton Textile Imports and Production

Year	Imports (thousands of bales)	Production (millions of yds.)
1958	80.3	8,974
1960	301.4	9,366
1962	370.8	9,248
1964	325.0	8,966
1966	688.5	8,840
1968	559.6	7,476
1971	569.5	6,149
1973	686.3	5,086

SOURCE: U.S. Department of Commerce, *Business Statistics, 1977* (Washington, D.C.: U.S. Government Printing Office, 1978), p. 173.

an average drop in textile jobs of nearly 17 percent, and the south as a whole a loss of 14 percent.[5]

The south was not Kennedy's only worry, however. Every New England and mid-Atlantic state, except for Vermont, Maryland, and Delaware (in addition to midwestern states Ohio and Illinois), were among the top sixteen states in textile employment and demanded special consideration regarding their demands for import limitations on cotton, wool, and synthetic textiles. With employment having dipped by a staggering three-fifths of the number of workers in factories in 1951, and down 12 percent—15,000 jobs—from the levels of 1958, New England had experienced 278 mill liquidations in all textile categories. In the mid-Atlantic states, nearly half of the textile workers had lost their jobs since 1951, and even in the midwest, employment had tumbled in Illinois alone by one-quarter.[6] Kennedy expected opposition from these states to a liberal trade program.

Indeed, the industry comprised a powerful and vocal lobby. Since hearings on the textile import problem in 1958, even such efficient, "Big Textile" concerns as Burlington Industries, J. P. Stevens, and Cannon Mills denounced imports. They were members of the peak political cotton textile organization, the American Cotton Manufacturers Institute (ACMI), which represented 80 percent of the industry. The ACMI compelled the National Cotton Council, an association of cotton growers, to endorse protectionism, and the Textile Workers Union of America joined them. Thus, except for textile importers, the entire industry—management, labor, and raw material producers—united against higher imports. In general, the industry backed freer trade, but not when competition was "unfair" due to low-wage production abroad. Such now seemed to be the case, as the industry joined other manufacturers who were hard pressed by foreign competition to condemn imports of cheap goods from the Third World. This view sidestepped the real culprit of the problems—inefficiency—that was responsible for difficulties in many declining industries like textiles. But management preferred to capitalize on the highly emotional (and more visible) import issue rather than blame themselves for not reinvesting their profits into plant modernization. Nevertheless, textile interests combined their leverage on the representative element, for as one of Lyndon Johnson's secretaries of commerce later remarked, "There is *no* industry that is better organized and more forceful and clever than the textile industry on the trade issue." [7]

The textile industry quickly, and effectively, took up the call for protectionism in the halls of Congress, but the occupant of the White House was perhaps the most attentive listener. Possessing a keen appreciation of the industry's political strength, Kennedy centered his textile program on cotton manufactures in order to win TEA votes from southern congressmen. Petersen's task force, and House majority whip Carl Albert (D-Okla.), calculated that the president needed support from southern Democrats, who chaired twelve of twenty House committees and ten of sixteen committees in the Senate, since he could not depend on Republicans. Kennedy knew that a trade policy that hurt a regional industry with such "political muscle" as textiles would bode ill not only for his TEA but for agriculture, civil rights, and social spending bills that faced congressional committees dominated by southerners. Antagonism toward liberal trade by mill owners influenced southern congressmen, noted a Georgia businessman, and even many legislators from non-textile districts were sympathetic to restraints on imports. [8] Interest group logrolling by Congress seemed in the offing.

Six votes on trade from 1948 to 1961 hinted at the probable response to the TEA by textile-state politicians. The sixteen top textile employment states sent 132 representatives to the House, of which 81 voted against the RTA at least twice, and 50 voted for protectionism in 1958. In addition, many of the 128 members of a thirty-five-state bipartisan "textile group" did not even reside in major textile states, including all but one of the twenty-two congressmen from Florida, Mississippi, South Dakota, and West Virginia. House members who had conditioned their support for the last RTA on assurances of protection for the industry were upset at recent import trends. John Dent, the leading protectionist congressman, opened hearings in 1961 in order to investigate the causes of decline in such industries as textiles, by cynically quoting Senator Kennedy's remarks about cutting imports when producers faced extinction. To be sure, only seven of the thirty-two senators from textile states voted for a restrictionist amendment to the 1958 RTA. Yet thirty-four senators, including at least one from all but Tennessee, one each from Alaska, Kentucky, Mississippi, Oregon, South Dakota, and both from Texas and Wyoming, signed two letters to the president expressing concern over imports. Senator Edmund Muskie (D-Me.) warned that without a "realistic solution to the problem of textile imports," Kennedy faced "real difficulty" on the TEA.[9]

A subcommittee, under Senator John O. Pastore (D-R.I.), took up the industry's cause by beseeching the administration to impose import quotas and federal assistance. Pastore admitted that industry health was cyclical, but still implied that inaction on textile imports might lose his vote on the TEA. He urged a reappraisal of the import question by the cabinet-level Interagency Textile Committee (ITC), which had earlier rejected his subcommittee's suggestions. But he, like producers, remembered Kennedy's pledge during the 1960 campaign for a "comprehensive industry-wide remedy," which, incidentally, had backed Pastore's previous recommendations. They all now urged the president to make good on his promises.[10]

The President Responds

Kennedy tried unsuccessfully to head off this pressure. In February 1961, he appointed his secretary of commerce, Luther Hodges, who as governor of North Carolina had called for textile import quotas, as head of the ITC in order to find a solution to the import problem. Before Hodges could act, however, the Amalgamated Clothing Workers of America threatened a boycott on cut cloth from Japan. The textile industry, Hollings, and Congress recommended quotas, but the president warned that such action invited retaliation from other nations, and would worsen the payments deficit. The union stopped the boycott, but labor, management, and Congress had made clear, once again, their protectionist leanings.[11]

Kennedy felt decisive pressure in the following months. Representatives Carl Vinson (D-Ga.), a key source of southern support for the New Frontier, Kennedy's enemy W. J. Bryan Dorn (D-N.C.), and a nucleus of protectionists, formed the 128-member Textile Conference Group. After meeting with the president on March 27, 1961, the Group wrote him a letter that predicted congressional rejection of a new trade bill unless there were safeguards for textiles. In April the ITC, sweeping aside its free-trade member George Ball's protests, reinforced the Pastore subcommittee position. Hodges recommended controls modeled after the 1957 voluntary export restraint on Japanese cotton textiles, which had slashed Tokyo's sales to America by one-quarter.[12]

On May 2, 1961, Kennedy bowed to congressional and industry pressure, and proposed a seven-point agenda of assistance for the cotton textile industry. He called for federal aid to help modernization, including revised depreciation allowances, loans, and research and development programs. He asked for a study of the two-price global cotton system and the possible imposition of an eight-and-one-half cents "equalization fee" on cotton textile imports. That is, restraints on raw cotton imports made textile manufacturers captives of higher domestic cotton prices, while foreign manufacturers bought cotton at the lower world market cost. The fee balanced out the differential. The seven-point plan also allowed for easier resort to the escape and national security clauses. Most important, Kennedy directed Ball to arrange a GATT meeting in order to negotiate a protective trade agreement. The seven-point program, Kennedy hoped, would protect domestic producers and slowly expand Japanese and Third World exports.[13]

Both Kennedy and Ball knew better, however, in that they

recognized that protectionism would take precedent over export expansion. Nonetheless, against his will, Ball began organizing a new GATT trade regime for cotton textiles. He had long sought export expansion for the LDCs in such light manufactures as textiles. These products were not as susceptible to price downswings as agricultural or semiprocessed goods, permitted higher export earnings than raw materials or farm foods, and thus were critical to Third World development. A GATT study in 1961 concluded that industrialization would be more rapid if the LDCs "were enabled to expand in sectors" in which they had a comparative advantages in production, by permitting an "intensive flow of manufactured exports."[14] But as Ball admitted, this "logic was no match for the realities of domestic politics."[15]

As he grudgingly shuttled between the South and the North to round up participants for the GATT meeting, Ball sought to protect core textile industries without cutting off major exporters—Japan, Hong Kong, Taiwan, Korea, India, Pakistan, and the United Arab Republic—from their overseas markets. He also hoped to distribute the LDCs' cotton textiles more equitably than in the past by asking the Common Market to buy a greater share of imports. Somewhat disingenuously, he later admitted, Ball requested that the Third World accept "voluntary" export restraints so that the North could "stabilize" exports from the South in an "orderly" fashion.[16] Such terminology was a euphemism for protectionism, and such policies were deleterious to efficient textile producers in the periphery.

But Ball's refusal to go further—he opposed unilateral quotas, included only cotton goods, and set import levels higher than desired by the U.S. producers—angered wool, synthetic, and apparel manufacturers, unions, and the ACMI back home. A letter issued by the House and Senate textile blocs censured Ball's effort as a "piecemeal and totally inadequate program," which could embarrass the president's trade proposals.[17] Senator Pastore added that the alternative to satisfactory quotas was certain defeat of a trade bill in 1962 by the concerted efforts of the textile bloc.[18] A quick, interbranch compromise between Congress and the president was in order to stave off a future political disaster, but a deal seemed a remote possibility in the late spring of 1961.

International Negotiations

Other nations also threatened to upset the plan. Exporters feared that GATT was headed for a quota system that would clamp down on imports. Japan already had a voluntary export agreement with the United States, while limits on exports from Hong Kong and India to Britain were also in effect. Exporters demanded trade liberalization. Meanwhile, most countries were skeptical of the Ball meeting; only Canada and West Germany, with textile problems similar to America's, endorsed the GATT conference. Britain particularly chafed against Asian imports, which reduced production in its Lancashire mills to the point where the country had become a net importer in 1958. The British posited that bilateral accords, not a global regime, would better serve its interests. To appease Kennedy, however, London supported "orderly" import growth, but only on the condition that other nations, namely the Six, accepted comparable shares of textile imports.[19]

Such burden-sharing lay at the heart of the British and American attack on Common Market textile protectionism. While imports from Japan and the periphery totaled 34 percent and 26 percent, respectively, of U.S. textile imports in 1960, the Six took in a paltry 9 percent from these nations, even well below the EFTA's purchases. The Common Market "agreed on the principle" to ease quotas, but domestic pressures prompted France, Belgium, and Italy to seek a weak textile regime that would permit them to invoke future restrictions. Prior to the textile negotiations, not surprisingly, Hickman Price, Jr., assistant secretary of commerce, noted the foot dragging by all of the EEC members but West Germany. *The Economist* warned that "the prospect of a liberal outcome at Geneva does not look good."[20]

Nevertheless, the resultant GATT Short-Term Arrangement satisfied the United States. The seventeen nations agreed that starting October 1, 1961, an importer who suffered "market disruption" from imports could ask an exporter to reduce textile shipments to the levels of the previous year ending June 30, 1961. If denied its request, the importer could apply for a GATT waiver to limit imports. Market disruption was a novel concept in discrimination against the periphery, but it had the same harmful effect on exporters as more traditional forms of protectionism. The United States also attached a clause that, pending the signing of a Long-Term Arrangement, would assure that the EEC "share fairly" in the growth of cotton textile imports.[21] The new regime, forged at the behest of the trade system's hegemon, stretched the intention of the fair-trade doctrine to its limit, because the agreement came dangerously close to closing the door unfairly to Third World imports.

And there was another flaw; all sides attacked the accord. It impressed the U.S. textile industry and congressmen Vinson and Dorn by its recognition that import curbs were in order. But they considered it merely a "first step," and wanted Kennedy to end the two-price cotton system, reduce quotas, and limit other fibers. Although lukewarm in its reception, the Six accepted a 60 percent expansion of import quotas. Hong Kong expressed uncertainty about the categories of textiles under restraint, while Japan predicted that restrictions would allow Hong Kong to fill the export gap at Tokyo's expense. Japan was bitter, justifiably calling the Short-Term Arrangement a "backward step in world trade."[22]

Japan and United States Trade

Recent U.S. trade policy lay at the root of Japan's unhappiness with the GATT accord. In short, Tokyo complained that it was a scapegoat for the problems of declining American industries. Japan was America's major source of cotton textile imports, occupying approximately one-quarter of the United States market. Yet these imports comprised less than 1 percent of American production in 1960, and actually shrunk by 5 million square yards from 1958 to 1960. Meanwhile, the sales of Spain, Portugal, Egypt, and France as a group rose by 3.3 billion square yards, Taiwan, Korea, Pakistan, and India by 1.2 billion, and Hong Kong by 321 million. Japan purchased three times more U.S. cotton, moreover, than it sold textiles to America. And, on the well-worn issue of unfair labor practices, Japan's wage rate in the textile industry was as high, or higher, than all of the aforementioned countries, except France.[23] Surely, complained Japanese producers, they had suffered enough from American protectionism.

To be sure, the era of Japan's huge trade advantage with the United States was still years away, and, thus an unknown quantity in bilateral relations of the 1960s. Japan indeed had doubled its exports to the United States from 1956 to 1961, beginning the trend that created huge surpluses from the late 1970s onward, but America maintained a surplus of almost $800 million in bilateral trade at the time. Admitting the need to liberalize its import policy, Japan worried about "signs of regression" in U.S. trade policy. Visiting Washington in June 1961, Premier Hayato Ikeda declared that his businessmen were losing enthusiasm for the American market. Other officials charged the United States with holding a hypocritical view of trade; America restricted Japanese exports while at the same time asking Western Europe to lower its barriers.[24] The United States was not acting like a fair-trader in textiles.

Avoiding conflict with Congress, Kennedy promised Ikeda only an "orderly expansion of trade," and rather weakly repeated to U.S. listeners that Americans could not expect to sell and never buy overseas. But he could also turn the table, citing Japan's foreign exchange controls and America's economic and military support for its Pacific ally, both of which aggravated the U.S. payments deficit. Yet Kennedy comprehended realities. Japan needed markets for growth, and the president wished to discourage Tokyo from finding these markets outside of the West, especially in communist People's Republic of China. Japan also suffered from its own payments deficit, so increased trade was a must. In addition, Japan bought more U.S. agricultural exports than any other nation, a key consideration especially as the Common Market readied its restrictive CAP against imports into Western Europe. And America had enjoyed an export surplus with Japan—its second biggest customer—every year since the war, and would continue to do so until 1965. In short, Kennedy opposed restricting Japanese imports, noting that trade with its Asian ally must be a matter of "balance."[25]

None of these arguments, however, swayed the U.S. textile industry, which dubiously complained about Japanese "dumping" of its products on the American market. The administration acquiesced to this sentiment, renewing the bilateral cotton agreement of 1957, under which the United States raised its import quota ceiling only 6 percent, instead of the 30 percent demanded by Tokyo. The textile industry grumbled even over this hike, which took effect in January 1962. Also, contrary to Japanese interests, Kennedy ordered the Tariff Commission, in November 1961, to study an equalization fee subsidy, which would allow the textile industry to buy cotton at the low world price. The industry deemed the fee crucial to textile votes for the TEA; Japan viewed it as a tricky non-tariff barrier.[26] Kennedy's help to the industry hurt his reputation as a liberal trader. He chose, however, to deviate temporarily from the principle of comparative advantage for the political goal of passing the TEA, which would bring long-term benefits by cutting tariffs in the future. Such were the fair-trade tactics involved in making compromises with societal interests and Congress.

Protectionism and the LTA

In short, Kennedy preferred protection to an imminent "boomerang action" from Congress against his proposed trade bill. Textileman Robert Stevens denounced the TEA to Senator Pastore because Kennedy seemed willing to "sell" the industry "down the river." The watchdog House Textile Conference Group, and a letter on January 23, 1962 from over one-third of the Senate, criticized the outline of the Long-Term Cotton Textile Agreement, which replaced the short-term accord. The textile bloc wanted ceilings on imports of all fibers until U.S. consumption of textiles rose.[27] Consistent with interbranch politics, Congress now expected cooperation from the president, or Kennedy would jeopardize his TEA. Although Ball might claim later that the short-term accord was an exception to, and not the rule in, U.S. trade policy, Howard Petersen acknowledged the stress on local, instead of national and international, trade priorities within the White House during the battle for the TEA. "The mentality was Boston," said Petersen later. "You want the votes, you give the guy the post office."[28] Kennedy was accustomed to the give-and-take of ward politics. Now relentless pressure from textile interests—producers and congressmen alike—obliged him to act like a political boss in order to save his trade bill.

Kennedy did not meet all demands, but the five-year Long-Term Arrangement (LTA) restricted cotton textiles. The LTA froze imports in 1963 and 1964, followed by a controlled rise in quota levels based on the concept of market disruption over the next three years. The arrangement also targeted the Common Market as having a major responsibility for increasing cotton textile exports from the South. Citing the inordinate rise of American textile imports as the reason for these limits, Willard Wirtz, undersecretary of labor, admitted that the plan might be interpreted as camouflaged protectionism.[29] He was certainly right.

Approved on February 9, 1962, the LTA favored America and prompted a cool reaction from others. Although winning more access into the Common Market, Asians correctly feared greater limits by the core on their exports. Assuming a larger burden of imports, the EEC began to hedge on trade liberalization by suggesting a more liberal use of the market disruption clause than desired by America. Taking a tough, neomercantilist approach, Kennedy refused to change the LTA, requiring the Six to raise their share of cotton textile imports. Plus, by diverting cotton textiles bound for America to Western Europe, the accord allowed a "standstill" of U.S. imports. Except for the United States and Britain, other nations expressed their disgust by not signing the accord for nearly seven months, or just before it took effect on September 30, 1962.[30] Among other evils, the LTA simply contradicted Kennedy's aim to boost Third World export earnings.

American treatment of Hong Kong under the LTA revealed this contradiction when the colony refused to restrain its textile exports. Hong Kong paid a price. Under pressure at home, Kennedy prohibited importation of eight categories of cotton textiles in April 1962, knocking a third of Hong Kong's textile laborers out of work. Although the United States did not adequately demonstrate market disruption under the terms of the GATT textile agreements, or intend such a serious blow, Washington claimed that Hong Kong would make up for its loss by its competitive superiority.[31] Such an explanation was a bitter pill for Hong Kong's unemployed to swallow.

The TEA Vote

In meeting resentment abroad, the LTA served Kennedy's political purpose; it cleared the way for the trade bill. By March 1962, the president had realized, or would soon fulfill, all seven points of the textile program, had weighed applying the national security clause to imports, and had pledged to consider other fibers. Such attention earned an acknowledgment from the journal *Textile World* that Kennedy had "gone to bat for the industry."[32] The National Cotton Council announced its support for the TEA because of the "exceptional treatment" given by Kennedy to the textile import problem. Victory was definitely his, however, when the ACMI thanked him on March 31, 1962 for his "unprecedented degree of thoughtful consideration and constructive action for textiles." The ACMI then endorsed the Trade Expansion Act.[33]

Congress reacted positively to the implementation of the seven-point program. *Business Week* wrote of Kennedy's neutralization of the textile bloc when Senator Pastore announced his appreciation for the administration's help in limiting imports, and Congressman Vinson told the textile industry to back the TEA. When some industry leaders complained about government neglect of imports, Vinson slapped them for their ingratitude. He asserted that the president had placed the industry "in a unique, preferential, and beneficial position—a position not enjoyed by any other segment of American industry." Vinson then heeded Hodges' request to keep the House textile bloc "in line" for the upcoming vote on the TEA.[34]

Disapproval of the LTA and the rest of the seven-point program also proved Kennedy's adept political maneuvering. Importer William Bernhard, now restrained by the LTA, scornfully applauded the textile industry for its political "efficiency," but warned Kennedy that further concessions to protectionists might turn the TEA campaign into a disastrous "economic Bay of Pigs." Another importer, Jerome Pitofsky, expressed shock when the ACMI endorsed the TEA, the first time to his knowledge that the headlines of the textile industry's newspapers declared support for a liberal trade bill. Pitofsky rhetorically asked what "backroom political deal" by Kennedy had been necessary to accomplish "the miracle" of textile industry support for the TEA.[35] Kennedy's interbranch accommodation with Congress was the answer.

Unease from backers of the TEA also surfaced in Congress. In June 1962, Kennedy signed a bill to limit cotton textile imports from nonsignees of the LTA in order to slow U.S. textile imports from all sources. The legislation wooed the industry, but stung liberal traders. Congressman Thomas B. Curtis (R-Mo.), disgusted by the "raw political deal" that epitomized Kennedy's textile program, denounced the "gross inconsistency" of the bill to liberal trade. Senator Paul Douglas (D-Ill.) asserted that the textile bloc "in a very genteel fashion has held a pistol to the head of the President," extorting concessions for its vote on the trade bill.[36]

Although morally correct, the charge—denied by the administration—that Kennedy bought off the textile bloc to pass the TEA, was politically naive. Vinson had warned of growing unrest in the textile bloc over the trade bill, and counseled the president to enforce the LTA without modification or dilution. Thus, Kennedy told Senator Pastore that although freer trade was his goal, he would stand by the protectionist seven-point program. Therefore, just four days before the Senate voted on the TEA, Kennedy met with eleven senators led by Pastore, who had the support of Senator Harry Byrd, chairman of the Finance Committee, and reaffirmed his intention to limit textile imports.[37]

The president reaped rewards from his promises. In June 1962, the TEA passed the House 298–125, and the Senate in September, 78–8, with textile-bloc support. The sixteen top textile employment states yielded 158 of a possible 213 votes in the House, and 28 out of 32 votes in the Senate in favor. Many bloc members were liberal traders or voted the Democratic party line, so they backed the TEA regardless of the textile program. The main opposition was Republican. In Eisenhower's first RTA in 1953, 95 percent of the Democrats backed him. By contrast, only three-quarters of the opposition party accepted the TEA. Thus, four "nays" in the Senate, and 40 of the 55 in the House, came from Republican stalwarts. They either retained vestiges of traditional

GOP protectionism, or hoped to embarrass Kennedy by vetoing his legislative centerpiece of 1962, thereby gutting the New Frontier. The textile strategy did not matter in their case.

Also significant were the votes of the various textile groups. For instance, 87 of the congressmen who had joined Vinson's 128-member Textile Conference Group, and 28 of the 34 senators who had signed the textile letter to the president, voted for the TEA. Forty-one congressmen voted against it, but well over half were Republicans, as were five of the six opponents in the Senate. The other nay vote came from Strom Thurmond (D-S.C.), who soon switched parties. In addition, 77 members of the House bloc, and a majority of the Senate faction, opposed protectionist amendments or motions to recommit the old RTA, including a narrowly defeated attempt by Senator Prescott Bush to restore the broad powers of the peril point.

The vote also showed regional trends of support. From the south, White House staffers were amazed that Congressman Dorn, who had voted for only 4 of 43 administration bills in 1961, acted "totally out of character" and "not only voted for us, but worked with a large number of members" to gain their approval.[38] Eighty-two of 105 House southern Democrats followed Congressman Vinson and sanctioned the bill, including all of those from Georgia, Tennessee, and Virginia, and a large majority from Alabama and North Carolina. In the Senate, 19 out of 20 southerners voted for the TEA. New England backers, including Senator Pastore, whose subcommittee had led the fight for protectionism on textiles, tripled the number of those opposed to the bill. The concessions on textiles were not the sole reason for the favorable outcome, but as many observers claimed, they were major factors.[39]

Thus, the seven-point program attained its objectives. The LTA violated GATT principles, but restricted trade in order to help American producers. Liberal traders recognized the hypocrisy of Kennedy's professed aim for freer trade when measured against the textile accords. Kennedy overstretched his fair-trade doctrine, but he had his reasons. Among these were his sympathy with textile industry problems and, most of all, the battle he faced in Congress over the trade bill. He won the conflict by submitting himself to an interbranch compromise, colored by logrolling, that

TABLE 3.2
United States Lumber Trade, Production, and Consumption
(billions of board feet)

| Year | Softwood | | | | Lumber imports from Canada |
	Imports	Exports	Production	Consumption	
1959	3.8	.6	30.5	33.7	3.7
1960	3.6	.7	26.7	29.6	3.6
1961	4.0	.6	26.1	29.5	4.0
1962	4.6	.6	26.8	30.8	4.6
1963	5.0	.7	27.6	31.8	5.1
1964	4.9	.8	29.3	33.4	5.0
1966	4.8	.9	28.8	32.8	4.9
1968	5.8	1.0	29.3	34.0	5.8
1970	5.8	1.2	27.5	32.1	5.8

SOURCE: U.S. Department of Commerce, *Historical Statistics of the United States, Colonial Times to 1970* (Washington, D.C.: U.S. Government Printing Office, 1975), pt. 1, p. 541; Commodity Research Bureau, *Commodity Yearbook, 1972* (New York: Commodity Research Bureau, 1972), p. 200.

satisfied textile interest groups and their congressional representatives, and earned him his Trade Expansion Act.

The Softwood Lumber Industry

The administration's only other explicitly formulated import protection program was assistance for softwood lumber producers. The Pacific northwest (Washington, Oregon, and northern California) and "Inland Empire" (Montana and Idaho) lumber industry appealed for restrictions of lumber imports from British Columbia, Canada. These were states that Kennedy had lost in 1960, and needed in order to offset foes of the New Frontier and assure his reelection. Some pine and hardwood regions mobilized behind them. Senator Karl Mundt (R-S.D.), for instance, said that imports had placed lumbermen "in a serious fix" for "precisely the same reason that the textile mills" were in trouble.[40] Like the textile industry, lumber tested Kennedy's political skills in responding to congressional protectionists while preserving his liberal trade bill.

A flood of cheap softwood imports from British Columbia to America's East Coast market instigated complaints from the industry. U.S. lumbermen supplied 70 percent of eastern consumption in the 1950s. But Canada, the world's top softwood exporter, depended on America to buy over half of its output, especially after 1954, when other nations began to compete with Canada in its traditional British market, and as Canadian consumption leveled out during the 1950s. A burst of Canada's softwood exports from 1959 to 1963 seized over 57 percent of the United States' Atlantic market. Ten years earlier, British Columbia had occupied only 15 percent of this market, while the U.S. West Coast lumber industry held the rest.[41] Now the trend had reversed.

This situation naturally affected U.S. production. The construction surge of the previous decade had spurred a "boom" period for American producers, noted the National Lumber Manufacturing Association (NLMA), the industry's umbrella organization. Consumption had remained even, despite occasional lags in housing starts. But by 1961, production had fallen off 16 percent from 1959; only once in the next decade would production climb above the 1959 mark. Such sluggishness was particularly serious for Oregon and Washington, where the forest industry accounted for 60 percent and 40 percent, respectively, of the manufacturing payroll. Industry employment had dropped 44 percent between 1947 and 1961, making many counties in lumber states eligible for federal Area Redevelopment assistance.[42]

The lumber industry simplistically blamed imports for its problems. Declining U.S. production, and soaring consumption, had attracted Canadian lumber at the expense of American mills. Despite an upswing in housing in 1962, claimed the new Lumbermen's Economic Survival Committee, imports had caused prices to plunge, creating an "awful" state of affairs. The Simpson Timber Company of Seattle, for instance, estimated a loss to West Coast sawmill communities of $10 million a year because of imports from Canada. An Idaho banker remarked that he had never witnessed such a decline in the industry since the Depression. The cause was clearly "foreign competition," inaccurately wrote Congressman Jack Westland (R-Wash.) to Kennedy.[43]

The Canadian Edge

In reality, Canadian imports were only a symptom of U.S. lumber problems. Canada certainly enjoyed advantages in lumber trade. To correct its payments deficit with America, Ottawa devalued its dollar in June 1961 to make imports more expensive and exports cheaper. Its currency reached a subpar value of 92.5 cents (U.S.) before stabilization by the IMF. Depreciation had a "devastating" effect on the U.S. lumber industry, admitted the State Department, and Canada later added an import surcharge that curbed U.S. exports. Also, British Columbia enjoyed its second most active year in logging history in 1961, prompting the industry there to lobby for higher export quotas in order to boost sales abroad. Lower wages and operating costs, and a more liberal allowance of national forest cuts relative to the United States, also helped Canadian lumber. In 1962 Canada had the lowest stumpage prices (cost of uncut marketable timber) in its postwar history, allowing mills to pay less for timber from British Columbia than America. Meanwhile, willing to pay a premium for logs, Japan drove up the cost of timber for U.S. mills. The nominal U.S. softwood lumber tariff, compared to Ottawa's higher duty, also boosted Canadian competition.[44]

Transportation laws also gave British Columbia an edge over U.S. lumber. The method of selling cars of lumber in transit, the "freehold" system, allowed for cheaper Canadian railroad costs. Of more bearing was the United States Merchant Marine Act of 1920, known as the Jones Act, which required goods bound for domestic markets to be shipped in U.S. vessels. Northwest lumbermen paid the more expensive American rate of $36 per thousand board feet, while British Columbia sent its lumber to the East Coast in world charter bottoms at $6 to $11 below that price. In addition, the number of ships engaging in intercoastal trade had dwindled since the mid-1950s, leaving American lumber without adequate service. For instance, only one vessel ran every forty-five days from Portland, Oregon to Puerto Rico. Not bound to U.S. ships, Canada doubled its share of waterborne exports to the Atlantic seaboard and Hawaii, and monopolized service to Puerto Rico.[45] In sum, Canada had advantages in lumber trade that went beyond mere import levels.

Pressure on the Administration

Nonetheless, the lumber industry asked the administration to address some of these problems, but emphasized curbing imports as a solution. Thus, like textiles, lumber imports became a national trade issue. Over fifty industry spokesmen—including the NLMA and lobbyists from softwood areas, seven U.S. senators, and fourteen congressmen—visited the secretary of agriculture on February 21, 1962. They requested that Freeman target timber sales at fair stumpage prices and permit additional access roads into, and more efficient use of, the national forests, which were the major sources of timber and were under the USDA's jurisdiction. A letter from nine senators to Freeman, and a congressional hearing in April, prompted the USDA to investigate lumber conditions. A poll by *Crow's Lumber Digest* regarding Canadian softwood exports found unanimity among producers and wholesalers that palliatives such as tariffs or quotas were necessary. Both groups backed a modification of the Jones Act, continued prohibition of the railroad freehold, and a requirement that the Buy American preference be used on homes insured under the Federal Housing Act. Imports were also the major topic at the annual meeting of the West Coast Lumbermen's Association (WCLA) in March 1962.[46]

The WCLA and NLMA concurred on two remedies. First, Congress should amend Section 22 of the Agricultural Adjustment Act to qualify forest products for quantitative import limits, or quotas. Second, they recommended removing tariffs on softwood lumber until imports from either Canada or the United States reached 10 percent of domestic consumption, at which time the importer could assess a duty of 10 percent. The plan was a thinly veiled protectionist measure. A removal of lumber tariffs would not harm America, since its duty was minimal. More revealing, since Canadian imports had already reached 13 percent of U.S. consumption, the 10 percent duty would go into effect automatically.[47] Northwestern and Inland Empire interests had drawn the line of protectionism clearly for the representative element and the foreign policy executive.

The congressional bloc championed the proposals. In the spring and early summer of 1962, Congresswoman Julia B. Hansen (D-Wash.) introduced the Section 22 amendment, House members Walt Horan and Thomas M. Pelly (R-Wash.) the 10 percent plan, and Hansen and Congressman Clem Miller (D-Calif.) a provision to discriminate against lumber exporters by requiring a country-of-origin label on all wood product imports. Senator Mundt tried to attach a protective timber import agreement to the same bill that subjected nonparticipants of the textile accords to quotas. All of these logrolling measures on behalf of interest groups met eventual defeat.[48] But they alerted Kennedy to disgruntlement on Capitol Hill, which could easily transfer to his TEA.

Liberal Trade with Canada

Kennedy listened to the U.S. lumber industry because the trade bill was moving through Congress, but he wished to avoid another restrictive international agreement like the LTA. Thus, he aimed for a fair-trade balance of assistance, while keeping trade open. Sending Dean Rusk, the secretary of state, to Seattle in order to investigate the import problem, Kennedy told the industry that protectionism was not in the United States' interests. Canadians held an advantage in lumber trade, but America had run an overall trade surplus with its neighbor since the war, supplying such key products as almost 90 percent of Canada's agricultural implements, and over one-third of its steel and iron. Simply put, Canada was America's most important customer; bilateral trade comprised the largest volume of merchandise exchanged by any two nations in the world.[49] For America to raise tariffs against such a good trade friend would be shooting itself in the foot, because protectionism would merely invite retaliation from Ottawa.

Thus, in order to aid the lumber industry, the administration stressed federal assistance, not trade restrictions, against which Canada would impose its own. Although sympathetic to West Coast problems, Rusk said that a voluntary export restraint by Canada was the most that could be expected, because harsher measures might provoke a trade war or upset cooperation on defense matters. Sensitive to U.S. domination of their economy, Canadians, under unpopular leader John Diefenbaker, sought to insulate themselves, to an extent, from American power. The import surcharge and a restrictive revision of their Tariff Law were manifestations of this sentiment. But beyond the unlikelihood of Canada trying to cut itself off from the United States, Ottawa's willingness to lower trade barriers once the TEA passed hinged on America's commitment to liberal trade.[50]

Howard Petersen spelled out administration policy by backing restrictions only as a "last resort." Trade figures revealed that softwood imports from Canada amounted to only 13 percent of U.S. consumption; American lumber supplied 87 percent of the United States' use. A more "durable solution" than limiting imports, he wrote Senate lumber bloc leader Wayne Morse (D-Ore.), was to increase demand at home and abroad by Keynesian productionist growth measures. Under the fair-trade approach, the administration placed "primary reliance on encouraging domestic industries to become more competitive by the adoption, where necessary, of appropriate domestic measures," and not by the "essentially negative step of restricting imports."[51] The foreign policy executive, therefore, enunciated a lumber trade policy that considered aggregate national and international concerns over specific interest group demands.

The Six-Point Lumber Program and the TEA

These explanations fell on deaf ears within the industry. Not all producers opposed the TEA; pulp and paper manufacturers, multinational loggers, and plywood wholesalers hoped to boost exports through liberal trade. But the NLMA disliked the trade bill because it abolished the escape clause, lowered the already minimal tariff on lumber imports, and offered inadequate help through adjustment assistance. When the NLMA advocated the 10 percent plan, several producers of hardwood and plywood in the midwest, south, and New England—the latter which opposed imports from Canada, Japan, the Philippines, and Finland—supported its position.[52] This opposition incited congressional appeals. Legislators weighed liberal trade against the rise in unemployment that they predicted would occur under the TEA. They also considered the upcoming November elections. Senator Morse, the chief critic of lumber imports, cringed at a handbill circulating around mills in his home state of Oregon that asked foreign workers to apply to him for jobs lost by Americans if the TEA passed. Although supportive of the TEA, and realizing that imports were not the cause of lumber problems, he wanted some interbranch, "conscionable compromise" by Kennedy, whom he perceived was sympathetic to the import problem.[53] Fresh from the cotton textile battle, Congressman Dent claimed he would vote for the TEA when Kennedy informed him of the fate of several thousand unemployed lumber mill workers. Others recognized that the TEA would expand lumber exports, but until then, they wanted restrictions. One journal reported that Kennedy faced the "greatest barrage of protectionists against Canadian lumber that has ever been fired" from Capitol Hill.[54]

Most noteworthy were the forty-three congressmen, concentrated in the west and south, who wrote Kennedy a "lumber letter" on June 12, 1962. This message, urging federal aid and quotas, concerned the president, since it was issued just two weeks before the House would vote on his trade bill. Eighteen of the signees had voted against the 1958 RTA, although it turned out that he had little about which to worry. Surprisingly, the House tally on the TEA disclosed that only legislators from Washington state cast a majority of votes against the bill. The lumber letter adherents also split along party lines; seventeen of the forty-three congressmen rejected the TEA and nineteen voted for Senator Prescott Bush's protectionist amendment, but they were mostly Republicans. The House vote showed that societal interest groups had not prevailed in Congress, but Kennedy still anxiously eyed the Senate, the seat of lumber bloc discontent.[55]

Attuned to NLMA demands for import limits, the Senate lumber bloc included such administration friends as Democratic whip Mike Mansfield of Montana, which was part of the Inland Empire. Although a liberal trader, Senator Warren Magnuson (D-Wash.), chairman of the lumber hearings, complained that the administration had not considered quotas, despite the import injury suffered by the lumber industry. The major outburst came from Morse, who pledged to oppose the TEA on behalf of the lumber industry. He was impatient with the president's delays, especially since Kennedy had acted so swiftly on the textile issue. "I cannot vote for the President's foreign trade bill," Morse pronounced, unless "we get comparable justice for lumber as was given the textile industry" under a "fair" trade program.[56]

On July 26, 1962, Kennedy issued a six-point program of assistance for lumber in order to win Morse and others to the TEA. He ordered new loans and depreciation schedules to upgrade mills and promote productivity. The plan provided for more access roads, a USDA study on more cuts, and efficient transport of logs in the national forests, and an immediate increase in cuts in Bureau of Land Management areas. Kennedy sought to modify the Jones Act to overcome the high cost or lack of ships available for U.S. producers, and ordered the government to buy more American lumber. In trade, he promised talks with Canada and a Tariff Commission investigation on imports requested earlier by the industry.[57] Kennedy hoped to contain Congress with these measures.

In fact, most lumbermen and the lumber bloc were happy. The only criticism came from the liberal Committee for a National Trade Policy, which claimed that the prospective restrictive agreement with Canada, Buy American preference, and Tariff Commission action were inconsistent with the principles of the TEA. Most lumber groups expressed their gratitude, although they warned about laxity with Canada regarding import barriers. The NLMA still wished to tack to the trade bill authority for an emergency quota, but thanked the president anyway at the Senate's TEA hearings for his program. Congress was also appreciative. Representative Hansen analyzed the six-point program, and lauded the administration's tireless efforts on behalf of the industry. She declared that Kennedy had taken every possible action under the RTA by urging a Tariff Commission investigation and naming a negotiating team to Ottawa. Despite the positive views, the Senate closely watched the president's efforts at the trade talks with Canada.[58]

Since consultations with Ottawa were scheduled for August 27, 1962, just weeks before the Senate vote on the TEA, Kennedy could not ignore the lumber issue. The lumber industry hoped for a voluntary export restraint, because it knew Kennedy was reluctant to contradict his commitment to freer trade by imposing import quotas.[59] But by stubbornly refusing self-imposed restrictions, Canada deflected Senate lumber bloc attacks away from Kennedy, and helped eased passage of the trade bill. And it was already evident that the administration was unwilling to bow to lumber interest group protectionism by forcing Canada into a quota agreement.

British Columbia based its arguments against restrictions on the principle of comparative advantage. Canada had lower operating and transport costs and wages than the United States, Canadians explained. The problems of American producers were internal, not external; it was ironic that the best customer of the United States should find itself the scapegoat for America's economic difficulties. Canadians also shrewdly observed that the talks were the product of American congressmen who wished to use the import issue as political capital in the November elections. Demand had mounted in America for lumber, moreover, and Canada had not exactly begged East Coast builders to buy its lumber. British Columbia believed it had every right to sell as much as possible to America, in light of Canada's increasing failure to correct its payments deficit with the United States and the world as a whole.[60]

Dragging out the specter of a potential trade war, by warning of a return to the "bad old days" of Smoot-Hawley, Canada refused America's requests for restraints. Ottawa noted that it had never adopted a voluntary export restraint, and only once (for zinc) had it permitted an industry to do so. In words that could be attributed to the president of the United States, as much as Canadian producers, the latter hoped that "the U.S. lumber industry will not persuade liberal-minded Washington to play once more the same kind of disastrous protection against the country's main customer" as it had during the Great Depression.[61] In agreement, the Kennedy administration pressed no further.

Nothing came of the negotiations or subsequent talks with Diefenbaker over the next two years. Canada was stubborn, but clearly Kennedy did not insist on restrictions. Both sides merely pledged an agreement of "mutual interest," without instituting quotas. In early 1963, after the Tariff Commission rejected the industry's plea to invoke the escape clause—the first case heard under the TEA—the administration opposed even any hint of retaliation against Canada.[62] Kennedy received credit with U.S. lumbermen for seeking restraints, yet did not jeopardize trade relations with Canada or his liberal trade goals.

His reward was the Senate lumber bloc's overwhelming support for the trade bill. The voting record of the nine senators who visited Freeman in February 1962 gives an indication of the success of the six-point program. These legislators, all from the northwest and Inland Empire, voted unanimously for the TEA, as did the two senators from Alaska, who were active on the import issue. The bloc voted ten to one against the Bush amendment to restore the peril point, and opposed three other protectionist measures. Again, many reasons existed for the lumber faction's acceptance, including the fact that all but one of its members were Democrats who endorsed their president. Yet both parties had soundly defeated Mundt's proposal to negotiate a protective lumber agreement similar to the textile accords. Furthermore, Wayne Morse, the most outspoken member of the Senate lumber bloc, voted for the TEA. Less than half of Kennedy's legislative requests passed Congress in 1962, but thanks to such adept presidential politicking as his lumber policy, the TEA did not become one of the casualties.[63]

Politics motivated Kennedy's actions on textiles and lumber. The TEA was in the hands of large congressional blocs, which acted on behalf of powerful import-competitors. Congress required protection for these interests before giving Kennedy his trade bill, in a game of pluralistic, political-economic trade-offs. Appeals for protection came from labor-intensive industries that promoted, contrary to Kennedy's policy, import restrictions rather than export expansion. Even the peak associations that represented industry elites as well as declining firms—the ACMI for textiles and the NLMA for lumber—advocated protectionism. Thus, gaping differences existed between the private and public sectors. Indeed, protectionists won many of their aims, but rather than creating informal networks with the foreign policy executive, societal interests exerted pressure through Congress. Decision making was politicized, confrontational, and pluralistic, as statist scholars argue.

Pluralism, therefore, applied to the textile and lumber cases, although interest group pressure was more decisive in the former than in the latter. Cotton textile interests effectively pushed legislators to pressure the president. Indeed, the textile industry's more extreme demands were not met, such as creating a more restrictive LTA that included other fibers, or securing an equalization fee before the TEA passed. But Kennedy's seven-point program and the GATT agreements accomplished the industry's objectives. Thus, some logrolling accompanied the eventual interbranch deal, which compelled the foreign policy executive to act and allowed legislators to vote for the TEA, safe from condemnation from their constituents back home. Such was not the case in the lumber sector. The lumber industry also sought limits on imports and pressured Congress. But the 10 percent import limit plan and restraints on Canada did not muster support from the foreign policy executive, or even the representative element. In fact, the congressional lumber bloc was satisfied with the six-point program, and did not endorse a Canadian voluntary export restraint. Instead, Congress and the administration laid their demands on the table and reached an accommodation that addressed constituent interests, but ultimately maintained the president's drive for liberal trade. In short, the statist interbranch model applies to the cotton textile and lumber cases through a pluralist bargaining process among elected elites.

In sum, although different in content and outcome, both cases exemplified pluralist horse-trading in trade policy. A politically open issue such as trade, as well as the president's weak position on Capitol Hill, forced him to compromise by using, in correspondent Carroll Kilpatrick's words, "favors, pork, patronage, and charm" to win the TEA.[64] In the textile case, pork was more obvious; in lumber trade, favors and charm worked best. Not insulated from coercion from the electorate or the representative element, Kennedy responded. Pluralist pressure was so prevalent, in fact, that Reverend Theodore Hesburgh, a social activist and president of the University of Notre Dame, even linked the trade bill to civil rights, claiming that Kennedy skirted the desegregation issue in 1962 out of a fear of losing southern votes on the TEA. This analysis seems plausible after considering the great lengths to which the president went in order to woo various congressional blocs to his liberal trade goal. In the end, his tactics, called brilliant by experts and aides alike, cut out "the heart" of two major protectionist coalitions and preserved his aim of promoting liberal trade.[65]

Even before the TEA passed, however, Kennedy's record of pushing liberal trade was somewhat mixed. In lumber, the president managed to achieve his overall aim of keeping trade as free and open as possible between America and Canada; fair-trade policy helped producers, without diverging from trade liberalism. In fact, during the next five years under the TEA, trade in lumber, and bilateral commercial relations in general, benefited Canada. Softwood imports from Canada rose throughout the 1960s, and jumped in 1968 by 16 percent, the biggest increase of the decade, after the United States eliminated its lumber duty at the Kennedy Round of GATT. That same year also marked the first time since the war that America suffered a trade deficit with Canada.[66] In sum, the United States was so generous with Canada that it lost its trade surplus. The statist school is accurate in that American leadership reaped advantages for all.

In cotton textile trade, such was not the case. The United States created a restrictive trade regime through the LTA, which countered trade liberalism and the principle of comparative advantage. Indeed, the Kennedy program was a compromise in a long-disputed problem in world commerce, and the reasoning behind protectionism had at least some economic foundation, since several nations had virtually flooded the U.S. market with cotton goods. Their superior comparative advantages caused a quickening decline of American textile employment. Kennedy interpreted the fair-trade doctrine to mean that freer trade would not destroy a domestic industry. Considering the economic factors and the political restraints on Kennedy as he pushed through the trade bill, the LTA was a viable alternative, although no paragon of liberal trade.

In some ways, though, the LTA was a positive factor for some traders, like Hong Kong. The colony had captured about 28 percent of America's cotton textile market by the 1960s. Its exports had shot up 67.8 million yards, a stunning thirty-two-fold increase from 1958 to 1961, amounting to nearly $11.2 million in value. This rise was crucial to its cotton textile industry, which employed 45 percent of Hong Kong's manufacturing workers, accounted for 50 percent of industrial exports, and made the textile industry the top export sector. Throughout the 1960s, textile jobs and exports expanded. Hong Kong's overall production also rose, diversifying the economy and fueling development. The LTA provided the nation with more market opportunities in Western Europe, Canada, and Australia, while America took an increasingly larger share of Hong Kong's exports, at just a slightly slower growth rate than before. Thus, Hong Kong rebounded from the U.S. restrictions of April 1962, and became one of the most profitable textile exporters under the Long-Term Cotton Textile Arrangement.[67]

The regime in no way *reduced* LDC exports. Only Japan's share of the cotton textile market declined, but Tokyo would soon make up the losses in other sectors. During the period 1961–1965, the periphery's share of global cotton textile exports increased from 21 to 24 percent, and exports to the core outpaced the overall growth rate for all countries. Again, this rate was inadequate for meaningful development efforts; the renewal of the LTA in 1967 slowed this increase, and additional limits followed during the Nixon years. Yet as a result of the Kennedy initiative, the Third World's share of cotton textile markets in the North expanded to 28 percent by 1969, and brought a more equitable sharing of imports within the core. Furthermore, the LTA compelled importers to relax restrictions over the next five years. While the Common Market lagged behind America in liberalizing barriers, the Six reluctantly increased access. Meanwhile, the United States led all nations, until the mid-1970s, in filling quotas and importing cotton textiles from the South. Asian textile exports to the United States increased by half in value during the second half of the 1960s, while U.S. textile and apparel imports from all sources tripled from 1961 to 1970. Over the same period, the ratio of imports to domestic consumption more than doubled.[68] America, at least, lived up to the terms of the restrictive cotton textile accord.

That textile exporters as a whole benefited, and America created a less restrictive cotton textile regime than might have been the case, were positive outcomes, but these results are not the whole story. In essence, America behaved like an unfair, selfish hegemon. The pact stunted growth in exports for the developing nations—Hong Kong's overall trade deficit grew in the 1960s, for instance—and America resorted to the market disruption clause more than any other importer. Without the LTA, exporters could have enlarged their share of the U.S. market at a faster and larger rate.

And, as foreigners increasingly penetrated the U.S. market, America again clamped down. The Nixon administration slowed imports by imposing stringent quotas under bilateral accords in 1971, and again with the Multifiber Agreement of 1974.[69]

The textile case, unlike lumber, showed Kennedy's retreat from the principle of comparative advantage. America indeed flexed its neomercantilist trade muscle, turning protectionist to the detriment of other nations when imports became too competitive. But focusing solely on the economics of trade misses the overall intention of the president's cotton textile policy. Kennedy did not back away from his goals of liberal trade or aiding Third World development. And most important, the flood of textile imports warranted some measure, especially in light of the campaign for the Trade Expansion Act. Protectionism was not the desired course, but a political expedient made necessary by the vote for the trade bill in Congress.

The statist school recognizes that Kennedy had to manage the international textile regime in order to meet the domestic requisites of his fair-trade approach. He had to protect the TEA from defeat in Congress. By acquiescing to protection in 1962, he hoped to pass the trade bill and use its authority to boost exports for textile exporters at later GATT negotiations. And enhancing America's exports at the same time would not only aid the U.S. economy but, above all, would provide correctives to the balance-of-payments deficit. In essence, the American political system determined his decisions and U.S. policy in the external environment. The same held true for coal, oil, carpets, and glass producers.

CHAPTER FOUR

Political Trade-Offs on Oil and Tariffs

The president astutely judged that the TEA would encounter further problems on Capitol Hill without attention to the oil, coal, glass, and carpet industries. As with textiles and lumber, Kennedy deviated from a defense of liberal trade by forging a private deal with Congress in order to limit oil imports, and by raising tariffs against glass and carpet imports. But conceding protectionism with statist, fair-trade tactics won him the TEA, and guaranteed his liberal trade program.

Background to Kennedy's Oil Policy

This achievement was impressive, considering the diversity on the oil issue. Divided into producers, refiners, and sellers, and between vertically integrated, multinational majors and independent domestic producers and refiners, the oil industry was complex. Among protectionists were independent oilmen who relied on strong domestic production and coal producers who sought limits on imports of residual fuel oil, used for heating on the Atlantic seaboard, in order to expand coal sales. On the liberal trade side, residual fuel ("resid") users demanded freer trade in order to lower fuel prices. Also, exporting nations sought more access into the

United States for their oil. And Kennedy backed liberal trade in oil not only for efficiency but because American security depended on reliable supplies of petroleum imports to conserve U.S. deposits. He faced a tricky job of satisfying all interests and passing the TEA.

Kennedy's oil import problem stemmed from the immediate postwar era. Its booming industry in need of oil, America, in 1948, became a net importer of petroleum for the first time since World War I. Meanwhile, the cold war increased oil imports; the United States hoped to keep this vital commodity available to its allies, conserve its own deposits by importing from foreign sources with secure access to America, and buoy the oil-dependent economies of Middle Eastern and South American nations. Yet rising imports displaced U.S. independent oil and domestic coal producers in the American market, causing production to stagnate.

As a result, organized forces pressured Congress to limit imports. Oil-state legislators attached the national security clause to the RTA of 1955 in order to restrict imports when they impaired domestic production required in an emergency. Two years later, Eisenhower imposed "voluntary" controls on U.S. importers, but soon replaced these ineffective restraints with the Mandatory Quota Program of 1959. The program limited imports to 9 percent of estimated domestic demand, but exempted Canada and Mexico from quotas in order to maintain their safely transported, overland supplies for national security purposes. The plan also placed a ceiling on fuel oil imports at their 1957 level. Inimical to liberal trade, the quota program was well ensconced when Kennedy moved into the White House.[1]

His prior stand on oil burdened him, however. Of all the presidential aspirants, Kennedy had been singled out by the oil industry as the most "openly hostile" to American producers. Opposing quotas and the depletion allowance tax break to producers, he was among twelve members of the New England Senate delegation who denounced restrictions on resid. Failing to persuade Eisenhower to exempt fuel oil from limits, Kennedy censored the quota program as a "completely unjustified, uneconomic and short-sighted action," which not only raised prices, but "cuts athwart our trade position, unnecessarily damages our relations in this hemisphere, and does not contribute to our national defense and security."[2]

Such a view did not sit well with U.S. producers, so he toned down his rhetoric during the campaign of 1960. Wary of inviting "howls" of complaints from the industry, where his support was weak, Kennedy did not depart from the quota program. Yet his views hurt him; he won only Texas among the oil states—and this thanks to his vice-presidential running mate Lyndon Johnson—and lost nine of the ten major coal states. Energy interests hoped that the pro-oil Johnson would temper Kennedy's stand on imports. Although Stewart L. Udall, the secretary of the interior, revised quotas and increased fuel oil imports in early 1961, the new president was careful. Asked about the future of resid controls, Kennedy the fair-trader responded that "we have to consider the needs of the coal industry and domestic producers, the needs of New England, and we are trying to reach a balance that will protect the public interest."[3]

Nevertheless, oilmen worried that he would shift import policy away from protectionism, and toward freer trade. Former oilman John M. Kelly, now the assistant secretary of the interior, argued for protectionism. Petroleum imports had risen over 63 percent since 1954 and U.S. crude production had not kept pace with foreign output. But Kennedy rejected Interior's plan to cut import quotas by 50,000 barrels a day because he opposed high fuel prices and trade restrictions, which injured Third World producers. As oilmen feared, the foreign policy executive focused on the international level in order to meet the national security aims of ensuring friendly trade relations and preserving American supplies.[4] Both Moscow and Washington viewed petroleum as a critical commodity in the cold war, and the Soviet Union had emerged as the second-ranking producer behind the United States by the 1960s. Italy had already responded to Soviet overtures by selling and bartering construction materials for East-bloc oil. The State Department now worried about Soviet penetration in the politically unstable LDCs, many of which turned to Russian financing for exploration and drilling when U.S. multinationals refused such help.[5]

Venezuela

Kennedy feared that Venezuela, the largest source of U.S. oil imports, would fall prey to communism. With the highest per capita income in Latin America, Venezuela was the world's top oil exporter and the sixth best customer for U.S. goods, buying over $1 billion worth with earnings from petroleum revenue. Without the addition of Venezuelan oil exports, moreover, the trade of Latin America as a whole would have run a deficit since the war. The bellwether of the region's oil industry, Venezuela's economy suffered, however, through a severe recession in 1959–1960, an unemployment rate of 12 percent, a decline in drilling by 42 percent since 1959, and a budget deficit of over $800 million. Because of a world oil glut, and consequent weakening of prices, oil sales—comprising one-fourth of Venezuela's GNP and over 90 percent of its total exports—were sluggish.[6]

In fact, Latin America received much of Kennedy's attention as a testing ground for his development programs, most notably the Alliance for Progress. To be sure, industrialization would help U.S. exports by increasing purchases of manufactured goods in the region. Yet modernization was the only way out of "colonial servitude," wrote aide Arthur Schlesinger, and a means of staving off left-wing revolutions. The time had arrived, he wrote, for a change in U.S. trade policy, which had been "geared too long to the thesis that Latin America should be essentially a producer and exporter of primary commodities."[7] Thus, Washington backed regional integration as a means to further productionism and augment trade. Kennedy stressed that the U.S. market must remain open to Latin America "because the security of the United States is tied up with the well-being of our sister republics."[8]

But economics jeopardized political stability. Venezuelans remembered Eisenhower's tolerance of the brutal dictatorship of Pérez Jimenez, expressing their disfavor to Vice-President Nixon in 1958 by attacking him in Caracas. Now Kennedy courted the government of moderate President Romulo Betancourt in order to protect Venezuela's new democratic institutions. Betancourt had recently survived a bombing attempt on his life from left-wing insurgents. From the right, he faced an entrenched, oligarchic ruling class that chafed at reforms. As Schlesinger warned, Betancourt's downfall might guarantee his replacement by either left- or right-wing extremism; a Fidel Castro or a Juan Perón. To keep him in power required a strong economy, particularly in the oil sector.[9] But since its inception, the U.S. quota program had threatened Venezuelan petroleum production, a development that enraged Juan Pablo Pérez Alfonzo, the country's minister of mines and hydrocarbons.

Pérez Alfonzo agreed with economist Raul Prebisch, who claimed that North–South terms of trade hurt the periphery and benefited the core. The minister attacked this problem by trying to raise world oil prices, reduce output, and control exports. To these ends, he helped form the Organization of Petroleum Exporting Countries (OPEC) in 1960. And although he understood the pressure on Eisenhower and Kennedy, and recognized that U.S. quotas had stabilized prices and allowed exports to grow, he criticized the program. Venezuela feared losing its historical position in the U.S. market to Mideast and Canadian oil; Caracas complained that it did not receive an exemption from the program like Canada and Mexico. In 1961, Pérez Alfonzo had Betancourt send a letter to the departments of Interior and State, which noted the harmful effects of quotas, and asked America's United Nations ambassador Adlai Stevenson to end the "abuses and injustices" of the U.S. oil restrictions.[10]

Oil was a chief topic of conversation during Kennedy's visit to Venezuela in December 1961, the first by a U.S. president. Drawing on Interior's arguments, the president said that the oil program helped Venezuela. Because of the overland exemption from U.S. controls, Canada's western provinces sold oil profitably in the American upper Midwest. Thus, Canada did not need to build a pipeline to its eastern provinces, a large market dependent on Venezuelan oil. Also, decontrolling resid would lower prices and impair Caracas' exchange rate. And fuel oil, of which Venezuela provided almost all of America's imports, was not overly limited, and Kennedy had abandoned plans to reduce crude quotas. In sum, Venezuelan oil was not in bad shape in the American market. But Kennedy recognized the dangers inherent in Venezuela's economic and political situation. He thus doubled loans to Caracas to

$100 million in 1961, and hoped Venezuela would take part in a regional common market in order to promote its exports. He also promised to hold consultations with Caracas before changing the oil quota program, installing a "hot line" to Betancourt's office to effect such communications.[11]

Interest Group and Congressional Pressure

Back home, Kennedy prepared to net votes for the TEA. Returning from the Army-Navy football game in early December 1961, he announced that the Office of Emergency Planning (OEP) would review the quota program. This study, due out in mid-1962, worried the oil industry about the future of controls, but won praise from the coal industry, which thought the quota program was inadequate. In general, the energy sector believed that 1962 would be a "showdown year" over trade issues.[12]

Well before the TEA campaign, interest groups voiced their grievances regarding oil imports. Indeed, the coal industry was in a sad state. While world coal production had risen by 35 percent from 1950 to 1962, U.S. output had dropped 13 percent over the same period. Of the ten principal coal-producing states, only Virginia, Tennessee, and Missouri mined more coal in 1962 than 1950. Meanwhile, nearly one-fifth of American mines had closed, causing employment to plummet by 65 percent, or 272,000 workers nationwide. These conditions existed mainly because coal exports to Canada and Europe had been halved, while railroads had shifted to diesel and consumers to natural gas. To be sure, resid imports had captured the eastern seaboard, but that market provided only a minor part of coal's traditional purchasers.[13]

The industry hoped to stake out a certain portion of the eastern market for coal. Kennedy supported modernization plans to achieve these ends, which led a West Virginia legislator to point out that "the President is killing us with kindness," but "we're not going to get what we really want."[14] The industry wanted export increases and fewer imports. On the export side, West Germany and Canada discriminated against U.S. coal, while both got special treatment for their key exports to America, including Canadian oil. But observers perceived imports as a bigger problem. Coal associations, companies, and the United Mine Workers (UMW) cited resid imports as injurious to Appalachia, a testing ground for the New Frontier domestic agenda. Supported by management, the UMW, demanding a "permanent rigid quota on residual oil imports," opposed the president's trade bill.[15]

The oil industry linked up with coal interests. Since independents supplied only 10 percent (900,000 barrels a day) of the resid used in America, they cared more about crude than fuel oil imports. Yet they allied with the coal industry mainly out of a fear that decontrol of any petroleum product implied an easing of crude quotas. The Independent Petroleum Association of America (IPAA) and state groups expressed disappointment that Kennedy refused to cut quotas by 250,000 barrels a day, or even by 50,000, following Udall's recommendation. Independents claimed that imports had absorbed market growth, and thus caused domestic stagnation. They complained that the overland exemption enabled Canada to dominate the U.S. upper midwestern market. And they also criticized the "Brownsville shuffle," a crafty Mexican sea-to-land-to-sea transshipment maneuver that skirted American customs houses at the south Texas port, and permitted Mexico to squeeze more of its oil, free of charge, into the United States. In the interest of "national security," the IPAA offered a plan to limit imports to 14 percent of domestic production, instead of estimated demand. Oilmen girded for a "tough fight" with Kennedy, willing to trade support for the TEA for this new restriction.[16]

Oil imports were partially to blame for industry hardships. Indeed, domestic crude output still more than doubled that of the closest competitors, Russia and Venezuela, and in 1961 topped the previous boom year of 1957. Resid production fell by choice, since independents preferred to refine the more profitable crude. Nonetheless, world surpluses and eroding prices boosted imports, which took an increasing share of U.S. demand. Excess capacity, coupled with rising imports, idled drilling and prompted worker layoffs. In Texas, exploration fell 44 percent from 1958 to 1961, as the glutted market limited production from an average of twenty-one days a month in 1952 to just over eight days a month in 1961. Louisiana, Kansas, Oklahoma, and New Mexico suffered similar fates.[17]

TABLE 4.1
U.S. Oil Production, Yields, and Imports
(millions of barrels)

	Production		Yield of resid from production	Imports		
Year	Crude	Resid		Crude	Resid	Total
1956	2617.3	426.7	14.7%	341.8	162.8	525.6
1958	2449.0	363.4	12.9%	348.0	182.3	620.6
1960	2574.9	332.1	11.2%	371.6	233.2	664.1
1962	2676.2	295.7	9.6%	411.0	264.3	759.8
1965	2848.5	268.6	8.6%	452.0	345.1	900.8
1968	3160.9	275.8	8.0%	472.3	409.9	1039
1970	3350.7	257.5	6.6%	483.3	557.8	1248

SOURCE: Douglas R. Bohi and Milton Russell, *Limiting Oil Imports: An Economic History and Analysis* (Baltimore: Johns Hopkins University Press, 1978), pp. 22–23; Commodity Research Bureau, *Commodity Yearbook, 1963* (New York: Commodity Research Bureau, 1963), pp. 245, 248; *1971*, pp. 253–254.

Congressmen heeded the calls for import restrictions. Many of them faced reelection; many in the southwest relied on oilmen to bankroll their campaigns. Although gratified by Kennedy's attention to Appalachia, the House coal bloc soured on oil import policy. Congressmen Arch Moore (D-W.Va.) and John Dent, who began hearings on coal and resid problems, led the coal bloc, which included such powerful members as Thomas Morgan (D-Pa.), chairman of the House Foreign Affairs Committee. The House oil bloc marched with its coal cohorts. Representative Tom Steed (D-Okla.) led oil protectionists, holding a hearing on oil imports in late 1961 as a platform from which independents castigated the failures of the quota program. Steed and Moore proposed an amendment to the TEA that endorsed the IPAA plan of limiting imports to 14 percent of domestic production. Both legislators described the Steed-Moore amendment as a weapon with which the oil–coal alliance would make a "final" stand against oil imports.[18] Societal groups had sounded the alarm.

Interest group pressure united oil protectionists by April 1962. For instance, thirty-three congressmen introduced measures identical to the Steed-Moore bill. Also, a bipartisan group of seventy-nine House and thirty-one Senate members endorsed a pamphlet published by the National Coal Policy Conference calling for import restrictions. An additional eighty-four congressmen from twenty-three states expressed similar disgruntlement in the *New York Times*. Kennedy noted the outcry, especially since it involved some of the most powerful members of Congress.[19]

If the revolt against oil imports had been as clear-cut as the textile case, Kennedy might have responded promptly with restrictions. But Venezuelan interests, and more immediate, the position of a "consumer" bloc, prevented a hasty move. The New England Council and the Independent Fuel Oil Marketers of America spearheaded efforts toward relaxing quotas. They argued, as Senator Kennedy had, that resid imports were not responsible for coal problems. Instead, consumers used fuel oil on the Atlantic seaboard where coal was no longer a significant source of energy. Besides, the U.S. oil industry did not produce enough resid for consumers' needs. Import controls only raised fuel prices, and had bankrupted three large New England marketers. Consumers had a plausible case. Since 1950, production of resid in the United States had fallen by 30 percent, as railroads, utilities, and ships switched to other energy sources. Also, since independents earned about $1 per barrel less for resid than crude, they focused on producing the latter. Before the war, resid accounted for over half the output of U.S. refineries; in 1962, production was a paltry 9.6 percent. Even the *Oil and Gas Journal* conceded that removing fuel oil controls would have little effect on producers, would hurt coal interests only if prices dropped appreciably, and that Venezuela should supply America's fuel oil demand.[20]

The illogicality of import controls on resid prompted pressure for their removal by the House consumer bloc, led by Silvio Conte (R), Hastings Keith (R), and Thomas Lane (D) of Massachusetts. In all, the bloc numbered roughly seventy-five members from the Atlantic coast states. They urged the president to "show his genuine belief in freer trade by removing barriers to residual oil imports" and ending "protection gone wild."[21] Consumers, and their congressional supporters, did not make Kennedy's decision on oil any easier.

The line-up of conflicting interests placed Kennedy in a difficult position. Udall raised the resid ceiling by 10 percent in April 1962, enraging the coal bloc, but pleasing consumers. Refusal to accept the Steed-Moore limit brought "rumblings" from Steed, who visited the president in March 1962. Kennedy opposed the Steed-Moore amendment because it would invite a slew of similar protective clauses for other commodities, and because oil imports could be slowed "administratively," he said, through the quota program. Although aware of oil-state conditions, he believed security interests would be better served by not cutting off LDCs from the U.S. market and throwing them into the laps of the Soviets.[22] As a general policy, fighting the cold war outweighed protectionism.

For the political short term, however, Kennedy decided that passage of the TEA took precedence. To pacify the oil interests, Kennedy retained the national security provision. Although Steed refused to back off his 14 percent amendment, Kennedy assured him privately that the quota revision plan was under consideration. The president's "understanding," replied Steed, encouraged the congressman. In addition, recovery programs for Appalachia, as well as a tariff hike on glass imports, convinced coal-state legislators of Kennedy's concern for their region. And Kennedy's ally, Wilbur Mills, engineered a defeat of the Steed-Moore amendment in the Ways and Means Committee by a vote of 15–10, on May 23, 1962. Arguing that the measure would tie the president's hands in trade policy, Mills kept the TEA unfettered by protectionist amendments.[23] Interest groups had not completely gotten their way in the House.

On June 28, 1962, the trade bill sailed through the House, in part due to fair-trade tactics. Of the 108 representatives who petitioned for oil import limits, 71 voted for the TEA. Among those who opposed it were 24 anti–New Frontier Republicans, and such intractable protectionists as Steed, Moore, and Dent. Coal-state congressmen backed the bill, including two-thirds of the West Virginia delegation and over half of Pennsylvania's members. Two-thirds of the oil-state legislators from Louisiana, Oklahoma, Texas, Kansas, and New Mexico sided with Kennedy, as did 20 of the 33 cosponsors of the Steed-Moore amendment. To no surprise, four-fifths of the consumer bloc favored the bill.[24]

The Kennedy-Kerr Deal

Kennedy's tightrope act faced a similar challenge in the Senate. Since the OEP report on the quota program was due out in a few weeks, and might draw a hostile response from oil interests, Kennedy wisely delayed its release until September. Not to be fooled, oilmen criticized his "vague promises that never seem to materialize," and looked to the Senate as their last "thin thread of hope" for protection.[25] The various groups squared off. The twelve-member New England delegation represented the consumer bloc. The voice for coal producers was newcomer Robert C. Byrd (D-W.Va.), while Robert S. Kerr (D-Okla.) led the oil bloc. Earlier, twenty-seven oil- and coal-state senators complained to Secretary Udall about oil imports, eighteen warned the president that imports jeopardized national security, and thirty endorsed the pamphlets signed by their House counterparts. Senator George Shipley (D-Ill.) noted that "grave concern is being expressed throughout the land over the serious impact of imports affecting the energy industries."[26] The oil-coal bloc comprised thirty-nine senators from half the states in the union.[27]

Kerr commanded the Senate oil-coal forces. The second-ranking Democrat on the Finance Committee, and part owner of Kerr-McGee Oil Company, he had reached the apex of power by 1962. The so-called King of the Senate had set back the New Frontier by defeating the Medicare bill in 1961, which made a big impact on the president. As the story goes, Kennedy, looking ahead to his legislative agenda for 1962, announced that he would visit Kerr's ranch in late October 1961. Before the trip, a jealous Oklahoma Governor J. Howard Edmondson, a possible replacement for Lyndon Johnson as a vice-presidential running mate in 1964 and a Kennedy intimate, flew to Hyannisport, found the president on a golf course, and demanded to know Kennedy's purpose for scheduling the visit. The president responded, "Why Howard, I'm going to Oklahoma to kiss Bob Kerr's ass."[28] Kennedy knew he was Kerr's "legislative captive."[29]

This relationship gave Kerr leverage. His congressional allies, senior senators called "whales" by LBJ, dominated the president's "minnow" friends. Kerr's power of persuasion with these veterans was a card he played ruthlessly. For instance, one day he discreetly, but pointedly, explained to the president that he could not break the logjam in Congress over the tax bill of 1962 unless Kennedy backed the senator's pet public works scheme, the Arkansas River Navigation Project. A smiling Kennedy replied, "You know, Bob, I never really understood the Arkansas River bill before today," and accepted it. Kerr also chaired the Aeronautical and Space Sciences Committee, which funded NASA, and thus had a decisive role in determining whether Kennedy would ever achieve his dream of sending a man to the moon.[30] He could also make or break the Trade Expansion Act.

In order to win favors for Oklahoma, and promote himself in the Senate, Kerr championed the cause of the oil industry. He had opposed the last two trade bills, helped write the protective national security clause, and pushed for the Mandatory Quota Program. But he was willing to abandon protectionism if Kennedy tightened oil quotas. Kennedy agreed. Thus, Kerr advocated liberal trade as beneficial to Oklahoma, and responded tepidly to the Steed-Moore amendment.[31] Visiting the White House during the spring and summer of 1962, Kerr revealed that his only "understanding" with the president was an avowal that Kennedy was interested in an accommodation. Kerr made this easy for Kennedy, by holding a new quota over the president's head as the trade bill came to a vote in mid-August. Yet he received heat back home for not backing Steed. When the oil press reported that he would guide the TEA through the Senate—which meant he abandoned Steed's plan—Kerr claimed that the amendment was politically impossible, he still sought import limits, and he would oppose the TEA if he thought Oklahoma might suffer.[32] A bargain between the foreign policy executive and representative element was in the making.

The eventual deal lived up to Kerr's assurances. Taking 1961 as a base period, Kennedy agreed to limit crude imports to 12.2 percent of domestic production in order to prevent imports from growing faster than U.S. output. The revised program adopted the Steed method of allocating quotas, reduced imports an estimated 70,000 bbls./day, limited imports from Canada, and expanded consumption of domestic crude on the West Coast. In return, Kerr corralled votes for the TEA by persuading thirty-four of the thirty-nine senators who had endorsed restrictions, and all of the south-western oil-state delegations, to accept the trade bill. Every senator but two from the coal states followed suit, while nine of the twelve New England delegation members sided with Kennedy. Dissent came from either staunch protectionists or the president's Republican foes.[33] The fair-trade strategy of conceding protectionism in oil for general trade liberalization under the TEA was a success.

Two loose ends remained to be tied before the administration could relish its victory. The first dealt with the OEP report, released in September after the Senate vote. When the OEP recommended liberalizing quotas, the watchdog Kerr readied a special bill to make them even more restrictive. At once, the president told reporters that the OEP proposal was "not acceptable," and on November 30, 1962, he had Udall announce a revised Mandatory Quota Program identical to his deal with Kerr. Earlier, the IPAA gave Kerr a standing ovation for his efforts, and thanked Kennedy for the special treatment.[34] The Kennedy-Kerr dialogue verifies the statist decision-making process; without the interbranch deal, interest groups would not have gotten their way.

The other loose end was the foreign response. Canada raised its oil exports to America despite the new restrictions. Still enjoying the overland oil, Canadian sales to the United States surpassed those of the Middle East by 1966 and top exporter Venezuela by 1976, resulting in an overall rise of 21 percent since 1962. The United States also worked out an agreement to sustain Mexico's negligible exports, permit the clever "Brownsville shuffle" to continue, and retain the overland exemption until 1971.[35] Oil trade was fair; a steady expansion of oil imports into the United States from Canada and Mexico continued to the advantage of both of them.

United States-Venezuelan Dialogue

For Venezuela, the situation was more complicated. In 1962 Betancourt had stabilized his democracy by quelling dissent and increasing oil output after a recent depression. As relations between Washington and Caracas grew more cordial after the Kennedy visit, even Pérez Alfonzo toned down his recriminations against the import quota program during a trip to the United States in April 1962. Indeed, he realized Venezuela benefited from the raise in the fuel oil ceiling. Yet the Kennedy-Kerr deal threatened to derail these positive trends. The American embassy reported Caracas' indignation over the new restrictions. Betancourt "had worked up quite a head of steam" after a briefing on the revised program by Pérez Alfonzo, and was allegedly reconsidering his proposed visit to Washington in early 1963 unless concessions were forthcoming.[36] Kennedy immediately dispatched White House aide Myer Feldman to Venezuela for consultations.

Betancourt and Pérez Alfonzo issued a list of grievances to Feldman. The revised program contradicted Kennedy's pledge never to change the system unilaterally, they asserted. Also, Venezuela was one of America's oldest and largest suppliers of oil, yet did not enjoy an exemption from quotas like Canada and Mexico. The lack of preferences not only "disregarded" Venezuela as an "integrated Sister-Republic," but restricted profitable crude sales, leaving Venezuela with the mere "bones" of the American resid market. They directed another complaint at "quota trading." The revised system cut the percentage of imports allocated to "historical" importers, those U.S. companies who bought foreign (mostly Venezuelan) oil before 1957. The rules now allowed "inland" refiners, which did not directly use imported oil, to swap their quota allotments for domestic petroleum. Thus, quota trading reduced imports; Venezuela estimated a loss of revenue of $35 million. Betancourt wished to eliminate this process, charging that the allocation of permits for imports encouraged speculation by greedy refiners. He desired that Americans use Venezuelan oil.[37]

Feldman defended Kennedy's program. Regarding preferences, he repeated that without the overland exemption, Canada would have cut off Venezuelan exports to the Montreal area by piping in oil from its western provinces. Besides, Canada's position in the U.S. market was fixed under the quota program, while Caracas could increase sales once American consumption expanded. And Venezuela's rising exports during 1962 confirmed the nation's competitiveness in the United States. The revised quotas would slow Venezuelan crude sales, admitted Feldman, but Caracas could look forward to higher demand in Europe and in the Caribbean and Canadian markets it dominated. Although resid did not reap as high profits as crude, it still offered "attractive opportunities." Venezuela virtually owned the American fuel oil market, supplying about 86 percent of the resid consumed there either directly or indirectly, through the Netherlands Antilles. These exports had climbed 30 percent over the past three years, and would most likely rise still further.

Kennedy also did not like the speculation involved in quota trading. But Feldman explained that the method aided domestic producers, who were required to expand sales to inland refiners penalized by the allocation advantage of historical importers under the previous system. Phasing out this competitive edge for importers was only fair. Besides, an elimination of quota trading would hurt Caracas by forcing inland refiners to transport oil from the coast at an uneconomical cost, thereby depressing prices and cutting revenue for Venezuela.[38]

In the end, Betancourt and Pérez Alfonzo accepted Feldman's explanation. Purely for home consumption, Betancourt pledged in January 1963 to end the "Sword of Damocles," by which the United States could unilaterally make decisions taken that affected Venezuelan oil in the American market. But the following month he privately expressed to the president his satisfaction with the revised program. Meeting Betancourt in Washington a month later, Kennedy promised to inform him of any changes in the import program.[39] Fair-trade bargaining at home and abroad accomplished Kennedy's goals in oil.

As time would tell, Venezuela's exports to America grew impressively. Since Venezuela also produced nearly all of the oil from the Netherlands Antilles, its sales to the United States increased by 18 million barrels a year, from 1962 to the first oil crisis in 1973. Venezuela remained America's top oil supplier until 1976. Also, although Kennedy rejected an OEP recommendation in February 1963 to eliminate controls on resid, limits on fuel oil ended in 1966. As American imports of crude rose by 15 percent, fuel oil imports more than doubled by the end of the decade. And the ratio of resid imports to U.S. domestic consumption leapt from 48.2 percent in 1962 to 69.4 percent in 1970. Since it sent nearly

TABLE 4.2
U.S. Petroleum Imports from Venezuela, Canada, and Mexico
(millions of barrels)

Year	Venezuela*	Canada	Mexico	Total U.S. oil imports
1955	307	—	23	470
1960	451	44	6	687
1962	440	91	18	760
1963	442	97	17	775
1964	464	109	17	827
1967	473	164	18	926
1970	536	280	15	1248
1973	627	484	6	2283

* Including petroleum imported from the Netherlands Antilles.
SOURCE: Stephen G. Rabe, *The Road to OPEC: United States Relations with Venezuela, 1919–1976* (Austin: University of Texas Press, 1982), p. 198.

nine-tenths of this fuel oil to America, Venezuela profited considerably.[40]

Spiraling U.S. oil imports showed that the controls imposed by Kennedy's fair-trade approach were limited in their effect on trade, but not on Congress' treatment of the TEA. The revision of the quota program was a sop to the oil industry; the refusal to junk restrictions on residual fuel a bone to coal interests. In the end, Kennedy's oil import policy, based on the delicate balance of international, national, and parochial concerns, satisfied all parties. Oil and coal producers got protection, while consumers enjoyed the general trend toward trade liberalization. Canada and Venezuela initially criticized, but accepted and gained from, the revised program. And Kennedy's strategy helped win his trade bill, thus placing America on the road to correcting its payments deficit and strengthening its cold war defenses.

Troubles in the Carpet and Glass Industries

Well before he signed the TEA, Kennedy granted his most protectionist concession to societal interests by raising tariffs on glass and carpet imports. Based on a unanimous recommendation by the Tariff Commission to invoke the escape clause, the action was the first and only tariff hike he ever made. The duties were too drastic to éxplain away as mere economic assistance, especially since the administration was in the midst of trying to inject liberalism into the international trade regime through the Dillon Round and, it was hoped, by passage of the trade bill. Instead, they indicated the lengths to which Kennedy went to pass the TEA. Increasing tariffs for wilton and velvet carpet imports served as further aid for the textile industry. The inflow of carpets from abroad reached a record high of 8.2 million square yards in 1961, almost double the level of 1958, and induced congressmen, particularly Samuel S. Stratton (D-N.Y.) of upstate New York, to ask the president for limits. The textile industry joined this appeal, which made Stratton's request all the more compelling for the administration.[41]

Just as the carpet problem influenced Kennedy, so did the issue of sheet glass imports. Eisenhower had twice rejected Tariff Commission recommendations for higher duties on sheet glass, which was used for windows. Kennedy kept the glass industry in mind during the 1960 election campaign as a source for, as he said, a "trade adjustment bill." Whether he meant these producers would benefit from adjustment assistance or greater tariff protection was not clear, but it was apparent that the industry's sagging health was serious enough to warrant his attention. He lost, however, a majority of the top nine glass-producing states, including West Virginia and Oklahoma, two of the three largest. As in oil, he did not succeed in the presidential politics of glass trade.[42]

He got another chance to aid producers, however, when the Tariff Commission convened a hearing on sheet glass imports in May 1961. Complaints emanated from major companies—Libbey-Owens-Ford, Pittsburgh Plate Glass, and American-St. Gobain—as well as the United Glass and Ceramic Workers of North America, the Window Glass Cutters League, and the Ohio-Pennsylvania-West Virginia-Indiana Glass Workers Protective League. Management and workers testified that declining tariffs since the war, cheaper labor and material cost for foreigners, and parity in technology and productivity among domestic and overseas firms gave imports a competitive edge. The industry admitted that "successful competition will be met only by increased mechanization and continued lowering of production costs," but also knew that "tariff relief" was a viable option.[43]

The Tariff Commission blamed a decline in sheet glass production partly on imports. Sales fell by one-quarter between 1955 and 1960, employment by 16 percent, and the four big manufacturers had losses of over $1.1 million. A discriminatory distribution system, which drove many buyers to turn to imports in order to compete with "recognized" (but higher priced) factory and consumer distributors, caused part of the problems. Yet the industry had also lost one-quarter of its market to imports over the past decade. Belgium, Japan, and others had accounted for 32 percent of these sales in 1959, when nine years before they had occupied less than 3 percent of the market. Based on its findings, the commission recommended invoking the escape clause.[44]

But suspicious of non-trade factors that inhibited the industry, especially discriminatory distributor practices, the president postponed his decision to act on the Tariff Commission finding. Aware of a tariff hike's potential serious impact to America's foreign relations, he sought more time to consider the "national interest" without "unduly restricting fair competition" from abroad. Kennedy figured that an imminent economic recovery from recession, fueled by expanding production in the automobile, construction, and aircraft sectors, would benefit window-glass makers. By delaying, he also hoped to avoid inciting Congress to override him in the event that he rejected the commission's recommendation.[45] Glass imports fully tested the political skills of the foreign policy executive.

Protectionists Rally

The postponement merely angered Congress, however. Senator Styles Bridges (R-N.H.) reacted with a bill that made Tariff Commission recommendations binding on the president. That three presidents had accepted only thirteen of thirty-six recommendations for tariff raises since 1950 frustrated protectionists. The House members at the commission hearing also concurred with the four-state Glass Workers Protective League's demand to ascertain, "plainly and promptly," where Kennedy stood on the sheet glass import issue, for they had received to date "no encouragement—only the opposite" from the White House.[46] Congressman

Dent also undertook a self-proclaimed "crusade" on behalf of domestic producers. An irreconcilable protectionist, Dent would never vote for the TEA but might rally legislators who accused the administration of giving "second-class consideration" to American workers and industries. The sheet glass problem was an example of Kennedy's "perverted" trade policies, Dent said, that allowed in goods in which there already existed a surplus, particularly in the congressman's home district in Pennsylvania, where the world's largest glass factory had recently closed. Not very subtly, Dent blamed the president for such economic difficulties, acidly proclaiming that "it does not take a Harvard graduate to make two and two equal four" in relating imports to stagnation.[47]

Dent rounded up House and Senate backers of a higher sheet glass duty. These legislators hailed from the nine major glass-producing states, and included Kennedy allies such as senators Estes Kefauver (D-Tenn.), J. William Fulbright, Robert Kerr, and the entire Oklahoma congressional delegation, minus House majority whip Carl Albert, who perhaps felt obligated to remain behind the president's trade program. This informal "glass bloc" paralleled, to an extent, the regional make-up of the coal-oil forces, and potentially numbered around ninety House and fifteen Senate members.[48] Again, protectionists had thrown down the gauntlet.

By postponing action in June 1961, Kennedy had time to weigh the implications of a tariff hike on international relations. Such an action could spur Japanese premier Ikeda, already disgruntled over cotton textiles, to retaliate. Belgium also required delicate handling; Brussels was in the midst of a civil war in its former Congo colony, and was also the sole member of the Common Market with a lagging economy, which rendered it sensitive to trade harassment. The United States counted on Belgian foreign minister Paul-Henri Spaak to sustain a liberal trade bent in the country. But powerful Belgian carpet and glass interests could cause a protectionist backlash against America as the Dillon Round of GATT ended in early March 1962, about the time Kennedy would decide the tariff issue. Higher tariffs, warned the State Department, would be "counterproductive, both psychologically and practically" to participants at the Round, might set off a "chain reaction" of retaliation, and would hurt the emerging trade relationship of the United States and the Six.[49]

Once again, Kennedy was caught between liberal trade and protectionism. He preferred to close out the Dillon Round, pass the TEA, and open the next GATT round without raising tariffs. But timing was on the side of protectionists; the desire of the president to gather votes for his trade bill brightened the prospects of escape clause action. Besides, glass interests adamantly opposed liberal trade. The president of Libbey-Owens-Ford, for instance, stated that "we're in favor of protection," and his company joined three other major producers in rejecting the TEA. The congressional bloc followed suit. Dent foresaw "nothing but disaster" for producers—and presumably the trade bill—unless Kennedy protected jobs.[50] It now seemed appropriate for Kennedy to activate the protectionist half of the fair-trade doctrine.

The Tariff Hike

Faced with the TEA vote, the president decided to raise tariffs on March 19, 1962. He refused to boost duties on baseball gloves and ceramic mosaic tiles, on the grounds that imports had not directly affected production in these industries. But these products also lacked the organized protectionist blocs that sheet glass- and carpetmakers enjoyed. Adviser Theodore Sorensen explained that Kennedy acted on the behalf of the latter two in order to show that the administration exercised a selective approach in granting protection under the fair-trade doctrine.[51] Since neither product contributed much to the gross national product, or to the trade balance relative to other goods, however, this choice had a distinct political meaning when applied to carpets and glass. In short, Kennedy traded protectionism for TEA votes.

That politics overrode other considerations is borne out by the subsequent reaction of the parties concerned. To be sure, the sheet glass industry continued, despite the tariff hike, to resist the trade bill. In fact, the day that Kennedy announced the new duties, nine industry witnesses testified against the TEA. When Kennedy delayed the tariffs for ninety days to give importers a chance to find new sources of supply, manufacturers criticized him. But they then turned around and raised prices—contrary to the president's wishes—thereby selfishly garnering the benefits of owning a greater share of the market.[52] Glass interests won their demands, but they were still at odds with the White House on general trade policy.

Kennedy and Congress were not out of step, however, because legislators noted the linkage of the new tariffs to the upcoming vote on the trade bill. *Time* responded that the duties cast in doubt Kennedy's sincerity for promoting liberal trade, but admitted that they won him votes. Many congressmen expressed their "delight" with the move. Cleveland Bailey (D-W.Va.), a founder of the escape clause, pointed out that since Kennedy had shown a genuine concern for injured industries by raising tariffs, the congressman would vote for the TEA. Congressman Ed Edmondson (D-Okla.), like Bailey, one of the six House members who attended the Tariff Commission hearing, said after the hike that "I feel that I can not only go along with the [trade] bill, but work for its passage."[53] The fair-trade dealing had worked.

Neutralizing protectionists was the administration's intention. The duty hike on carpets earned the votes of the two New York congressmen, Samuel Stratton and Steven B. Derounian (R), who had pushed for restraints. Senator Harry Byrd later attributed the passage of the TEA to the seven-point textile program, coupled with the carpet duty action. Legislators from glass-producing areas in West Virginia, Pennsylvania, Ohio, and Illinois who, as *Business Week* claimed, had been "100 percent against" the legislation earlier, now divided. In the House, four of the six members who demanded an escape clause ruling by the Tariff Commission voted with Kennedy. The ninety-member glass bloc split down the middle, with the intractable Dent and congressmen from the nine glass states in opposition. Yet four-fifths of those against the TEA were Republican foes. In the Senate, all but two of the fifteen-member bloc tallied in favor. One was liberal trader Fulbright, who did not record a vote, and the other was Republican Homer Capehart of Indiana.[54] Kennedy chalked up another win.

The Common Market implicitly acknowledged the politics of glass trade in criticizing the tariff hike, which occurred just twelve days after the Dillon Round ended. The Six denounced the action, which raised tariffs on wilton and velvet carpets from 21 to 40 percent, and on sheet, crown, and cylinder glass from 1.3 to 3.5 cents per pound. Belgium recalled its delegate to GATT and its ambassador to the United States for consultation, while Maurice Brasseur, the Belgian trade minister, called the hikes a "brutal" and "immoral" step. France joined Belgium in claiming that the new tariffs gave further evidence that any European industry that competed successfully in America would be penalized. In its entirety, the EEC issued a more restrained response, although still dismayed that the measures were "not in the spirit of the recent [Dillon Round] talks or of the coming talks" to be held after the passage of the TEA.[55]

The Common Market might have recognized the constraints on Kennedy, however. Quite justifiably, the Six retaliated in June 1962 by raising tariffs from 19 to 40 percent on certain U.S. chemical, synthetic fiber, and paint exports. Yet the reprisals were not politically injurious to the president. That is, the American chemical industry, primarily an exporter, incurred the brunt of the new European duties. The few protectionist chemical makers cared more about retaining more restrictive non-tariff barriers than high tariffs. Chemical producers also viewed Western Europe as a temporary outlet until the U.S. market could better absorb their products. Thus, the Six possibly picked on the healthy chemical industry, and not more vulnerable producers, so as not to arouse protectionists in Congress against the TEA.[56] The EEC tacitly understood that pressure from interest groups, and above all, the representative element, underlay Kennedy's decision to raise tariffs.

The Six, though, questioned the utility of negotiations with America if Kennedy could be so blatantly protectionist just after a round of tariff cuts. U.S. imports of wilton and velvet carpets never increased during the decade above the level registered in 1961, and the new tariffs caused severe cuts in sheet glass imports. Belgium's share of these imports actually rose during the decade, but did not register real gains since this market had actually become much smaller. In addition, Brussels ran alternative trade surpluses and deficits with the United States, but when in the red, Belgium's deficits were quite large.[57] Trade favored America, and the tariff raises portrayed the United States as a liberal trade hypocrite that shut out imports that were too competitive with its domestic goods.

For Kennedy, though, the economic effects of the tariffs ranked second to the trade bill. He vainly tried to justify the duties by citing Belgium's favorable payments balance at the time, and its healthy glass and carpet industries. More convincingly, he said that the tariffs were necessary to win the TEA, which would stimulate employment on both sides of the Atlantic. After the Common Market retaliated, Kennedy added that protectionism was regrettable, but, reminding Americans of the importance of the trade bill, he stressed that if the TEA had been in effect, "we could have then offered an alternate package which I think would have prevented retaliation."[58] As the foreign policy executive, he was concerned above all with freer international trade.

Clearly protectionist, the carpets and glass tariff hikes won adherents to the trade bill. Indeed, it is difficult to determine exactly how heavily economic motives weighed in the president's actions, but politics took precedence. Aide Myer Feldman in August 1962 echoed his boss in writing a chemical industry leader that it was precisely to avoid the type of mini-trade wars that had occurred during the carpets and glass episode that the TEA must be passed.[59] It is unlikely that Kennedy would have risked upsetting his carefully cultivated relationship with Western Europe, and future trade negotiations, for the sake of selfishly protecting two rather minor industries. Instead, he decided on a statist school compromise; lose a battle to protectionists, and infuriate the allies now, and win the war later, by passing the TEA and reducing overall trade barriers in negotiations with all GATT members.

The tariffs on carpets and glass, like the measures for oil and coal, lumber, and cotton textiles, indicated that Kennedy was no ideologue in foreign trade. Instead, he pragmatically balanced the domestic and international elements inherent in the fair-trade doctrine. The president mastered domestic politics, learning that success depended on compromises that broke down resistance to major legislation. Further evidence for his tactics appeared in an incident reportedly involving Senator Russell Long (D-La.). After giving a pitch for the TEA to a group of senators, Kennedy fielded their questions. Long, upset about the administration's intention to shut down some military bases around the country, demanded an explanation about the closure of Louisiana's Fort Polk. An irritated Kennedy informed Long that the meeting concerned trade, not bases. "I understand trade and I hope you do too," replied the senator, "I'll trade you that fort for a vote on the Trade Expansion Act."[60] Long knew that the president understood the importance of deal-making.

Decision making reflected such pluralistic exchanges. Independent oilmen and glass makers did not enjoy an informal relationship with the Kennedy administration. In fact, Kennedy's deal with Kerr was at odds with the elite, multinational "Seven Sisters," who wished to sell unlimited amounts of petroleum to U.S. consumers. Even neocorporatist historian David Painter singles out the domestic oil industry's incompatibility with the supposed network of the international petroleum structure.[61] And leaders in the glass industry won their aims, but did not agree with Kennedy on trade policy. Thus, elitist arrangements do not explain decision making in these cases.

Instead, the key interaction in the internal environment occurred because of negotiations between societal interests, the representative element, and the foreign policy executive. In the glass and carpet case, interest groups achieved their goals by pressuring congressmen. Except for divergences in opposition to or support for the TEA, their demands jibed with those of their bloc on Capitol Hill. Logrolling succeeded; Kennedy then accommodated these protectionists with tariffs. The interest group model applies to the carpet and glass tariffs.

The oil import issue reflected, however, statist interbranch bargaining. The oil industry came very close to getting the full slate of its requests, including import levels and the method of limiting foreign oil. Coal interests got government attention to overseas export barriers and to economic development, while Washington assured consumers of freer trade and lower prices in fuel oil. Yet the very tangle of rival parties regarding oil imports also demonstrated that the decision-making process was much more complex than can be explained by simple interest group pressure. Instead, facing diverse demands, Kennedy juggled all concerns satisfactorily. The oil case represented interest group politics succeeding *through* interbranch bargaining, a process epitomized by the deal with Kerr. All sides were happy, but Kennedy particularly so, because he preserved his goal of fair-trade by winning votes on the TEA from the major political blocs, giving foreign producers a slowly growing share of the U.S. oil market, and offering the potential for more access on other goods once the TEA helped lower trade barriers through GATT.

In short, Kennedy perceived he had little choice but to forge protectionist agreements with oil, carpets, and glass, and, for that matter, lumber and cotton textile interests. By resisting protectionists, the TEA would surely lose. By meekly submitting to them, as Eisenhower had done, the trade bill could be altered, and thus its effectiveness as an instrument of trade liberalization undermined. Kennedy's fair-trade tactic was a middle course that preserved the basic outline of the TEA and appeased Congress at the same time. Interest group activism, but mostly interbranch bargaining on the trade bill, signified, as scholar Theodore Lowi wrote, a most "vulgar pluralist view of American politics."[62] However distasteful, such a characterization described accurately the facts of trade politics in the United States.

The external effects of this protection were mixed, but on the whole, as availing as possible under a neomercantilist, global commercial system. Statists point out that trade remained remarkably open and competitive, considering the internal dynamics of pressure politics in the legislative process. Thus, the seemingly blatant protectionism undertaken to win the TEA did not upset the general liberalization of the trade order. Surely, Belgian carpet and glass producers suffered from tariffs, as had many Third World cotton textile exporters, although the Belgians received some compensation in the form of Common Market retaliation against certain American goods. In effect, the interdependence of the domestic and international parts of the fair-trade doctrine necessarily placed politics above economics and efficiency, at least until the TEA passed Congress. But the fair-trade approach also resulted in repeated gains for foreign producers.

Actually, the United States was often not responsible for the economic hardships of others, and even more telling, America frequently lost in trade. American oil import limits certainly stymied rising Venezuelan crude oil exports, and thus hindered that nation's lack of diversification of its oil-based economy. But Caracas deserves blame, too, for its persistent problems. The country's high cost structure, due to lofty tariffs and overvalued exchange rate relative to other nations, restrained growth in export sectors other than petroleum. Venezuela was not successful in using its considerable earnings from oil exports to build a solid industrial base necessary for economic diversity and growth.[63] Kennedy's deal with Kerr was not the only reason for this LDC's underdevelopment.

In addition, U.S. imports rose at America's own expense. In the petroleum sector, for instance, fuel oil imports climbed, while coal exports to Western Europe and Canada continued to plunge until 1970. Oil imports grew by 65 percent from 1962 to 1973, the U.S. share of world production dropped, and purchases from overseas filled a growing percentage of demand and consumption, taking more of the market away from domestic producers and giving it to other nations.[64] The door remained ajar to imports, and American oil and coal producers bore the harmful costs. At the same time, the effects of the TEA sent American trade into the red, and not only with Venezuela. Critics contend that America's overall world trade surplus, and its domination of the Venezuelan economy, warranted this deficit. Yet as Secretary of State Rusk informed Betancourt in late 1962, the oil import program would in no way effect the growing tide of other Venezuelan exports to the United States. He was right. The U.S. trade deficit with Caracas more than doubled between 1960 and 1976, when it reached $896 million. By 1976, moreover, the United States suffered a *global* trade deficit of almost $6 billion, when fifteen years before it had enjoyed a $5 billion surplus.[65] The benefits brought to others in commerce, the injury suffered by domestic producers, and the political constraints on Kennedy proved that trade was as fair as possible under U.S. leadership, thus confirming the statist school view.

Kennedy's protectionism, essentially a neomercantilist response to competition, therefore strayed from the comparative advantage principle but did not always hurt others. To be sure, cotton textile policy undermined export growth in the Third World. But Hong Kong's textiles, like Canadian oil and lumber, registered gains in trade with the United States, and Ottawa earned an overall trade surplus. In carpets and glass, and in cotton textiles, Belgium and Japan respectively were hurt, yet the former used the muscle of the Six to bargain down tariffs later in the decade, and Tokyo enjoyed a steadily mounting trade surplus with America by 1968.[66] These nations were, moreover, guilty of their own protectionism against U.S. exports. And the halving of the American merchandise trade surplus by the end of the 1960s testified to the fact that they did not unduly suffer from U.S. trade policies. On the contrary, to a large extent, America was the country that often lost out.

As statist scholars contend, the United States frequently sacrificed its home markets to foreign competition in order to retain its leadership over the world trade order. Kennedy believed such a trade-off worthwhile because he sought a reciprocal opening of doors abroad for American exports under the authority of the TEA, which would, in turn, help correct the payments deficit. The drive for exports undergirded his hope that most Americans would understand the importance of the TEA in promoting U.S. sales abroad and helping the country achieve the domestic and foreign aims envisioned by the New Frontier. Kennedy focused, therefore, not just on protecting certain import-competing industries but on persuading Americans to look overseas in order to sell their goods for the sake of national and international prosperity, strength, and unity.

CHAPTER FIVE

Kennedy Drives for Exports

After mollifying protectionists, Kennedy assumed he could round up TEA votes from liberal trade legislators, since exporters were efficient producers who would benefit under the law of comparative advantage from tariff cuts. By the early 1960s, a wider acceptance of liberal trade existed in trade and political circles than ever before. Western Europe, particularly, presented trade-biased enterprises with attractive opportunities. America seemed primed to export. Yet two traits among societal interests constrained the export effort. First, many ostensibly liberal traders preferred to exploit markets at home rather than abroad. Second, disagreements over policy existed among broad economic sectors, within specific producing groups, and with the foreign policy executive. An analysis of export sectors reveals the weaknesses of neocorporatist elitism as an interpretation of decision making, and the accuracy of the pluralist view and statist theory. That is, many producers chose to ignore or oppose Kennedy's calls for more exports, thus compelling the president to base his appeal for the trade bill on congressional concerns about the cold war, and not just profits.

In short, Kennedy prodded Americans—although not always successfully—to sell abroad in order to augment U.S. wealth, power, and security. In other words, he placed exporters at the service of the nation. Through export promotion, the president tried to display the economic and political benefits of a united capitalist world under an "Atlantic partnership." Ultimately, exports would reverse the balance-of-payments deficit, thereby maintaining a strong Western alliance in the cold war. Although many producers did not heed his appeal, his export drive reflected political and military, as well as economic, goals.

Export Promotion

Since export expansion lay at the heart of the TEA and the fair-trade doctrine, it could be assumed that efficient, rising producers would not only support, but more significant, help decide and formulate, Kennedy's trade agenda. But a public-private partnership on trade, in which corporate leaders forged policies in a similar fashion to the way that the privately led Randall Commission made them during Eisenhower's "industrial administration," did not exist in the New Frontier. Even the Petersen TEA task force, although drawn from the private sector, limited its activities to the campaign in Congress. The only organization that came close to, but was still not an example of, neocorporatism, was the Committee for a National Trade Policy (CNTP), the major lobby for liberal trade and exports.[1]

Founded in 1953 to support low tariffs, the CNTP comprised two thousand mostly capital-intensive members, who exported and invested abroad, and included Ford Motor, Standard Oil, Chase National Bank, International Business Machines, General Mills, International Telephone and Telegraph, Pillsbury, H. J. Heinz, and Crown Zellerbach. Led by founders George Ball, Paul Hoffman, and William Clayton, who were also architects of America's postwar trade policy, the CNTP contained elements of neocorporatism in that it was a quasi-public organization that fulfilled the demands of a supposed "aristocracy" of exporters. Although most of its corporate associates backed the TEA, however, the CNTP had *no* decision-making power. Ball, of course, pursued liberal trade as an official in the State Department, yet elected government officials (the president and Congress) already embraced this ideology, or negotiated over policy by interbranch bargaining. Thus, to conclude that corporate America, under the CNTP, enjoyed a privileged position within White House councils is stretching the issue. This free-trade forum was merely an interest group, with views similar to Kennedy's on trade, and which competed with other lobbies over trade policy, including the protectionist industries that the president listened to very closely. In short, the CNTP engaged in educating the public, giving its opinion, and acting as one of Petersen's liaisons with Congress and the private sector. However prestigious its membership, the CNTP did not have a neocorporatist decision-making role in trade policy, nor, for that matter, did other private organizations.[2]

The president appreciated the CNTP's export promotion efforts, however, because he hoped to convince Congress *and producers* to redirect their natural proclivities to turn inward solely in order to exploit the U.S. economy. Yet the export drive had a limited appeal, since many producers believed that GATT tended to increase imports, not exports. Kennedy could also not ignore a most telling fact about U.S. trade; only an estimated 5 percent of all American manufacturers were sold abroad.[3] There was hardly a widespread desire to export in the nation, a fact that liberal trade proponents such as the CNTP more than recognized. Liberal traders thus were only one of many voices on the foreign trade issue, a reality that presented Kennedy with many headaches in his campaign for the Trade Expansion Act.

Although Kennedy advocated the TEA as a means to boost the profits of corporate America, he stressed overall statist security imperatives. That is, although promoting exports for productionist ends, he linked sales abroad to foreign policy. "Be export-minded," he told NAM, in order to reverse the payments deficit and "meet our commitments" in the alliance.[4] The TEA was a foreign policy, echoed Petersen, while policy planner Walt Rostow added that sagging trade expansion harmed the Atlantic community and the periphery, and heartened the Soviets, who feared a resurgent West. Kennedy agreed. America could either "trade or fade" from power, warned the president.[5] In selling the TEA on television in May 1962, he said that "we talk about the economic, but there's also the political" elements of confronting the Soviets, European competition, and Third World instability. Trade, he added, "involves our national security as well as our economic well-being."[6] In December 1961, he introduced the "E" (export) flags in recognition of businessmen who built up exports. The flags had flown over productive factories during World War II; now the president asked Americans, "in a new and constructive context of national urgency," to "regard the new 'E' symbol as an incentive to their best efforts." Tying higher overseas sales to a healthy balance of payments, Kennedy declared that "more exports will mean a stronger America; a more prosperous America, and greater assurance of a free world."[7] Thus, he stressed business' responsibility of enhancing U.S. power, but under the framework of security through export expansion.

In 1961, he also instructed Secretary of Commerce Hodges to boost Eisenhower's export promotion program. Hodges tried to shake the complacency of businessmen and his department by opening trade fairs, conferences, and centers abroad, and revitalizing the overseas commercial services organization, which was under the State Department's jurisdiction. Such services as country surveys, directories, product lists, and export advice to businesses had suffered from neglect. Now Hodges got the State Department to enhance the prestige of the commercial service by elevating its employees to ministerial rank. Kennedy also expanded credit for exporters through Export-Import Bank credit guarantees. Under Eisenhower and Kennedy, the concerted export expansion program, in part, helped raise merchandise exports.[8]

But appeals and programs had little effect on changing attitudes toward trade. Douglas MacArthur II, the U.S. ambassador to Belgium, attributed America's poor showing in foreign markets to the U.S. business sector's loss of "vigor," while an Export-Import Bank official called the export performance "pathetic." Hodges complained that even American ambassadors downgraded the importance of the commercial services. Furthermore, in May 1962, at a White House conference on export expansion, trade associations focused not on exports but on protection, prompting Petersen to conclude that Americans were "not strong seekers of export opportunities."[9] Parochialism and reaction to imports undercut the export drive, while many producers were simply unaware of markets abroad, or simply opposed liberal trade. Asked if they had even heard of the EEC, for instance, over three-quarters of those polled by George Gallup responded "no." Nearly half had no knowledge of Kennedy's trade bill in January 1962; by April, after Petersen's intense informational campaign for the TEA was well under way, this figure depressingly worsened. Of those that did know about the TEA, 60 percent saw no reason to change or lower duties, or had no opinion at all. The lack of knowledge was even comical at times. When asked about the Common Market, one New York City commuter queried if the reference was to a new supermarket in suburban White Plains. Failure to win the TEA, acknowledged Petersen's staff, would not be due to a lack of persuasiveness by the administration, but because of public ignorance.[10]

The figures that Petersen compiled showed the reason behind this indifference. Exports accounted for 10 to 19 percent of the GNPs of the Common Market, Britain, Sweden, and Canada. The world leader in export volume, the United States earned nearly $20 billion from sales in 1961, or one-sixth of the global total. But only 3.8 percent of the its GNP in 1962 was attributable to exports; this figure had not moved above 6.8 percent since 1920, and rose to only 4.4 percent by 1970. An "export origin" study by the Commerce Department showed that all fifty states benefited from exports, but agriculture was the only sector reliant on them. Only eight states accounted for 60 percent of industrial exports, and fewer than one of every twenty-five manufacturers exported. With justification, protectionists complained that the study, which they saw as propaganda for the TEA, was misleading since only a small percentage of America's industrial output went abroad. In short, America did not need to export out of necessity, and producers did not resort to selling abroad in order to reduce gluts on the domestic market.[11] Still, Kennedy wished they would export more for productionist and security reasons.

Agriculture and the Chicken War

Exports were important to one group: farmers. The agricultural export total of $5.1 billion (out of $35 billion produced) accounted for 14 percent of farm income in 1962. Such a total was

TABLE 5.1
Trade Related to Production
(percentages)

Year	Total exports to GNP	Total imports to GNP	Farm exports to farm income
1955	3.9	2.9	10.8
1960	4.1	3.0	14.3
1962	3.8	2.9	14.0
1965	4.0	3.1	16.0
1970	4.4	4.1	14.3

SOURCE: U.S. Department of Commerce, *Historical Statistics of the United States, Colonial Times to 1970* (Washington, D.C.: U.S. Government Printing Office, 1975), pt. 2, p. 887.

impressive, although almost $2 billion went abroad as aid or gifts. An overall farm commodity surplus of $1.4 billion in 1962 grew larger, but America ran a deficit in dollar exports until 1970. Nonetheless, farmers were export champions. One of every six acres, and 15 percent of farm goods, as opposed to 8 percent for nonagricultural production, went abroad. Broken down, exports as a percentage of production ranged from 57 percent for rice to 20–49 percent for barley, tobacco, cotton, soybeans, and wheat, and 14 percent for sorghum. Said Secretary of Agriculture Free-man to Congress, the "prosperity and stability of the American farmer is directly dependent upon our exports."[12]

As a result, "Big Agriculture"—large-scale, efficient produc-ers—demanded more access into the lucrative Common Market. The Six took close to 30 percent of U.S. farm goods, but the common agricultural policy threatened these exports. Farmers pressured the representative element to fight CAP restrictions, and Kennedy feared that legislators would sour on the TEA when they perceived little chance for reciprocity from the Six. In order to secure votes for the bill, he staked the success of his crusade for exports on increasing American poultry sales into Western Europe. Unfortunately, he encountered rough opposition from the EEC over American chicken exports, and a lesson in the politics of exports at home.

The celebrated "chicken war" grew from a squabble into a dramatic stand by America against the CAP. The problem stemmed from a sixfold upturn in U.S. poultry (broilers and eggs) exports, beginning in 1959. Advances in breeding and management glutted the chicken market at home and prompted a search for new outlets. The explosion was ill-timed; exports confronted the Common Market's integration process and Europe's own poultry revolution. After difficult intra-EEC talks, the Six readied CAP levies on poultry imports for July 30, 1962, which would harmonize internal poultry prices, restrict imports, and reserve the big West German chicken market for Common Market producers. Americans controlled one-quarter of the West German market, with exports valued at $49.5 million, and growing. In effect, the CAP set a minimum import price, raising the cost of chicken imports by nearly 10 cents per pound. The Six refused to negotiate the poultry CAP, which emerged during the Dillon Round, and as a result, the "standstill agreement" of 1961 on poultry did not assure the United States of its historic share of the EEC market. As agricultural expert Ross Talbot explains, this stalemate allowed the chicken issue "to fester and irritate." [13]

By the time the levy was in place, at the end of July 1962, just before Senate hearings on the TEA, conflict was inevitable. The American Farm Bureau Federation and the National Farmers Union demanded that the Six maintain America's share of the West German market. The influential Institute of American Poultry Industries, a combination of producers with offices in Washington and Frankfurt, West Germany, mobilized producers to lobby for "fair play" from Europe. The subsequent visits and mail to the White House from the poultry industry, delegations of governors from seventeen states, and chicken bloc legislators, were considerable. [14] The foreign policy executive was made well aware of discontent.

Kennedy took action because, like textiles, the poultry industry was centered in the south. Congressmen from the region oversaw New Frontier legislation and demanded solutions to the chicken problem. For instance, Congressman Harold Cooley (D-N.C.), chairman of the House Agriculture Committee, could tie up the beleaguered Kennedy farm program indefinitely. And no less than Wilbur Mills, from a top chicken state, warned the president that the TEA would not pass if the Common Market retained the CAP on poultry, or granted inadequate compensation to America if

EEC tariffs rose. He refused to grant tariff authority that would be dissipated by bargaining down the very barriers that the Six had arbitrarily inflated. Another ally and Arkansan, Senator Fulbright of the Foreign Relations and Finance committees, called the CAP "trade strangulation." Other powerful southern veterans— LBJ's "whales"—agreed. Kennedy also expected pressure from the Atlantic states, particularly Maryland.[15] The representative element showed its willingness to advocate export help for the trade-biased sector.

Congress sent White House aides scampering for a poultry program. Not that the administration had been silent; Freeman, Petersen, and Kennedy spoke out against the CAP at the Dillon Round. Now they plotted a strategy to avoid congressional recriminations. Not surprisingly, White House political aide Myer Feldman opposed waiting until the TEA vote before working out a bargain with the Six. He ruled out appeals for liberal trade to the EEC, knowing they would be ignored, and also turned down an option calling for a meeting of Common Market agricultural ministers. To discuss unfair trade barriers at a conference table would put Kennedy in an uncomfortable spot, believed Feldman, since the Six could turn around and criticize America's inopportune tariff hikes on carpets and glass.[16]

Instead, the president opted to send a letter to Chancellor Konrad Adenauer in June 1962, before activation of the poultry levy. Calling the levy "unfair and inconsistent" with GATT principles, Kennedy warned that it impaired alliance relations and might doom the TEA on Capitol Hill. Difficulties with the EEC, he wrote, were "an important adverse factor in the consideration of the Trade Bill now before Congress." He asked Adenauer to defer the imposition of the levy from July 30 until after passage of the TEA.[17] On the chicken issue, Kennedy was willing to attempt hegemonic persuasion in order to ensure liberal trade.

Adenauer was receptive but West German politics constrained him. Promising to look into the levy, he explained that only the EEC Commission could change it. Indeed, on July 20, 1962 he requested that the Common Market preserve lower poultry duties until the end of the year. The administration was delighted; the State Department remarked that Bonn's effort would at least "earn

us some credit in this matter" with Congress.[18] The EEC Commission, also resisting pressure from farm organizations in Europe
that sought a high levy, authorized the cut in the West German
levy, subject to approval by the West German Bundestag. America's earlier exultation was short-lived and premature; protectionist
West German farmers possessed much political influence over their
parliament, which never acted. The levy went into effect on schedule.[19] The Chicken War erupted.

Over the next year, the poultry trade issue cursed Atlantic trade
relations. As scholar John Evans has written, the image of plucked
chickens being at the center of diplomatic conflict provoked even
the most serious commentators to make such jokes as America
crying "fowl" over EEC policy. But although the Chicken War
proved a field day for pundits and cartoonists, American government officials were not at all amused by Europe's poultry protectionism. The congressional poultry bloc appreciated Kennedy's
understandably limited actions against the Common Market,
choosing to censure the Six instead of the president's trade bill.
Meanwhile, Secretary of Agriculture Freeman met with EEC leaders and futilely berated them for the levy, while in June 1963,
chickens entered into diplomacy when Kennedy mentioned the
problem during his trip to West Germany. The Common Market
retorted that poultry was relatively unimportant to U.S. trade;
chicken exports were only 1.2 percent of America's total exports.
In addition, America still enjoyed an overall trade surplus with the
Six. Acting for Kennedy, LBJ retaliated in December 1963 in order
to curb protectionism in the new EEC, and sought more exports
to correct its payments deficit. America raised tariffs amounting to
$26 million on items that particularly injured West Germany,
France, and the Netherlands, the main protectionists.[20] Kennedy
showed his support for poultry interests.

In the external environment, at the very least, the Chicken War
pointed to future limits on agricultural imports under the CAP. By
1971, U.S. poultry exports to the Six fell to less than one-fifth of
their high levels of 1962, and almost half of sales in 1959. Although overall farm exports to the Common Market rose in value,
they declined as a percentage of EEC imports. Thus, the United
States did not retain its historical share of access into Western

Europe.[21] America had a comparative advantage in chickens, but the Six refused to trade fairly. The United States could not force Europe to remain open, despite the threat and reality of retaliation. The Chicken War revealed that the United States sought trade according to comparative advantage, yet was stymied in its pursuit by the Common Market's integration. As statist writers assert, the EEC, like America, could also exercise its neomercantilist muscle, placing politics, power-seeking, and protection above economic theory and the free interplay of markets.

Mixed Farm Support for the TEA

Most farmers took a liberal trade position like the poultry industry, but many did not support the TEA right down the line. The American Farm Bureau sought greater access into the Common Market, although as an advocate of laissez-faire, disliked the adjustment assistance provision in the trade bill. Other organizations backed trade expansion but they disagreed on the details.[22] The family-farmer National Farmers Union, for example, supported adjustment assistance for its import-competing members. Some farmers were also protectionists, including those from livestock and dairy states, whose legislators accounted for two-thirds of the votes against the TEA. California specialty crop farmers, Pacific Coast fishermen, and vegetable and fruit growers from all over the nation, opposed Kennedy. Even cotton producers, who exported half their production abroad, but feared upsetting the textile industry or the two-price cotton subsidy, denounced liberal trade. The timber industry also sought restrictions.[23]

Legislators listened to these farmers. Senators from New York noted that their state sold only 1 percent of its produce abroad, while agricultural imports displaced workers. The inflow of strawberries provoked outcries from congressmen from several states, noted the TEA task force, while Representatives Al Ulman (D-Ore.) and Clair Engle (D-Calif.) pressed for restrictions on a host of specialty commodities. The lumber bloc pushed for restraints, and Senator E. L. Bartlett (R-Alab.) sought to limit fish imports. The representative element agreed with the Western Growers Association that "foreign trade should be fair trade."[24]

Thus, a certain pluralism on trade issues best characterizes the farm sector. Some questioned the utility of exporting as a means to lower domestic surpluses, while a Farm Bureau official admitted he had a "damn tough job" of even interesting farmers in trade expansion. As political scientist Lauren Soth warns, those who generalize about opinions in the farm sector stand on "dangerous ground."[25] To be sure, Kennedy got solid support from the farm bloc; the Farm Bureau, for instance, delivered all but one member of the Kansas delegation. Kennedy did not buy votes by concessions, as he had with protectionists, although his efforts for the poultry industry helped. Yet he carefully cultivated TEA votes from the agricultural sector because of its divisions among exporters and producers who were susceptible to import pressure. Beyond the trade bill, he hoped to alleviate his political weakness in the midwestern farm states, which he lost in the 1960, and use overseas farm sales to right the payments balance.[26] Still, protectionism and impatience from exporters showed that the agricultural sector was far from unified in its support for his goals.

Labor's Response to the TEA

In the labor sector, contrary to farm states, Kennedy's political stock was high and he had solid support for the TEA, but union backing came with a price tag, qualifications, and deep disagreement with the business community. It was also unclear if workers cared much about exports, although they certainly realized the effects of imports on jobs. Like farmers, many workers disagreed with the administration over trade policy. More often, however, they clashed with business; a neocorporatist, business-labor alliance was not the rule in trade policy. Thus, labor also comprised pluralistic interests, some of which united with business, others with the administration, and still others that opposed both management and the foreign policy executive.

Administration and labor leaders acknowledged the employment benefits of foreign trade but exaggerated the effects of exports on lowering the jobless rate. In theory, liberal trade improved allocative efficiency and the international division of labor, and thus employment benefits in the long run for society. But in

America's case, only about 3.1 million workers—nearly one-third on farms—relied on exports. As George Harrison, vice-president of the AFL-CIO, admitted, since the percentage of employment attributable to exports and imports (7.5 percent) was small, the United States was not reliant on trade for domestic economic security. But the GNP absorbed a "vital" percentage of trade. "High wages are important to keep sales up at home as well as abroad," he told workers.[27] Yet such remarks clouded the facts about labor and exports. Figures revealed that large rises in employment did not depend on an increase in foreign trade. For instance, only 5 percent of nongovernment, nonagricultural jobs, and 7.7 percent of industrial workers, depended on exports. Senator Albert Gore (D-Tenn.) agreed with Kennedy that merchandise exports stimulated the economy, and thus created jobs. But, he added, exports were not of such great magnitude as to lower unemployment to an acceptable level.[28] Thus, productionism brought benefits for the economy, yet the specific gains in employment from exports remained small.

Kennedy appealed to workers by stressing the traditional Democratic party support for government intervention in the economy. Since unions were one of his political bases, he tried to satisfy them on trade policy by advocating adjustment assistance. "Big Labor" backed the RTA, but without unemployment compensation to cushion workers after the TEA gutted the "no-injury" criteria, union leaders vowed that they would oppose the bill. At the 1960 Democratic convention, moreover, the AFL-CIO had lobbied, in fact, for the strengthening of the escape clause. Now its endorsement of the TEA was "wholly contingent" upon adjustment assistance.[29] Of course, Kennedy obliged, since adjustment assistance was a centerpiece of his fair-trade doctrine. But union demands for adjustment assistance showed that workers were in no way unabashed liberal traders. And AFL-CIO adamancy also restricted Kennedy's flexibility in packaging the provision to suit conservative, anti-labor industry leaders and congressional foes.

Labor's views showed the split with management, and thus the tear in any possible neocorporatist fabric of consensus regarding trade policy. A reporter goggled as union and business leaders walked into the Capitol together when the TEA hearings began, but this episode belied the tension within an expedient alliance against protectionism. AFL-CIO president George Meany denounced the "powerful forces in and out of Congress" who claimed that the payments deficit had "arisen because we had priced ourselves out of the market" with high wages. The deficit, competition abroad, and cheap imports were favorite "fronts" for "those" corporate leaders who advocated wage restraints on labor, he argued.[30] "Honest businessmen and bankers," said AFL-CIO vice-president Harrison, knew that corporate inattention to exports explained the persistent deficit. America's reputation for know-how and supersalesmanship was "a myth if industry pretends that it does not have to try to sell because it can excuse its failures by blaming everything on wages."[31] The TEA laid bare the fundamental business-labor schism over the economy, ideology, and specifically, Kennedy's liberal trade program.

Pluralism existed within the labor movement as well. Although not numerous, some unions opposed freer trade, and they possessed considerable influence. Carpenters and joiners, shoemakers, potters, and glass and textile workers rejected the AFL-CIO stand on liberal trade; the glass tariff hike and GATT textile arrangements showed the weight of the latter two. The 1.7 million-member Teamsters brotherhood expressed "serious reservations" about the TEA because it made "no provision for fair trade" by attempting to equalize international wages, or issuing an assault on non-tariff barriers. Like others, the union accused Kennedy of being inconsistent on trade; the Teamsters perceived him as a former protectionist who had switched over to liberal trade once he became president.[32] The Teamsters misunderstood his fair-trade stance, but along with some other workers, they resisted Kennedy's efforts to build a unified coalition for his trade bill.

Yet Kennedy counted on labor because he shared Meany's aim of prosecuting the cold war with the TEA. Fervently anti-communist, the AFL-CIO president linked liberal trade to a unified Atlantic community, joined by Third World allies. The Soviet bloc was anathema; he opposed, for instance, inviting Moscow to discuss a code of fair labor practices. For Meany, the essence of foreign affairs was capitalism versus communism. "In this struggle," he told Congress, "the economic well-being of the free nations, our own included, is of paramount importance."[33] This cold war perspective, issued by a major societal interest, reflected, as the statist school contends, the president's motive for issuing the Trade Expansion Act in the first place.

In sum, regarding the workers who backed the TEA for economic or security reasons, those who opposed it, and the squabbling with the business sector, the only firm conclusion that can be drawn is that pluralism pervaded the labor view of trade policy. Workers were not "free traders in the usual sense," explained Solomon Barkin of the Textile Workers Union. Their support was qualified, both by demanding adjustment assistance and, for some, import protection. Kennedy responded to both desires and won the majority to liberal trade. As Meany declared, "I would support any legislation that would be helpful to our country's position in the world, and at the same time find some way to help protect our own workers."[34] Kennedy could not have agreed more with this statist, fair-trade view of trade, a position that was necessary to win labor votes.

Business/Industry Divergence on Trade

Because, like the other two sectors of the economy, business and industry also showed pluralistic divisions on trade policy, Kennedy struggled to win many industrialists to his trade bill. Some manufacturers feared that hurting local economies by tariff reductions might provoke a backlash of consumer boycotts. Others were apathetic. Elmo Roper pollsters found that although most sided with Kennedy, only 27 percent of the 500 largest corporations answered their survey. A Research Institute of America survey of 30,000 businessmen discovered 57 percent in favor of the TEA, but one-quarter against, and 17.3 percent undecided. A *Business Week* sampling of 150 executives found one-half undecided, but concerned about the effects of the TEA on local industry, and the other half split on the bill. Of 262 industrialists polled in Cleveland, Ohio, 164 opposed the bill, or had no opinion at all. Historian Jim Heath noted a "solid minority" of opposition businessmen to the TEA, and when added to fence-sitters, they exposed the diversity in the business sector.[35]

Despite vigorous efforts, the administration battled to get businessmen to export. The lumber industry, for instance, sent a trade mission to Europe in 1963, yet giants Weyerheuser and Georgia-Pacific remained skeptical about overseas markets. Labor and management, groaned Kennedy, were "largely unconcerned" about opportunities abroad. Only a handful of companies, he told bankers in February 1963, gave the export market "the attention it deserved." The rest thought the risks greater than the potential benefits, the profit margin much less than in the domestic market, and foreign protection too high to overcome.[36] In the business sector, there was no unanimity on exports.

As scholar Robert Dahl discovered, the TEA troubled the U.S. Chamber of Commerce and the National Association of Manufacturers. A representative for small merchants and trade, business, and professional groups, the Chamber included exporters and industries affected by imports. It backed the TEA in order to help U.S. companies penetrate the Common Market, but only with protective safeguards. In fact, the trade bill provoked a rebellion at a Chamber meeting in early 1962 when protectionists rallied against adjustment assistance as an answer to import injury. The board of directors managed to win support for the TEA, but many members agreed with Monsanto's Thomas J. Dewey that such a "wide diversity" existed within the Chamber that no policy statement could be made. In the end, the Chamber retained its opposition to federally funded adjustment assistance, but went ahead and supported the TEA, albeit with dissenting opinions.[37]

The voice of "Big Business," the National Association of Manufacturers, took no stand. Split between export- and import-competitors and firms with no interest at all in tariffs, this 22,000–member organization had remained consistently neutral on trade since the 1940s. In fact, NAM's Economic Advisory Committee discussed all foreign economic policies except tariffs, of which it left the "widest discretion" to its membership. Rejecting both extremes of free trade and protectionism, NAM sought trade expansion, but not at the expense of U.S. producers. Although offering no resolution on the trade bill, NAM, in general, opposed adjustment assistance, sought a one-year extension of the RTA, and desired to reduce presidential authority over tariffs.[38]

The lukewarm reception from NAM and the Chamber revealed the lack of neocorporatist consensus on trade within the industrial sector and, even worse for the president, the discord between industry and the White House. Recent scholarship portrays Kennedy as a neocorporatist who pursued tax and trade policies to assure business hegemony in the domestic and foreign economy. But in reality, he met business resistance over steel prices, investment policy, and trade, to name but a few areas of conflict. If anything, Kennedy had to appease businessmen regarding his plans. The president sportively, but accurately, told NAM in December 1961 that he knew its members had not "approached the New Frontier with the greatest possible enthusiasm."[39] As Jim Heath notes, when agreement occurred, Kennedy acted not for particular businessmen or sectors, but in the national interest of invigorating the American economy as a whole. A foreign observer noted the close business-government relations in other countries, but admitted that such alliances in the United States were not as prevalent.[40] Erecting bridges between the private and public sectors was a task that Kennedy found difficult and unrewarding, especially in trade policy.

To be sure, much of the business community, and certainly many capital-intensive and service industries, fell in behind the TEA. Transportation, consumer goods, and heavy machinery manufacturers joined banks and insurance firms in stressing the "amazing opportunities" opening up in Western Europe. The CNTP and the Committee for Economic Development, a business think tank, added to these forces. Business sought an end to the "vicious circle" of trade restrictions that cut profits. Take away the national income derived from trade, said one industrialist, and the margin between profit and loss would be eliminated. James Lindeen surveyed testimony on the RTAs since 1934 and found that the more competitive producers were inclined toward liberal trade. Political scientist Stephen Krasner also discovered that support for freer trade reached a high in the early 1960s, although this enthusiasm soon waned as American economic power declined, and producers were subjected to increasing foreign competition.[41] But many exporters, consumers, and internationalist-minded businessmen supported the TEA and urged Congress to pass the bill.

Even among capital-intensive enterprises, however, support varied in intensity. One trend was clear: the TEA represented a "sweeping change" in attitudes in favor of liberal trade, said business analyst Gene Bradley. For many, though, tariffs were not important. Chrysler Corporation, for instance, admitted that road and other taxes doubled the price of its cars in Europe, so duty cuts would make little difference in sales. Aircraft giant Boeing remarked that tariffs were irrelevant, since most of its buyers were government-owned, and therefore paid any price regardless of the added cost of duties. Installing subsidiaries overseas concerned Caterpillar Tractor, and other multinationals, much more than exports. And other industries that stood to gain from the productionist TEA seemed apathetic to the Kennedy cause. The CNTP bemoaned, for instance, the delinquency of some of its members in donations, including Texaco, Coca-Cola, American Radiator and Standard, and F. W. Woolworth. Furthermore, competitive, high technology industries in the chemicals, coal, steel, and aluminum sectors wavered between the TEA and protectionism.[42] Divergences existed among manufacturers, as did apathy or indifference, toward the president's export objectives.

A fitting example of the split in opinion over trade was the fast-growing electronics industry. With exports accounting for 6 percent of its output, the industry would enjoy free access into the Common Market under the dominant supplier clause of the TEA. Predicting that rising European firms would squeeze out U.S. competitors, however, producers focused on the home market for sales of televisions, radios, and semi-conductors. Thus, much to the anger and disappointment of the administration, the Electronics Industries Association called for American trade restrictions because its high-tech competitors threatened production. Manufacturers requested quotas to limit these foreign products, and sought to add more protectionist devices to the TEA.[43] Here was a capital-intensive industry that turned inward, when it should have looked toward trade expansion, and it was not the only one of its kind.

TABLE 5.2
U.S. Chemical Trade
(billions of dollars)

Year	Imports	Exports	Balance
1958	.78	1.36	.58
1960	.82	1.77	.95
1962	.77	1.87	1.10
1965	.78	2.40	1.62
1968	1.12	3.28	2.16
1972	2.01	4.13	2.12

SOURCE: U.S. Department of Commerce, *Statistical Abstracts of the United States, 1962* (Washington, D.C.: U.S. Government Printing Office), p. 874; *1967*, pp. 829, 831; *1974*, pp. 795, 797.

The Anomalous Chemical Industry

This tendency also surprisingly held true for the chemical industry. A prime candidate for the export club—with 6 percent of sales going overseas—the industry ranked fifth in total sales, fourth in assets among American producers, and boasted a growth rate three times the national average. It accounted for nearly 9 percent of U.S. exports, with overseas sales tripling imports. Market surveys predicted rapid growth in investment and trade, especially in competitive but capital-starved Western Europe. "Never before has the chemical industry played so heavy a role in the U.S. export trade," proclaimed *Chemical Week* in April 1961.[44]

Chemical producers were a paradox, however. A knee-jerk response to imports dominated their trade views. Protectionism stemmed from a reaction of forty years before against German dye makers, who dumped chemicals on the American market after World War I. In order to protect themselves, fledgling U.S. producers asked the government in 1922 to impose the American Selling Price (ASP) customs valuation. Reinforcing the prohibitive 60 percent chemical rates of the Fordney-McCumber tariff of 1921, the ASP undercut the price advantage of foreign manufacturers in organics (dyes) by basing duties on the current U.S. price of chemicals instead of the value of the imports. Over the next four decades, the ASP limited organics imports to 20 percent of their potential in the U.S. market. The revival of British and Common

Market chemical cartels exacerbated fears of competition. West Germany, France, Italy, and Great Britain had enjoyed tremendous growth in chemical output since the late 1950s, and as a result, cut into America's world market-share. Liberal traders pointed to the surplus of exports over imports in the American ledger, but U.S. producers predicted a leveling off of overseas sales, and a sixfold jump in imports. They hoped that Kennedy would increase access for chemicals in Western Europe, while protecting dye makers, and other synthetic organic producers, at home.[45]

But the administration and industry were at odds on economic policy. For one, producers were ambivalent about the export credit guarantee program, which issued Export-Import Bank coverage for private loans to exporters. Since their main markets were low-risk areas, chemical makers did not need the program. Kennedy's confrontational rollback of steel prices in May 1962 also upset industry leaders, as did the lack of more liberal depreciation allowances for plant modernization and his plan to change the overseas investment tax deferral privilege. Regarding the latter point of discord, corporations were not taxed until their subsidiaries remitted their earnings to the parent firm, but often affiliates held on to their earnings and reinvested them so as to avoid paying taxes. Kennedy sought to assess these multinationals in order to slow capital flight, which aggravated the payments deficit. But between 1957 and 1960 investments in Western Europe and Canada exceeded the dividends remitted to parent companies by $655 million. Kennedy withdrew the tax plan after an angry chemical industry claimed that producing at home was more expensive than in Western Europe, where labor, transportation, and manufacturing costs were cheaper. Thus, American producers competed by skirting around the common external tariff to set up fifty-five new plants in Western Europe from 1957 to 1962, augmenting the output of American subsidiaries by 84 percent, and countering Kennedy's desire to slow down multinational investment.[46]

The foreign policy executive and societal interests also disagreed on trade. At the Dillon Round, the Synthetic Organic Chemical Manufacturers Association (SOCMA) and the umbrella trade organization, the Manufacturing Chemists Association (MCA), revolted when many chemical products appeared on the list of goods

eligible for tariff cuts. Demanding higher tariffs, the MCA sardonically remarked that the list looked like it had been prepared by
foreigners eager to enter the U.S. market. *Chemical Week* cautioned against such sarcasm, but pointed out that the synthetic
organic sector would not survive without tariff protection, and
thus implored negotiators to remember that "there is no stigma
attached to considering U.S. interests."[47]

The Dillon Round also provoked animosity among Atlantic
chemical traders. Charges of dumping flew both ways; the Six
protested the flood of U.S. polyethylene into Western Europe,
while Americans denounced cheap imports of antibiotics from its
allies. A British producer called Americans "two-faced" because
they wished only to sell without lowering their own protective
barriers. The ASP was particularly nettlesome because it more
than doubled the price of imports. Anyway, argued the Europeans,
the reasons for U.S. protectionism in chemicals had disappeared
long ago, since other products had assumed a greater significance
in trade than those under the ASP, which covered just a handful of
goods.[48]

Despite getting a good deal at the Dillon Round, many U.S.
chemical producers still opposed liberal trade, and hence the TEA.
As a result, they girded for one of their "stiffest battles with the
government in years" over tariff policies.[49] Linear tariff cuts would
leave them in "complete uncertainty" in the future, and discourage
development of new products. Other spokesmen accepted tariff
reductions as long as Kennedy did not water down the escape
clause and peril point provisions—but, of course, he did the opposite. In opposition were, to no surprise, synthetic organic producers, who predicted an evisceration of the ASP valuation if the
trade bill passed Congress.[50] SOCMA and its allies readied for
battle with the president.

Diverse opinion on the TEA ran through the ranks of the chemical industry, but regardless of the "split personality" of exporters
and militant protectionists, the industry leaned toward more restrictions. Welcoming the bill were, among others, American Cy-
anamid, Cabot Corporation, Pfizer International, and Baird
Chemical, who confidently believed that U.S. chemical products
could penetrate the Common Market. Others, such as Reichhold

Co. and National Distillers and Chemicals, resigned themselves to
tariff cuts, as long as they were gradual. Opposition was overwhelming, though, even from exporters. Two of the biggest companies, Dow Chemical and Monsanto, both with large foreign
sales, opposed the trade bill. Dow wanted controls on imports and
perceived a "definite peril" to employment and research from
liberal trade. Monsanto actually proposed a five-point program
designed around item-by-item reductions. Criticizing the TEA for
its failure to ensure true reciprocity, Monsanto took its cue from
founder Edgar Queeny's prevailing forty-year-old emphasis on
protectionism.[51]

Just as startling, another chemical behemoth, DuPont, also sided
with the protectionist cause. DuPont's exports comprised 6 percent of total sales, yet its dye division dominated trade policy.
Vowing to "fight for our very existence," dye makers had president Crawford Greenewalt offer four "safeguard amendments" to
the TEA that strengthened the escape clause, reinstated the peril
point, eliminated adjustment assistance, and assured reciprocity in
negotiations in which industry advisers would be present. DuPont
endorsed Senator Prescott Bush's extremely protectionist amendments, and the industry predicated its support for the TEA on the
DuPont clauses.[52] It would be extremely difficult for Kennedy to
ignore these chemical protectionists, especially when they included
in their ranks such powerhouses as Dow, Monsanto, and DuPont,
all of which had a ubiquitous presence in several states of legislators on Capitol Hill.

Protectionists were influential. As expected, synthetic organic
producers denounced the trade bill as "reckless" legislation that
squandered U.S. economic strength. By March 1962, the MCA,
representing 182 producers who accounted for 90 percent of
chemical sales, edged toward a revised TEA. Indeed, chairman
Robert Semple sided with export expansion as a goal and, like
Kennedy, sought to establish "fair trade rules so that the U.S.
manufacturer operating abroad has an equal break with the foreign competition delivering his products to our shores."[53] But
Semple stood in the way of the TEA, backing the four DuPont
amendments and opposing the president's request for more au-

thority to lower American tariffs at GATT.[54] Congress and the president listened closely to this disgruntlement.

Such interest group pressure distressed the administration. Like the CNTP, Kennedy erroneously believed that, save for organics, producers would be at the "vanguard of liberal trade." Howard Petersen told the MCA that the industry epitomized the law of comparative advantage: it possessed substantial investment capital, cheap raw materials, and efficient production and marketing resources. Imports were also negligible, accounting for only 5 percent of U.S. consumption.[55] According to Petersen's calculations, the industry was a perfect example of the efficient producer being able to trade with success in the world economy. But for chemical producers, liberal economic arguments came second to the desire for protection from imports.

The president reiterated Petersen's message—but to no avail—when Semple and General John Hull, president of the MCA and a former aide to General George C. Marshall, visited the White House on April 9, 1962 in order to discuss the four DuPont amendments and the ASP. Kennedy promised to take the four amendments under "earnest consideration," and make a careful determination of which chemical items to exempt from tariff cuts at future negotiations. Upon the advice of Petersen, the president also pledged to retain the ASP. Although disappointed by the industry's position, he agreed not "to disturb" the chemical sector. Hull later thanked Kennedy, and Semple gave qualified approval of the TEA, but as Petersen's aide Myer Rashish concluded, the chemical industry was "one of those squeaky wheels that [got] the grease."[56]

Kennedy now banked on Congress to deal with any remaining recalcitrant chemical producers. When organics producers complained, Wilbur Mills chided Carl Gerstacker, the chairman of SOCMA and president of Dow Chemical, for being selfish, declaring that inefficient sectors must adjust to competition or bow under for the good of the industry. Congressman Sidney Yates (D-Ill.) also utilized the export origin study in order to display the benefits of chemical exports for every state. To Kennedy's relief, House and Senate conferees refused to attach the DuPont amendments to the TEA, and in the end administration allies in Congress secured the chemical votes for the trade bill. Although resigned only to "make the best" of the TEA, *Chemical Week* conceded that the bill had a "silver lining," since it would lower Common Market restrictions.[57]

Interaction on the chemical issue reflected pluralist, interest group, and interbranch politics, as Kennedy made a deal with the MCA, but liberal traders in Congress also fended off pressure from producers and gave him the TEA. Like electronics, steel, and some other strong industries, the chemical industry defied the neocorporatist assumption that efficient producers gravitated toward an alliance with the foreign policy executive. Instead, all of them contested the president, and forced him to grant concessions. Such were the process and results of his fair-trade push for industries that, to most observers, seemed confirmed and natural liberal traders.

Congress and the Grand Design

Kennedy appeased protectionists, and even some exporters, in order to win votes for the TEA, but the foundation of his congressional strategy banked on solid support from liberal traders. These legislators could counter intractable protectionists, and also hostility or apathy to his trade policy. A defined bloc is hard to discern exactly, since many legislators feared that by supporting Kennedy, they would arouse producers back home who were sensitive to imports. An unidentified midwestern congressman revealed this worry. He recognized the need for the bill, yet preferred to cast his vote with Kennedy, and then "keep quiet about it and hope nobody notices."[58] On the other hand, other liberal traders boldly rallied for the TEA, such as the twenty-two congressmen who lobbied for trade liberalization in August 1961. The president counted on legislators from major farm and manufacturing export states for votes.[59] But most of his loyal allies hailed from a bipartisan group that looked beyond local problems to national and international economic, political, and security interests. These legislators grasped that a trade war with Western Europe and an escalating payments deficit would impair America's security. Thus, like the foreign policy executive, they sought freer trade in order to strengthen the Western alliance under U.S. leadership.

The liberal trade bloc therefore supported Kennedy's all-encompassing diplomatic scheme for the NATO alliance, called the "Grand Design," which sought an Atlantic partnership between America and the Common Market, soon enlarged, it was hoped, by the addition of the Outer Seven. Eisenhower had most recently enunciated the idea of a partnership, which had actually brewed in the minds of politicians and thinkers on both sides of the Atlantic for years. For the Kennedy administration, the partnership concept, as applied to commerce, accepted the Six as an equal with the United States; "two pillars," one American, the other European, would be joined by the common purpose of liberal trade. The Grand Design implied that America was no longer the sole hegemon in the global trade order, and thus must undertake cooperative endeavors in foreign economic policy. As Kennedy wrote a journalist, "We have sought among our European allies not a band of followers, but a strong partnership capable of sharing with us the leadership" of the West.[60]

In a "Declaration of Interdependence" on July 4, 1962, he publicly acknowledged this goal by announcing that the Grand Design would in no way retain U.S. hegemony. Guided by the fair-trade doctrine, Kennedy sought American-Common Market trade "on a basis of full equality." Confessing that he was under no illusions that the United States could "please all of our European allies," the president said that he just wanted "the benefits of this kind of union to be shared."[61] In order to further this end, he sought trade expansion. Under the TEA, the Atlantic powers would create "the greatest market the world has ever known . . . a trillion dollar economy, where goods can move freely back and forth."[62] To be sure, dissent intensified against the Grand Design, especially abroad. Gaullists, for instance, viewed the blueprint for an Atlantic partnership as a disguise for continued U.S. dominance of Western Europe. After all, Kennedy balked at giving up the dollar's dominance in the global monetary system, so why would America abandon its control of the GATT order? Regardless of this opposition, however, the Grand Design mustered a broad appeal. Most notably, top EEC officials endorsed Kennedy's call for productionism, unity, and liberal trade under a united Atlantic community.[63]

As the statist school contends, the Grand Design for America and its allies emanated not just from economic motives, but from cold war imperatives. A trade partnership would spread to the aid and military spheres, where Western Europe would assume more of the financial burden to ease the U.S. payments deficit, while America would share control of nuclear weapons. Without the TEA, American leaders feared, the Atlantic economies would drift apart, fulfilling the goals of Moscow's foreign policy. The Soviets opposed a United States-Common Market front, which strengthened Western European integration, NATO, and the LDCs, reported security adviser Roger Hilsman of the State Department. A partnership would frustrate communist hopes for a capitalist trade war and fund the military deterrent of the alliance, and thereby, assured Kennedy, doom Moscow's "efforts to split the West" to "failure." As Roswell L. Gilpatric, deputy secretary of defense, summed up, "While defense provides the essential security of the alliance, trade provides the substance."[64]

If a consensus on trade policy, and particularly exports, existed among those active on trade issues, then it evolved not from neocorporatist economic alliances, but from a regard for "free world" defense. Thus, the liberal trade bloc in Congress understood the fundamental link of the TEA to national security. Senator Fulbright declared that a trade partnership was more than a dream, it was a cold war necessity. A trade war with Western Europe, added Senator Vance Hartke (D-Ind.), would "only delight the communists." Congressmen John R. Lindsay (R-N.Y.) claimed that Soviet inroads in the Third World merited a liberal trade program, and William S. Moorehead (D-Pa.) argued that cold war threats outweighed those of import injury in forging the nation's trade policy. "Much more [was] at stake" than U.S. employment and expansion, said Senator Jacob K. Javits (R-N.Y.). The TEA addressed, he continued, "the economic strength and military power of the nations confronted today by a massive and multi-faceted Soviet challenge."[65] As statist scholars argue, the foreign policy executive and representative element focused, above all, on the cold war as they settled the politics of trade.

If cold war ideology undergirded the TEA, the fair-trade doctrine defined the practical use of the bill. Critical to passage were amendments—worked out by House and Senate conferees—that ensured a liberal trade bias, but also some protection. On the latter, for instance, Wilbur Mills changed the congressional votes needed to override presidential escape clause decisions, from two-thirds to a majority, making it easier to resort to the provision. Also, Congress added to the trade bill an assurance that the president would not reduce tariffs for five years on import-sensitive items. In addition, the TEA provided a bipartisan delegation of two House and two Senate members to accompany the new Special Representative for Trade Negotiations (STR) to the upcoming tariff talks, in order to voice and ensure congressional priorities concerning export expansion, and also protectionism.[66]

The STR itself comprised a key element of the fair-trade doctrine. Working out of the White House, the novel STR replaced the State Department as chief GATT negotiator. Rusk and Ball grudgingly accepted the creation of the position, while the Commerce Department and Kennedy saw it as a counter to accusations that State was too generous at tariff talks. To be sure, the STR would be a liberal trader, as the president selected an ailing former secretary of state, Christian Herter, to fill the post. Some disliked the choice; Congressman Henry Reuss (D-Wis.), for instance, wanted a tough bargainer, someone capable of confronting the Six "who smokes a cigar without lighting it and doesn't smile very often," rather than the genteel Herter.[67] Yet Herter would remain mostly in Washington coordinating policy, leaving the bargaining to his seasoned deputy, W. Michael Blumenthal, who had helped negotiate such difficult agreements as the GATT cotton textile accords.[68] The STR, administration officials believed, would appease protectionists, but make sure that export expansion, hence lower tariffs, assumed precedence in American trade policy.

Ironically, the administration defeated liberal traders on a key issue. Congressman Reuss and Senator Douglas tried to extend to the British-led Outer Seven, the TEA's dominant supplier clause, which was designed to eliminate tariffs on items in which the United States and Six provided 80 percent of world trade. Noting that Britain made many of these goods, the Douglas-Reuss amendment would still permit large-scale duty cuts, even in the event that the EEC rejected London's application into the Common Market. But Ball opposed the amendment, fearing that the Six would interpret it as an interference in the delicate UK-Common Market talks. Others believed that the provision might signal that the United States had lost confidence in Britain's bid. When Reuss and Douglas retorted that America had already injected itself into the talks by siding with Britain, Petersen disagreed, arguing that Washington had stayed aloof of the negotiations and that the dominant supplier would achieve a truly Atlantic partnership. The administration blocked the amendment but the debate simmered into 1963.[69]

In the end, although some liberal traders sought more power for the trade bill, they passed the legislation with, to be sure, the help of protectionist converts. After defeating thirty-seven potentially crippling protectionist amendments offered by Senator Bush, liberal traders gave the president the fifth highest total in the House, and the most votes ever in the Senate, for reciprocal trade legislation. Senator Eugene T. McCarthy (D-Minn.) described the TEA accurately the day it passed the Senate. The Trade Expansion Act, he said, was "in reality, a 'fair trade' bill. It is designed to protect the American businessman in his right to compete fairly around the world [while] it protects American workers and firms from unfair competition."[70] Added to the Atlantic integrationist and security underpinning of the new trade legislation, this summation aptly portrayed the intent of the statist fair-trade doctrine.

When Kennedy looked back on the TEA campaign, he recognized the wearisome task of convincing Americans of the importance of exporting as a way to win votes for the bill. He did not always succeed, as apathy or opposition to the TEA showed, although many Americans leaned toward freer trade. Some had little interest in overseas markets, while intra- and interindustry divisions, an occupation more with foreign investment than exports, and the relative unimportance of exports to the U.S. economy, undercut support for the bill. The chemical and electronic sectors, consisting of exporters but dominated by protectionists, were cases in point.

So were NAM and the Chamber of Commerce and, for that matter, *all* sectors of the economy, to some extent.

Such diverse opinion compelled Kennedy to command the export drive himself, rather than rely on interest groups. In other words, *he,* not exporters, determined policy. To be sure, powerful economic interests lobbied the president and Congress, yet these groups, and their agents such as the CNTP, did not have power over decisions. And, contrary to neocorporatism, exporters did not join the foreign policy executive to decide policy "outside parliamentary channels."[71] Rather than being the captive of export interests, Kennedy tried to persuade producers of the importance to sell more goods abroad. The export drive was difficult, however, because of the economic pluralism of society on trade matters. For instance, chicken exporters pressured him to oppose EEC protectionism, while chemical producers resisted his prodding to focus on exports. The pluralistic private sector thus obliged Kennedy to rely on congressional liberal traders. In the politics of exports, as in the politics of protectionism, Congress and the White House comprised the decision-making medium.

The arena of export politics differed from protectionist battlegrounds, however, because interbranch bargaining was not usually required; both sides agreed on the need for higher export profits, but above all, on the importance of combating communism by productionism. The foreign policy executive and representative element essentially agreed along economic and ideological lines, although the Chicken War showed that congressional liberal traders could, on occasion, pressure the president to take measures beyond which he initially was willing to go. Still, although the pursuit of higher profits from exports accounted for part of the export bloc's support for the TEA, Congress, led by cold warriors, united behind the notion that national security depended on a liberal trade policy that raised revenues for overseas financial commitments. Through the so-called Grand Design of freer trade, claimed President Kennedy, Europe and America could "combine their resources and momentum to undertake the many enterprises that the security of free peoples demands."[72] When the TEA passed, he again emphasized that a "vital expanding economy in the free world is a strong counter to the threat of the world Communist movement. [The TEA] is, therefore, an important new weapon to advance the cause of freedom."[73] Congress agreed, and joined Kennedy in an interbranch, security-conscious alliance in order to defeat protectionism. The statist school is correct that political-military aims coincided with, if not overrode, economic motives as the major influence on trade policy decisions.

The support of congressional liberal traders, and shrewd maneuvering with protectionists, gave Kennedy a well-earned triumph, which allowed him to proceed with his foreign policy agenda. Upon signing the bill on October 11, 1962, he proclaimed that the TEA was "the most important international piece of legislation, I think, affecting economics since the passage of the Marshall Plan."[74] Just as the Marshall Plan had aimed to strengthen the West in the cold war, the new trade law also was a tool with which to confront the Soviet Union. The Trade Expansion Act not only promoted exports, but closer political relations with Western Europe, the economies of the less-developed nations, and, ultimately, the alliance's defense against communism. With these goals in mind, Kennedy prepared for the GATT trade negotiations named in his honor.

CHAPTER SIX

Round One to Europe, 1963–1964

Kennedy expected to lower trade barriers at the sixth round of GATT, dubbed the Kennedy Round, using the new powers of the Trade Expansion Act, but the talks quickly became entangled in the divergent aims of the Atlantic powers. The Six understood the benefits to world trade of tariff cuts, but its customs union also sought protection for European producers. Meanwhile, America had its own import restrictions. This seemingly impassable state of affairs reflected the neomercantilist self-interest of both powers during the rule-making stage of the GATT talks in 1963 and 1964. The consequent rising tensions showed the EEC's emerging leverage over, and resistance to, U.S. trade and diplomatic policies. Indeed, the Six sided with the efforts of Kennedy and Lyndon Johnson to boost productionism, alliance cooperation, and thus, national security. But the Common Market wished to do so on its *own* terms, a fact that the EEC made ever more evident to the United States as American power came under increasing attack.

The French Veto

Signs of America's ebbing powers of persuasion over Western Europe appeared just after the trade bill passed Congress. To be sure, the EEC Commission applauded the TEA, but the nationally minded Council of Ministers, which controlled the commission, was less enthusiastic. The ministers worried that large tariff cuts by the Six might weaken EEC institutions. France led the others in stressing this danger, although even Chancellor Adenauer of West Germany, who allied with Washington on most economic issues, feared a "monstrous" influx of U.S. goods if Europeans lowered their trade barriers. Citing the EEC's trade deficit with America, Valèry Giscard d'Estaing, the French minister of finance, revealed the Common Market's partial divergence from Washington by cautioning against the dominant supplier provision, and even the "doctrine of integration" implied by the Grand Design.[1]

Charles De Gaulle dealt the most serious blow to American policy when, demonstrating his skepticism toward the Atlantic partnership, he vetoed Britain's application into the EEC on January 14, 1963. He scoffed at the Grand Design, presuming that Europe would disengage from America once the Soviet threat abated. During the Cuban missile crisis in October 1962, Kennedy had not consulted the allies, validating de Gaulle's belief that the hegemonic United States would act unilaterally on important matters. And doubting America's will to defend its allies, he sought a Western European nuclear "third force" that would offset the superpowers, and closer relations with West Germany. London's exchange of Polaris missiles for U.S. control over NATO's nuclear force in December 1962 confirmed de Gaulle's belief that Britain's loyalty lay with Washington, not the Common Market. The U.S.-UK nuclear deal also revealed, at least for the French, the true intention of the United States. A headline of the newspaper *Le Monde* in early January 1963 announced, "President Kennedy Has Decided to Direct the Western Alliance without Bothering Himself Too Much with Possible Objections of his Allies." Thus, the French president decided to exercise his power in the EEC and stop Britain from "dragging the West into an Atlantic system" under U.S. domination.[2]

Economic and European integration issues also caused the veto. Concerned about mounting U.S. investments in Western Europe, smaller French producers complained that they could not compete with big American firms. Also, the TEA portended an invasion of cheap U.S. exports, and an attack on the common agricultural policy, of which France was the main beneficiary. Thus, to no surprise, Paris denounced U.S. Secretary of Agriculture Orville Freeman's criticism of EEC farm protectionism during his visit in November 1962. De Gaulle also feared that Britain would encourage U.S. penetration of European markets even further, which would worsen France's trade deficit with America. Arguing that EEC integration, and an arrangement with Europe's former colonies (most of them ex-French African countries) must proceed before the Six could discuss lowering the industrial external tariff or the CAP, de Gaulle resisted Kennedy's trade plans.[3]

Furthermore, Kennedy had misjudged de Gaulle. For one, the impressionistic Grand Design offered few concrete guidelines on how to achieve a partnership, so de Gaulle could point to its impracticality and vagueness. More significant, the heroic general of the Free French forces in World War II believed that his mission now revolved around voicing a growing European feeling of pride and independence in the EEC, and on bolstering his own, and France's, grandeur. To an extent, de Gaulle's view of Europe determined his veto, and Kennedy, perhaps because he thought that EEC leaders could sway de Gaulle, failed to anticipate the French president. De Gaulle aimed to control the Common Market, with West German help, but feared that Britain would alter this plan. Once Britain—and presumably the rest of the EFTA—joined the Six, and majority voting replaced the veto power of each member, the EEC could easily align against his policies.[4] To a large extent, Kennedy failed to consider that de Gaulle chafed at such a possibility of losing power and prestige.

Most nations reacted against the veto, but de Gaulle had substantial enough influence over EEC and Atlantic trade policy to counter such sentiment, at least for the time being. The veto caused shock waves within the EEC. For one, after Konrad Adenauer visited Paris the week after the veto to sign the Franco-German alliance, Ludwig Erhard, Bonn's economics minister who would replace Adenauer in October 1963, publicly demanded that the chancellor retire, in part because the treaty implied that West Germany had sided with France's anti-American position. A disappointed British prime minister Macmillan, who could not recall "going through a worse time since Suez," reported scathing denouncements of Gaullist obstructionism by the Italians and others. And Paul-Henri Spaak, Belgium's respected foreign minister, blamed the veto on de Gaulle's haughty personality, warning his EEC partners of the danger of permitting the Frenchman's "childish" and "even ludicrous . . . autarchical, inward-looking, [and] selfish" policies to guide the Common Market in the future. The rest of the Six agreed with West German legislators that January 14 was "a black day for Europe."[5]

Officials and businesspeople reaffirmed their support of the Atlantic partnership. Still, because France was an important trade partner, the Commission was reluctant to confront de Gaulle. Across the Atlantic, most Americans regarded the veto as an affront. Some proclaimed that the Grand Design had miscarried, while protectionists applauded the veto, since it vitiated the TEA. The administration avoided a shouting match with de Gaulle, but Ball urged Kennedy to make clear to EEC president Hallstein that America intended to defend its trade interests. Kennedy decided to get tougher on the Six by holding France accountable for any future trade restrictions, which could spell "disaster" for the alliance. Pressured by exporters to attack Common Market barriers, the president announced that "the day of free traders around this administration was over," and that Americans must "sort out our priorities" at the Kennedy Round.[6]

The veto had numerous repercussions. One was that it set back the U.S. export drive by nullifying the dominant supplier. Congressman Reuss and senators Douglas and Javits proposed anew that zero duties apply regardless of the veto. Believing the administration too obsessed with the EEC, they argued that Washington should use the clause to reduce tariffs with all GATT members. Because of Kennedy's "toadying" to Europe, said Reuss, America had punished itself by making large duty cuts impossible; the dominant supplier amounted to "all sound and fury, signifying nothing." Kennedy accepted the Douglas-Reuss amendment, but viewed it as inessential to the negotiations, and it soon died on Capitol Hill. But anger toward de Gaulle and the Six did not wither away, and Eric Wyndham White, the director of GATT, scrambled to restore confidence in trade cooperation.[7] The fair-trade doctrine was in jeopardy because Western Europe had blocked U.S. objectives.

Strategy for the Kennedy Round

The veto also frustrated efforts to rectify the payments deficit, which had worsened in 1962. In response, Kennedy proposed an interest equalization tax to reduce overseas loans, an investment tax credit for modernization, and a renewed export drive. White House aide Carl Kaysen reminded him of a paramount concern; that without a bigger trade surplus, the United States would have to cut its huge share of military and economic expenditures. Treasury Secretary Dillon echoed that the export drive had to pay off in 1963, or "we're heading for trouble" on the deficit.[8] The president needed no prompting. He still opposed a substantial reform of the monetary system as a means to solve the deficit, refusing to devalue the dollar or accept a new reserve currency in order to allow others to share world financial leadership. But he had a clear sense of Special Trade Representative Christian Herter's job. Comparing the STR's responsibility to Herter's former post as secretary of state, in that both "had ties into our security," Kennedy said that the STR must help America pay its $3 billion a year in "national security expenditures" through higher exports. The issue of trade was "vital," he added, because it went "to the heart of our ability to keep more than one million Americans in uniform who now are serving the United States outside [its] borders."[9] He hoped to overcome Gaullism, and other Common Market obstacles, by using the fair-trade doctrine against the deficit.

United States-Common Market agreement at GATT was central to this ambition. Failure at the Kennedy Round, the largest tariff negotiations in terms of participants and trade volume in GATT history, would invite divisive trade practices and destructive protectionism. But encouraged to keep its external tariff low, the Six would permit outsiders to share its markets. Said STR deputy William Roth, "Trade liberalization and expansion," which had enriched the industrialized world and were essential to Third World development, would assure this outcome. Building a vibrant and unified Western alliance, he furthered, was "what the Kennedy

Round was all about."[10] This statist view bears out the prevailing objective, and the underlying concern, of the Kennedy trade program.

Thus, America's Kennedy Round strategy, conducted by Herter but developed by the State Department's George Ball, concentrated on the Common Market. The United States aimed to halve tariffs in rising industrial sectors, minimize exceptions to the linear, across-the-board cutting rule, and integrate agriculture into GATT negotiations for the first time ever. Recognizing that the United States required more concessions than it could give the Six, Ball advised that American negotiators accept less than the 50 percent tariff cuts called for in the TEA. Instead, he sought "maximum" reductions in tariffs in the 10–20 percent range, in which most of Europe's duties fell. He also knew that getting "fair access" on farm goods into the Common Market would be an arduous task, since the CAP was a keystone to European integration. Without a doubt, the Common Market had leverage, primarily because it bought one-third of America's total exports. Furthermore, U.S. agriculture relied on the EEC market, enjoying a five-to-one edge in trade, and, since demand had boosted American sales of manufactures, the external tariff was a valuable bargaining chip for the Europeans. In addition, the Six knew the importance of the round to President Kennedy, who counted on the TEA to realize his diplomatic aims.[11] Europe held many cards in the bargaining process but America still hoped to achieve its objectives of promoting industrial and food exports.

Strategy varied with other nations. Since the EFTA's primary market was in Western Europe, America had all the more reason to focus on trade with the Six, because concessions granted to the United States by the EEC would be applied on an MFN basis to the Outer Seven. Ball also hoped that Japan would exchange less restrictions on U.S. farm goods for growth in Atlantic, particularly Western European, markets, but Tokyo refused to lower barriers by the linear method until export restraints ended. Canada and the LDCs exempted themselves from across-the-board cuts in order to protect their small industries. Constituting economies that produced mostly primary goods, these nations doubted that 50

TABLE 6.1
U.S. Payments Balance with Western Europe
(billions of dollars)

Annual avg.	Current account*	Net capital outflow**	Payments balance***
1960–1965	1.14	−1.11	−.13
1966–1969	−.54	−1.31	−1.89

* Trade, military spending, government grants, tourism, etc.
** Outflow of U.S. long-term private and government capital.
*** Sum of current account and net capital outflow.
SOURCE: UN, *The European Economy from the 1950s to the 1970s* (New York: United Nations, 1972), p. 35.

percent tariff reductions on manufactures would be of much benefit anyway. Canada preferred instead selective duty cuts of equal value to the linear offers. The United States agreed; lowering farm sector protectionism, noted Ball, would win concessions from Canada and others. He also knew that the Third World was a special case because the South required careful treatment for its exports and needed more access into core markets for its tropical goods and light manufactures.[12] Still, successful bargaining with these nations hinged on a viable deal between the United States and the Six.

Although progress with the Common Market was conceivable, recent trade patterns foreboded much resistance to the American trade program. In 1962 growth in the EEC slowed, in part because lagging exports caused a trade deficit of $1.9 billion, which degenerated even more by 1964. Much of the deficit was attributable to an unfavorable trade balance with America; the Six's share of the U.S. market decreased 71 percent, while American exports to the EEC shot up by 93 percent, between 1958 and 1964. France particularly harped on these figures, and the EEC trade deficit, throughout the Kennedy Round. But the Six unfairly slighted the notion that not only would their deficit most likely shrink as they integrated, grew, and gained more power, but the United States had run, and would continue to suffer from, an *overall* payments deficit in Western Europe, due to the America's total goods, services, and aid transactions in NATO nations. This deficit essentially nullified the U.S. trade surplus with the EEC.[13]

Nevertheless, in order to correct its deficits, the Six had already begun to reserve more of their own market for EEC producers, to the detriment of U.S. export interests. Of 177 items made in the Atlantic community, for instance, 97 American-made products lost their marketshares from 1960 to 1962. Some decreases, such as for cotton, eventuated from European purchases from other countries, but rising intra-Six trade hurt U.S. exports of transportation goods and electrical machinery. America also faced adverse competitive conditions in cereals, fruits, coal, chemicals, and aluminum. Thus, despite the Common Market's decision, in July 1963, to accelerate the reduction of its external tariff by an additional 30 percent, it was still too high for the United States to benefit in many sectors.[14] Washington hoped that the Kennedy Round would slow its declining economic power in Western Europe by lowering EEC trade barriers.

French–West German Trade Conflict

But de Gaulle set out to hinder this goal. The State Department reported that the French president would not torpedo the Kennedy Round, for fear of angering liberal trading West Germany and upending his scheme for a Paris-Bonn axis in the Common Market. But France sought only limited success for the GATT talks in order to protect Common Market institutions, prevent a flood of imports from America into the Six, adjust to internal EEC competition, and enable its farmers to dominate European food markets. This policy placed the other EEC members in a dilemma. They opposed Gaullist obstructionism, but also felt vulnerable to U.S. export policy. Thus, they preferred to negotiate on imports that were not only important for Western Europe but sensitive for America, and also suggested separate talks on farm goods, in direct opposition to U.S. policy. In general, however, the other five (although Italy less so), supported Kennedy's objectives, and looked to West Germany's new chancellor, Ludwig Erhard, to confront France, the black sheep in the EEC, on the matter of trade liberalization.[15]

In effect, running underneath the Kennedy Round was a current of French–West German conflict on Common Market issues. Erhard was an Atlanticist who knew that West German industry relied on the U.S., as well as Western European, markets. And Bonn depended on America's nuclear deterrent and troops for its defense. It was an "incontestable fact" to Erhard that the Atlantic community was critical to the defense of Europe. Going even further, he argued that although the EEC was no longer a "junior partner" in this community, the United States was "destined to play the leading role" in the "historical task" of "gathering together the forces of the free world" under its trade and military policies. Thus, as France tried to distance the Six from the United States, West Germany sought closer Atlantic relations. As EEC official Paul Luyten noted, both nations favored reciprocal tariff cuts, but agreement stopped there; Paris and Bonn were "diametrically opposed" on the foreign trade policy of the Common Market.[16]

This rift centered on agriculture. Within the Common Market, France sought to trade West German sales of manufactured goods for French control of intra-EEC farm trade by both a low, unified price for grain and an export subsidy to be paid by the entire Six. Low prices would discourage production elsewhere, and therefore foster French exports. But pressure on Erhard from protectionist West German farmers, the same ones who had effectively opposed U.S. chicken exports, heightened his resistance to low prices, at least until after West German federal elections in 1965. In addition, Bonn frowned at financing an inordinate share of the EEC food export subsidy. The Kennedy Round forced these issues, however. On one side, France counted on the CAP for protection, and balked at TEA authority to reduce industrial tariffs. On the other, Erhard, endorsing the TEA, guarded against French sabotage of the GATT talks by offering de Gaulle a "synchronization" plan. Under the measure, West Germany would permit the imposition of the CAP, in exchange for French acquiescence to industrial tariff cuts. The proposal neglected a unified grains price, though, and France refused the deal.[17] Soon Franco–West German disagreement caused a shutdown of the Common Market, as well as the Kennedy Round; a crisis that American power was tellingly helpless to prevent.

TABLE 6.2
Comparison of U.S. and EEC Tariff Rates

Rates of protection	United States		EEC	
	Number	Percent	Number	Percent
Free	990	20	270	10
0.1–9.9%	894	18	538	19
10–19.9%	1510	29	1624	56
20–29.9%	775	15	358	13
≤30%	895	18	45	2

SOURCE: U.S. Department of State *Bulletin* 46 (May 7, 1962):774.

The Industrial Sector in 1963

Bickering within the EEC was not the only way in which Paris delayed progress on the reduction of trade barriers. From the start, France also exerted its influence at GATT by compelling the Six to back away from linear tariff cuts, due to supposed "disparities" between American and European duties. Halving the many high U.S. and the more medium-range EEC tariffs, as called for in the TEA, would result in an unfair bargain for the Six, claimed the EEC Commission under French persuasion. As a consequence of this view, by March 1963, the commission adopted a disparity formula, seeking to cut the "peaks" off high U.S. tariffs in order to "harmonize" them with the Common Market's lower rates. Herter rebuffed this plan, which obligated America to reduce duties more than other nations, and invited outcries at home about "give-aways" at GATT. The disparity issue plagued the negotiations for over a year and at this point in the rule-making stage, bogged down the GATT contracting parties with innumerable delays.[18]

At first glance, the Six seemed justified on disparities, but a closer look at tariff levels disclosed the pernicious neomercantilism of the harmonization formula. Herter argued that the de-peaking did "not agree with the facts."[19] Indeed, the Common Market possessed 45 tariffs at 30 percent or more, to America's 895 tariffs at this prohibitive level of protection; high tariffs encompassed 18 percent of U.S. dutiable imports but only 2 percent of the Six's imports. Yet more U.S. imports were completely free of duties, and over half of the EEC's tariffs provided middle-range protection, which hurt a majority of U.S. exports, while 30 percent of America's were grouped at this level. In other words, both sides were guilty of high tariffs at various levels, and disparities were just too complex to solve by imposing rules at this early stage of the GATT conference. Above all, halving duties, according to the authority vested in the TEA, would net both traders $3.8 billion in receipts. The difference between tariff rates could be adjusted during the tariff bargaining period of the Kennedy Round, concluded Herter, and did not warrant deviations from the 50 percent linear cut method. Every GATT member except the Six agreed.[20]

At the tense GATT ministerial meeting in May 1963, where the contracting parties set rules for the negotiating stage of the Kennedy Round, a compromise eventuated on disparities, but only after Herter warned of ensuing "political implications" if the negotiations broke down over the matter. France withdrew the depeaking formula, while America allowed a departure from linear cuts when a "significant" disparity existed. Although such a deal erased the chance for 50 percent reductions, Kennedy had to accept the "Geneva Compromise," or risk the breakdown of the GATT talks. The compromise, admitted Herter, showed that all traders recognized a common purpose at the Kennedy Round, but also that the "major countries in the Atlantic area are free to speak out and defend points of major interest to them."[21] The bargain injected new momentum into the first stage of the Kennedy Round, but once again confirmed the emerging ability of the Common Market to influence major policy decisions.

The ministers also discussed non-tariff barriers (NTBs), of which all nations were guilty. Herter hoped to eliminate many NTBs, such as European taxes on car imports, but also offered to modify the U.S. escape clause and the Buy American provision. Led by West German chemical makers, the Six insisted on ending the American Selling Price. Other nations criticized U.S. restraints on steel imports under the Anti-Dumping Act, which America imposed when it discovered that certain imports were priced well below their original cost. A committee formed to recommend ways to deal with NTBs, yet a concerted attack on them awaited later GATT talks in the following decades, when they had replaced industrial tariffs as the main protective devices in international trade.[22] For now, traders focused on adjusting tariffs to the new Common Market.

Deadlock in Agriculture in 1963

Agricultural sector rule-making mirrored the conflicts over industrial tariffs, but was even more trying, as the United States confronted EEC resistance to its policies. All nations had farm barriers, yet over 80 percent of the goods of the Six and Outer Seven enjoyed protection, rendering dim the prospects for more food export access in Western Europe. American farm exports had soared in recent years to the Common Market. Leading the way were feed grains, wheat, and oilseeds (soybeans), which comprised $650 million of the $1.5 billion in EEC food imports from the United States. But since agricultural employment was substantial in Western Europe, protectionist farmers there had political influence. Imports of oilseed by the Common Market from former colonies threatened U.S. sales, which also suffered CAP restrictions that transformed American farmers into residual suppliers.[23] Being secondary exporters in Atlantic community markets was a role desired by neither U.S. farmers nor President Kennedy.

The Department of Agriculture, as the representative element for farmers at GATT, attacked the CAP; Secretary Freeman demanded a suspension of the Kennedy Round if no access guarantees were forthcoming from the Six. He told Congress that "there can be no misunderstanding of the firm intention of our Government to resolve trade problems" in a "fair and equitable manner," and he also reminded Kennedy that "all agriculture is watching carefully" for a defense of U.S. farm exports.[24] The CAP could modify the Dillon Round standstill agreements by breaking tariff bindings, and thus raising import barriers. Even worse, Freeman discovered a "very disturbing" trend in EEC policy. Each Common Market country had staked out its market in particular commodities—France in wheat, Italy in rice, Holland in dairy products—and now strived to minimize outside penetration. Edgar Pisani, the agricultural minister of France, tried to justify this policy, which rang alarm bells in the USDA. Western European farmers needed years to develop their production, reasoned Pisani, sheltered from outside competition. This "infant industry" excuse for protectionism did not escape the acuity of many observers, even among the Six. Acknowledging the CAP's restrictiveness, for instance, Sicco Mansholt, Common Market vice-president for agriculture, warned that without American pressure, grain prices within the Six would climb to the high West German level, boost EEC production, and thus curb U.S. exports.[25]

Upon returning to Washington, Freeman devoted his efforts to circumventing the CAP. He, and the president, understood their weak bargaining position, since the United States sold one-third of its crops to the Six, but purchased only 10 percent of the Common Market's produce. Pressure mounted from American farmers to end foreign restrictions, however, and Kennedy knew that he must take action since, after all, he had sold the TEA on a pledge to expand agricultural exports. Although the principle of comparative advantage was an "ideal," Freeman urged Herter to insist on minimum guarantees in order to ensure a "fair sharing of markets" abroad. If not granted, asserted the secretary, the United States should "let the people in Western Europe and their governments know what we really meant about agriculture" by threatening to retaliate as it had during the ongoing Chicken War.[26]

The foreign policy executive agreed with the USDA on gaining access assurances, although less vehemently. For instance, the chief STR negotiator, W. Michael Blumenthal, cautioned against unrealistic expectations in the agricultural sector. He reminded Americans that high productivity and static wheat consumption in Europe were not new, but antedated the CAP. Therefore, the United States should keep prices low through world commodity agreements, and sell feed grains, meat, tobacco, and fruit in which it was most efficient, and in which Common Market consumption was growing. Above all, he said, farmers should not expect to "sweep away the elaborate structure of agricultural protectionism in the next two years," but seek greater—"although in many areas still controlled"—access into the Common Market.[27] Americans, in other words, should not hold high aspirations for significantly expanding food sales into Western Europe.

The president, meanwhile, spurred on by domestic sentiment

and foreign policy imperatives, supported Freeman's efforts. He stressed that farm trade exports helped the payments balance; agricultural sales abroad have "really meant that our balance of payments has not been in [a] more difficult position than it has been."[28] The president pledged "to take every step to protect the full rights due American agricultural exporters," and that "a fair agreement [was] an essential first part" of the trade talks.[29] If not, U.S. troop levels overseas, Third World aid, and thus defense efforts, would have to be pared back.

Yet fair-trade was going to be difficult to attain in the bargaining over agriculture at the Kennedy Round. The CAP was a structural support of European integration, and the Common Market had not yet worked out arrangements for farm financing and pricing policy, which were foundations of its political and economic unity. Farmers in Western Europe also pointed out that technological advances, made possible partly by U.S. postwar aid, had reduced employment, but raised output and surpluses, in their region. And the Six, like America, was not bereft of pressure from domestic sources. For example, the Bureau of the Committee of Farmers' Organizations, a collective of EEC agricultural groups, urged protection for European producers. Anyway, the Six countered, America protected dairy products, wheat, cotton, and peanut products. Thus, instead of knocking down barriers to international food imports, the Common Market offered a novel, but equally protectionist, suggestion. Developed by Sicco Mansholt, the plan proposed that all nations set price supports for their farmers, and once they were in place, the GATT members would reach an agreement on maintaining certain levels of protection.[30]

Mansholt offered this controversial "margin of support" plan in February 1964. Assuming protectionism and price controls in all countries precluded the possibility that food prices would ever reflect free-market realities, the Six endeavored to raise world prices, end subsidies, and protect their farmers. In order to do so, each nation of GATT would set its own level of protection, determining tariffs by subtracting the initially lower world "reference" price from the higher internal farm price of each food product. Among themselves, the six nations of the EEC would then unify grain prices, and finally bind the high-level prices of domestic support, which had resulted from the subtraction process, in trade agreements with other nations for three years. Thus, Common Market producers would receive more protection, although without subsidies, which would no longer be needed since global agricultural prices would be higher than before. The EEC viewed the margin of support offer as a realistic proposition and a concession to others at the Kennedy Round, agreeing to limit domestic farm supports if its trade partners did likewise.[31] In essence, however, the measure permitted a substantial level of protection by instituting the CAP's high, prohibitive price structure.

By no means did the entire Common Market share in the enthusiasm for the margin of support, which became an issue that further opened the breach between West Germany and France over trade policy. West Germany resisted the necessary unifying of low grain prices under Mansholt's plan, especially because its farmers received sizable subsidies that would be cut under the margin of support. France, however, pursued the unified price agreement in order to seize a greater share of the EEC farm market. De Gaulle won this skirmish. In May 1963, the Six linked the CAP to the Kennedy Round by deciding to consolidate cereal prices. But West Germany then resisted changes in its domestic support levels, to the dismay of France. An increasingly irate de Gaulle threatened trouble at the Kennedy Round if Bonn persisted in opposing Mansholt's plan.[32]

More than any other nation, however, America denounced the plan because it universalized the hated CAP variable levies, set prices at prohibitively high levels, and thus impaired access for U.S. agriculture into the Common Market. The margin of support also disregarded existing GATT concessions by fixing new, three-year bindings.[33] In short, the Mansholt plan exemplified the fundamental disagreement between the United States and the Six in farm trade. America, a fading hegemon, wanted to maintain its food sales abroad, but the strengthening Common Market sought to wrest its market from outsiders and protect its own farmers. Very possibly, the Six now had a tool, with the margin of support scheme, with which to accomplish these goals.

Domestic Discontent with Kennedy Round Preparations

The Mansholt plan, and other Common Market policies, brought pressure on Kennedy from farm interests. Legislators fretted about Western Europe's drive for self-sufficiency, and believed that the president was either too naive about exports, or had falsely inflated their hopes about a European dream market for American food in order to sell the TEA. Said Congressman E. Y. Berry (R-S.D.), "The bubble [the administration] painted as a gold nugget has blown up in [its] face"; food sales would not double, as Freeman had pledged, but would be slashed by the Common Market.[34] Anyway, farmers had already rejected Kennedy's supply management program in the spring of 1963, opposing stricter controls, but adding to U.S. trade problems by permitting continued overproduction of food, which required outlets abroad. Declared Congressman Durward Hall (R-Mo.), if "this administration is in water over its head, perhaps the Congress should ruffle its own feathers and develop guidelines for firmer policy" toward the Six.[35] The foreign policy executive was now caught between the CAP, American farmers, and legislators, and its own promises.

Farmers did not monopolize discontent over the GATT talks or trade policy; labor and industry also grumbled. When the Tariff Commission rejected three petitions for adjustment assistance in 1963, the AFL-CIO blasted the decision, and threatened to withdraw its backing of the Kennedy Round. The lumber bloc urged limits on Canadian softwood imports, but to no avail, while the textile bloc pressured for an agreement similar to the LTA in order to restrain woolen textiles from Britain, Italy, and Japan. England refused, although Kennedy closed some loopholes in wool import laws and considered reserving woolens from the Kennedy Round offer list. Yet other industries pointed to the LTA as an example of the protectionism that was possible if the administration showed "sufficient will." The president stepped delicately, reiterating that fair-trade required letting in imports to expand exports.[36]

But such statements did not appease protectionists, and now even some Kennedy allies dissented, annoyed by the ambiguous results of the May 1963 ministerial talks, which favored the Six on disparities and agriculture. Liberal-trade Senator Javits, for instance, called the meeting a failure for U.S. objectives. Others vowed to block a removal of critical NTBs, particularly the highly prized American Selling Price, as long as Europe strangled farm imports. GATT congressional adviser Thomas Curtis, struggling with Herter over the right to join the STR at American trade policy planning sessions in Geneva, reminded Kennedy that the TEA granted no power to deal with NTBs. Even more ominous, Wilbur Mills issued warnings that Congress "would legislate toughness" against the Common Market if Herter did not. Mills had heretofore beaten back protectionist bills on Capitol Hill, but a "soft position" at GATT would warrant their serious consideration. In no uncertain terms, Mills declared that "there would be hell to pay" if the Kennedy Round "resulted in an unequal agreement" for the United States.[37]

Finding suitable answers to this criticism would be exacting for the president, however, because he wished to push ahead with his liberal trade agenda in order to coax reciprocal tariff cuts from the Common Market. Pursuant to the TEA, Kennedy submitted to the Tariff Commission the items that America would "table," or offer, for tariff reductions. He sought to minimize the goods withheld from the list in order to promote liberal trade, although certain "exceptions" were mandatory under the national security and escape clauses. In October 1963, he submitted six thousand products for tariff cuts, the largest list ever presented by America at negotiations. About 87 percent of U.S. dutiable imports were included; by comparison, Eisenhower had sent only 25 percent to the Dillon Round. As anticipated, a parade of manufacturers tried to remove certain products from the negotiating list at Tariff Commission hearings beginning in late 1963, while the administration tried to temper resentment toward Western Europe and GATT. At the same time that these hearings occurred, Herter asked exporters at separate hearings to identify foreign trade barriers that restricted their products. Meanwhile, Kennedy appointed thirty-five advisers from industry, agriculture, and labor to help the STR formulate a negotiating plan in each sector. He also picked two congressmen and two senators to accompany the U.S. delegation to Geneva.[38] The STR, and American trade policy, would be closely watched by societal and representative interests.

As a fair-trader discouraged by EEC protectionism, but equally as a politician for whom the 1964 election loomed, Kennedy listened to the disgruntlement at home. The timing of the Tariff Commission hearings, and the scheduled opening of the Kennedy Round tariff-negotiating phase for May 1964, placed protectionists in a politically favorable position, considering that the presidential election was just months away. If forced to give in, Kennedy risked upsetting negotiations on which he had staked his prestige, but when he counted votes, he perceived that his reelection in 1964 was no certainty. The civil rights issue had hurt him in the south, where he had carried seven of eleven states in 1960. If he lost ground there (and polls showed him in trouble in Alabama and North Carolina), he would not be reelected, assuming the other states voted the same as four years earlier. Furthermore, he had won four midwestern farm states in 1960—Illinois, Michigan, Minnesota, and Missouri. But if he lost the former and any of the other two—perhaps due in part to his failure to curb the effects of the CAP—he would also lose. The president could not forget, moreover, that he had won Illinois with special help from Chicago mayor Richard Daley, and captured Minnesota riding on the coattails of Senator Hubert Humphrey. In eleven states, he had earned less than 51 percent of the votes, and worse, states that had voted for him in 1960 would have ten fewer electoral votes in 1964.[39] Foreign trade policy might in fact play an important role in Kennedy's reelection bid.

Assessing the extent to which trade policy affected votes is problematical, but the Kennedy Round probably entered the president's election strategy. Kennedy hoped to win industrial regions again, where his strength lay, and he needed farm-state support, where he was weak. Thus, he backed agricultural export expansion, in part for political reasons. He told Freeman that he understood the need for access into Western Europe, although he knew that the prospects were not good because of EEC protectionism. The president also complained that he had bent over backward in order to help farmers with special programs and export incentives, but "then they vote Republican," anyway. Perhaps, lamented the president to Freeman just before leaving for Dallas in mid-November 1963, he had oversold the Kennedy Round. His failing attempt to retain U.S. farm markets in Europe, writes historian William Borden, was perhaps the most disappointing (and perhaps politically dangerous) aspect of his foreign economic policy.[40] But the problem persisted for his successor, resulting in a major setback at the Kennedy Round and a point of discord in international trade in future decades.

Lyndon Johnson Takes Up the Liberal Trade Banner

Nevertheless, Lyndon Johnson continued the campaign for tariff reductions at the Kennedy Round. Among other topics in his first address to Congress as president, he "rededicated" America to trade expansion as a safeguard against depression, an integral part of allied cooperation, and a bulwark against communism.[41] To be sure, Johnson arrived at his trade principles by a different route than Kennedy. But his record of defending local economic interests *against*, instead of by, protectionism, permitted him to step easily into the role of promoting the Kennedy Round and trying to carry out his slain predecessor's fair-trade policies.

While Kennedy observed the Depression from the comfort of Hyannisport, Johnson had grown up in rural poverty, although he later lived in town among the lower middle class. His background, and an attachment to his mentor, House Speaker Sam Rayburn, instilled in him a populist bent. Ignored by Washington in the 1920s and early 1930s, farmers had been ruined by falling commodity prices and the high cost of farm machinery, while eastern manufacturing and banking interests prospered behind the high tariff walls that made agricultural equipment so expensive. Rayburn hated the supposed "Eastern Establishment" and the protective tariff, which he called the "robber tariff, the most indefensible system the world has ever known."[42] Johnson agreed, and in 1948 he denounced tariffs as subsidies for northerners at the expense of farmers. Texas was reliant on exports, he said, but for a century, the Republican tariff had incited foreign retaliation, which had choked off the state's overseas sales. He therefore supported the RTA throughout his career, sardonically admitting that it was "not pleasing to rich northern and eastern industrialists. They want to bring back the high tariffs which keep the South in a state of economic dependency."[43]

Johnson also promoted liberal trade for national and global interests. Although oil imports hurt Texas independents, freer trade improved the U.S. economy. Protectionism alienated allies, he argued in the early 1950s, and also resulted in depressions. As Senate majority leader, he implored Eisenhower to resist protectionism during the RTA renewals, and opposed Senator Robert Kerr's attempt in 1960 to prevent further tariff cuts at the Dillon Round. "I realize the large part that international trade plays in the economy of our country, and that world trade is a two ways street. I have never been in favor of erecting high tariff barriers," he told a constituent.[44]

Yet Johnson was a fair-trader. He backed "prudent" tariff cuts, and reportedly, but astutely, joked that a liberal trader should never reveal his true identity because there were no votes in it. Thus, applauding the RTA in 1951, he warned about reducing duties while others raised barriers; at times it was necessary "to stop, look, and listen before making further concessions" to nations that did not reciprocate in trade.[45] He favored freer trade, but "this does not mean, however, that special circumstances do not call for special measures" to protect domestic producers.[46]

Oil interests, a major concern for Johnson, exemplified his occasionally protectionist bent. Despite being a strong advocate of reciprocal trade, Johnson said that the president should be obligated to protect the domestic oil industry by using the national security clause as it was intended. Fearing bad times for independent producers, who, incidentally, had bankrolled his political career, the senator told Eisenhower that "a mule team cannot pull a wagon up a hill when it is too heavily loaded, and this is one case in which a far-too-heavy [sic] load may have been dropped in the wagon." If the president did not insist on "treating our own people as well as we treat others"—in this case, by protecting oilmen—"the wagon may break down."[47] Like his predecessor, he balanced the demands of protection-biased and export-oriented interests at the state and national levels.

Since oilmen were so important to his career in both a financial and political sense, petroleum imports drew his attention, but he retreated from blatant protectionism. Believing that a "keystone of our security is our domestic petroleum industry," he backed the quota programs of the late 1950s, but rejected the more stringent Neely amendment quotas in favor of the national security clause.[48] Strict import limits, Johnson feared, might provoke easterners to eliminate the depletion allowance tax break, impose price controls, and begin rationing of crude oil. He preferred a middle course that prevented the national security clause from becoming a "toothless tiger" but preserved liberal trade on a "fair and equitable basis." Said Johnson, "I think that it ought to be possible for us to relate the domestic needs of our country to those of our friends throughout the world."[49] These were the words of a fair-trader.

Johnson's pursuit of oil protection was a parochial concern that earned him an unjustifiable reputation as a tepid supporter of liberal trade. *Business Week* even claimed that his efforts on behalf of the oil industry were a reason why a growing protectionism had mounted on Capitol Hill in the early 1960s. In reality, he was merely a liberal trader worried about "unfair competition" from abroad. White House political aide Myer Feldman distinguished between Kennedy and Johnson in that the former promoted freer trade and then approached each industry to accomplish this aim, while the latter started with each producer and tried to arrive at a general liberal trade posture.[50] Regardless of tactics, the two ended up as statist fair-traders, seeking to aid vulnerable producers in order to achieve the overall goal of export expansion.

Like Kennedy, Johnson, as president, worried about the payments deficit. His efforts to boost exports, discourage the outflow of dollars, and tie aid to purchases of American goods helped reduce the deficit slightly, and halted the gold drain entirely in 1964. When the interest equalization tax went into effect in September 1964, Johnson instituted capital controls on overseas investors instead of relying on the fading Atlantic partnership to solve America's payments woes through European cooperation. Like his predecessor, Johnson also tried to avoid giving up the dollar's hegemonic position in the Bretton Woods monetary system, although he failed to do so by the end of his administration. Although the conflict in Southeast Asia was not yet draining the treasury, some discussion also ensued in late 1963, and after the Gulf of Tonkin incident in August 1964, about minimizing expenditures for the Vietnam War so as not to exacerbate the deficit and further subvert confidence in the dollar. As the decade wore on, spending skyrocketed on Vietnam and the Great Society social welfare system, and became a serious drag on U.S. finances. But in 1964 England's sagging pound, and the continued French push for a new IMF reserve asset to supplement the dollar, concerned the administration more than inflation or overspending.[51]

Thus, Johnson preferred to approach the payments deficit problem through export promotion. In December 1963 he established the Interagency Committee on Export Expansion, and partly as a result of its efforts, the merchandise trade surplus hit its peak of the decade in 1964, at $6.7 billion, the highest level since 1948. He also opposed protectionism, vetoing a restrictive lumber origin labeling act, and despite pressure, refusing to limit woolen imports.[52] Thus, as part of the foreign policy executive, he strived to maintain momentum for liberal trade. Johnson, moreover, clearly demonstrated his commitment to this end during the first trade crisis of his administration, regarding beef imports.

The influx of beef from Australia and New Zealand jumped 106 percent from 1961 to 1963, and cut domestic meat prices. Although overproduction affected the cost of beef, cattlemen sought import quotas to boost prices. The Senate narrowly defeated a quota bill in March 1964, but the Finance Committee held hearings, and one-quarter of the Senate proposed protectionist amendments. Senator Mike Mansfield, the majority leader, then introduced the Meat Import Law, which set ceilings above which imports could not climb without triggering quotas. Johnson opposed quotas and went into action. As a Texan familiar with beef problems, he hoped to woo Republican cattlemen in the 1964 election by promotional schemes, including a "June Barbecue Month" with he and his wife hosting a cookout at the LBJ ranch. He also ordered government agencies to buy more beef, told Freeman to expand American exports to the Third World, and instructed Herter to negotiate "voluntary" export agreements, under which Australia and New Zealand promised to lower their exports. After realizing the agreements, they actually reduced imports more than the Mansfield Meat Act, which passed Congress, but was now, of course, unnecessary. By fall of 1964 the president had rolled back imports to pre-1962 levels, with few complaints from Australia and New Zealand, which turned back to Western European markets for their beef sales.[53] Johnson had skillfully weathered the beef crisis by using the fair-trade doctrine.

1964: Dark Clouds in the Trade System

But by this time protectionism had increased in Congress. A total of seventy-five congressmen from thirty-eight states spent two hours in April 1964, just days before the Kennedy Round opened, discussing import limits. The STR feared an uprising against GATT, and the liberal periodical, *The Economist,* pronounced that 1964 would be known as the "year of retraction" in trade, due to restrictive bills pending on Capitol Hill. These included the Mansfield Meat Act, the Buy American clauses attached to the Urban Mass Transportation and Food Stamps acts, and quotas on shoes, wool, lead, zinc, steel containers, and electron microscopes. The Tariff Commission also imposed anti-dumping duties on Canadian steel.[54] Substantial numbers of societal interests, and their congressional counterparts, seemed dangerously close to revolting against the TEA and the Kennedy Round.

The foreign policy executive tried to temper protectionism. The Tariff Commission heard testimony from hundreds of industries opposed to the extensive list of items available for 50 percent duty cuts. But heeding Herter's advice, Johnson refused to place more products on the exceptions list. Yet he made clear his intention of fighting for American interests at the Kennedy Round, and that he no longer wanted the United States to be pushed around by the Common Market. Although he realized the need for patience and firmness with the Six, and supported the Atlantic partnership, Johnson reiterated the demand for reciprocity in the industrial sector, and fair access in agriculture. As a fair-trader, he explained that the negotiations were "not the kind in which some nations need lose because others gain."[55] The president would be fair and understanding, and he expected other nations to follow suit.

By early 1964, however, the Kennedy Round seemed no longer a grand, cooperative effort, but a quibbling, tough discussion between business rivals. The STR realized that U.S. objectives might be unattainable, and even liberal-trade Chancellor Erhard of West Germany cautioned that Washington exaggerated the chances for large tariff reductions by the Common Market. Indeed, the Six withdrew the tariff disparity formula, but sought to link duty levels to the removal of America's closely guarded American Selling Price. Europeans also managed to make linear cuts merely a "working hypothesis," and not a formal commitment, at the GATT talks. This weak resolution, and the continuing disparity issue, were victories for the Common Market.[56] But as EEC triumphs, demands, and leverage at the conference grew, so did American pessimism at home toward the Kennedy Round.

Much of this negative attitude was an indirect product of Franco–West German tension, centering mainly on agriculture. Bonn had rejected the Friendship Treaty with France, and increasingly criticized Gaullist ambitions. The American ambassador to France, Charles Bohlen, reported that de Gaulle still sought a judicious approach on tariff cuts and, above all, insisted on the common grains price and settlement of payments into the farm subsidy fund as a prerequisite for French participation at the Kennedy Round. France threatened to walk out of the EEC in December 1963 without West German acquiescence on these matters. Erhard, however, still balked on prices and the fund, but feared that disagreement might break apart the Common Market, and upset the Kennedy Round. Despite appeals from the EEC Commission for a settlement of farm issues, the lack of agreement prevented the Six from tabling exceptions in agriculture along with industrial goods, as the GATT contracting parties had planned in September 1964. The Common Market's unwillingness to lower the CAP was another stumbling block; its large farm lobby even deemed the variable levies off-limits at the Kennedy Round. France's ambassador to the United States, Hervé Alphand, told Americans that a guarantee of access for outsiders' exports was simply not possible.[57]

Such was the bad news for angry U.S. farmers, who relied on exports more than ever for their economic well-being. Johnson lifted their spirits, stressing on the campaign trail in 1964 the record rise in agricultural exports of $1 billion over the past year, a 35 percent gain since 1960. Yet farmers feared that Herter was selling them out by not insisting on rules for agriculture, as he had for industry. Congress responded by castigating foreign protectionism. But some legislators even called for the termination of the TEA, two years before its expiration, in order to evaluate the Kennedy Round, which many now called an "unforgivable economic stupidity."[58] Farm-state congressmen, part of the representative element most favorable to freer trade, censured the foreign policy executive's trade program.

Nevertheless, except for Freeman, the rest of the administration continued to give way to the Common Market. This retreat was no more apparent than when EEC recalcitrance softened U.S. policy on the issue of food access guarantees. The USDA wanted either trade based on comparative advantage or withdrawal from the Kennedy Round. Persuaded by Herter, Johnson refused Freeman's fatalism, which placed the United States in the awkward role of criticizing European integration. To be sure, the president did not wish to deviate from linking farm with industrial products, nor did Herter accept Mansholt's margin of support proposal. But the STR did propose a "flexible, pragmatic" plan in order to negotiate tariff cuts on fixed duty items, and access on grains and variable levy goods by any method, including world commodity agreements.[59] America seemed to be reaching for any solution, just so it represented progress in the farm sector.

Furthermore, in a major turnabout, Herter also opted to proceed with agricultural negotiations without waiting for a cereals price accord within the Common Market. With Johnson's approval in October 1964, the STR tabled the industrial exceptions list, without a companion farm list, contrary to the U.S. strategy of negotiating in both sectors together. The move reflected the deadlocked EEC talks on grains, which prevented the Six from negotiating, and a concern that the Kennedy Round would lose momentum if farm issues further delayed bargaining. Also, by not tabling industrial products, the Common Market might postpone decisions on its farm organization. But there was a tactical advantage as well. By proceeding without agriculture, Washington could shift the burden of responsibility for possible failure of the Kennedy Round to the Six, and especially France. Although Erhard finally gave into unified prices, Herter's decision irked France because it took pressure off Bonn to proceed with talks on the export subsidy fund. Agriculture, asserted *The Economist,* seemed "more than ever like the sick man of Europe."[60]

Like the French, Americans also criticized Herter's retreat, but for far different reasons. Freeman had assured farmers that access would remain a priority at GATT, but now admonished the president that the Farm Bureau was as "anti"-Johnson as ever, and had vowed to block his farm program as a result. When added to attacks on his trade policy by William E. Miller, the Republican vice-presidential candidate, prior to the 1964 election, this dissent might have been troublesome. Thus, if not for Johnson's insurmountable edge over Senator Barry Goldwater (R-Ariz.), the opposition nominee, the president might have taken more vigorous action against Western Europe. But as the election turned out, Johnson handily won rural, and industrial, region votes in a landslide victory. Yet the agricultural standoff in Geneva still dampened enthusiasm for the Kennedy Round and darkened the hopes among the contracting parties for a successful outcome.[61]

The Exceptions Lists

The industrial sector also portended future disputes when the GATT participants presented their lists of "exceptions," or goods that they would withhold, from the 50 percent linear tariff reductions. Much of the Outer Seven did not reserve any products, but retained the right to cut their offers if they did not receive reciprocity. Canada also had no exceptions but drew up a list of an equivalent value of goods open to tariff cuts. In order to protest the "voluntary" export restraints imposed by other nations, Japan reserved from the tariff negotiations the most goods, about one-quarter of its dutiable imports. Britain's list covered 10 percent of its tariffs. After hearings on American exceptions ended in the spring of 1964, the administration eliminated additional items from its list in order to demonstrate its commitment to liberal trade. The United States included 18 percent of its dutiable imports, exempting cotton textiles and some products that fell under the escape clause. Oil comprised eight percent of the list, but was not significant in GATT, since Venezuela was not a member of the organization. And, since Canadian petroleum enjoyed an exempt status from quotas, America considered the inclusion of oil unrelated to the upcoming debate on reciprocity at the Kennedy Round.[62] In sum, the amount of goods in which the United States was willing to lower tariffs, especially when compared with most other nations' exceptions, showed Johnson's sincere desire to facilitate a liberal reduction of trade barriers at the Kennedy Round.

This liberal trade bent was even more evident when America placed its exceptions alongside those of the Common Market. The EEC's exceptions, in short, stirred controversy. To be sure, the process of creating the list was complex. Each of the six EEC nations, and the commission as a whole, came up with separate lists that were pared down, added to, and then combined into one final roster of reserved goods to be presented by the Common Market. Not surprisingly, the freer-trading commission and West Germany proposed a modest list, while French exceptions were numerous. After a marathon Council of Ministers' session, a compromise provided a list between the two extremes. Intended to be comparable to America's schedule, the list covered 10 percent of the EEC's dutiable imports, but it encompassed more—thus was more restrictive—than those of other GATT members. The list was divided into three categories. There was a section for full exceptions, including machinery, vehicles, and other items that were of major importance to U.S. exporters. Partial exceptions, in which the Common Market offered less than 50 percent cuts, contained aluminum and magnesium. Finally, conditional exceptions would be removed on chemicals if America eliminated the ASP; on autos, when Britain took them off its list; on watches as soon as Switzerland stopped banning imports of watchmaking equipment; and on cotton textiles, if all nations put them up for bargaining. The Six argued that its list ensured reciprocity, but Americans saw it as another impediment to the Kennedy Round.[63] Rule-making, which had absorbed all of 1963 and 1964, ended in a tense, negative atmosphere, with the Common Market assuming a dominating presence in Geneva.

For two years de Gaulle had confronted America. In the diplomatic realm, his veto of British entry into the Common Market undermined U.S. efforts to integrate the West on a more intimate basis than before. Most Europeans did not share his opinion that America plotted to preserve its hegemony over Western Europe through a trade partnership, and viewed the veto as an abuse of power. But without a doubt, de Gaulle stymied the Grand Design, weakened the TEA, and put the allies on notice that the Kennedy Round would be a difficult affair. With the veto, Kennedy's death, and Johnson's mounting focus on Vietnam, the Atlantic community was, as historian Frank Costigliola writes, "gone in a flash."[64] American power did not disappear so quickly, but it began to wane, as certainly as the Common Market rose.

De Gaulle shaped much of the EEC's policy, or at least had a major influence on the other five nations, although he often found his path blocked by West Germany. Ludwig Erhard was able to confront him just when de Gaulle had seemingly achieved his goal of placing Paris and Bonn at the helm of the Common Market. Erhard's support for tariff cuts at GATT, protection of West German farmers, and general Atlantic bias contradicted French policy. Thus, de Gaulle found himself mired in a two-front economic war, against West German aims within the Common Market, and U.S. liberal trade designs without. Yet remarkably, it was clear that by the end of 1964, the French president seemed to be winning on both fronts. Erhard acquiesced to low grains prices, while the Six submitted an exceptions list that prohibited large tariff reductions, just as France desired. Meanwhile, de Gaulle stymied American plans, insisting on the tariff disparity formula and making sure that the CAP remained intact in order to restrain American farm exports into the Common Market. By no means was French input uncontested by other EEC members, but the Six took many cues from Paris in formulating their internal and external trade policy.

The impact of Gaullism on trade and the Kennedy Round was largely negative. America indeed enjoyed a trade surplus with the Six, and growth in agricultural exports to Western Europe, but these were facts that justified, for de Gaulle, his resistance to U.S. trade policies. His position was compelling, for the Common Market's trade deficit with America worsened to $2.3 billion in 1963, and improved only slightly in 1964.[65] The deficit, added to the domestic pressure on EEC members to reserve markets for their citizens, gave the Commission and Council of Ministers every right to request rules and table exceptions that were in the Common Market's best interests. Washington found it a bit arduous at times quarreling with de Gaulle, who seemingly represented the demands and aspirations of the new, but still fragile, European Common Market.

But the United States was bargaining with an eye on future patterns of trade, the entire GATT trade system, and the cold war. Cognizant that the CAP could limit farm imports, and that France could curb the inflow of manufactures by preventing cuts in the Common Market tariff, Kennedy and Johnson urged liberal trade on all the contracting parties, but especially the Six. The CAP already restricted some exports and would soon cover other commodities. Also, the share of U.S. manufactured exports to the Six tumbled, as Western European industries became more efficient. In sum, EEC integration and productivity were positive signs of European recovery and strength, but they could also hurt outsiders.[66] France might succeed in forging a Common Market that looked inward, to the detriment of non-members' economies and, ultimately, to the cohesion of the Western alliance.

The Six, therefore, might subordinate their commitment to freer trade to the evils of protectionism, thereby ruining the Kennedy Round, jeopardizing the openness of GATT, and undercutting efforts to correct the U.S. payments deficit and prosecute the cold war. It was no shock that in the rule-making stage, as statist scholars acknowledge, neomercantilism had prevailed. Two self-interested traders, the United States and the Common Market, squared off in order to achieve their sometimes mutual—but oftentimes disparate—economic, political, and military objectives. America, with larger global aims in mind, appeared to be losing to the more narrow policy of the Six.

In essence, America's world leadership trapped Washington. Military assistance for the defense of Europe, which was several times the amount paid by any other ally, was a drain on the U.S. treasury. As a consequence, America ran a payments deficit with Western Europe. No doubt security commitments boosted American power, but the deficit threatened overseas aid and domestic social programs and weakened the U.S. economy relative to other core nations. It also made the United States more reliant on exports, and thus susceptible to pressure from the Common Market. Calls for the withdrawal of troops and aid had mounted in Congress, but few allies, not even de Gaulle, desired such a retreat. Thus, the economic stability and military protection of *all* core nations depended, in large part, on the expansion of U.S. exports to Western Europe. But this necessity clashed with the ambitions of the EEC, the emerging powerhouse in the region.

Thus, Common Market policy in the preparatory stage of the Kennedy Round dispelled the idea that a hegemonic America dictated trade policy. While the TEA called for 50 percent linear tariff cuts, the Six made a major conflict out of a subsidiary issue, by harping on tariff disparities. When Freeman pressed for access guarantees in agriculture, the EEC denied his request. The Six postponed the agricultural exceptions lists and, in general, determined the agenda in the farm sector talks because of their unfinished CAP. Also, when Herter minimized U.S. industrial exceptions, the Six devised a three-category list that penalized their trade partners. The United States had an edge in bilateral trade, but the EEC tried to undo this advantage by seeking negotiating rules in its favor. A neomercantilist America, shackled by a French-dominated, neomercantilist Common Market trade policy, grew increasingly frustrated at the GATT negotiations.

Common Market policy took its toll on support for the Kennedy Round. Pressured by interest groups and Congress for action against the Six, President Johnson remained "prudently confident" about success at GATT. This statement was a far cry from the bounding optimism after the TEA's passage, however. The STR warned that France could kill the Kennedy Round, while there was growing momentum in the EEC Commission for a slower pace at the talks, in order to consolidate Common Market institutions. Like Ball before him, Herter, moreover, predicted smaller tariff reductions than the original 50 percent authorized by the TEA.[67] The GATT trade environment, regulated, to an extent, by the Six, seemed more and more hostile to U.S. policy.

By late 1964, gloom pervaded the GATT talks. The submission of exceptions lists was a positive sign, claimed the *Wall Street*

Journal, but the conference would probably be prolonged at least one and a half years by disputes. *Business Week* placed no bet that the contracting parties would even reach a final agreement. Secretary of State Dean Rusk also deflated hopes by remarking that "the Kennedy Round, like all great enterprises that are underway, could come to nothing."[68] The administration noted that the United States could no longer "press, persuade, and cajole its major trading partners" as effectively as before, and feared that one nation's selfish trade policies would meet certain retaliation by others as the Kennedy Round entered its bargaining phase.[69] Washington's fear was that now, in the mid-1960s, America would be unable to retaliate, an enfeebled leader too weak to confront the Common Market and fully attain its objectives. Included in these worries and goals was not only the desire to persuade Western Europe and other industrial nations to accept American trade policies, but also the Third World.

CHAPTER SEVEN

The Third World Revolt

Although the Kennedy Round was largely an Atlantic community affair, Third World trade entered the negotiations. According to the less-developed countries of the periphery, however, their needs seemed secondary to the concerns of the North. Although this claim was arguable, the American-led GATT system had indeed failed to spur the substantial growth in LDC exports required for their development. Industrialization, and its consequent effect on boosting social welfare and employment, had simply not transpired for many nations of the South. America's traditional preoccupation with the theory of comparative advantage in commercial dealings with the Third World was the problem; the United States repeatedly blocked attempts to reform trade relations by granting the LDCs special export "preferences." The Third World went on the offensive, changing the global trade system's rules and norms through the United Nations Conference on Trade and Development (UNCTAD) in 1964, after overcoming the opposition of the United States. Still, America was on record for hindering a much-needed revamping of trade policy for the South. The neomercantilism of the system hegemon was largely to blame for the persistent obstructionism of the periphery's policy, although America's emphasis on cold war security explains why the U.S. often slighted meaningful reforms that would help poor countries.

The North Searches for Solutions

All leaders of the advanced industrial nations, including Kennedy and Johnson, noted that the South was not keeping pace with the North in terms of wealth and development. Old dilemmas persisted; raw material prices had fallen relative to manufactures, impairing the South's terms of trade. In other words, LDC exports earned less while imports into their countries cost more. As scholar Steve Chan explains, poor nations were in a similar situation that the Red Queen had described to Alice in *Alice in Wonderland,* in that "you have to run as fast as you can simply to stay in the same place. If you want to get somewhere else, you must run at least twice as fast as that."[1] As Third World export earnings stagnated, Kennedy warned core allies that the West might soon find itself "a rich area in a poor world," open to exploitation by the Soviet Union.[2]

The president asked his Kennedy Round task force to suggest ways to ameliorate conditions in the South, although he did so not just out of genuine sympathy for the periphery, but because of pressure from the United Nations Conference on Trade and Development. Communists and the South viewed UNCTAD, which convened in March 1964 in Geneva, Switzerland, alongside the Kennedy Round, as a counterweight to GATT, which they believed favored capitalists in the North. The popularity of UNCTAD worried the Kennedy Round task force, but obviously had little impact, because the administration still proposed a traditional, although stepped-up, plan to aid poor countries. In order to foster the foreign exchange reserves of the LDCs, suggested the task force, the North must cut its tariffs, open markets by curbing trade barriers and preferential treatment, end imperial trade systems, permit price stabilization agreements, and even allow the South to forgo granting full reciprocity at the Kennedy Round. But since the periphery also had to conform to GATT rules, the remedies essentially retained the status quo in the trade system, to the dismay of Third World producers. Thus, since the top priority of the TEA was obviously not the Third World (it was the Common Market), and because reductions in core tariffs were contingent on reciprocal concessions from the South, the periphery would have to look beyond the United States for assistance in raising export earnings.[3]

The South could rely more on the Common Market, for instance. An enhanced role for the Six in boosting Third World exports was a key ingredient of the Kennedy Round task force plan, but as in Atlantic trade relations, the EEC diverged, to some extent, from U.S. policy. First, Kennedy designed his Atlantic partnership as a joint American-European venture to fight poverty in the periphery, but Gaullism upset his plans to stabilize commodity prices, increase aid, and reduce restrictions against Third World goods. Second, the Six already furnished "preferences" to associated countries—many of them former colonies tied to Western Europe—by granting them concessions on many of their exports without requiring reciprocity in return. Although non-associates would gain from a 40 percent cut in Common Market tropical duties, the preferences to associates created a discriminatory system against outsiders. Robert Marjolin, vice-president of the EEC Commission, added that once the North reduced tariffs at the Kennedy Round, it could then pass on the concessions to the entire periphery. Thus, the Six, also worried about the threat of UNCTAD to the trade order, proposed some viable alternatives to American policy for the South but still focused on panaceas through traditional GATT mechanisms.[4]

Another possible avenue of relief for the periphery was the GATT Program for the Expansion of Trade of 1961, although it, too, disillusioned the poor nations. Although amounting to a majority at the Kennedy Round, the LDCs, in general, attacked GATT policy. Their grievances included, above all, restrictions by the core on trade in manufactures. As a solution, the South intended to resort to the development norm of GATT, which permitted import protection and preferential export treatment, that is, tariff concessions not conferred on advanced nations, in order to force the North to open its markets to more Third World products. The South's impatience with the North led twenty-one LDCs to propose a GATT "Action Program" in October-November 1962. This eight-point plan called for the core to eliminate new tariffs and NTBs, remove quantitative restrictions and tariffs on primary products by 1966, accord free entry for tropical commodities by

1964, cut tariffs on semi-processed and processed goods by at least 50 percent within three years, abolish internal taxes, and adopt a yearly reporting procedure to chart progress on the program. Their attitude toward the Kennedy Round, admonished the South, hinged on the North's adherence to the Action Program.[5]

Opposition to the plan actually came not from the trade system leader, but from the Common Market. The Six as a whole balked at the standstill on NTBs, while individually, West Germany wished to retain internal taxes on coffee and Belgium argued that Third World exports disrupted its economy. Yet it was France that led the dissent against the Action Program, but for mostly selfish reasons. Paris agreed that trade restrictions partly explained the export problems of the South, although low commodity prices, ineffective commercial techniques, and lack of diversification and regional cooperation also impaired the LDCs. But above all, de Gaulle sought to preserve the recent Common Market arrangement with the Associated Overseas Countries (AOCs) under the Yaoundé Convention of 1963, which perpetuated France's special economic and political relationship with eighteen of its former African colonies, and clashed with the intention of the Action Program (and America) of ending preferential arrangements.[6] De Gaulle compelled the entire Common Market to adopt the AOCs.

Non-AOC poor countries opposed the arrangement, but to no avail. Latin Americans, for instance, did not get the favorable duty rates enjoyed by AOC competitors, and although their exports to the Six grew during the 1960s, they began to lose their market-share to the former African possessions. But like the United States, the EEC also noted the decline of Third World export earnings, and so logically focused on taking care of its old colonies. Furthermore, when the AOCs shrewdly accused the EEC of being a rich man's club neglectful of African needs, the Common Market, ever sensitive to this reproach, gave them preferential rates on tropical goods, applied to them the same uniform duties possessed by the Six, set up a stabilization fund in order to offset fluctuating commodity prices, and augmented loans.[7] The Six would not abandon the AOCs.

To be sure, the AOC system created conflict between France and West Germany. The latter, with no colonial possessions, held that preferences contradicted the MFN principle, and were of limited value for development. But, since most AOCs were former French holdings, which remained in the franc-based African Community Financial Zone, Paris insisted on the association because France would benefit from cheaper foodstuffs. Also, France argued that preferences were only part of the "sum of advantages" available for the AOCs; the system ensured faster growth. But de Gaulle also had a diplomatic and personal agenda. By adeptly handling the bloody Algerian independence issue in 1962 and afterward, by supporting anti-colonialism during visits to Latin America, his appeals in favor of the Yaoundé Convention promoted his grandiose image within the Third World.[8] The AOC system was a prerequisite to French cooperation in the Common Market, and with the United States at GATT.

Although initially ambivalent to the EEC-AOC system, Washington disliked the preferences in general because they harmed non-associated nations, particularly Latin America. Preferences countered America's plan to boost *all* Third World exports within a multilateral, nondiscriminatory framework. Kennedy feared that Europe's "closed shop" with former colonies might "freeze out" non-AOC exports, and thus curb foreign exchange earnings. His stance reflected U.S. self-interest as well as his desire to help the periphery. To be sure, the EEC-AOC agreement encouraged African development and lessened the American aid burden to the region. But the system also curbed Latin American banana and coffee exports to Western Europe, not only diverting these products to the United States, but compelling America to recapture the losses in Latin export earnings by increasing aid, thereby aggravating the balance-of-payments deficit. In short, the Yaoundé arrangement carved the periphery into spheres of influence and undermined the fair-trade intention of enlarging access in the core for all traders. The Common Market's AOC system stalled the GATT Action Program, and American designs, at the Kennedy Round.[9]

The Problem of Exports of Manufactures

By late 1963, the GATT Action Program's demands for tariff preferences on manufactured goods had become a rallying point for the Third World as it prepared for UNCTAD. The United States seriously weighed the advantages of preferences, but ended up disparaging UNCTAD, described by the State Department as "one of the most unpleasant propaganda efforts of the decade."[10] Yet administration officials could not ignore some disturbing signs in the trade balances of the periphery. An estimate of trade flows showed, for instance, that the difference between the South's declining exports and its rising imports would amount to a $15 billion debit by 1975, which would lead to a doubling of the gap between incomes of the core and periphery from 1950 to the mid-1970s. The percentage of LDC exports of industrial products was pitifully small—just $2.6 billion of the $62.3 billion world total in 1961—and falling. And, despite a 9 percent rise in export earnings from 1962, the periphery's trade balance for 1963 (excluding petroleum exports) suffered a sizable $5.5 billion deficit.[11] The South suffered from serious trade problems that the North had to address.

But trade preferences as a remedy clashed with the inherent political conflict in America's fair-trade policy. As an administration member summed it up, "It is easy to say that the economic solution is to let in more of [the LDCs'] exports, such as textiles, and close down some of the plants in this country and go into other, perhaps more sophisticated products. But it is difficult politically to attempt that."[12] As the foreign policy executive wrangled with the problem of Third World exports and development, it also had to consider the power of protectionists at home, knowing that societal interests and the representative element would protest higher imports.

Thus, influenced by the constraints of the fair-trade doctrine, Kennedy's staff proposed to increase exports of manufactures from the periphery, but do so in time-honored, more acceptably free-market ways. First, the South must diversify its industries. Second, the North should buy Third World exports on a country-by-country basis—and not according to commodity—in order to promote faster development in certain areas. Third, the United States must encourage regional integration, especially in Latin America, which paid a "double dividend" of export expansion within, as well as outside, the South. Fourth, the LDCs must realize that

Congress frowned on extending more aid to countries that traded with communist nations, while Congress, in turn, should recognize that periphery–Soviet bloc trade did not imply a Third World alliance with Moscow.[13] Although well-intentioned, the proposals constituted uninspired, traditional alternatives to the problems of the South, ones which the LDCs had already censured.

To no astonishment, neither America nor GATT strayed far from these suggestions. Just months before UNCTAD convened in 1964, America still insisted on 50 percent reciprocal tariff reductions as the guide to help the Third World, and denounced preferential trade blocs and commodity stabilization plans. President Johnson stayed aloof, advising only a traditional, bland "commercial basis" for development in the South. Meanwhile, in a scramble to make the Kennedy Round more amenable to the periphery, GATT ministers decided to study the feasibility of preferences for manufactured exports, and agreed to exclude, as much as politically possible, products of special interest to the South from the Kennedy Round exceptions lists.[14] Faced with these insubstantial gestures, the poor nations threw up their hands and turned to the United Nations Conference on Trade and Development.

UNCTAD I

The United Nations, transformed by the addition of thirty-six Third World countries by 1960, became the avenue for change in North-South trade relations through UNCTAD. In 1961 a panel of economic experts issued the Posthuma Plan, which recommended stabilizing commodity prices through a development fund, and proposed a compensatory financing scheme that would reimburse LDCs when prices dropped and reduced their earnings from exports. Later, Yugoslavia, Cuba, the Soviet Union, and twenty-five African and Asian nations called for a meeting to discuss Third World economic issues. Kennedy's push for an annual growth rate in the periphery of 5 percent, added to the Cairo Declaration of July 1962, in which thirty-one poor nations requested a trade conference that would address their special demands, speeded up momentum for talks under the United Nations. UNCTAD thus convened in March 1964, with 2,000 delegates from 120 nations and several international organizations.[15] The major core nations attended, including the United States and the Common Market. The guiding force of UNCTAD was its secretary-general, the head of the UN Economic Commission for Latin America, Raul Prebisch. His "structuralist" philosophy held that liberal trade enriched the core, and not the periphery. Protectionism in the North, and worsening terms of trade for the South, caused a "trade gap" that diminished the Third World's foreign exchange earnings needed to finance imports of capital goods for development. Basing imports on the 5 percent annual growth rate set by the UN, he estimated that the trade gap would swell to $20 billion by 1970. The Kennedy Round would help expand the gap; tariff cuts would mainly help the North and impair the periphery's exports. Biased against the Third World, GATT, claimed Prebisch, instilled "an abstract notion of economic homogeneity which conceals the great structural differences between industrial centers and peripheral countries."[16] The LDCs had to change world trade rules or create a new organization that would obtain their needs.

Prebisch's structuralism amounted to a call for a profound alteration in international trade policy. He focused on increasing exports of manufactures, which he viewed as a responsibility of the North, and raising commodity prices. Farm self-sufficiency in the core made LDC commodity exports, except for oil, a losing source of earnings. Thus, "real reciprocity" could only occur when infant Third World industries got trade preferences. And, when the terms of trade deteriorated, Prebisch suggested that the core step in with the compensatory finance plan in order to help the South recoup its losses. Continued adherence to liberal trade theory would simply perpetuate the unequal North-South relationship, concluded Prebisch.[17] UNCTAD provided an alternative that would correct the imbalances, but unlike GATT, it would do so at the expense of the advanced industrial nations.

These proposals received varied reactions from the participants at UNCTAD. Communist countries hoped to use UNCTAD to pressure the West, since the periphery depended on capitalist markets for exports, and earn propaganda points in the Third World for the Soviet bloc as a result. The Soviet Union and Yugoslavia won credit for supporting the conference, while the South noted the resistance of the "imperial powers" of the Western alliance. The communists also offered to buy commodities at fixed, instead of free-market, prices, thereby assuring the LDCs of a stable profit for their goods. Seeking to disrupt the existing Western trade order, and the Common Market's "colonial" relationship with the AOCs, the Soviet bloc offered attractive inducements and moral support to the periphery at UNCTAD.

A fear of communist inroads in the periphery drove the United States to respond to UNCTAD. The CIA derided the Soviet overtures, noting that East-South trade was not as lucrative, or as reliable, as North-South commerce. The capitalist nations, for instance, provided convertible currencies to the LDCs, rather than nontransferable rubles. Also, prior East-South economic deals had sputtered from bad management or inefficiency. A cotton trade agreement between Moscow and Egypt had not enhanced the influence of the Soviet Union, for instance, nor had a shoddily built steel mill in India, which had clearly shown the disparity between low communist and high Western construction standards.[18] Still, the Soviet bloc, by aligning with the South, stood to gain politically from the highly charged atmosphere of UNCTAD.

The periphery viewed UNCTAD as the most significant international conference of the decade, although there were divergences over certain issues within the South. For example, the AOCs and Commonwealth contested non-associated countries over the necessity of preferential trade systems. Also, while more developed Third World nations pressed for new markets for manufactures, the very poorest nations eyed agricultural commodity exports as their main concern. Yet unanimity overrode any initial fissures at UNCTAD. All less-developed countries wished to institutionalize their objectives in a permanent organization, and agreed on the Prebisch formula for manufactured preferences, commodity prices, and compensatory financing. Above all, they remained pessimistic concerning the potential gains of the Kennedy Round, calling instead for a "new deal" in the international trade regime, separate from the unprofitable GATT system.[19]

Trade patterns merited this attack on GATT, and the push for UNCTAD. Third World export expansion was less than half that of the advanced nations from 1950 to 1962, despite a boom in

TABLE 7.1
Exports Between and Within the North and South
(percentages of world exports)

Origin	Destination:	Year	North	South	Total world
North		1960	42.3	16.4	63.7
		1962	44.5	14.9	64.1
		1964	45.7	14.0	64.9
		1966	47.6	13.9	66.6
		1968	49.1	13.4	67.5
		1971	51.8	13.0	69.6
South		1960	15.0	4.9	21.5
		1962	14.3	4.6	20.5
		1964	14.2	4.3	20.1
		1966	13.6	4.0	19.1
		1968	13.4	3.8	18.5
		1971	12.9	3.5	17.7

SOURCE: GATT, *International Trade, 1967* (Geneva: GATT, 1968), p. 4; *1971* (Geneva: GATT, 1972), p. 3.

commodity sales. The "striking feature," said Prebisch, was the fall in the periphery's share of world exports due to shrinking purchases of their goods by the core. If oil exports are ignored, Third World export growth dropped from 11 percent to 6 percent from 1963 to 1964, while the overall merchandise trade deficit of the periphery grew to a sizable $6.3 billion during these years. Even with oil exports included, the South was still in the red by $1.6 billion in 1964. Exports of commodities (except oil) fell well short of the increase in comparable sales by the North. Clearly, global trade favored the core, not the periphery, and would continue to do so.

Regional, bilateral and industrial trade figures were just as bleak, due to the South's adverse terms of trade with the advanced countries. In 1964 Latin American export earnings rose 9 percent, slower than the world total of 12 percent. Excluding Venezuelan oil, the region ran a deficit of $475 million (although an improvement from 1963), with the United States importing less from Latin America as the Common Market retained its share. Asia's exports rose 3.5 percent in 1964, but its trade deficit spiraled down to $3.1 billion, and even larger when the substantial Indonesian oil exports are not considered. Africa enjoyed the highest export growth

of any Third World area, and as a result, lowered its deficit to
$210 million in 1964. Oil exports boosted Middle Eastern profits.
But the periphery's share of industrial exports peaked in 1963,
and declined thereafter, while the world registered an 117 percent
rise from 1955 to 1964. In addition, the North's expansion in
manufactured exports of 114 percent, to $80.8 billion by 1964,
contrasted sharply with the South's rise of 83 percent, worth only
$5.5 billion.[20] Clearly, the LDCs felt justified in demanding pref-
erential treatment for their exports.

Maurice Brasseur, the Belgian minister of foreign trade, set out
to reverse these trends by meeting the demands of the Third World
at UNCTAD. He proposed to stabilize commodity prices, permit
compensatory financing, and most important, install tariff preferences. Promoting "selective and controlled" North-South trade,
this "Brasseur Plan" replaced the free-market approach, which
America pursued, with an inherently discriminatory "organization
of markets" scheme. Because it kept the EEC-AOC arrangement
for select African nations, but would, in general, appeal to the
South, France endorsed the plan. As American officials noted,
however, the neomercantilist Brasseur Plan contradicted GATT
principles. West Germany agreed with the U.S. assessment, and
also opposed the Brasseur Plan because it accentuated France's
"independent" foreign policy and made Bonn, which was a beneficiary of the South's adverse terms of trade, liable for large payments into the finance fund. Yet Erhard again gave way to
de Gaulle, especially after the EEC Commission, hoping to protect the EEC-AOC system, called the Brasseur Plan a pragmatic
first step in extending trade preferences to all developing countries.[21]

The United States fought a rearguard action against its allies in
order to maintain the status quo by making improvements in
GATT's nondiscriminatory order, instead of abandoning the system in favor of tariff preferences. But in the face of obstinacy from
most of Western Europe, Washington's was a losing cause. A
major blow had come from the EEC's endorsement of the Brasseur
Plan. Then, Great Britain shifted by issuing a ten-point program,
similar to the GATT Action Program, but with the addition of
compensatory finance, price floors, greater access for commodities,

and most significant, a "generalized" system of preferences, which would be applied to the entire periphery. Even GATT's Wyndham White, who admitted that GATT had been too doctrinaire on preferences, sanctioned this proposal. Other nations did, too. The United States was now virtually alone in its resistance to trade preferences for the Third World.[22]

Although Washington stood increasingly isolated, George Ball, the U.S. delegate at UNCTAD, would not give up easily, vowing to undermine Prebisch's appeal. He suggested a "relaxed role" for the United States, so as not to appear to sympathize with the South, and thereby give Republicans a reason to portray Johnson, during an election year, as too generous to other nations on import issues. But America should not seem too skeptical either, because the periphery had placed great hope in UNCTAD, an organization that was dangerous to U.S. policy because it threatened GATT and increased Soviet influence in the South. Yet for these very reasons, Ball also detested UNCTAD, to the extent that McGeorge Bundy, the president's national security adviser, cautioned him about making the United States a target of recrimination by being close-minded on preferences. Still, Ball retorted that the LDCs were "victims of a high-class confidence game conducted in elegant economic jargon," which did not help their interests. He hoped that UNCTAD would end with a "whimper, not a bang."[23]

Realizing that domestic politics, lack of authority in the TEA, and support of GATT principles prevented an acceptance of preferences, Ball proposed his own remedies. In order to close the North-South trade gap, he rehashed the old suggestions of sound fiscal measures within the Third World, trade based on comparative advantage, and freeing poor nations from making reciprocal tariff cuts at the Kennedy Round. As a sop to the South, the United States would also accept a permanent secretariat and budget for UNCTAD. But Ball wanted to limit commodity agreements, compensate LDCs that did not enjoy special access to markets, and curb tariff preferences. He remained firmly opposed to the big issue of preferences, claiming that the "LDCs want alot, . . . and they want it for nothing." Unfortunately, argued Ball, the South stressed more "the highly charged political UNCTAD," than the "practical possibilities at the Kennedy Round" of tariff cuts.[24] He added that preferences were "logical" in theory, but disregarded the "political reality" that such concessions were impossible on sensitive imports. Thus, desperately wielding the fair-trade doctrine, he urged trade based on efficient production and marketing, rather than transferring resources to the periphery by the artificial means of preferences, which would anger American protectionists in the process.[25]

Indeed, preferences contained economic and political pitfalls. They seemed too complex to implement for all LDCs, and by their very nature, impossible to apply on a nondiscriminatory basis, especially since some Third World countries already enjoyed them, and some did not. They also smacked of spheres of influence, and a bit of colonialism. And, as political scientist Ronald Meltzer maintains, the foreign policy executive feared that preferences would neutralize multilateral tariff reductions and jeopardize the support of business and Congress at the Kennedy Round. Above all, he writes, such a system sabotaged the traditional "GATT theology" embraced by U.S. officials, who strived to uphold the MFN norm, and GATT as its tool of enforcement.[26] In sum, Washington perceived the preference idea as an attack on America's historic efforts to build a liberal trade order, and an assault on the principles of this system, which protected the hegemonic position of the United States. But just as alarming, by annulling GATT rules and allowing more competitive imports into the North, UNCTAD also threatened trade solutions to the American balance-of-payments deficit.

At UNCTAD, Ball voiced America's opposition to deviations from the free-market system. In fact, he ignored White House pleas to give just a "sympathetic waffle" on the Prebisch program so as not to upset the South.[27] Instead, he implored the North not to dismantle GATT rules, under which 80 percent of trade now moved on a nonpreferential basis. Describing his speech to the president, Ball claimed that many LDCs viewed his presentation as honest, yet disappointing, although others now recognized that the "Prebisch gimmickry" was not the answer to their problems, nor was UNCTAD the "dawn of a golden age."[28] Johnson, perhaps sensing that Ball's "cold rain" speech was not sound diplomacy, pledged his "strongest cooperation" with UNCTAD. Yet he could not undo the bad press within much of the Third World caused by Ball's statement.[29]

Indeed, when it became clear by late May 1964 that the major accomplishment of UNCTAD would be merely the creation of the secretariat post—a result that Ball exulted was "a mouse not a mountain"—the South expressed its keen displeasure. The periphery had hoped, said UNCTAD president Abdel Moneim El Kaissouni, to put into effect Britain's plan for generalized preferences. Given America's refusal to grant them, he said, the Third World had grown lukewarm to the Kennedy Round. Other LDCs were more strident, calling U.S. policy "grossly inadequate," and a "watering down" of existing commitments by the North.[30]

America would not abandon its stance against preferences, although Ball prepared to back a generalized system, that is, one applicable to all periphery nations in the capitalist core and East bloc, in the event that UNCTAD forced his hand and imposed one. Generalizing preferences would counter both Soviet efforts and the Brasseur Plan, the latter which he criticized as Gaullist "grand-standing." Although the TEA authorized tariff preferences only for the Philippines, STR Christian Herter was also open to a generalized regime, but only if it was nondiscriminatory, very selective, and temporary. But since these conditions were impossible to meet, and thus unacceptable to the other UNCTAD participants, America emerged from so-called UNCTAD I as the archdefender of the extant system that had failed the periphery, and the major obstacle to Third World desires. In a sense, the United States served as a scapegoat for the North; the Common Market's Brasseur Plan would benefit mainly the select group of AOCs. Without a doubt, though, Ball raised the suspicions of Third World nations that LDC trade problems were still subsidiary issues in American eyes.[31] This view was largely correct. The United States cared much more about the main show regarding Atlantic community tariffs at the Kennedy Round than for the sideshow of North-South trade, since a reversal of the payments deficit depended on a meaningful trade accommodation with the Common Market, not the South.

The Road to a Generalized System of Preferences

Nevertheless, after UNCTAD I, the State Department accepted a generalized system of preferences as a necessary evil. The impetus to change was the new undersecretary for economic affairs, Anthony Solomon, who focused on the problem of Latin American development, his field of expertise. Solomon recognized that preferences were a hot domestic political issue—Congress might not authorize them unless they were selective, or might cut back aid or impose quotas in exchange for them. Preferring the principle of nondiscrimination in trade, he conceded, nonetheless, that if all nations dispensed preferences, America should follow suit, and thereby reverse a 189–year-old policy of upholding the MFN rule in its conditional or unconditional form.[32]

In essence, Solomon accepted the inevitable. Latin American pressure for preferences, in order to offset the EEC-AOC system, necessitated their adoption. And not only would America's acceptance of preferences overcome the negative press that Ball had generated at UNCTAD, but it would also deter the Common Market from becoming a discriminatory trade bloc with its AOC arrangement. Besides, the United States participated in two preferential systems, although the one with the Philippines would end in 1974, and the U.S.-Canadian Automotive Agreement was not prejudicial to third countries. But a decision by Australia to seek a GATT waiver, in order to grant its own system of preferences to Third World nations, built more momentum for a new approach to the trade difficulties of the South. The State Department denounced Australia for opening "the door to administrative anarchy in world trade," but America remained out of step with the rest of the world.[33]

Solomon sought a generalized system of preferences (GSP), but his economic affairs bureau was the only branch of the State Department willing to accept it. He thus turned to the OECD in order to fashion a blueprint for the GSP. Meeting in late 1965 and 1966, an OECD Special Group of senior Atlantic community trade officials forged the system. The Six accepted it when France agreed to build the GSP around tariff quotas, instead of the EEC-AOC arrangement, while America held its nose and approved the GSP out of compulsion. The decisive turnabout in U.S. policy came in response to an overwhelming show of support for preferences in GATT. With the United States as the lone dissenter, a vote of 51–1 in the supposedly American-led GATT in favor of the Australian waiver had shocked senior State Department officials. Ball, the most prominent foe of preferences among them, then abandoned the fight, resolving to revise U.S. policy.[34]

America accepted the GSP in August 1966. Ball admitted that the United States had lost the initiative in North-South trade, and thus had to give the Third World a "headstart" by special tariff treatment. He hoped the GSP would appeal to Congress on humanitarian grounds, since it would surely injure industries that were susceptible to import competition. Ball suggested sending a revised MFN bill to Capitol Hill, preferably after the 1968 presidential election. In order to head off another call by Latin Americans for solely hemispheric preferences and garner support at home for the change in trade policy, the administration tested U.S. opinion on the GSP. The Chamber of Commerce, NAM, the AFL-CIO, and most legislators favored it, as long as American producers and workers received safeguards. Bolstered by domestic backing, and hoping to reawaken the crippled Alliance for Progress, the president announced America's readiness to explore temporary preferences at the Organization of American States summit in Uruguay in mid-April 1967. This cautious declaration, which disappointed Latin Americans, aimed to discourage discriminatory trade blocs in world trade.[35]

Agreement on the GSP was one of the few bright spots of UNCTAD II, which met in 1968 in New Delhi, India. By this time, many Americans saw UNCTAD as a way to update U.S. trade policies toward the periphery. Yet Arab-Israeli and black African–South African conflicts cast a shadow over the talks, rendering resolution of key issues among Third World countries impossible. Also, many LDCs sought even more concessions from the core, including duty-free entry for manufactures, but the position of the advanced nations hardened. Not only did the North refuse to remove tariffs from the manufactured exports of the South, but the core countries withheld preferences on some products, stymied commodity agreements, and refused a pledge to donate 1 percent of their GNPs to the periphery. UNCTAD II, noted some LDCs, witnessed "plenty of platitudes and evasions but little in the way of firm commitments from the participating nations."[36] The GSP finally went into effect in 1976, but was supposedly only temporary, exempted key imports, and placed ceilings on others. As political economists Rolf Langhammer and Andre Sapir have concluded, the ineffectual administration of the GSP by neomercantilist core nations, and their concurrent resort to NTBs as tools of protection, prevented the stimulation of Third World exports through preferences in later decades. The South's victory in the GSP battle, and even at UNCTAD, was dubious.[37]

The South at the Kennedy Round

In part because of the difficulties over the preferences issue, the trade problems of Third World nations persisted in the 1960s; their terms of trade did not improve and their share of world exports plummeted. From 1964 to 1967, the South's trade deficit, which had shown signs of improving, worsened from $6.3 to $8.2 billion, despite rising Venezuelan and Libyan oil exports. Stagnating interregional trade was partly responsible, but core-periphery commercial patterns were also to blame. Although the value of total exports from the South rose by $4.4 billion, the LDCs' share of imports into the North fell, thus hindering reversals in regional deficits, except for Africa. Trade with the periphery also favored individual core countries, especially the United States. In fact, from 1965 to 1968, America's surplus with the South was the one of the few positive signs in the U.S. trade balance.[38] Clearly, the entire core held some responsibility for the deteriorating trade balances of the Third World nations, and the United States, as the GATT system leader, was the logical target of reproach by the periphery.

The market and, to an extent, the statist school profess that internal problems within Third World nations explain LDC trade imbalances, and stress that America's large foreign aid payments to the periphery partly offset the U.S. trade surplus with the South. In other words, underdevelopment resulted not from a systemic bias against the periphery, but from internal political, social, eco-

TABLE 7.2
U.S. Trade Balance with the Third World
(billions of dollars)

Year	All LDCs	Latin America	Africa*	Asia*
1958	1.7	.43	.09	1.18
1960	2.3	.08	.25	1.80
1962	2.5	.25	.26	2.04
1964	2.7	.14	.34	2.30
1966	2.7	.07	.37	2.26
1968	2.4	.19	.14	2.10
1971	2.4	.39	.45	1.55
1973	1.8	.31	−.27	1.80

* Includes South Africa and the Middle East.
** Includes Australia and Oceania, but not Japan.
SOURCE: U.S. Department of Commerce, *Business Statistics, 1977* (Washington D.C.: U.S. Government Printing Office, 1978), pp. 108–109, 113–114.

nomic, and cultural problems within the Third World.[39] Their arguments are valid, but they cannot deny that U.S. trade policy failed to enrich most of the periphery. Regardless of the setbacks for the Third World, however, statists affirm that the North-South unequal relationship was an inevitable, although unfortunate, occurrence in light of America's focus on Western Europe and, above all, on Washington's preoccupation with its ability to pay for its national security.

Nonetheless, the United States led the core nations at the Kennedy Round in confronting the problems of the periphery. The North opened the Kennedy Round in May 1964, resolved to make "every effort" to cut tariffs deeper than 50 percent on goods of interest to the South, and compensate those LDCs that did not enjoy preferential trade benefits. For its part, the United States pressed for the elimination of duties on tropical products once the Six did the same, and urged others to keep exceptions to import-sensitive goods to a minimum. The periphery received a longer period to table offers, and the exceptions lists of the advanced nations underwent the scrutiny of the GATT Trade Negotiations Committee in order to comb out key Third World exports. In February 1965, GATT strengthened its development norm by not compelling the periphery to grant reciprocal concessions at trade negotiations.[40] Such were the concerted efforts by advanced nations to offset the impact of UNCTAD at the Kennedy Round.

Yet these measures dissatisfied the South. As negotiations with the LDCs began in May 1965, the periphery remained pessimistic about the potential benefits of GATT and the Kennedy Round. Still on the agenda, the GATT Action Program of 1962 went unfulfilled because of Common Market reservations. And, despite efforts by a Tropical Products Group to maximize tariff cuts, the core was actually unwilling to reduce duties on most items. America tabled a large number of offers for tariff reductions on tropical goods, but the Six did not reciprocate because they wished to maintain preferential access for AOCs by restricting imports from other Third World nations. And, although twenty-two LDCs offered tariff concessions, the North's exceptions lists, which included major exports from the South, such as lead, zinc, oil, copper, and cotton textiles, convinced them that GATT would grant them few tangible benefits.[41]

Cotton Textiles

Cotton textiles talks confirmed this view. One of the five products under separate industrial sector discussions at the Kennedy Round, discussions on cotton textiles concerned not only tariff cuts, but the administration of the Long-Term Arrangement. Exporters used the GATT Textile Committee's major review of the Arrangement in 1965 to castigate the disguised protectionism of the LTA accord. Although their exports and shares of import markets had climbed from 21 to 26 percent from 1961 to 1964, imports into the core had not matched the relative rise in consumption. Due to the "intensive use of restraint provisions" by the core, noted the committee's chairman, the LTA punished efficient producers. As a result, India, for one, complained that the textile arrangement had "brought complete satisfaction to importing countries and growing gloom to the exporting countries," and that ironically, signees of the LTA suffered from *slower* export growth than nonparticipants. The mere existence of imports, accused the periphery, was taken by importers in the core as a sign of market disruption.[42] In sum, the neomercantilist LTA had worked exactly as America had planned; it limited cotton textile imports in an "orderly" fashion, and thus guarded politically powerful, but inefficient, protectionists textile producers at home.

Yet exporters had little choice but to accept the renewal of the LTA once it expired in September 1967, since possible alternatives included even more prohibitive unilateral import restraints. In addition, Pakistan, India, Korea, and the UAR had taken over markets previously held by Japan and Hong Kong. Thus, these latter two in particular now had a stake in the LTA because it guaranteed them a fixed share of U.S. and European markets without having to compete against "newcomers." Nevertheless, exporters demanded the LTA's liberalization and more access in bilateral trade North-South, warning that the core's response would affect their cooperation, and that of most LDCs, at the Kennedy Round.[43]

The American foreign policy executive supported their position. The State Department and STR accused the importing nations, including the United States, of abusing the "market disruption" clause by invoking restraints even when imports rose minimally. This rigid interpretation undermined America's liberal trade "image" in GATT. The North had lived up to the "letter but hardly the spirit" of the LTA, said Herter, especially now that domestic producers enjoyed an upswing in production and employment. Criticizing America for diverging from the fair-trade approach, Herter argued that the United States should administer the LTA liberally so as to expand, not restrict, trade. The State Department added that the continued protectionism of the LTA might further convince poor nations that GATT would not work in their favor.[44] Yet these admonitions were pointless. Societal interests, and their representative element, still controlled America's textile trade policy.

The well-organized U.S. textile industry wanted restraints on imports and, as in the Kennedy years, forced the foreign policy executive to oblige. Admitting that the industry was in decent shape, William E. Reid, the president of the American Textile Manufacturers Institute, nonetheless asked that the growth ceiling for quotas remain at 5 percent, and also demanded more than a three-year extension of the LTA without liberalization. The request, at first, did not appear excessive in light of recent economic trends. Kennedy had pledged to hold imports to 6 percent of domestic consumption for the five-year duration of the LTA, but imports had grown to 8.3 percent by 1966, a record high. But this rise hid the rather severe limits on world cotton textile exports, of which 60 percent came from Third World nations that depended on export growth for their own development. The American delegate to the GATT review bluntly stated, however, that the United States "did not intend to dismantle its textile industry" by letting in a flood of imports.[45] Trade, according to American producers, was as fair as possible.

Washington believed that an answer to the textile stalemate rested on pressing the Common Market to buy more imports, but the Six resisted this course. America had long asserted that Europe's overprotected market diverted Asian textiles into the United States. Yet the Six, like the United States, had placed cotton textiles on their exceptions list, making tariff reduction conditional on a renewal of the LTA. Since neither Atlantic partner would liberalize the sector before it received assurances that the LTA would continue past 1967, GATT director Wyndham White, the head of the Cotton Textile Sector Group, stepped in with a "package deal" in 1965 that, he hoped, would become the eventual basis of a Kennedy Round agreement.[46]

Wyndham White linked tariff cuts and liberal implementation of the LTA to a renewal of the arrangement, because without a deal, the North would impose further restraints, the South would then refuse to renew the LTA, and trade in cotton textiles would become more restrictive. America was willing to pay the "price" of easing the LTA's bilateral quota ceilings and controls on yarn, and then reduce tariffs at the Kennedy Round, in return for another five years of the LTA. Without an extension, warned Secretary of Commerce John T. Connor, the administration would face a hostile Congress in the process of weighing new trade legislation and other key Johnson bills. This consideration was all the more noteworthy when figures released in September 1966 showed cotton textile imports at an all-time high.[47] Again, the White House faced domestic textile protectionists, this time in selling them Wyndham White's compromise proposal.

The protectionist side of the fair-trade doctrine still determined American policy on cotton textiles. In short, societal interests and Congress constrained Johnson from liberalizing the LTA, and the administration was not happy. White House aide Francis Bator suggested lowering import barriers because many poor countries accused America of violating the spirit of the LTA. While the U.S. textile industry took advantage of restrictions to expand capacity at "break-neck speed," the United States was "paying a foreign policy price" in such locales as Singapore, where there were anti-American riots. But, although Bator knew that the retention of a rigid LTA was "bad economics [and] bad foreign policy," he acknowledged it would also be "bad domestic politics" not to renew it because textilemen would blame the president for higher imports. They expected Johnson to keep his 1964 campaign pledge to limit imports. Indeed, the president had already trod on dangerous electoral ground by resisting calls for a wool textile agreement and attempts to tighten the LTA. Now he had little choice but to stretch the fair-trade doctrine by not liberalizing the LTA.[48]

It still remained for the administration to sell this continued protectionism at the Kennedy Round. Since many exporters from the South opposed a renewal of the LTA before being granted tariff cuts at the Kennedy Round, Washington sought to buy them off with bilateral accords to increase quotas after they agreed to extend the arrangement. This complicated "policy of encirclement" won Third World consent. Unfortunately, the EEC nations could not agree on a common textile policy—the Six bargained separately on the LTA, but collectively on tariffs—and struggled with the bilateral agreements. To the irritation of the other participants, the Common Market delayed the LTA renegotiation until March 1967. By that time, powerful Senator John Pastore had joined the protectionist crowd at home, which now wanted to tighten the LTA. Bator explained that the Kennedy Round was at "an extremely delicate stage," at which renewal of the LTA rested on at least modest tariff cuts by the North. Any hint of additional protectionism, he warned, "would derail a train which stretches through the whole range of commodities on the table, in agriculture as well as industry." Although promising no "laxness in LTA enforcement," Bator asked the president to resist the Pastore interests that sought not only to prevent the LTA's liberalization, but make it more restrictive.[49]

Johnson stood his ground, but American protectionism still

prevailed. The GATT parties did not liberalize the LTA, and cotton textile tariffs were reduced at the Kennedy Round a meager 21 percent, with American duties falling 15 percent and the Common Market's by 20 percent. The periphery rightly complained, since the package deal impaired its exports. Short of junking the LTA, however, and causing a domestic backlash that could upset the entire Kennedy Round, no better alternative existed. To his credit, Johnson staved off pressure at home for the inclusion of all fibers in the LTA, and refused a demand by American producers not to reduce tariffs at all. Also of note, U.S. imports in all textile materials rose until 1972, which helped the LDCs because they began to concentrate on exporting synthetic fabric instead of cotton.[50] But as it had in creating the LTA in 1962, America curbed Third World exports at the Kennedy Round five years later. Domestic political restraints on the president compelled him to strain the bounds of the fair-trade doctrine, and continue a malignantly neomercantilist trade regime at Geneva.

Kennedy Round Results for the LDCs

Cotton textiles exemplified the South's plight at the Kennedy Round. A study of concessions by America, Britain, the EEC, Switzerland, Sweden, and Japan—representing 65 percent of the North's dutiable imports on Third World goods—revealed tariff cuts on over half of these products. Yet on key Third World manufactures—textiles and steel, to name but two—core importers still enjoyed significant protection. In addition, tariff reductions on industrial goods from the periphery amounted to 29 percent, as compared to an average of 35 percent for all participants at the Kennedy Round. The LDCs would also, quite evidently, not reap advantages from large reductions in high-tech sectors, such as chemicals and machinery. And quantitative restrictions like the LTA, and the unrealized GATT Action Program, further impeded their exports. Regarding primary commodities and semi-processed foodstuffs, moreover, eventual tariff cuts were unimpressive; concessions on tobacco, oils and fats, and foodstuffs, for instance, were smaller than initially sought by the South. Food aid increased, but the insistence of the AOCs on the retention of Common Market preferences curbed the Trade Expansion Act's considerable authority to eliminate duties on tropical products. Also, although the Third World pressed for implementation of the concessions in advance of the schedule for tariff reductions, the Common Market and the United States accelerated them on very few products in 1968, or afterward. *The Economist* aptly summed up the results for the periphery by calling the Kennedy Round a "rich man's deal," in which concessions to poor nations were merely "apologetic."[51]

America's specific offers to the South were also somewhat disappointing, although there were some bright spots. To its credit, the United States exercised the TEA's authority to drop tariffs on $45 million worth of tropical products (without corresponding EEC cuts), reduced $252 million worth of duties that applied to Latin American goods, and, for the region's additional benefit, temporarily suspended another $68 million in tariffs. Overall, America's concessions to the Third World amounted to $900 million, and almost all reductions were by half, while only 3 percent of cuts by the periphery that applied to American products equaled this percentage decrease. But the United States resisted tariff preferences until after the negotiations, a policy that particularly hurt Latin America. In addition, America's advocacy of the Long-Term Cotton Textile Arrangement hurt Asian producers, and other efficient manufacturers. Furthermore, by viewing North-South trade as a secondary issue, and by trying to uphold the MFN principle, the United States was as much to blame as any nation for the meager gains won by the periphery at the Kennedy Round.[52]

In the international trade system, the two avenues open to the South for development in the 1960s proved unsatisfactory for development. One option, UNCTAD, won a pledge for preferences from the North, but the administration of the system failed to boost Third World exports in any meaningful fashion. And the modified GSP was a long time in coming, not taking effect until 1976, twelve years after UNCTAD I. Meanwhile, GATT was the other way for the South to develop, but the Kennedy Round focused on core trade and the periphery remained a background issue. And when LDC trade was important, as in cotton textiles, the North protected its producers. The Kennedy Round did not reverse the deteriorating terms of trade and insufficient export earnings of the South, in large part because of core policies.

Surely, all core countries were at fault. The EEC's Brasseur Plan amounted to a disingenuous diversion from liberal trade. It did not provide realistic answers to Third World problems because it sought mainly to attain the integrationist goals of the Common Market by consolidating the AOC preference system. But the Six at least tried to adapt to new conditions by accepting tariff preferences, which is more than can be said for the United States. America only rolled over on the preference issue when international politics made resistance inexpedient. But both Atlantic core trade powers approached the Third World in a similar, statist fashion, accruing the benefits of North-South trade to achieve neomercantilist goals. The loser in these EEC and American designs was the periphery.

For its part, to be sure, the United States did not purposefully try to hinder Third World development. Rather, traditional assumptions of liberal trade, which applied more logically, effectively, and equitably to core trade, but not to North-South commerce, trapped American policymakers. To overturn the carefully cultivated postwar trade regime of the past twenty years would have been difficult and foolish, for GATT had served the United States well. And, as economist Bela Belassa argues, GATT trade liberalization benefited newly industrializing LDCs, because tariff reductions led to productionist growth in the core, and thus higher demand for Third World manufactures.[53] Yet a more flexible approach to the special circumstances of core-periphery trade relations was in order. That America eventually bent on generalized preferences is admirable; it could have persisted in its hegemonical refusal to grant them to the periphery. Still, the American trade edge with the South, and the stagnating performance of LDC exports, shows that Kennedy and Johnson did not use the fair-trade doctrine properly to help Third World development.

Yet judging American trade policy is more complex than just deciding whether the Third World gained or lost in its relationship with the United States. Indeed, America was neither too benevolent nor overly malicious toward the South. An unequal and dependent core-periphery relationship persisted because of some pernicious American policies, most notably in cotton textiles. But this was due not necessarily to the inherent exploitative nature of capitalism against weak nations, but because of the tangled web of trade, diplomacy, and domestic politics that constrained the liberal trade bent of the foreign policy executive. And, to be sure, the newly industrialized countries, many of them textile exporters in Asia, succeeded in climbing out of poverty through export-driven development, aided by the United States. But, trade patterns revealed that the gains from liberal trade did *not* always trickle down to all nations, whether rich or poor, as many LDCs remained destitute and underdeveloped.

Instead, U.S. policy toward the periphery reflects the complexities of the statist interpretation. U.S. neomercantilism often punished weak and strong traders in the South, but America resisted Third World demands because of overarching security aims. That is, Washington believed that it could achieve its goal of correcting the payments deficit two ways. First, it had to adhere to the liberal trade norms of GATT, and thus oppose preferences for the LDCs, in order to expand its own exports. Second, the United States had to forge, ironically, protectionist arrangements, such as the renewed LTA, in order to maintain domestic support for its liberal trade policy. North-South trade was in no way immune to the priorities of the fair-trade doctrine, or irrelevant to the national security considerations of the foreign policy executive that also typically represented the American approach to its core partners.

Thus, both presidents pursued a trade policy that hurt the LDCs, but at the very top of their agendas was the statist goal of promoting national security through a growing export surplus. Although not excusing American behavior, the defense imperative explains why the United States often found itself at odds with periphery desires. As scholar Phillip Darby writes, postwar leaders understood that the cold war "had taken an economic turn" regarding the Third World. Nikita Khrushchev, the leader of the Soviet Union, asserted that Moscow valued trade "most for political purposes." The same could be said of American leaders. Kennedy understood the "subtle relationship between [Third World] development and anti-communism," while the Johnson era "saw a renewed emphasis on security considerations plainly conceived," which intertwined the cold war with the necessity of stimulating growth and development.[54] The interests of the United States came well before those of the South, or any other trade partner, for that matter. America's trade policy aimed to boost primarily *U.S.* power and wealth, in order to defend the LDCs against communism. Thus, the revolt of the South was a nuisance to America's interrelated trade and security policies. Opposition from the periphery also threatened to divert attention from the center stage: tariff bargaining between the United States and Common Market at the Kennedy Round.

CHAPTER EIGHT

America Retreats, 1965–1968

Negotiations over tariffs at the Kennedy Round began in December 1964, and culminated two and a half years later. In the interim, the Atlantic traders increasingly viewed the bargaining process not in terms of cutting tariffs to benefit nations with comparative advantages, but according to statist aims of maximizing exports. By the end of the talks, moreover, in mid-1967, it was clear that EEC internal and external trade policies had clearly stymied U.S. strategy in Geneva, and as a result, efforts to correct the payments deficit through export expansion. The Common Market's neomercantilism had grave implications for American power. The fair-trade doctrine kept the GATT regime open, but did not halt America's tumbling trade surplus or its growing payments deficit, both of which, in the end, vitiated U.S. strength.

The Bargaining Stage Begins

During the first half of 1965, the exceptions lists of the nations that had decided to reduce their tariffs on a linear basis occupied the contracting parties at GATT. Some of the lists were troublesome, for if not whittled down, the extensive rosters of the Six and Japan would undermine the TEA's authority to lower duties by 50 percent on a reciprocal basis. But as in the earlier rule-making stage of the GATT talks, a typical stalemate ensued among the core powers. Again, GATT director Wyndham White intervened, this time suggesting separate discussions in industrial sectors that comprised a large volume of trade in sensitive imports. This "sector" approach had the potential for both positive and negative results; it might facilitate solutions to protectionism in key product categories and force the Six to abandon their hopes of reducing tariff disparities, but also might encourage cartels and quotas. Nevertheless, in order to address specific trade problems, the United States endorsed the sector plan in aluminum, pulp and paper, cotton textiles, steel, and chemicals. For, having examined the industrial offers, STR Herter found room for many "meaningful" concessions by all nations, which would counter the dangers of resurgent protectionism. Outlines of the five sector agreements did not emerge until late 1966.[1]

Meanwhile, agricultural trade predicaments persisted. America's pursuit of access guarantees from the Common Market for feed grains seemed doomed to Mansholt's margin of support plan. USDA Secretary Freeman still sought a commitment on access from the Six, particularly after hearing predictions that U.S. wheat exports to the Common Market would be halved in 1965. Herter told EEC Commission president Hallstein "in no uncertain terms" that America wanted access pledges, and opposed the margin of support.[2] But the Six's chief negotiator, Jean Rey, replied that the common agricultural policy and Mansholt's price plan would stay. "Surely," Rey assumed, "the United States does not expect real liberalization" of the CAP and EEC farm policy, but merely sought instead assurances that the Six would not become more restrictive.[3] This view worried the administration, most of all because it seemed to vindicate Common Market agricultural neomercantilism.

To no surprise, the agricultural talks stalled in the face of Western Europe's resistance to American demands. Refusing access guarantees because the EEC did not give them to its own producers, Mansholt urged the United States instead to curb its own surpluses. But America preferred to boost exports. Vice-President Hubert Humphrey warned Mansholt that the Kennedy

Round would "flop" without progress on food goods because Congress would not stomach American concessions on manufactures without benefits for U.S. farmers. Mansholt replied that America's trade surplus weakened its appeal against Common Market protectionism, to which Humphrey countered that the problem was not just economic, but political and psychological. That is, the Six gave the impression that they were not interested in liberal trade, thus "undermining the internationalist policy of Europe and the U.S." Humphrey warned that President Johnson had no choice "but to take stern measures unless Europe is willing to play fair on agriculture."[4]

In order to test the EEC's willingness to compromise, Herter persuaded Johnson to forgo the tedious process of fixing farm trade rules, and set September 16, 1965 as the date for tabling non-grain offers in the agricultural sector. This maneuver would force the Common Market's hand, compelling the Six to subject their agricultural offers to the scrutiny of the other contracting parties. In doing so, the STR, by judging the concessions (or lack thereof) to be gained by America from the EEC offers, could then demonstrate to farmers and Congress the administration's resolve to link manufactures with agriculture in tariff bargaining. The STR also hoped to prevent the Six from offering a bare minimum of concessions, obliging Washington either to suspend the Kennedy Round or acquiesce to meager duty reductions on food products. Thus, head negotiator J. Michael Blumenthal suggested that the United States should withhold its offers until the Common Market proposed acceptable agricultural concessions.[5]

In mid-1965, talks also began—but soon were afflicted with obstacles—on an International Grains Agreement (IGA). Wheat made up only 15 percent of U.S. sales to the Six, but feed grains amounted to 42 percent of America's booming exports to the region. Trade expansion prospects were dim, however, for these latter crops used for feeding animals because of the CAP. Estimates showed that France would seize a greater share of the EEC market, limiting not only U.S. feed grains, but other nations' meat and dairy exports.[6] The United States decided to use its negotiating muscle—diminishing as it was—in order to block Common Market protectionism through a liberal IGA.

The IGA talks fell into three categories, in which America had three aims. First, the United States sought more access into the Common Market. The Six based access for exporters on a "self-sufficiency ratio," in which the EEC would provide 90 percent of grain needs and outsiders 10 percent. Seeking a higher percentage, the United States confronted the margin of support, which impeded this goal. Second, America wanted a realistically low price for wheat. The United States opposed Canadian, Australian, and Western European plans to set a high minimum price for feed grains, which encouraged production by inefficient farmers, and thus hurt U.S. exports. Third, Washington sought a multilateral program of food aid to the periphery for two reasons. First, there was the desire to shift the Common Market's excess grain production from selling on commercial markets to Third World assistance, so that it would not compete with U.S. exports. Second, a higher donation by the Six to the LDCs would also relieve America of some of its substantial aid burden to the South, and therefore help reverse the U.S. payments deficit. Urging the Six to give more aid, the United States set an annual target of 10 million tons, of which it would supply 40 percent, the Common Market 25 percent, and others the remainder. In short, the IGA would provide exporters with more trade outlets through enlarged access, stable prices, and a rising aid commitment. The IGA sparked optimism in the otherwise negative farm sector negotiations.[7]

The EEC Shuts Down the Kennedy Round

GATT bargaining ceased altogether, however, when France shut down Common Market operations, in part due to trade issues. Paris held that the Kennedy Round threatened French welfare, although this argument seemed specious because the country had clearly survived the earlier reductions in EEC internal tariffs. Actually, wrote American observers, Gaullism really caused the crisis of 1965–1966. De Gaulle sought to dominate the Six, and pushed his own "Grand Design" of European nationalism, led by a glorious France, in order to counter U.S. "hegemony." Disengagement from NATO, overtures to the Soviet Union and China, and delays at the Kennedy Round were manifestations of his policy.[8]

So was securing his influence over the other five members of the Common Market.

Debate over the Six's farm program was an impetus to this new, and ultimately most disruptive, round of Gaullism. France disposed of 90 percent of its growing wheat surplus through exports, financed by a subsidy, to non-EEC nations. In order to compete with such major historic grains exporters as the United States, the French had coerced the Six to unify and reduce wheat prices, while France maintained export subsidies for its farmers. Yet the combination of price cuts and subsidies placed a strain on the treasury in Paris, compelling de Gaulle to search for relief through the Common Market. He found a suitable solution for his budgetary dilemma by asking the other EEC nations to help France pay for its subsidy. In sum, the unified grain prices accord had won France greater control of the Common Market's cereals market. De Gaulle next sought to shift more of France's share of the export subsidy fund to his European partners, mainly West Germany. Then he hoped to stabilize global wheat prices at a high level to boost profits for EEC farmers. Although the rest of the Common Market generally disapproved of managing the international agricultural economy in this way, the commission, under the influence of de Gaulle, proposed an ambitious program of financing farm subsidies in March 1965.[9] France's was not a total victory, however, because the commission required political concessions from de Gaulle in return for the subsidy plan. This proposed trade-off instigated an acrimonious debate within the Six, which resulted in closing down the EEC for nearly a year.

The deal involved the subsidy payments in exchange for a greater supranational role for Common Market institutions than ever before. First, the commission required that the European Parliament—the EEC's political representative body that met in Strasbourg, France—determine the budget of the Six under the guidance of the commission. Second, the Common Market would proceed with a timetable to install majority voting in the Council of Ministers by 1967, replacing the unanimous voting requirement that had given de Gaulle his veto power over such critical decisions as the British application for membership in the Six. The French president opposed abdicating control to the council and enhancing the supranational role of the commission, both of which would now act more independently from France's designs. But led by West Germany, the other five countries countered him. Since France would be the beneficiary of the farm fund, they logically requested, in exchange, expanded authority for the commission in budgetary and political matters. In essence, de Gaulle was willing to grant more power to the Six over economic issues, but not over political decision making. In short, he refused to link the farm program with supranational integration; West Germany's Erhard and the other five EEC nations refused to separate them, and in the ensuing standoff, France announced that it would boycott Common Market activities beginning June 30, 1965. Without the required full membership on voting matters, the Six suspended operations, including participation in the Kennedy Round, until the end of May 1966.[10]

The crisis, which occurred as the tabling date for agricultural offers neared at the Kennedy Round, threatened U.S. trade policy. America feared that as food importers, the Outer Seven and Japan would jump on the crisis as an excuse to withhold concessions, and that the Six would follow suit once the French boycott ended, thereby prompting a withdrawal of offers and unraveling the entire conference. Thus, after hearing Freeman's plea to postpone farm sector talks until the Common Market was ready, the White House decided instead to proceed with U.S. offers. The STR reasoned that the USDA's "stiff-necked" approach was useless. Blumenthal argued that since "agriculture in the Kennedy Round [was] not going to be a success story" anyway, Johnson should prevent the failure from being marked as "our fault."[11] The STR worked out a compromise with Freeman. Herter suggested withholding items of interest to the Six, and when farmers and legislators agreed, Johnson permitted the STR to offer tariff reductions on $500 million of $2.1 billion dutiable imports, and withhold an additional $250 million, pending reciprocal actions by the Common Market.[12]

After this tabling exercise, the Kennedy Round went dead. The contracting parties hoped that the Six would soon grant concessions, but this scenario appeared unlikely, since de Gaulle still denounced his EEC partners and adjourned the Common Market.

The postponement worried GATT officials, particularly in agriculture. Wyndham White, for instance, called farm sector trade a "ghastly problem" that would destroy the Kennedy Round if not solved. But there was little hope for progress as long as the EEC crisis continued. By December 1965, to the delight of American protectionists, the Geneva talks had reached a low point in morale and activity. As one European journalist noted, the Kennedy Round had "run out of gasoline," and with it, America's trade, diplomatic, and security agenda.[13]

A break in the crisis seemed imminent, however, when de Gaulle failed to win a majority on the first ballot in the French national elections, partly because of voter disapproval of his obstruction in the Common Market. After his reelection, in January 1966, he agreed to discuss his problems with the other members of the Six. Out of these talks emerged the "Luxembourg Compromise," in which he acquiesced to the new budgetary and voting procedures of the Common Market, lower internal tariffs, and the EEC's negotiating position at the Kennedy Round. Erhard, in turn, conceded on the organization of the Common Market agricultural program, including the subsidy that would assist French farm exports. In the end, save for the subsidy and, most aggravatingly for the United States, delaying Johnson's fair-trade program, de Gaulle's dramatics won him few rewards.[14]

Disappointment in the Agricultural Sector in 1966

After the eleven-month delay in the Kennedy Round, the authority of the TEA was due to expire in just over a year, on June 30, 1967. But finishing the tariff negotiations before the United States would need new powers in order to reduce duties was no certainty, especially after the reborn Six presented their disappointing agricultural offers in July 1966. As expected, the offers centered on consolidating the protectionist CAP, now the bane of American export policy. In response, Freeman again urged cutbacks in American concessions so that the Common Market would buy more U.S. exports, and in order to head off Third World demands for preferential trading arrangements. He also cautioned that if the United States gave into the CAP, without first receiving reciprocal concessions, the president would provoke "swift and serious domestic repercussions" from societal interests and their representative element, including the Department of Agriculture.[15]

Indeed, farmers disparaged the Kennedy Round because of the Six's agricultural import policy. The American Farm Bureau warned that maintaining CAP protection might prompt another retaliatory episode like the Chicken War. Exports to the Common Market of fruits and vegetables, which had risen earlier in the decade, but had recently fallen, were already one casualty of the CAP. The National Fruit Export Council blamed this drop on the Six, adding that "it would be unthinkable for the United States to lower its tariffs on industrial products from the EEC without achieving its objectives with respect to agricultural trade liberalization."[16] According to the Senate Agriculture Committee, admonished Senator John Sparkman (D-Ala.), the patience of Congress, and "the millions of businessmen, ranchers, and farm families whom we serve" was not "inexhaustible" toward a U.S. trade policy that acquiesced to Common Market protectionism.[17]

The administration reacted, but not to an extent that would anger the Six at the Kennedy Round. For instance, Herter warned of retaliatory measures if U.S. tobacco exports to Western Europe dwindled, but he resisted a tit-for-tat response of withdrawing concessions, which might lower others' offers and diminish the scope of the negotiations. Soon, many farmers themselves began to concede to the STR's logic that beating the Six with a stick was useless. The Common Market, they realized, had not only committed to protect its own farmers, but was still in the process of forging its agricultural organization. Thus, high expectations from the Kennedy years for export expansion now had to be lowered. In fact, by mid-1966, Herter, and some societal interests, realized that even their prior hopes for access guarantees were unrealistic.[18]

This emerging belief, however, did not ease frustration over the weak offers presented by the Common Market in the non-grain sector in September 1966. The Six granted concessions of less than 10 percent on one-sixth of their total dutiable farm imports; that is, tariff cuts on only $40 million of $1.5 billion worth of U.S. non-grain exports affected by duties. Herter confessed to Russell Long, chairman of the Senate Finance Committee, that "we have done everything possible to persuade the [Six] to negotiate genuine reduction in agricultural trade barriers," but with little result.[19] The STR also confided to Dean Acheson that he was "frankly, none too sanguine as to the final outcome" in the farm sector.[20] Above all, the Johnson administration, like most Americans, was gradually realizing the Common Market's ability to dictate terms at the Kennedy Round, to the detriment of U.S. interests.

The Five Industrial Sectors

Discussions were also strenuous in the five industrial sectors, in which America worried that the GATT contracting parties—and particularly the Six—would substitute neomercantilist, market organization schemes for multilateral tariff cuts. The EEC, for instance, perceived the U.S.-Canada Automotive Products Act of 1965, which removed barriers on automobiles and parts in order to create a single North American market, as a model of how trade might be controlled, rather than freed. The sector talks would be difficult, although America had a secondary interest in all but cotton textiles, steel, and chemicals. In pulp and paper, the United States was not a major trader, but still rejected Western European plans to tie tariffs to prices in a preferential arrangement. In aluminum, the American firms of Reynolds Metal, Alcoa, and Kaiser were not significant exporters but backed reductions in Japanese and Common Market restrictions. And, as explained earlier, efficient cotton textile exporters endured the renewed LTA, which was not liberalized, and the only slightly lowered tariffs at the Kennedy Round.[21]

Steel was important, since many nations had experienced difficulties in this sector, including the United States, which had become a net importer in 1959. Once a supporter of the TEA, the industry now pushed for quotas on European, Japanese, and Third World imports, the U.S. import ratio to consumption tripled from 1962 to 1968. Figuring into the influx were high prices, which prompted Kennedy's confrontation with steelmakers in 1962 and also spurred consumers to buy cheaper imports. Britain and the European Coal and Steel Community (ECSC), which represented the Six, also suffered from inefficient organization, overcapacity, and costly raw materials. Any discussion at the Kennedy Round would have to consider the needs of many powerful countries.

In steel trade, export subsidies and taxes were bigger problems than moderate tariffs, yet failure to lower duties, which ranged from 9 percent in the ECSC and United States, to 15 percent in Japan, could cause withdrawals in other sectors at the Kennedy Round. America suffered a distinct disadvantage, however, because its steel tariffs were bound, and thus could not increase without compensation to other nations, while British and ECSC duties were unbound, and could therefore rise without fear of retaliation from others. The Six offered to halve tariffs, but from the rate of 14 percent from the pre-ECSC era, and not from the present level of 7 percent. Britain, meanwhile, opposed all duty reductions. For its part, America sought fair trade under a proposal by Herter, who recommended that the contracting parties "target," or fix, tariffs at similar levels. The scheme provided an impetus to unify Common Market steel tariffs, compel British cooperation, help America bring its high duties in line with the more average rates of other nations, and quiet protectionism in all countries. In short, the target plan offered an equitable solution in steel trade, and its success hinged on intensive bargaining undertaken in early 1967.[22]

The focal point of the sector negotiations was chemicals. At issue was the American Selling Price, which based tariffs on the higher U.S. price, and not on the actual value of the goods, and imposed prohibitive duties on four products: canned clams, wool knit gloves, sneakers, and certain synthetic organic chemicals. The ASP became the Common Market's "cause célèbre" in the latter stages of the Kennedy Round because of its blatant protectionism, the uncertainty of its application, and the French and West German trade deficit with America in synthetic organics. The Six and Britain conditioned reductions on chemical tariffs on the ASP's removal, and Japan concurred in order to augment its footwear exports to the United States. The Common Market would also use the ASP as a bargaining counterweight to the American assault on the CAP. As J. Robert Schaetzel, the U.S. ambassador to the

Common Market, reported, the ASP was a sensitive topic in Geneva, although foreign "preoccupation [was] substantially unrelated to the facts."[23]

In other words, Schaetzel believed that the Six exaggerated the effect of the ASP, although it was truly an anachronism. Actually, the ASP was insignificant in trade, applying to only 108 of over 800 U.S. chemical tariffs, and $43 million of $958 million of imports. Yet American chemical exports rose by nearly two-thirds between 1962 and 1967, while imports increased only 20 percent, from $765 to $958 million. With a three-to-one ratio of exports to imports, the industry was simply not in need of protection. Thus, White House aide and trade adviser Francis Bator noted that the ASP was a "protectionist gimmick entirely out of line with our liberal trade posture."[24] Indeed, the Six had not yet offered concessions on chemicals, rejecting a U.S. proposal to convert ASP tariffs to ad valorem rates in order to proceed with 50 percent cuts and responding instead with a long list of withdrawals of concessions in the event that GATT did not narrow disparities in chemical duties. And the EEC had leverage, since it imported from America a much larger amount of chemicals than it exported.[25] Western Europe insisted on fair trade.

But Congress, led by Congressman Peter Rodino (D-N.J.), warned the president not to abolish the ASP at the Kennedy Round. By 1967, 134 House and 17 Senate members had written Johnson to keep the ASP, and 40 legislators, mostly from New England, exerted pressure for the footwear industry. The Senate adopted a resolution, sponsored by Abraham Ribicoff (R-Conn.) and 12 others, which mandated that all NTBs, including the ASP, should not be negotiated without congressional consent. Legally, they argued, the TEA did not authorize the elimination of the ASP, a position that seemed fair since Kennedy had pledged to the chemical industry to retain the system. Although there was no support for the ASP in the House Ways and Means Committee, noted STR deputy William Roth, the Senate Finance Committee wanted it "for its own sake." The ASP, he concluded, had become the "trickiest political issue."[26]

But in the interest of liberal trade, America offered a two-part plan, labeled "découpage," or "cutting apart," by separating tariff cuts from the ASP system. By tying the two together, the adminis-tration feared with good reason, the Kennedy Round might be canceled if Congress refused to annul the ASP. Under the decou-page idea, Washington proposed reductions of Common Market and American chemical duties. After these were agreed upon, Johnson would then abolish the ASP, in exchange for concessions from the Six on some of their NTBs that hampered U.S. exports. Découpage was a compromise, but, ironically, because the Six—especially France—had made a big deal over the ASP, the United States now viewed it as a bargaining chip. By the end of 1966, only Switzerland and Britain had made tariff offers in line with the découpage package. As in the other sectors, a chemical deal would have to be thrashed out during the Kennedy Round "crisis" in the spring of 1967, before time ran out on the Trade Expansion Act.[27]

The Diplomacy of Trade and the Payments Deficit

In general, the Kennedy Round had betrayed the schisms among the allies in Atlantic affairs. France, as usual, led the way in exemplifying the deteriorating relations among Western Europe and the United States. De Gaulle attacked U.S. investments and the dollar, and opposed the cultural "Americanization" of Europe, which convinced Treasury Secretary Henry Fowler that Paris hoped to chase America from the region. In March 1966, France also began to withdraw troops from NATO, a development that rocked the alliance. U.S. preoccupation with the Vietnam War also im-paired Atlantic diplomacy. While West Germany lent support to the war, many Europeans decried Johnson's increasingly single-minded focus on Southeast Asia. Denying the charge, Johnson acknowledged that he had a public relations problem in Western Europe, not to mention with many LDCs, over the Vietnam issue. A National Security Council report explained that discord in the alliance was an indication of Western Europe's desire for a "voice" in world affairs, and was "fed by increasing European strength."[28] The Common Market, in other words, tested American leadership in the alliance and the trade order.

U.S. trade patterns clearly exposed this challenge to American hegemony, and stimulated calls for a response among many Americans. Reaching a high of $6.8 billion in 1964, America's overall trade surplus plunged to $3.8 billion by 1966. A stronger Common Market caused part of the decline. In 1964, for instance, the United States enjoyed a $2.28 billion edge in trade with the Six, but by 1967 the EEC halved this surplus, and by 1968 it was a mere $41 million. In addition, Common Market imports from America grew 5.2 percent from 1964 to 1966, but the exports of the Six across the Atlantic jumped by an impressive 20 percent. The higher industrial output of the EEC, relative to the United States, also showed that it was a potent competitor. Washington therefore realized that U.S. hegemony was no longer a given. As a result, many Americans believed that Western Europe should pay more of the aid and military burden of the Western alliance. Bator reminded the president that the payments deficit could be reduced if America scaled back defense expenses, and he noted the rising support at home for such a course. Johnson initiated financial talks with America's NATO allies on burden-sharing. But in trade, he acknowledged that a "showdown in this country is coming soon" if the Kennedy Round failed, thereby preventing the United States from paying for its national security expenses with export earnings.[29]

Quite simply, the payments deficit still overrode all other considerations in international economic affairs. As scholar Fred Block has written, Kennedy's optimism of erasing the deficit gave way, in the mid-1960s, to Johnson's hope for a "holding action" in order to prevent the payments imbalance from degenerating further. Due to restraints on capital outflows, Federal Reserve Board limits on dollar sales, and export promotion, the sagging trade surplus at first did not worsen the deficit. In fact, in 1965 America enjoyed its first quarterly payments surplus since 1957. For the year, the deficit fell to a heartening $1.3 billion, down from the $3.1 billion mark of 1964. Furthermore, the gold drain ceased. During the next few years, however, these encouraging trends were reversed. Inflation, caused by domestic spending under the Great Society and the rising cost of the Vietnam War, pushed up demand for imports, which grew by 12 percent during mid-decade. Meanwhile, higher prices and deflation by other nations slowed American exports. In addition, the elaborate bureaucracy established to promote exports stopped meeting by 1966, ending coordinated efforts to boost trade. By 1967, as spending increased and the trade surplus dipped, the payments deficit rose again above $3 billion, prompting another run on gold.[30]

Yet America still refused to abandon the dollar's hegemony as a way of reversing the deficit, instead preferring clever ad hoc arrangements. In 1967, for example, the United States agreed to maintain its costly troop levels in West Germany in return for Bonn's promise not to convert its dollar holdings into gold. Washington also tried to prop up the British pound, fearing a run on sterling would lead to speculation against the dollar and subsequent devaluation. But Johnson's "holding action" on the pound failed by late 1967. Also, foreign pressure succeeded in creating an additional IMF reserve currency, which would, it was hoped, increase international liquidity. Introduced in September 1967, this new asset, called Special Drawing Rights (SDRs), cushioned traders and financiers against runs on the pound and dollar, but also enabled the United States to maintain large-scale domestic and overseas spending. The Six gained more leverage over world finances through their veto power over the body that issued SDRs. Nevertheless, SDRs permitted the dollar to remain the basis of the world monetary system, which allowed the U.S. hegemon to prolong its payments deficit.[31] America still presided over global finance in order to attain statist political and security objectives, as well as expand its domestic economic programs.

Instead of relying solely on financial means to right the deficit, the foreign policy executive opted for exports, too, but Kennedy Round problems stifled the effort and brought recriminations at home. Johnson tried to curb protectionism; by January 1967 he stripped the escape clause from six of the eight products under its authority. Included in the escape clause rollback was Kennedy's sheet glass tariff hike, which then induced the Six, in turn, to free American chemicals from the higher EEC duties imposed in June 1962. But such cooperation was rare in U.S.–Common Market trade. In a congressional hearing on the Kennedy Round in 1966, chairman Leonard Farbstein (D-N.Y.) lamented that Kennedy's hopes for Western unity through liberal trade had stalled. "On the face of it, in view of the apparent setbacks to our political and military policies in Europe in recent years," he said, "we seem to have misjudged the impact that [the TEA] would have" on Atlantic relations.[32] In order to drive home the point of aborted objectives, Senators Long and minority leader Everett Dirksen (R-Ill.) censured the White House for its giveaways at GATT, and Vance Hartke (D-Ind.) called the TEA a "colossal failure." Republicans warned of a sellout of farmers, and several experts predicted that the Kennedy Round would result in a bad bargain.[33] The GATT talks might result in dividing the Western alliance, not to mention undermining support at home for American liberal trade policy.

The Kennedy Round Crisis of April–June 1967

Even worse, in Geneva no end to prior difficulties seemed in sight, as ill will permeated the talks. A deal in agriculture could "be pulled off," said Ambassador Schaetzel, but only if the United States kept its "cool," and Johnson prevented "irate farm interests and legislators" from disrupting the negotiations. He pleaded for Herter to end his "bouts of dark gloom and excessive anti-EEC bias," developed by the STR's dealings with the Six.[34] The talks, however, did not encourage most Americans. For one, West German chancellor Erhard's ouster in November 1966 removed a liberal trade champion from among the Six; now Ball saw the EEC appealing to "the lowest common denominator," or protectionists, in its trade policy. Indeed, just before his death in December 1966, Herter was "guardedly optimistic" about the talks, but then congressional adviser Thomas Curtis' prior positive outlook faded by mid-January 1967. William Roth, the new STR, pledged to assure reciprocity, or, in a real possibility, he would reject the final agreement worked out at the Kennedy Round.[35]

Ostensibly hopeful developments amounted to false signs of progress. Johnson's rollback of the escape clause sparked praise from the Six, and boosted morale at GATT. Yet finding its Kennedy Round offers would result in a $2 million deficit for the United States if the Kennedy Round ended on the present terms, America prepared a withdrawal "warning" list to ensure reciprocity. Although justified, such muscle-flexing could have undone the negotiations if not for the EEC's refusal to submit a similar list. Fortunately, opting instead to improve their offers, the Six—with France hesitating—prepared to bargain on the "big issues." In order to leave time for an assessment of the final package before June 30, 1967, when the TEA would expire, Roth set an informal deadline of the end of March for an agreement. When this date passed, however, the Kennedy Round entered a "crisis" stage, from April to June 1967. When Roth flew to Geneva to take charge of the U.S. delegation, White House aide Bator set up a secret "Command Group" to give the STR "appropriate backstopping" at home, and the president enough time and advice to make critical decisions. This group of high-ranking officials communicated under the unlikely code name LIMDIS-POTATOES. This elaborate structure sounded "like a battle plan," wrote Bator to Johnson, but the Kennedy Round would face such a "crunch" in the coming weeks that it required close attention, "cool nerves, and fine negotiating judgment to pull it off." Concluded Bator, "Not only five years of work, but your entire trade policy is at stake."[36]

Industrial Sector Bargaining

The Kennedy Round crisis centered on bargaining between the United States and the Six. By early May 1967, frustration with the "big issues" forced Roth to issue another deadline of May 9, after which he would return home barring an agreement. At issue was the Common Market's submission of a list of withdrawals based on the old complaint about tariff disparities, which had hung over the talks since 1963. Blumenthal soon laid the matter to rest, reminding the EEC that no rules on disparities existed. He flatly threatened the Six with counterwithdrawals if they invoked the list, and there the disparity conflict ended. Although America had managed to shelve this contested issue, heated negotiations in the key industrial sectors still persisted.[37]

In the steel sector, America's proposal of target rates fell by the wayside because other nations feared that the projected tariffs did not provide enough protection. Instead, each country lowered duties to roughly an equivalent level, with Japan and Britain cutting more than America and the Common Market. The average duty reduction of 37 percent in the sector was a solid achievement. In bilateral results, Washington won concessions from the ECSC of $709 million, and three-quarters of these dropped tariffs by 25–49 percent. On the other hand, the subsequent outcry for quotas from the U.S. steelmakers indicated the extent of U.S. concessions. Partly due to the Kennedy Round, steel imports rose from 11.4 to 17.9 thousand tons from 1967 to 1968, a 63 percent hike with deleterious effects on the U.S. steel industry in the following decade.[38] Despite its higher tariffs, America was a fair-trader in steel.

Chemicals remained the thorniest problem in the industrial sectors, as the découpage plan had come to nothing. America insisted on unconditional cuts of Common Market duties, while the Six premised concessions on the ASP's elimination. The Common Market was unyielding, rejecting a suggestion by Wyndham White to reduce tariffs 20 percent, and then an additional 30 percent once America abolished the ASP. Noting that the resistance of the Six would undermine the TEA's intent of reciprocity at the Kennedy Round, Washington decided to play "chicken" with Western Europe by holding to the demand of unconditional cuts on EEC chemical duties. Clearly, warned Roth, the Common Market's policy of making the Kennedy Round contingent on congressional action on the ASP could be a "stopper" at the talks.[39]

Wyndham White broke the deadlock at a "marathon" meeting on May 15, 1967. His compromise entailed American tariff decreases of 20 percent on its low duties, while the Six reduced high tariffs by 20 percent, instead of 30 percent, and Switzerland and Japan maintained their offers. Under a separate découpage agreement, the United States would abolish the ASP by converting ASP duties to normal valuation, and then lower tariffs by an additional 30 percent. Then the Common Market would lower its high tariffs another 30 percent and grant concessions on some NTBs. The resulting reductions of 46–49 percent benefited the United States. Since its imports were small relative to exports, America gained by granting $314 million in concessions, and receiving $796 million in return. Although the possibility of the ASP's elimination threatened its dye industry, the United States enjoyed even more exports starting in 1968. Unfortunately, Congress refused to repeal the

ASP, and thus undercut the Kennedy Round agreement, to an extent.[40] But overall, in the chemical sector, freer trade brought positive results for America.

Negotiations in Agriculture

Contrary to the industrial sector, it appeared that in agriculture, trade liberalization was not realistic. Jean Rey, the Common Market's chief negotiator, merely advised that since all nations were farm protectionists, they should accept the margin of support, a restrictive plan, according to America, that he called a "courageous proposal." Indeed, the Six offered concessions on non-grain exports, but gave little on CAP variable levy items. There was also little progress in the dairy and meat sectors, due to the CAP in the former, and Common Market and British restrictions in the latter. U.S. fruit growers, and their representative element of Congress and the USDA, criticized the EEC's token offers. Nevertheless, Johnson realized that retaliation was senseless, even though he knew that the Common Market discouraged trade liberalization in the farm sector.[41]

The United States turned its hopes instead to the IGA talks, perhaps its last chance for a while to get the Common Market to provide food aid, set price levels, and allow outsiders to share in its future growth through access guarantees for grains. But the Six again resisted policies that they believed undercut the agenda of European integration, and America's conceptualization of the IGA threatened this plan by attempting to change the structure of the CAP. U.S. farm interests, caring more about economics rather than European politics, watched the now stalemated talks closely. Still, cautioned James Patton of the National Farmers Union, there would be "nothing more disastrous than having to face a closed door in Europe, carrying on the Vietnam War, and trying to give aid to all the underdeveloped nations of the world" because of an unacceptable deal in grains.[42] Societal interests, like Congress and the president, knew that a healthy balance of payments rode on an equitable settlement of the IGA.

But the administration backed away from a confrontation with the Six, acknowledging the neomercantilistic nature of farm trade, and thus eased the way for the IGA. Schaetzel wrote that the "nasty issue" of agriculture could be resolved only when U.S. farmers awoke from their "dreamland" of adhering to the law of comparative advantage. Furthermore, Bator urged the president to ignore pressure from Freeman to withdraw from the Kennedy Round, who advocated this course if the Common Market remained obstinate on the IGA. Washington still insisted on a fair deal in both the industrial and farm sectors, but realized that a fair-trade compromise in grains was in order. After digesting LIM-DIS-POTATOES telegrams from the STR in Geneva, the Command Group advised the president to drop the demand for access guarantees, in return for the Six doing likewise on the margin of support. This deal broke the deadlock in the cereals sector, although not to the advantage of the United States.[43]

The IGA brought mixed results for the United States. America had sought an annual ten-million-ton food donation from the Six, in order to keep the EEC's surplus grain off commercial markets and fix equitable levels of aid-sharing. The contracting parties agreed to the sharing percentages desired by America, with the Common Market providing almost one-quarter of the aid, the United States donating about 40 percent, and other nations the remainder. But America lowered the total commitment of donations to 4.5 million tons because the Six pressed for less, and Japan sought a smaller share, or some cash equivalent. On price levels, Canada, Australia, and the United States set a minimum price of $1.70 to $1.75 per bushel, but this level was too far above actual market prices, and thus distorted trade in favor of less efficient producers. Even worse for America, the Six rejected attempts to fix their self-sufficiency ratio at 87 percent by preserving the remaining 13 percent of their market for outsiders, and thus a larger share than before. Thus, in line with the deal to shelve the Mansholt Plan, the EEC refused America's key aim of access guarantees by retaining a smaller quota for outsiders.[44]

The IGA, which fifty-two nations signed, helped end the Kennedy Round but reflected U.S. concessions. The aid commitment fell short of its initial target, the high minimum price level penalized efficient exporters by stimulating production in Western Europe, and failure to obtain access guarantees diminished exports to the Common Market. Most striking, by 1969 U.S. grain sales to the Six were less than half those registered in 1966.[45] America, recognizing that further efforts to get its way in grains trade might lead to conflict with the Six, and upset the Kennedy Round, agreed to the IGA. The United States subordinated economic gains in agriculture to the goal of ending the GATT talks. Washington recognized that the IGA was the best that it could get from the powerful Common Market.

Kennedy Round Results

Despite the agricultural imbalance, Johnson endorsed the Kennedy Round accords. He did so after Bator warned that withholding U.S. consent could cause "spiraling protectionism with parliaments holding the whip hand."[46] The president might "take some heat" from chemical, textile, and farm interests at home, but the bargain could not be opposed after four years of haggling. To accept the results, however disadvantageous to the United States some of them were, placed the foreign policy executive's aims, which would help the nation as a whole, above those of the parochial representative element. After last-minute adjustments, the contracting parties signed the Kennedy Round agreement, just hours before the Trade Expansion Act expired on June 30, 1967.[47]

The outcome was impressive. Most experts and the press lauded the Kennedy Round as the "highwater mark of international trade cooperation," the "most successful trade negotiations in history," and a "historic compromise."[48] Successes included the chemical package, IGA aid, and an Anti-Dumping Code, which represented an initial stab at NTBs. Tariff reductions applied to $40 billion worth of goods, more than eight times that of the Dillon Round, and averaged 35 percent on industrial duties. Because two-thirds of the tariff cuts on manufactures were by half, industrial duties, now around 9 percent, became virtually meaningless in trade after the Kennedy Round. Disparities were no longer an issue; only 0.8 percent of U.S. duties were above 30 percent. Overall, U.S. tariffs fell 64 percent, while the biggest previous reductions had been 54 percent in 1947. And the tariffs of both the Common Market and Outer Seven ended up half of the level in force before the creation

TABLE 8.1
Post-Kennedy Round Industrial Tariff Distribution
(percentage of product categories)

Rate	U.S.	EEC	Japan	UK	Switz.	Sweden
0.1–10	68.0	83.3	66.1	63.1	87.9	89.6
10.1–20	25.5	16.5	31.1	34.8	10.9	10.4
20.1–30	5.7	.1	2.8	2.1	1.2	0
Over 30.1	.8	.1	0	0	0	0

SOURCE: Ernest H. Preeg, *Traders and Diplomats* (Washington, D.C.: Brookings Institution, 1970), p. 214.

of these two trade blocs. Above all, no nation gained inordinately in the industrial sector; the accord was balanced and reciprocal.[49]

The United States reaped many benefits. Japan was the only country that received more concessions from America than it gave to the United States. Indeed, the U.S.-Japan bilateral deal foretold of the trade competition of the next decades, which shot Tokyo to the top rank of trading nations. But accords with the EFTA and Canada favored America. In the overall final tally from the Kennedy Round, the United States granted concessions on $6.4 billion worth of imports of manufactured products, and received them on $6.7 billion of its exports, $2.7 billion of these from the Six. Cuts in tariffs of advanced technology items—transportation equipment, machinery, and chemicals—all helped America. The Kennedy Round also assisted the United States in food aid, which reduced Common Market cereals in commercial markets.[50]

Yet the GATT conference also fell short for the United States in many categories. In the industrial sector, STR Roth cited minor cuts in aluminum, steel, and such high-tech goods as business machines and electronics, as setbacks for the country. Excluding mineral fuels, U.S. exports to industrial nations would earn, at most, $541 million, while imports would rise $537 million over the next few years, only a $4 million surplus in the non-farm sector. Even this small margin of profit would fall, moreover, as congressional refusal to repeal the ASP would unravel the chemical sector deal, and thereby suspend many concessions by the Six. Thus, exports would drop to $487 million, actually netting America a loss from Kennedy Round tariff reductions.[51]

For the United States, agriculture was the biggest disappoint-

TABLE 8.2
U.S. Agricultural Exports to the EEC
(dollar amounts in millions)

Year	Variable levy commodities	Non-variable levy commodities	Total to EEC	Percent of commercial exports to EEC
1958	236	586	822	31.4
1960	299	800	1099	32.7
1962	479	672	1151	32.4
1964	525	891	1416	30.1
1966	642	922	1564	28.3
1968	475	892	1367	27.1
1970	454	1105	1559	25.1

SOURCE: U.S. Senate Committee on Finance, Executive Branch Study No. 4, *Effect of Regional Trade Groups on U.S. Foreign Trade: The EC and EFTA Experiences,* 93d Cong., 1st sess., 1973, p. 27.

ment, however, with the average tariff cuts amounting to only 20 percent of previous levels. The maintenance of CAP levies impaired a host of U.S. exports, including grains and poultry, and the United States won no access guarantees to assure future sales. America's share of the EEC farm market thus suffered; U.S. farm exports to the Six would stagnate starting in the mid-1960s, and those under variable levies would decline. USDA officials tried to remain optimistic, but only in order to keep in step with the administration's positive appraisal of the Kennedy Round. Undersecretary of Agriculture John Schnittker summed up the department's feeling, that the "negotiation was a moderate success—not a big roaring success, but a modest success."[52] But others were not so equable. One official, declaring that farm interests "share pretty conservative feelings on the Kennedy Round," lamented that now the Common Market had future U.S. exports "at its mercy."[53]

Although Orville Freeman also labeled the Kennedy Round a "modest success," he found its "lessons" largely negative. He learned that the pursuit of liberal trade ran up against philosophical divergences among food traders. Such exporters as the United States traded on the basis of comparative advantage, but the Six adhered to the law only in certain cases, while the LDCs hardly ever did, since they produced primarily to exist. These approaches created a "disturbing" conflict that prevented agreement in Geneva, and hurt American export prospects.[54] The secretary of agriculture could not deny, above all, that the rising Six could seriously hinder U.S. farm exports.

In sum, the Kennedy Round brought rewards for almost all core traders in the industrial sector, but few advantages for exporters in agricultural trade. Except in losing overall with Japan, the United States won in bilateral deals with the Common Market, EFTA, and Canada. Yet disappointments in the critical cereals sector undercut these gains, and prevented the large-scale trade surpluses that America required for its international payments. Also, even the 36–39 percent average reductions on industrial tariffs were less than the TEA's 50 percent target, a shortfall that further curbed efficient U.S. exports. In the larger picture, the Kennedy Round kept the trade order open, but failed to achieve America's aim of reversing the payments deficit through export expansion. The negotiations, in sum, did not boost the U.S. trade surplus; in fact, it steadily declined after 1964. As it sunk—while spending rose on domestic programs and the Vietnam War—so did hopes to correct the deficit, and so did American power.

Domestic Reaction to the Kennedy Round

The plummeting trade surplus, import pressure on producers, and difficulties with allies, spurred criticism of the Kennedy Round at home. Efficient grain dealers opposed the IGA because it interfered with the free market, and curbed liberal trade. In addition, since the Kennedy Round did not lower the CAP, claimed the Farm Bureau, the results were moderate, "at best." Industry opinion varied. The textile industry recorded its "deep disappointment" that the LTA did not include all fibers, while dyemakers sided with O. R. Strackbein, a leader of societal protectionists, who concluded that the ASP deal was a "time bomb loosed against the American economy."[55] Furthermore, many exporters were only mildly optimistic, expecting some increase in overseas sales, but no major gains. A number of producers predicted few rewards, either because NTBs had now emerged as effective restrictive devices, or because exports were small relative to the domestic market. The *Wall Street Journal* found that the business community had greeted the Kennedy Round with "fear, hope, confusion—and a big yawn."[56] Foreign trade was still not a big attraction for many producers, and for those who took an interest, the outlook for both lowering imports and expanding exports seemed bleak.

Trouble also brewed on Capitol Hill, as many legislators attacked the Kennedy Round. Although some reserved judgment, many, like Congressman Gerald R. Ford (R-Mich.), questioned concessions granted to foreigners in vulnerable American sectors. On behalf of the House Republican Task Force on Agriculture, moreover, Congressman Odin Langen (R-Minn.) called the Kennedy Round a "failure," blasted Johnson's giveaways, and agreed with other legislators that the U.S. farmer had been "sold out" in Geneva. By the end of 1967, no fewer than 729 House bills, and 19 in the Senate, proposed quotas on over 20 imports. At one count, 97 of 100 Senators endorsed at least one protectionist bill. Senator Vance Hartke explained that the Kennedy Round amounted to America's "unilateral disarmament," and until the administration grew tougher, he said, Congress would "insure that trade is fair" by matching foreign barriers with America's own.[57]

The administration countered with firmness. Treasury Secretary Fowler told Long that engaging in a "quota war" was a "fool's game," especially for a nation like America, which enjoyed a large (but shrinking) trade surplus.[58] Bator agreed that "an export-surplus nation can't win a serious war of import restrictions—it has too much to lose." If America slipped into protectionism, it would "tumble—into an economic cold war where nobody trusts anybody and everybody stagnates." The issue was "a matter of international politics as well as economics," he added. "We all recognize that this is a time of stress and redirection for the Atlantic Community. We can emerge stronger and more mature. Or we could dissolve into rival islands."[59] Not wishing to invite "massive retaliation" from abroad, Johnson sided with his advisers, and declared that the quota bills would not "become law as long as I am President and can help it."[60] The foreign policy executive expressed its intention of not allowing protectionism to undermine national and international statist objectives.

Yet such courage exacerbated a tricky legislative problem. The president sent a two-year extension of the Trade Expansion Act to

Congress in 1968, including an elimination of the ASP and liber-alization of adjustment assistance, which critics said had been an "abysmal failure" since not one petitioner had qualified for relief under the rigid criteria. The situation in Congress was "very rough," reported aides, and even "dismal" because of lack of Democratic party leadership for liberal trade. The sinking trade surplus weak-ened enthusiasm for trade liberalization, as did Vietnam and infla-tion for other Johnson endeavors in 1968. At hearings before the House Ways and Means Committee, the ASP became an insur-mountable obstacle. The threat of protectionist riders prompted Mills to delay reporting the bill until it was "clean." By July, committee members opposed it, as they watched the trade surplus fell to $611 million, the lowest level since 1955. Presidential aide DeVier Pierson reported a "Mexican stand-off" in the House; both the trade bill and quotas were stalled. In the end, the White House accepted the death of the TEA of 1968 (and the retention of the ASP) in the Ways and Means Committee, for defeat of the quota bills.[61] This accommodation drew the curtain on the liberal trade initiatives of the decade.

Post-Kennedy Round protectionism worsened the U.S. pay-ments deficit, now aggravated even more by the Vietnam War and Great Society expenditures. Controls on capital outflows, protec-tion of gold holdings, and talks on allied offset payments for shared funding of American troops abroad, did not provide an-swers. Despite promoting exports, moreover, the Commerce De-partment complained that "export-lazy" Americans still sold only 4 percent of their GNP abroad from 1963 to 1968. And old allies deserted the liberal trade camp, most notably organized labor, an erstwhile supporter now turned protectionist. Augmented by the falling trade surplus, domestic inflation, and an overvalued dollar, the American payments deficit eventually led to more drastic—and trade-restrictive—measures by the administration of Richard M. Nixon, which hastened the collapse of the Bretton Woods financial system in 1971. Soon afterward, the United States experienced its first trade deficit of the twentieth century.[62]

The United States had pushed for liberal trade and export expan-sion for the benefit of American producers, the world economy, and the defense of the Western alliance. But ironically, the Kennedy Round stirred up protectionism, did not increase America's trade surplus, and failed to reverse the payments deficit. The United States had witnessed the gutting of the Grand Design, tensions in the NATO alliance, dissent from the Third World, and inflation. GATT was not solely to blame for these problems, but the Kennedy Round had, long before its end, lost its luster. The conference often degenerated into a zero-sum game, in which one side's gain meant another's loss. At home, Americans reacted to this contest, and its results, by protectionism. This response disturbed not only the foreign policy executive, but the allies, too. Europeans feared that the United States might withdraw "into its shell," loosening its economic and military commitments around the globe.[63] The Kennedy-Johnson era of enthusiasm for liberal trade had come to an abrupt finish.

But the fizzling of enthusiasm for liberal trade did not obscure the accomplishments of the Kennedy Round. Large tariff reductions, the IGA agreement, and a first look at NTBs were some of its achievements. The talks tightened the bonds between the Outer Seven and the Six, and enhanced Japan's status as a major partner in the international trade order. Considering the disturbances in NATO, moreover, the GATT accord, wrote congressional adviser Thomas Curtis, "provided a sort of comforting continuity and momentum toward agreement in at least one area" of alliance relations.[64] "No monument to partnership," added scholar William Diebold in retrospect, the Kennedy Round nevertheless was a "landmark" in U.S.-EEC relations.[65]

But the negotiations also represented a distinct triumph for the Common Market. The Six overcame de Gaulle and worked as a "unit," thereby enhancing European regionalism and the unity of the Common Market. This integration, the United States had always believed, benefited the entire Western alliance by enhancing productionism, and increasing trade among all GATT nations.[66] Without a doubt, however, EEC solidarity built resistance to U.S. trade objectives. The Six's rough treatment of American agriculture, fewer concessions than predicted in the industrial sector, and Gaullist obstructionism to many U.S. objectives made the idea of an intimate Atlantic partnership seem overblown by the end of the decade. Simply put, the Common Market blocked the effectiveness of the Trade Expansion Act and, in essence, American foreign policy.

At the Kennedy Round, therefore, it was obvious that America had neither dictated terms, nor had been the innocent victim of European selfishness. Instead, the Six had confronted America, and both trade partners—as neomercantilists—had experienced gains and losses. The fair-trade doctrine, of reciprocal tariff reductions in conjunction with protectionism, guided behavior at the Kennedy Round. Statists correctly claim that America treated tariff cuts as costly concessions, to be circumvented as much as possible. Washington had hoped to expand its export surplus by capitalizing on its comparative advantages and curbing imports without provoking retaliation abroad. Such a policy would enhance American power in the face of the EEC's challenge to U.S. leadership, and help pay for arms and aid expenses. Thus, however lofty the vision of Atlantic cooperation under the Grand Design, the GATT talks boiled down to each trader trying to pry open the other's markets, without unduly exposing producers to import competition. Not surprisingly, this neomercantilism resulted in a standoff between two commercial giants, but the very fact that the Six were able to defy their Atlantic trade rival exposed the disintegration of American hegemony.

It would be an exaggeration, however, to argue that, due to the power of the Common Market, the United States essentially shrunk from its leadership role over the international economy. For one, America did not lose the Kennedy Round, at least not across the board. The United States gained in many sectors, and its sheer size and share of world trade enabled it to reap advantages at GATT. Furthermore, America also grew selfish after the Kennedy Round, and resurgent protectionism scared other nations because of its possibly deleterious effects on the trade order. In addition, the United States also held a positive trade balance with the Common Market and the world, although the former dwindled, and the latter soon turned into a deficit. A flagging giant, America was still a dominant force in trade.

Yet in the battle for export advantages, the GATT talks demonstrated that American hegemony had ended. The nation's inter-

ests would have been served by 50 percent tariff cuts in the industrial sector, a diversion to Western Europe of Latin American
tropical commodities, and assured access into Common Market
agricultural markets. The United States achieved *none* of these
objectives at the Kennedy Round. Also, liberal trade efforts had
unintended—in fact, often the opposite—effect of the aims Kennedy had strived for in 1962. For instance, in lowering import
barriers, Johnson touched off a protectionist backlash. And pursuing trade liberalization for the sake of national security and
economic health, the president forged an agreement at the Kennedy Round that hurt U.S. interests and did not accomplish the
key goal of correcting the payments deficit. An overvalued dollar
indeed slowed exports and raised imports, but the Kennedy Round
also expedited, in 1971, America's first trade deficit of the postwar
years.[67] The GATT negotiations were not so beneficial for the U.S.
trade balance or its power in the global trade system.

A significant indication of the end of U.S. hegemony was the
Common Market's new leverage over America in trade. As farm
historian T. K. Warley points out, America's assumption that
because Western Europe had an interest in reducing tariffs on
manufactured goods, the United States would enjoy equal bargaining power over EEC agricultural barriers, was simply wrong.
Washington was "defeated on grounds of its own choosing" in the
farm sector by European resistance, asserts Warley, leaving one of
its major trade objectives unrealized.[68] And, when checkmated by
the Six, the United States was unwilling to halt the Kennedy
Round because the foreign policy executive had staked too much
prestige on its success. The Common Market hindered many
American objectives in trade; the EEC was now a formidable and
effective challenger to U.S. power.

In sum, at the Kennedy Round, America met its match in international trade talks. The United States did not (and could not)
behave as a pernicious hegemon, nor as a selfless seeker of mutually profitable trade benefits for all nations. Instead, America
was one mighty neomercantilist nation competing against several
other strong or ascendant nations. But it was the Common Market
that was the real rival, and a successful one at that. For the first
time since World War II, Western Europe came to the bargaining

table equal in trade and political stature to America. The United States got many trade advantages but, in the final Kennedy Round tally, the EEC won *its* aim of lowering industrial tariffs while maintaining agricultural barriers. Clearly, as U.S. officials and producers came to realize, America, in scholar Isaiah Franks's words, could "no longer call the tune" at trade negotiations.[69] Not only was plurality in the global trade order an established fact, but Western Europeans had redefined the fair-trade doctrine to suit their interests.

CHAPTER NINE

American Trading Power
in the 1960s and Beyond

John F. Kennedy hoped that liberal trade would reinvigorate America's economy, balance its international payments, and help unify capitalist nations into a solid front against global communism. His trade program fell short of these expectations. Indeed, trade increased during the 1960s in dimensions not recorded since the Cobdenite era one hundred years before, giving the impression that under the New Frontier, as historian Allen Matusow has written, "American liberal capitalism still seemed capable of mastering any challenge."[1] Yet the falling trade surplus, an ailing economy at home, international financial problems, the Vietnam War, lagging Third World export earnings, and internecine conflicts among the allies destroyed this confidence by 1968. American hegemony declined, so too did the momentum for trade liberalization. A chapter had closed in the postwar trade history of the United States.

Kennedy's dream of prosperity and unity seemed fanciful just six years after he had announced his Grand Design. Inflation and an overvalued dollar not only ravaged the domestic economy, but exposed U.S. producers to more foreign competition. Many observers at home and abroad feared that the country might return to isolationism in response to its economic predicament. Tired of giving allies a "free ride," for instance, Congress, in the late 1960s and early 1970s, considered withdrawing troops from Western Europe and passing retaliatory trade legislation to counter Common Market import restrictions. Just days before leaving office, President Johnson asked Americans not to "drop our guard" against protectionism, explaining that the nation's economic difficulties could not be improved by erecting trade barriers that attempted to "insulate producers from the invigorating force of world competition."[2] His pleading seemed hollow in the face of a sagging economy, and drew disparaging responses from American societal interests and the representative element.

In 1973 hearings on a new trade bill, for instance, Senator Russell Long declared that the "history" of the Trade Expansion Act had been largely negative and unfavorable for the United States. America had counted, somewhat naively he thought, on GATT nations and its own negotiators to strike an equitable bargain at the Kennedy Round. But the outcome was the first U.S. trade deficit since 1894, a growing payments deficit, and a more protectionist European Common Market. Not only was "the bloom off the rose of the 'Atlantic partnership,' " Long said, but America had become the "least favored nation in a world full of discrimination." As a result, he pledged that "the next decade of our trading relations will be different from the last," after Congress passed tougher trade legislation.[3] The very name of the bill, the Trade Reform Act, indicated the swing in attitudes from a decade earlier, when the country had endorsed trade expansion. This transformation in the attitude toward liberal trade showed not only America's inability to win its economic objectives, but was a product of the simmering protectionism of previous years.

Protectionist, as well as liberal trade, sentiment had buffeted the foreign policy executive throughout the 1960s. In essence, U.S. trade policy was subject to pressure both from internal actors at home, who responded to changes in the external environment, and external actors, who sought power at the expense of the American hegemon. This study examined the influence of the internal and external factors on decision making, and the effect of those decisions on the global trade system. Although some questions remain unanswered, enough evidence exists to draw conclusions that, in general, confirm the statist interpretation of American foreign trade policy.

At the individual and ideological level, for instance, it was clear that policymakers adhered to the statist paradigm through their pursuit of the fair-trade doctrine. Kennedy combined a localized concern for declining Massachusetts industries with an internationalist drive for freer trade. His successor backed trade liberalism as a populist attack on high tariffs, although supported some protection, too. Johnson's stance meshed with Kennedy's, particularly since both were New Deal Democrats who feared a resurgence of Depression-era protectionism, and who perceived the cold war as the critical factor in U.S. trade policy. The need to build up America's economy and wealth, stabilize the West through freely exchanged goods and services, and attract the Third World to the capitalist countries' camp were all part of the effort to fend off Soviet aggression. Thus, concerned about American and international interests, the president, as leader of the foreign policy executive, advocated liberal trade in order to maintain and reinforce national security.

At first glance, the presidents seemed to face an insolvable conflict between their liberal trade ideology and practical politics, a struggle essentially over national and local objectives. To be sure, Kennedy expended political capital, and diverged from liberal trade principles, when he fought for the Trade Expansion Act. Yet the fair-trade doctrine rationalized this deviation, dealt effectively with protectionists, and at the same time guaranteed the overall goal of lowering tariffs at the Kennedy Round. Neither president was a doctrinaire free-trader, but neither had to be, since even the norms and rules of GATT recognized the inherent protectionism in the world trade system that arose from internal demands at home. Both were savvy politicians who knew how, and when, to accommodate powerful societal interests and their representative element on Capitol Hill. The policies of the foreign policy executive thus reflected the collective national interest *and* the local desires of certain constituents. In sum, liberal trade ideology guided the foreign trade policy of Kennedy and Johnson; fair-trade strategy and tactics fulfilled their objectives.

While individual ideology and experiences help determine the roots of policy, the governmental and societal levels explain the policy process. The class conflict school's neocorporatist view assumes that efficient exporters joined government officials in order to minimize interest group conflict and thereby channel benefits to corporate America. No doubt Kennedy had these capital-intensive exporters in mind, expecting them to take advantage of opportunities in the Common Market and expand sales abroad in order to boost the American trade surplus. Yet decision making did not function along elitist lines. Liberal trade lobbies, such as the Committee for a National Trade Policy, were no more than informational and support forums for administration policies. Also, the president actually angered "corporate liberals" by placating protectionists with concessions, or by advocating tax, investment, trade, and farm management policies that big, efficient producers opposed. In short, Kennedy did not take cues on trade policy from a supposed exporter-government network. Instead, his New Frontier, although sharing a similar ideology with corporate America, was often, in practice, at odds with rising sectors of the economy.

Furthermore, a neocorporatist consensus among societal interests did not exist in the foreign trade arena. To be sure, many firms, workers, and farmers backed the TEA, eager to sell (or invest) abroad. But despite being the world's largest exporter, America remained a relatively weak trader, its combined exports and imports remained under 8 percent of its GNP. Many producers were indifferent to trade, protectionist, multinational investors, or preferred domestic to overseas markets. As Ambassador J. Robert Schaetzel told Atlantic community leaders in 1971, Congress expressed a deep-rooted isolationist feeling espoused by many Americans. For a self-sufficient nation like the United States, he said, "it is all too easy to ignore the foreign scene, to say 'who needs foreign trade?' "[4] Thus, protection-biased members dominated several ostensible neocorporatist industries, such as electronics and chemicals. Farmers were export leaders, but the agricultural sector, too, divided on trade. And labor, beginning in the late

1960s, abandoned the liberal traders when adjustment assistance proved ineffective. Such apathy, opposition, and diversity—in short, pluralism—in the private sector, undercuts the neocorporatist argument about supposed consensual arrangements in American society and the political economy.

To be sure, agreement existed on the overriding objective of national security in the Kennedy-Johnson trade program, but this accord revolved around concerns about global defense, not just profits. Many producers, and much of the representative element, joined the foreign policy executive in promoting liberal trade as a way to fight the cold war. As a top priority, they all realized that the Trade Expansion Act would help provide funds for U.S. military and aid spending, and thus ease the payments deficit. Yet liberal trade would also prevent the alliance from disintegrating into hostile trade blocs, which were susceptible to Soviet influence, while a prosperous trade system would lure the periphery away from communism and toward the Western capitalist core. The TEA, as the linchpin of America's neomercantilist trade policy, indeed promoted economic gains for corporate America. But the goal was not primarily to boost profits for efficient producers, as neocorporatists assert. Instead, anti-communism and defense requirements lay at the basis of support for liberal trade.

Nor, it might be added, did a private-public partnership of class or economic alliances seem prevalent in the international trade regime, as neocorporatism assumes. Such global links might be found in the investment and financial spheres, which were controlled by central bankers, insurance companies, or multinational firms. But it is impossible to discern neocorporatism among the competitive, neomercantilistic GATT nations, despite the fact that they all accepted the productionist ethic. Instead, divisive squabbling over export concessions and advantages between trade rivals characterized the trade system. Gaullist labors to promote French interests, through the Common Market and over American (and oftentimes European) objectives, were the most dramatic examples of this trend. But mutual, cross-national protectionism also prevailed in agriculture, chemical, cotton textile, and steel trade, to name but a few major cases. Contrary to class conflict beliefs, clashes over policy objectives persisted at the Kennedy Round, just like contention endured in the internal decision-making arena in the United States.

Thus, typified by the various attitudes toward trade, protectionism, competition within the American economy, and electoral politics, the market and statist schools' pluralist interpretation best explains decision making. Elected officials obviously depended on their constituents to remain in office, thus giving societal interests considerable leverage over Congress and the president. Naturally, many legislators cast votes for Kennedy's trade bill out of traditional party affiliation and fear of recession, and in order to assist exporters and meet cold war exigencies. But many sought to garner votes by protecting their constituents. Less certain was the influence of presidential elections on trade policy, although Kennedy and Johnson apparently took into consideration export benefits and, more often, protectionism, in order to overcome political weaknesses in certain regions. In any event, that politicians acted on behalf of voters when making trade policy provides evidence for democratic pluralism.

Yet the decision-making process itself, not the specter of elections, explains the pluralist arrangement in the internal trade policy structure. Contrary to market school assumptions, congressional logrolling, leading to extensive tariff protection in the Trade Expansion Act, did not occur because the RTA had long before given the president, not legislators, authority to negotiate duty levels. Surely, as the market school contends, interest group demands on the representative element translated into pressure on the foreign policy executive. Kennedy's efforts on behalf of cotton textile, lumber, oil, and carpet and glass import-competitors, and for chicken and chemical exporters, echoed this process. Domestic politics—the fact that the president granted concessions to powerful congressional blocs to win his trade bill—determined policy in foreign trade. In fact, though, these trade-offs show that interbranch dealings, between the White House and Congress, usually settled trade matters, as statist scholars argue.

Despite voter influence, the relative autonomy of the representative element and the foreign policy executive from societal interests bears out the statist viewpoint. The market school's interest group model misleadingly portrays Congress as too malleable in the hands of private interests; if such was the case, then the supposed determinism of protectionist logrolling would put in question why the Trade Expansion Act ever passed Congress in the first place. Without a doubt, legislators listened to constituents, conveyed complaints to the White House, and the president acted. But Congress and the president sought a fair-trade accommodation, which preserved liberal trade. Thus, legislators won the seven-point program for the textile industry, but backed the TEA. The congressional lumber bloc followed suit, pleased by the six-point plan but refusing to press for import restrictions against Canada. The oil deal satisfied interest groups, yet came to fruition only through the Kennedy-Kerr talks, which persuaded the protectionist oil and coal blocs to pass the TEA. Even many confirmed protectionists voted for the bill after the tariff hikes on carpets and glass. And Kennedy quelled a revolt by poultry-state legislators by opting for resistance to EEC policy in the Chicken War. The president horse-traded concessions for votes on the Trade Expansion Act, and Congress obliged. In sum, as the statist school contends, a pluralist structure, under which government elites negotiated with each other, characterized the internal process of decision making on foreign trade policy.

In the external environment of foreign trade policy, namely in GATT and in America's bilateral relations with core and Third world nations, this study argues that the United States pursued, but not with uniform success, a statist policy of promoting exports, permitting certain restraints on imports, and keeping the trade system open in order to achieve its national security objectives. As a hegemon, albeit a declining one, America managed to maintain the principles of nondiscrimination, reciprocity, and limited protectionism in the GATT system; that is, the fair-trade doctrine. But in dealing with its trade partners, the United States increasingly ran up against resistance from others, which undermined its global power. A neomercantilist seeking trade advantages, America was also a degenerating hegemon. U.S. trade policies, and their effects on the GATT regime, exposed this status.

A balance sheet, which gauges the results of the Kennedy-Johnson trade policy on U.S. power and leadership in the international trade order, is useful in ascertaining the successes and failures of American foreign trade policy. In one major accomplishment, the TEA succeeded in lowering tariff barriers. Thus, despite some protectionist deviations for vote-getting purposes and the Common Market's restrictive agricultural policy, the United States perpetuated the openness, or liberalism, of the trade regime, as the statist hegemonic stability theory supposes. Although the regime underwent considerable strain during and after the Kennedy Round, major trading nations did not form into restrictive blocs (except in dealign with agricultural trade) that might undermine GATT principles. Reciprocal and equitable tariff cuts at the Kennedy Round kept the trade order open in later decades, thus signaling the effectiveness of the United States as the system leader.[5]

Except for Great Britain, and to some extent, ironically, the United States itself, this leadership had a positive effect on the advanced countries, especially in promoting productionism. Between 1960 and 1972, the GNPs of the Six, the European Free Trade Association (excluding Britain), and Canada grew an average of 5 percent, and Japan an impressive 10.3 percent. A survey of merchandise trade to 1973, when the Common Market enlarged to nine members, showed that core exports boomed. The share of world and industrial exports for every advanced nation, except from Britain and America, rose from 1960 onward. In addition, the EEC as a whole enjoyed a trade surplus, and only the Netherlands among the Six suffered a deficit. The Outer Seven were not as fortunate, but the United Kingdom and Denmark would soon benefit by joining the Common Market. Japan held a healthy surplus, soon to skyrocket, and Canada sustained its trade edge.[6] In general, the industrial nations of the core were better off by the early 1970s than they had been a decade earlier—and they added to their wealth over the next two decades—thanks, in large part, to America's productionist, fair-trade policy.

But in North-South trade, U.S. actions were less constructive; in fact, they were frequently disruptive and contrary to the fair-trade doctrine. Restraints on cotton textile exporters, for example, showed that America could brandish its neomercantilist power to punish nations that tried to trade on the basis of the principle of comparative advantage. For an extended period, the United States also disdained the Prebisch proposals at UNCTAD, and the GATT Action Program before them. When Washington finally gave way to calls for preferences, even the eventual generalized system was not as extensive, enduring, and liberal as the one initially sought by the South. Indeed, from 1950 to 1975, the average per capita income of the developing countries grew more rapidly than ever before, with resultant progress in industrialization, literacy, and the eradication of diseases. Yet these results were not uniform. Newly developing countries with 25 percent of the LDC population, such as Taiwan, Turkey, and much of Latin America, experienced rapid gains, while much of Southeast Asia and Africa, comprising 40 percent of the Third World's people, continued to suffer. Despite American rhetoric of aiding the periphery over the past eight years, many of the poorer nations were no closer to penetrating core markets in 1968 than they were when Kennedy took office. And most LDCs endured trade deficits during the next two decades, exacerbating their debt problems by the 1980s.[7] Surely, the United States wielded its hegemonic power to the detriment of the South, as class conflict scholars accuse. But as the statist school counters, the reason for American behavior toward the periphery was not so much purposeful exploitation, but benign or malign neglect, as the United States focused on core trade and cold war security as its top priorities. Regardless, the plight of the Third World was a blemish on the American record, a definite minus on the balance sheet.

U.S. trade policy also did not achieve initial diplomatic goals; de Gaulle's gutting of the Grand Design was an explicit loss for America. Although most Western Europeans opposed de Gaulle's veto of British membership and the French withdrawal from NATO, America could not recover momentum for the Atlantic partnership. Johnson's foreign policies, especially in Vietnam, and extended haggling at the Kennedy Round, heightened allied discord. Certainly, NATO without the French remained strong in the cold war, the thrust within the Common Market for integration continued, and allies later cooperated in order to attack multiplying trade and monetary problems. But the view, held by many observers at the time, as well as scholars assessing GATT history, that the Kennedy Round strengthened Atlantic unity in a period of great stress, is too optimistic. As political scientist David Calleo points out, the Kennedy Round "revealed an unexpected depth of trans-Atlantic economic tension."[8] The Kennedy-Johnson trade program engendered economic advantages in the alliance, but did not secure America's statist political aims under the Grand Design.

Despite the successes and failures of U.S. trade policy in international economics and diplomacy, America's *own* interests still were the chief consideration of Kennedy and Johnson. Both envisioned that liberal trade would maintain the country's competitiveness, bolster the trade surplus, and reverse the payments deficit. Behind these ambitions were the overarching statist objectives of enhancing national security and halting the relative decline in American economic power. As the 1960s came to a close, it was apparent that the two presidents had succeeded on the former, because America's defense posture remained strong and the superpowers entered a period of détente. But Kennedy and Johnson did not manage to end America's sliding influence in GATT. This deficiency was due, ironically, to the triumph of the United States' cold war objective of rebuilding Western Europe and Japan. But despite this fulfillment of postwar designs, America, contrary to the market school assumption, was not a selfless, generous nation in the Kennedy-Johnson years because it still practiced neomercantilism. Nor, as class conflict scholars contend, was the country extraordinarily selfish, as its declining hegemony also demonstrated. Rather, as the statist view concludes, the United States was a fair-trading leader of a competitive GATT commercial order, which was growing progressively weaker.

One indication of America's decline was in the performance of exporters and producers hurt by imports. The United States enjoyed comparative advantages in agriculture and high-tech products. In both categories, the nation stayed competitive over the ensuing decades, although the Common Market trimmed American farm exports, while other nations (namely Japan) grabbed larger shares of sales in markets previously reserved for U.S. advanced industries. To be sure, the United States still bought and sold in more volume than any other country, and its GNP remained large relative to others in subsequent years. Yet many vulnerable industries, such as textiles and steel, fought a losing battle against imports. Furthermore, the over-primed economy at the end of the 1960s subjected producers to more import pressure. Even more telling, America's share of world and industrial exports dropped throughout the decade and afterward, yielding to European and Japanese products.[9] Kennedy and Johnson were unable to maintain American competitive dominance in many trade sectors.

In order to promote rising sectors, Kennedy focused on lowering Common Market barriers, but his export drive ran headlong into Western Europe's efforts at integration. Exports of chemicals, transportation equipment, and machinery gained in Western Europe, but agriculture was a loser. Although U.S. farm exports rose after the imposition of the CAP, higher sales of non-levy crops and greater European consumption explain the improvement. The CAP almost halved U.S. grains, rice, and poultry sales, dropping by over one-fifth the American share of the Six's market by the last half of the 1960s. Just as portentous, the Common Market also began to compete with America in farm trade. The world's largest poultry importer in 1962, the Six became the biggest exporter within twenty years, and also gained on U.S. grain sales. Not surprisingly, America's agricultural surplus with the Common Market sank during the 1970s.[10] The CAP's trade-diversionary effects blocked penetration by outsiders of EEC markets, chalking up the most significant defeat for the Kennedy-Johnson trade policy and increasingly becoming key points of discord among the allies in subsequent decades at GATT negotiations.

In addition, the U.S. approach to the Third World sputtered, again revealing America's falling powers of persuasion. Refusing to end preferential tariff treatment for its associated territories, the Common Market nullified TEA authority to divert Latin American tropical goods exports to markets other than the United States. A more long-standing setback occurred through UNCTAD, in which all countries—except America—embraced the preference system for manufactures from the periphery. To his credit, Johnson eventually relented, but the generalized tariff arrangement advocated by Washington fell short of Third World hopes and needs. Just as significant, other nations either defeated or changed American policy toward the poor nations; the United States lacked viable

and universally acceptable solutions to the export and development problems of the South. Rather than America, other nations,
including the Common Market and the LDCs, had blazed the way
in the search for answers to poverty in the periphery.

Resistance to U.S. policy showed that Kennedy and Johnson
overplayed their global trade and financial cards in trying to accomplish American aims. Promising trade expansion once the Six
reduced tariffs, both presidents appeared either naive or unrealistic
in formulating international trade policy. They neglected domestic
restraints on European officials and the impact of Gaullist obstructionism on Common Market institutions. In a related fashion, the
foreign policy executive did not grasp the fact that the Six could
not—and would not—dismantle the CAP, the common external
tariff, or the AOC system for former African colonies for a vague
Atlantic partnership. The presidents slighted the very political
foundation of the Common Market and its emerging infrastruc-
ture, which, in trade, rested on French-West German quid pro
quos over control of internal farm and industrial markets.[11] In
addition, the two presidents would not devalue the dollar, abandon U.S. monetary hegemony, or accept the dollar as one of
several reserve currencies. Their refusals maintained an overvalued
dollar, curbed exports, and eventually led to the collapse of the
Bretton Woods system in 1971. Presiding over America in an era
of self-confidence, Kennedy and Johnson led the country down a
path of exaggerated hopes doomed to inevitable disappointment,
believing that the United States could maintain high levels of
spending and its hegemony in international finance and trade,
much as it had since the end of the Second World War. But they
soon discovered that times had changed, and so had American
power.

To be sure, the United States was no innocent victim of European manipulation, suffering unjustly at the hands of Common
Market protectionism and Gaullist political antics, as the market
school contends. The Six had legitimate reasons for protectionism,
especially in agriculture, in which employment was much higher
than in America. And, as statists argue, the neomercantilist United
States pursued its interests doggedly, seeking an edge in trade for
the sake of its own wealth and international payments balance.

Nor, clearly, did America coerce the Common Market into accepting U.S. policies, as class conflict scholars assert, because the United States was no longer capable of doing so. America confronted a Common Market trade bloc that was as liberal-minded, but also as neomercantilistic, as the United States.[12] Kennedy anticipated EEC protectionism, but presumed he could overcome it by shaping the policy of the Six with the fair-trade doctrine. He was wrong.

Thus, America could not permanently and greatly expand its trade surplus, a major goal neither Kennedy nor his successor ever realized, as other nations benefited in commerce with the United States. The merchandise trade surplus of $6.8 billion in 1964 plummeted to -$6.4 billion by 1972, with only a few aberrant surpluses afterward, before incurring the huge deficits of the 1980s. An inflated dollar, consumerism, imports of high-priced oil, and investment abroad hurt the trade balance. But the failure to lower Common Market trade barriers at the Kennedy Round, in order to help efficient U.S. competitors sell their goods, played a significant role in enlarging the deficits. Meanwhile, the exports of the Six, Outer Seven, Canada, and Japan outpaced U.S. overseas sales after the Kennedy Round. And, as America's trade deficit sprouted to tremendous proportions, the Common Market enjoyed an overall international trade surplus. The United States indeed had a bilateral edge with the Six, and this advantage actually expanded during the 1970s. Yet the surplus was not large enough to overcome either the nation's trade debit with Japan, Canada, West Germany, and several LDCs, or aid and NATO expenditures, which cost America so dearly as the alliance leader.[13] The figures reveal that, led by the Six, America's trade partners helped compromise the statist goal of boosting the U.S. trade surplus.

Kennedy and Johnson also failed to correct the balance-of-payments deficit. In 1962, this shortfall had amounted to $3.6 billion. Ten years later it was $11.2 billion, and boomed thereafter, despite periods of less military spending before the Reagan years. Again, higher oil prices, inflation, and the breakdown of the international monetary system were partly to blame, but the concessions granted at the Kennedy Round, and the rising strength of the Common Market and Japan, were also responsible.[14] Reducing the deficit had been the major goal in the foreign economic policy of Eisenhower, Kennedy, and Johnson. None of them could prevent it from swelling out of control. That trade was a panacea for the payments imbalance was another misplaced and overblown idea; the deteriorating American deficit was perhaps the most prominent loss on the Kennedy-Johnson balance sheet.

The inability of America to meet the goals of the Trade Expansion Act—enhancing competitiveness, penetrating the EEC, helping Third World development, boosting the trade surplus, and lessening the payments deficit—signified that U.S. objectives had not been achieved. To be sure, America accomplished some of its ambitions, in that the entire trade regime stayed open and most system participants benefited. But most other goals, both economic and political, fell short of attainment. The impotence of U.S. leaders to dictate terms at GATT, or forestall the nation's sinking trade and payments fortunes, attested to failure. And, unlike the early postwar era of U.S. hegemony, other nations in the alliance now constrained American actions. The Kennedy Round revealed this new predicament. As an example of muscle-flexing, writes political economist Andrew Shonfield, the GATT conference was "a curiously unsatisfying one for [America,] the hegemonial [sic] power."[15] The United States had grown weaker relative to others, a trend that would persist into the years ahead.

Surely, though, America was no weakling, but one of the strongest among the strong, as power had become more equitably distributed in the Western trade order due to the emergence of the European Common Market. Like other observers, historian Paul Kennedy views the decline in the United States' relative wealth, output, and trade as predictable, as competitors recovered from the war. In other words, America was not really producing less, others just made more. As political scientist Stephen Krasner adds, the United States was not a second-rater, but "became more like a normal nation-state. No longer does American power dominate in virtually every issue-area. No longer can the U.S. simply impose its will on others."[16] In sum, the United States was a victim of its own making, furthers David Calleo, in that the decline of American power was an inevitable product of the very triumph of the liberal, hegemonic economic system that the United States established after the war. The beneficiaries of this system were Ameri-

ca's major allies, which soon began to transform the postwar
hierarchy of power among the capitalist nations. Thus, the United
States responded to the Six by trying, according to columnist
Joseph Kraft, to plug "into the dynamism of Western Europe and
the Common Market: the Old World called in to redress the
balance of the New."[17] The flourishing trade regime attested to
the success of this approach, guided by the balanced fair-trade
doctrine. Yet by the end of the decade, such observers as former
White House aide Francis Bator wondered if the alliance could
"avoid the risk of an economic cold war between a growing EEC
and ourselves."[18] His anxiety addressed the arrival of the Common Market as a main player on the international trade stage.

The Common Market's power in the GATT trade regime fulfilled an important American postwar objective, even as the Six
became a trade rival for the United States. Justifiably content that
its leadership had made Western European (and Japanese) recovery complete, the United States nonetheless eyed the future, through
its foreign trade lens, with apprehension by the late 1960s. By this
time, it was clear that overseas trade with the allies and others was
not providing enough revenue to pay for America's international
expenditures, correct deficiencies in the domestic economy, further
Third World development, and maintain stability in the postwar
monetary system. The United States continued to trade, but could
not forestall its fading global economic fortunes, of which John
Kennedy had so fervently warned years before. At the time, however, he had not realized that the American retreat was already
underway.

NOTES

Introduction

1. For the relative decline thesis, see Geir Lundestad, *The American "Empire"* (Oslo: Norwegian University Press, 1990), pp. 85–99, 189n138; Paul Kennedy, *The Rise and Fall of the Great Powers: Economic Change and Military Conflict from 1500 to 2000* (New York: Random House, 1987); David P. Calleo, *Beyond American Hegemony* (New York: The Twentieth Century Fund, 1987); Richard Bolling and John Bowles, *America's Competitive Edge: How to Get Our Country Moving Again* (New York: McGraw-Hill, 1982). For dissenting views, see Joseph Nye, Jr., *Bound to Lead: The Changing Nature of American Power* (New York: Basic Books, 1990); Richard Rosecrance, *America's Economic Resurgence: A Bold New Strategy* (New York: Harper and Row, 1990).

2. David P. Calleo, *The Atlantic Fantasy: The U.S., NATO, and Europe* (Baltimore: Johns Hopkins University Press, 1970), p. x. See also Charles S. Maier, "The Politics of Productivity: Foundations of American International Economic Policy after World War II" in *Between Power and Plenty,* edited by Peter J. Katzenstein (Madison: University of Wisconsin Press, 1978), p. 46. Recent scholarship by "European revisionists" has argued that Western Europe, instead of following policy mandated from Washington, shaped much of its own foreign, economic, and political agendas in the early cold war years. Europeans often persuaded America to take a certain course, frequently leading the way on major issues, such as confronting the Soviet Union, forming NATO, establishing and operating the Marshall Plan, and easing export restraints on East-West trade. Although occasionally prone to exaggeration, this argument is noteworthy for its attack on prior American-centric scholarship and for its revelations about the pluralism in the Western alliance. For a sampling, see Fraser Harbutt, *The Iron Curtain: Churchill, America, and the Origins of the Cold War* (New York: Oxford University Press, 1986); Alan Milward, *The Reconstruction of Western Europe* (Berkeley: University of California Press, 1984); Geir Lundestad, "Empire by Invitation? The United States and Western Europe, 1945–1952," *Journal of Peace Research* 23 (1986):263–277; Tor Egil Forland, "Beyond the Numbers Game: A Reinterpretation of Cold War Economic Warfare Politics," paper given

at Society for Historians of American Foreign Relations meeting, June 21, 1991, Washington D.C. For excerpts from many of these and other works, see Charles S. Maier, ed., *The Cold War in Europe: Era of a Divided Continent* (New York: Markus Wiener Publishing, 1991).

3. This definition of hegemony is drawn from Christopher Chase-Dunn, *Global Formation: Structures of the World-Economy* (Cambridge: Basil Blackwell, 1989), pp. 169–170, 185; Immanuel Wallerstein, *The Politics of the World-Economy: The States, the Movements, and the Civilizations* (Cambridge: Cambridge University Press, 1984), pp. 38–40. Both scholars place the period of U.S. hegemony from 1945 to about 1970, although Chase-Dunn claims that American economic hegemony began to fall as early as 1950. Geir Lundestad prefers to describe American hegemony as an "empire." For a discussion of hegemony and empire, see Lundestad, *The American "Empire,"* pp. 37–39, and especially p. 181n18.

4. Richard N. Cooper, "Trade Policy as Foreign Policy" in *U.S. Trade Policies in a Changing World Economy,* edited by Robert M. Stern (Cambridge, Mass.: MIT Press, 1987), p. 292; Maier, "The Politics of Productivity," pp. 24–25; Robert Pollard, *Economic Security and the Origins of the Cold War, 1945–1950* (New York: Columbia University Press, 1985), pp. 11–14; Randall Bennett Woods, *The Changing of the Guard: Anglo-American Relations, 1941–1946* (Chapel Hill: University of North Carolina Press, 1990), chap. 1.

5. Bruce Cumings, *The Origins of the Korean War, Vol. II: The Roaring of the Cataract, 1947–1950* (Princeton: Princeton University Press, 1990), p. 12. Despite the sophistication of such interpretations as neocorporatism and postrevisionism, for instance, debate has not created a satisfied consensus (and perhaps never will) on the origins of the cold war, or, even more general, on the motives of American foreign policy. For a view that urges a new methodology using various levels-of-analysis as a way to solve some of the debate, see Stephen E. Pelz, "A Taxonomy for American Diplomatic History," *Journal of Interdisciplinary History* 19 (Autumn 1988):259–276.

6. For the four sources, see Pelz, "A Taxonomy." For a survey of decision-making factors, see James E. Dougherty and Robert L. Pfaltzgraff, Jr., *Contending Theories of International Relations: A Comprehensive Survey,* 2d ed. (New York: Harper and Row, 1981). Cumings, *Origins of the Korean War, Vol. II,* pp. 13–23, develops a similar "world systems theory" which integrates global, nation-state, and societal factors into his study of the Korean War.

7. Stephen E. Pelz, chap. 4 of unpublished manuscript; Jeffry A. Frieden and David A. Lake, "Introduction: International Politics and International Economies" in *International Political Economy: Perspectives on Global Power and Wealth,* edited by Jeffry A. Frieden and David A. Lake (New York: St. Martin's Press, 1991), p. 5. For a historiography of diplomatic history interpretations, see essays in Richard Dean Burns, "Overviews: Diplomatic Surveys, Themes, and Theories," in *Guide to American Foreign Relations Since 1700,* edited by Richard Dean Burns (Santa Barbara, Calif.: ABC-CLIO, 1983) and Jerald Combs, *The History of American Foreign Policy* (New York: Knopf, 1986).

8. Robert Gilpin, *The Political Economy of International Relations* (Princeton: Princeton University Press, 1987), pp. 26–30; Lake and Frieden, "Introduction," pp. 5–7. For market school analysis, see H. Peter Gray, *International Trade,*

Investment, and Payments (Boston: Houghton Mifflin, 1979); Cletus C. Coughlin, K. Alec Chrystal, and Geoffrey E. Wood, "Protectionist Trade Policies: A Survey of Theory, Evidence, and Rationale," in *International Political Economy*, edited by Frieden and Lake, pp. 18–33; and many economics textbooks.

9. Frieden and Lake, "Introduction," pp. 5–7; Robert B. Reich, "Beyond Free Trade," *Foreign Affairs* 61 (Spring 1983):777; Leland B. Yeager and David G. Tuerck, *Trade Policy and the Price System* (Scranton, Pa.: International Textbook, 1966), p. 42; Benjamin J. Cohen, *The Question of Imperialism: The Political Economy of Dominance and Dependence* (New York: Basic Books, 1973), pp. 170–218.

10. Maier, "The Politics of Productivity," p. 45, explains that U.S. leaders campaigned for productionism because agreement on growth and efficiency had worked in America to solve conflicts between business and government during the New Deal and wartime era. Class conflict scholars claim that America used productionism to disguise its pursuit of hegemony through "free-trade imperialism." See Thomas J. McCormick, *America's Half Century: United States Foreign Policy in the Cold War* (Baltimore: Johns Hopkins University Press, 1989), pp. 49–51. But Maier implies that McCormick's view is simplistic and ignores the domestic productionist political accommodation before the war. A continuity between the New Deal and postwar economic planning is found in Michael J. Hogan, *The Marshall Plan: America, Britain, and the Reconstruction of Western Europe, 1947–1952* (Cambridge: Cambridge University Press, 1987), pp. 2–25. For an explanation of the adoption of growth (productionism) by policymakers, see Alan Wolfe, *America's Impasse: The Rise and Fall of the Politics of Growth* (New York: Pantheon, 1981).

11. Benjamin J. Cohen, "The Industrial World," in *American Foreign Economic Policy: Essays and Comments*, edited by Benjamin J. Cohen (New York: Harper and Row, 1968); Gerard Curzon and Victoria Curzon, "The Management of Trade Relations in the GATT," in *International Economic Relations of the Western World, 1959–1971*, vol. 1, *Politics and Trade*, edited by Andrew Shonfield (London: Oxford University Press, 1976); Harald Malmgren, "The United States," in *Economic Foreign Policies of Industrial States*, edited by Wilfrid L. Kohl (Lexington, Mass.: D. C. Heath, 1977), p. 21; John Spanier, *American Foreign Policy Since World War II*, 9th ed. (New York: Holt, Rinehart, and Winston, 1983), pp. 132–145.

12. Chase-Dunn, *Global Formation*, p. 3, chap. 10; Gilpin, *Political Economy*, p. 263; Frieden and Lake, "Introduction," pp. 7–9; Walter Goldstein, "U.S. Economic Penetration of Western Europe," in *Testing Theories of Economic Imperialism*, edited by Steven J. Rosen and James R. Kurth (Lexington, Mass.: D. C. Heath, 1974), p. 214; James Lee Ray, "The 'World System' and the Global Political System: A Crucial Relationship," in *Foreign Policy and the Modern World-System*, edited by Pat McGowan and Charles W. Kegley (Beverly Hills, Calif.: Sage, 1983), p. 14; Thomas McCormick, "World Systems," *Journal of American History* 77 (June 1990):125–132; Immanuel Wallerstein, *Modern World System II* (New York: Academic Press, 1974–1980); Immanuel Wallerstein, *The Capitalist World Economy* (New York: Cambridge University Press, 1978); Wallerstein, *Politics of World-Economy*, p. 15.

13. D. K. Forbes, *The Geography of Underdevelopment: A Critical Survey* (Baltimore: Johns Hopkins University Press, 1984), pp. 71, 77, 92; Albert Szymanski, *The Logic of Imperialism* (New York: Praeger, 1981), pp. 69–83; Gunnar Myrdal, *Rich Lands and Poor: The Road to World Prosperity* (New York: Harper and Row, 1957); Raul Prebisch, *The Economic Development of Latin America and Its Principal Problems* (New York: United Nations, 1950); Samir Amin, *Unequal Development: An Essay on the Social Development of Peripheral Capitalism* (New York: Monthly Review Press, 1976); Arghiri Emmanuel, *Unequal Exchange: A Study of Imperialism* (New York: Monthly Review Press, 1972); Chase-Dunn, *Global Formation*, p. 80.

14. Stephen E. Ambrose, *Rise to Globalism: American Foreign Policy Since 1938*, 5th rev. ed. (New York: Penguin, 1988); Lloyd C. Gardner, Walter LaFeber, and Thomas J. McCormick, *Creation of the American Empire: U.S. Diplomatic History* (Chicago: Rand-McNally, 1973); David Horowitz, ed., *Corporations and the Cold War* (New York: Monthly Review Press, 1969); Gabriel Kolko, *The Roots of American Foreign Policy: An Analysis of Power and Purpose* (Boston: Beacon Press, 1969); Walter LaFeber, *America, Russia, and the Cold War: 1945–1980*, 5th ed. (New York: Wiley, 1985); Harry Magdoff, *The Age of Imperialism: The Economics of U.S. Foreign Policy* (New York: Modern Reader, 1969); Ernest Mandel, *Europe and America: Contradictions of Imperialism* (New York: New Left Books, 1970); McCormick, *America's Half Century;* William A. Williams, *The Tragedy of American Diplomacy* (New York: Dell, 1972).

15. McCormick, *America's Half Century*, pp. 49–51.

16. Gilpin, *Political Economy*, pp. 26, 32; David A. Lake, *Power, Protection, and Free Trade: International Sources of U.S. Commercial Strategy, 1887–1939* (Ithaca, N.Y.: Cornell University Press, 1988), p. 19; Susan Strange, "Protectionism and World Politics," *International Organization* 39 (Spring 1985):236.

17. Chase-Dunn, *Global Formation*, p. 76. See also Kal J. Holsti, "Politics in Command: Foreign Trade as National Security Policy," *International Organization* 40 (Summer 1986):644, 669; Gilpin, *Political Economy*, p. 32.

18. Lake, *Power*, pp. 9–10; Stephen D. Krasner, "State Power and the Structure of International Trade," in *International Political Economy*, edited by Frieden and Lake, pp. 49–67; Stephen D. Krasner, "The Tokyo Round: Particularistic Interests and Prospects for Stability in the Global Trading System," *International Studies Quarterly* 23 (December 1979):495. For the theory of hegemonic stability, which has come under attack by international relations theorists, see Gilpin, *Political Economy*, pp. 72–80.

19. McCormick, *America's Half Century*, pp. 5–7, 51.

20. Gilpin, *Political Economy*, pp. 74–90; John L. Gaddis, "The Emerging Post-Revisionist Synthesis in the Origins of the Cold War," *Diplomatic History* 7 (Summer 1983); David Calleo, *The Imperious Economy* (Cambridge, Mass.: Harvard University Press, 1982); David P. Calleo and Benjamin M. Rowland, *America and the World Political Economy: Atlantic Dreams and National Realities* (Bloomington: Indiana University Press, 1973); Pollard, *Economic Security;* Robert A. Pollard and Samuel F. Wells, Jr., "1945–1960: The Era of American Hegemony," in *Economics and World Power: An Assessment of American Diplo-*

macy Since 1789, edited by William H. Becker and Samuel F. Wells, Jr. (New York: Columbia University Press, 1984).

21. Raymond A. Bauer, Ithiel de Sola Pool, and Anthony Lewis Dexter, *American Business and Public Policy: The Politics of Foreign Trade,* 2d ed. (New York: Aldine, 1972), p. 1.

22. John Edward Ray, "Changing Patterns of Protectionism: The Fall in Tariffs and the Rise in Non-Tariff Barriers," in *International Political Economy,* edited by Frieden and Lake, pp. 339–340; Judith L. Goldstein, "A Re-Examination of American Trade Policy: An Inquiry into the Causes of Protectionism," Ph.D. dissertation, UCLA, 1983, p. 419.

23. Harry Shutt, *The Myth of Free Trade: Patterns of Protectionism Since 1945* (Oxford: Basil Blackwell, 1985), p. 3.

24. Ibid., pp. 16–17, 29–36. For GATT rules and norms, see Jock A. Finlayson and Mark W. Zacher, "The GATT and the Regulation of Trade Barriers: Regime Dynamics and Functions," in *International Regimes,* edited by Stephen D. Krasner (Ithaca, N.Y.: Cornell University Press, 1983), p. 287; Robert O. Keohane, *After Hegemony: Cooperation and Discord in the World Political Economy* (Princeton: Princeton University Press, 1984); John G. Ruggie, "International Regimes, Transactions, and Change: Embedded Liberalism in the Postwar Economic Order," in *International Regimes,* edited by Krasner, p. 215; Charles Lipson, "The Transformation of Trade: The Sources and Effects of Regime Change," in *International Regimes,* edited by Krasner, pp. 240–243; Vernon L. Sorenson, "Contradictions in U.S. Trade Policy," in *U.S. Trade Policy and Agricultural Exports,* Iowa State University Center for Agricultural and Rural Development (Ames: Iowa State University Press, 1973), pp. 184–185. Scholars agree that protectionism coexisted with trade liberalism under GATT. Ruggie argues that America "sought *some* notion of comparative advantage [but] *also* promised to minimize socially disruptive domestic adjustment costs as well as any national economic and political vulnerabilities" arising from freer trade. He terms this "embedded liberalism." Lipson, too, notes that the "GATT regime does not contemplate a world in which commercial policies are based on the austere pursuit of comparative advantage."

25. Lake, *Power,* pp. 73, 83–84; Frieden and Lake, "Introduction," pp. 11–15.

26. Lake, *Power,* pp. 71–72; Robert Baldwin, *The Political Economy of U.S. Import Policy* (Cambridge, Mass.: MIT Press, 1985), pp. 120–122; Cumings, *The Korean War, Vol. II,* pp. 20–21.

27. Lake, *Power,* pp. 13, 19, 69–70; Gray, *International Trade,* p. 198; Coughlin, Chrystal, and Wood, "Protectionist Trade Policies," pp. 27–28. On the terms *protection-* or *trade-biased,* see Robert L. Allen and Ingo Walter, "The Formation of United States Trade Policy: Retrospect and Prospect," *Bulletin of New York University Graduate School of Business Administration* (1971):5–6. The choice made by politicians to support protectionism because of voter pressure is called "endogenous tariff behavior."

28. Robert A. Pastor, *Congress and the Politics of U.S. Foreign Economic Policy* (Berkeley: University of California Press, 1980), pp. 10–48; Stephen D. Cohen, *The Making of United States International Economic Policy: Principles, Problems, and Proposals for Reform,* 2d ed. (New York: Praeger, 1981), p. 17;

Peter J. Katzenstein, "International Relations and Domestic Structures: Foreign Economic Policies of Advanced Industrial States," *International Organization* 30 (Winter 1976):1–45; Peter J. Katzenstein, "Introduction," in *Between Power and Plenty*, edited by Katzenstein; Stephen D. Krasner, "U.S. Commercial and Monetary Policy: Unravelling the Paradox of External Strength and Internal Weakness," in *Between Power and Plenty*, edited by Katzenstein, pp. 52–53, 57–65; Vinod K. Aggarwal, *Liberal Protectionism: The International Politics of Organized Textile Trade* (Berkeley: University of California Press, 1985), pp. 34–35; I. M. Destler, *American Trade Politics: System Under Stress* (New York: Twentieth Century Fund, 1986), p. xiii; Richard C. Snyder, H. W. Bruck, and Burton Sapin, *Foreign Policy Decision-making: An Approach to the Study of International Politics* (Glencoe, Ill.: Free Press of Glencoe, 1962), p. 6.

29. Baldwin, *Political Economy of Import Policy*, p. 176; Magee and Young, "Endogenous Protection," p. 45. Historians analyzing other topics have referred to the clash in objectives between the foreign policy executive and representative elements in a similar fashion, but with different terms. See, for example, Woods, *A Changing of the Guard*, pp. 1–8, multilateralism versus nationalism-isolationism, and Cumings, *The Korean War, Vol. II*, pp. 23–32, internationalism/imperialism versus expansionism/nationalism.

30. Theodore J. Lowi, *The End of Liberalism: Ideology, Policy and the Crisis of Public Authority* (New York: W. W. Norton, 1969), pp. 42–45; Theodore J. Lowi, "American Business and Public Policy: Case Studies and Political Theory," *World Politics* 16 (July 1964):679; David Knoke, "Power Structures," in *The Handbook of Political Behavior*, vol. 3, edited by Samuel L. Long (New York: Plenum Press, 1981), pp. 281–285; Katzenstein, "Introduction," pp. 17–18; Pastor, *Congress*, pp. 5, 13–14; Krasner, "U.S. Commercial and Monetary Policy," p. 65; Destler, *American Trade Politics*, pp. 2–3. Cohen, *Making of U.S. International Economic Policy*, pp. 85–104.

31. E. E. Schattschneider, *Politics, Pressures, and the Tariff: A Study of Free Enterprise in Pressure Politics, as Shown in the 1929–1930 Revision of the Tariff* (Hamden, Conn.: Archon Books, 1963); Stefanie Ann Lenway, *The Politics of U.S. International Trade: Protection, Expansion, and Escape* (Marshfield, Mass.: Pitman 1985), pp. 26–33; Pastor, *Congress*, pp. 43–48; Walker and McGowan, "U.S. Foreign Economic Policy Formation," pp. 212–213; William Zimmerman, "Issue Area and Foreign-Policy Process: A Research Note in Search of a General Theory," *American Political Science Review* 67 (December 1973):1204–1212. For an analysis of interest group behavior, see Bauer, de Sola Pool, and Dexter, *American Business;* Frieden and Lake, "Introduction," p. 7.

32. Knoke, "Power Structures" pp. 316–317; Stephen G. Walker and Pat McGowan, "U.S. Foreign Economic Policy Formation: Neo-Marxist and Neo-pluralist Perspectives," in *America in a Changing World Political Economy*, edited by William P. Avery and David P. Rapkin (New York: Longman, 1982), p. 210; Amos Perlmutter, "The Presidential Political Center and Foreign Policy: A Critique of the Revisionist and Bureaucratic-Political Orientations," *World Politics* 27 (October 1974):89–91; C. Wright Mills, *The Power Elite* (New York: Oxford University Press, 1959); McCormick, *America's Half Century*, pp. 7–16.

33. Ibid., pp. 8–10.

34. Calleo and Rowland, *America and the World Political Economy*, pp. 172–175; Louis Galambos, "Technology, Political Economy, and Professionalization: Central Themes of the Organizational Synthesis," *Business History Review* 57 (Winter 1983):479–484; Michael J. Hogan, "Corporatism: A Positive Appraisal," *Diplomatic History* 10 (Fall 1986):363–372; Hogan, *Marshall Plan*, pp. 2–3; Theodore J. Lowi, "The Public Philosophy: Interest Group-Liberalism," *American Political Science Review* 61 (March 1967):12, 17, 22; Thomas J. McCormick, "Drift or Mastery? A Corporatist Synthesis for American Diplomatic History," *Reviews in American History* 10 (December 1982):323–324; Philippe C. Schmitter, "Still the Century of Corporatism?," in *The New Corporatism*, edited by Frederick Pike (South Bend, Ind.: University of Notre Dame Press, 1974); Philippe C. Schmitter and Gerhard Lehmbruch, eds., *Trends Toward Corporatist Intermediation* (London: Sage Publications, 1979). For a dissenting view, see Robert H. Salisbury, "Why No Corporatism in America?," in *Trends Toward Corporatist Intermediation*, edited by Schmitter and Lehmbruch.

35. G. John Ikenberry, David A. Lake, and Michael Mastanduno, "Introduction: Approaches to Explaining American Foreign Economic Policy," in *The State and American Foreign Economic Policy*, edited by G. John Ikenberry, David A. Lake, and Michael Mastanduno (Ithaca, N.Y.: Cornell University Press, 1988), p. 13; Holsti, "Politics in Command," p. 669; Joanne Gowa, "Public Goods and Political Institutions: Trade and Monetary Processes in the United States," in *The State and American Foreign Economic Policy*, edited by Ikenberry, Lake, and Mastanduno, p. 15.

36. Katzenstein, "Introduction," p. 18; Pastor, *Congress*, pp. 5, 49–62, 345–348; William H. Becker, "American Manufacturers and Foreign Markets, 1870–1900: Business Historians and the 'New Economic Determinists,' " *Business History Review* 47 (Fall 1973):466–481.

37. Joan E. Spero, *The Politics of International Economic Relations*, 3d ed. (New York: St. Martin's Press, 1985), p. 122. Analyses of the conflicting political-ideological arena (multilateralism versus nationalism, internationalism versus isolationism, etc.) also point to a more general dualism in international affairs. See especially the constructs of Cumings and Woods in note 28. Other studies describe the dualism in trade: Aggarwal, *Liberal Protectionism*, "liberal protectionism"; Lenway, *The Politics of U.S. International Trade*, "pragmatic liberalism"; Ruggie, "International Regimes," p. 215, "embedded liberalism"; Robert W. Barrie, "Congress and the Executive: The Making of U.S. Foreign Trade Policy," Ph.D. dissertation, University of Minnesota, 1968, p. 192; Judith Goldstein, "The Political Economy of Trade: Institutions of Protection," *American Political Science Review* 80 (March 1986):165. See also Susan Strange, "The Persistent Myth of Lost Hegemony," *International Organization* 41 (Autumn 1987):572–574. Strange, like many scholars, sees the dualism as contradictory.

38. McCormick, *America's Half Century*, p. 125; Robert T. Green and James M. Lutz, *The United States and World Trade: Changing Patterns and Dimensions* (New York: Praeger, 1978), p. 1; William R. Thompson, "The World Economy, the Long Cycle, and the Question of World-System Time," in *Foreign Policy and the Modern World-System*, edited by McGowan and Kegley, pp. 40–41.

1. Seeds of the Fair-Trade Doctrine, 1945–1960

1. Richard N. Gardner, *Sterling-Dollar Diplomacy: The Origins and Prospects of Our International Economic Order*, 2d ed. (New York: McGraw-Hill, 1969), chaps. 1–2; Pollard and Wells, "1945–1960," pp. 333–339; Robert Dallek, *Franklin D. Roosevelt and American Foreign Policy, 1932–1945* (New York: Oxford University Press, 1979), p. 283; Pollard, *Economic Security*, pp. 10–17; Woods, *The Changing of the Guard*, chaps. 1, 5, 7, 8,

2. Pollard, *Economic Security*, p. 14. See also U.S. Department of Commerce, *Historical Statistics of the United States: Colonial Times to 1970* (Washington, D.C.: U.S. Government Printing Office, 1975), pt. II, p. 887; Harry S. Truman, *Memoirs: Years of Trial and Hope*, vol. 2 (Garden City, N.Y.: Doubleday, 1956), p. 111; Dean Acheson, "The Interest of the American Businessman in International Trade," *Vital Speeches of the Day*, no. 11, February 15, 1945, (New York: City News, 1945), p. 264; Woods, *The Changing of the Guard*, p. 13.

3. Burton I. Kaufman, *Trade and Aid: Eisenhower's Foreign Economic Policy, 1953–1961* (Baltimore: Johns Hopkins University Press, 1982), p. 16.

4. Spero, *Politics of International Economic Relations*, pp. 94–96; Gardner, *Sterling-Dollar Diplomacy*, chaps. 3, 8, 17 and pp. 348–361; 95–96; F. V. Meyer, *International Trade Policy* (London: Croom Helm, 1978), pp. 72–73, 136–141; Lipson, "The Transformation of Trade," pp. 240–243; Pastor, *Congress*, pp. 78, 98–99; William A. Brown, Jr., *The United States and the Restoration of World Trade* (Washington, D.C.: Brookings Institution, 1950), chap. 9; Clair Wilcox, *A Charter for World Trade* (New York: Macmillan, 1949), pp. 72–73, 199–200. GATT convened in Geneva, and with a few early exceptions, has met there ever since. It was more palatable to American leaders than the ITO, which, in addition to the areas of involvement mentioned in the text, also encompassed rules on trade policy, investment, and economic development. Not only did the ITO require American oversight, but in the charged anticommunist atmosphere of the late 1940s, such issues as employment and commodity agreements, under government management, smacked too much of socialism to make ratification by Congress possible. Thus, the more limited GATT was maintained and amended, though much to the disappointment of such ITO visionaries in the State Department as William Clayton and Clair Wilcox.

5. Wilcox, *Charter for World Trade*, p. 65; Kenneth W. Dam, *The GATT: Law and International Economic Organization* (Chicago: University of Chicago Press, 1970), p. 56; Gerard Curzon, *Multilateral Commercial Diplomacy: The General Agreement on Tariffs and Trade and Its Impact on National Commercial Policies and Techniques* (New York: Praeger, 1965). Italy joined GATT in 1949, West Germany in 1951, and Japan in 1955.

6. For international monetary issues, see Fred L. Block, *The Origins of International Economic Disorder: A Study of United States International Monetary Policy from World War II to the Present* (Berkeley: University of California Press, 1977); Alfred E. Eckes, Jr., *The Search for Solvency: Bretton Woods and the International Monetary System, 1941–1971* (Austin: University of Texas Press, 1975); William Borden, "Defending Hegemony: American Foreign Economic Policy," in *Kennedy's Quest for Victory: American Foreign Policy, 1961–1963*,

edited by Thomas G. Paterson (New York: Oxford University Press, 1989), pp. 57–59; Spero, *Politics of International Economic Relations,* pp. 41–44.

7. Ibid., pp. 42–43, 97, 126; Pollard and Wells, "1945–1960," p. 346; Hogan, *The Marshall Plan,* pp. 126–127; M. M. Postan, *An Economic History of Western Europe, 1945–1964* (London: Methuen, 1967), pp. 98–99; Merry Bromberger and Serge Bromberger, *Jean Monnet and the United States of Europe* (New York: Coward-McCann, 1969), chaps. 8, 10; Paul-Henri Spaak, *The Continuing Battle: Memoirs of a European, 1936–1966* (London: Weidenfeld and Nicolson, 1971), pp. 207–252.

8. William Diebold, Jr., "The Process of European Integration," in *The Common Market: Progress and Controversy* edited by Lawrence B. Krause (Englewood Cliffs, N.J.: Prentice-Hall, 1964), p. 34; Emile Benoit, *Europe at Sixes and Sevens: The Common Market, the Free Trade Association, and the United States* (New York: Columbia University Press, 1961), pp. 5, 29–30.

9. Harry G. Johnson, "Mercantilism: Past, Present, and Future," *Journal of World Trade Law* 8 (January-February 1974):12–13; Benoit, *Europe,* p. 24; Arnold Wolfers, "Integration in the West: The Conflict of Perspectives," in *The Atlantic Community: Progress and Prospect,* edited by Francis O. Wilcox and H. Field Haviland (New York: Praeger, 1964), p. 245; Meyer, *International Trade,* pp. 160–161. For details of the Treaty of Rome, see Richard Vaughan, *Twentieth-Century Europe: Paths to Unity* (London: Croom Helm, 1979), pp. 134–143.

10. Statistics are from Max J. Wasserman, Charles W. Hultman, and Russell F. Moore, *The Common Market and American Business* (New York: Simmons-Boardman, 1964), pp. 59, 69; B. R. Mitchell, *European Historical Statistics, 1750–1970* (New York: Columbia University Press, 1978), pp. 182, 308–309; Postan, *An Economic History,* pp. 11, 90–91; Alfred Grosser, *The Western Alliance: European-American Relations Since 1945* (New York: Continuum, 1980), pp. 177–178; Council on International Economic Policy, *Annual Report and International Economic Report to the President* (Washington, D.C.: CIEP, 1973), p. 4; Statistical Briefing: U.S. Trade and the Common Market, [1961]; Memorandum on Performance of U.S. Exports During the Past Decade, December 15, 1961, box 2, White House Staff Files-Howard C. Petersen, John F. Kennedy Library, Boston, Massachusetts (hereafter Petersen Files); *Historical Statistics,* pt. II, pp. 903, 905. The EFTA included the United Kingdom, Switzerland, Austria, Denmark, Norway, Sweden, and Portugal.

11. Report by the Subcommittee on Regional Economic Integration of the Council on Foreign Economic Policy to the Council, November 15, 1956, *Foreign Relations of the United States, 1955–1957,* vol. IV, (Washington, D.C.: U.S. Government Printing Office, 1986), pp. 482–486; A. W. Deporte, *Europe Between the Superpowers: The Enduring Balance* (New Haven: Yale University Press, 1979), pp. 175, 182, 189–190, 223; Pollard and Wells, "1945–1960," p. 378; LaFeber, *America,* pp. 205–209; Thomas A. Bailey, *A Diplomatic History of the American People,* 8th ed. (New York: Meredith, 1969), p. 847, chap. 54; Grosser, *The Western Alliance,* pp. 148, 168, 177; Shonfield, "International Economic Relations," p. 3; Kaufman, *Trade and Aid,* p. 188. On the undermining of British power, see Woods, *The Changing of the Guard.*

12. Benoit, *Europe,* pp. 68–71, 82–83, 92–93; Kaufman, *Trade and Aid,* p.

182; Pollard and Wells, "1945–1960," pp. 367, 387; Shonfield, "International Economic Relations," pp. 3–18; James R. Schlesinger, *The Political Economy of National Security: A Study of the Economic Aspects of the Contemporary Power Struggle* (New York: Praeger, 1960).

13. Roderick N. Grant, "The European Common Market and U. S. Trade," in *Public Policy: International Economic Problems,* vol. 11, edited by Carl J. Friedrich and Seymour E. Harris (Cambridge, Mass.: Harvard University Graduate School of Public Administration, 1961), p. 234; Randall Hinshaw, *The European Economic Community and American Trade: A Study in Atlantic Economics and Policy* (New York: Praeger, 1964), pp. 142–143; Edwin M. Martin, "New Trends in United States Economic Foreign Policy," in *Whither American Foreign Policy* in *The Annals of the American Academy of Political and Social Science,* edited by James C. Charlesworth (Philadelphia: American Academy of Political and Social Science, 1960), p. 29; Ernst H. van der Beugel, *From Marshall Aid to Atlantic Partnership: European Integration as a Concern of American Foreign Policy* (Amsterdam: Elsevier, 1966), chap. 5; Max Beloff, *The United States and the Unity of Europe* (Washington, D.C.: Brookings Institution, 1963), chaps. 6, 8, 9; Bela Belassa, "Competitiveness of American Manufacturing in World Markets," in *Problems of the Modern World Economy: Changing Patterns in Foreign Trade and Payments* (New York: W. W. Norton, 1964), p. 31.

14. Pollard, *Economic Security,* pp. 174–187; Pollard and Wells, "1945–1960," pp. 348–349; Holsti, "Politics in Command," pp. 648–652; Alfred K. Ho, *Japan's Trade Liberalization in the 1960s* (White Plains, N.Y.: International Arts and Sciences Press, 1973), pp. 5–6; Hugh Corbet, ed., *Trade Strategy and the Asian-Pacific Region* (Toronto: University of Toronto Press, 1970), pp. 51–59; *Historical Statistics,* pt. II, pp. 903, 905; Warren S. Hunsberger, *Japan and the United States in World Trade* (New York: Harper and Row, 1964), pp. 33–45, 51–55, 131–140, 257–275; Meyer, *International Trade,* pp. 142–143; Kaufman, *Trade and Aid,* pp. 39–41; William S. Borden, *The Pacific Alliance: United States Foreign Economic Policy and Japanese Trade Recovery, 1947–1955* (Madison: University of Wisconsin Press, 1984).

15. Gordon T. Stewart, " 'A Special Contiguous Country Regime': An Overview of America's Canadian Policy," *Diplomatic History* 6 (Fall 1982):348–351, 356; Harry G. Johnson, *Canada in a Changing World Economy* (Toronto: University of Toronto Press, 1962), pp. 5–6, 32, 50; Mitchell Sharp, "Canada's Independence and U. S. Domination," in *U.S.-Canadian Economic Relations: Next Step?,* edited by Edward R. Fried and Philip H. Trezise (Washington, D.C.: Brookings Institution, 1984), pp. 13, 16–17; Paul Wonnacott, *The United States and Canada: The Quest for Free Trade, An Examination of Selected Issues* (Washington, D.C.: Institute for International Economics, 1987), p. 16; B. W. Wilkinson, *Canada's International Trade: An Analysis of Recent Trends and Patterns* (Quebec: Canadian Trade Committee, Private Planning Association of Canada, 1968), p. 29; *Historical Statistics,* pt. II, pp. 903, 905; J. L. Granatstein, "When Push Came to Shove: Canada and the United States," in *Kennedy's Quest for Victory,* edited by Paterson.

16. Spero, *Politics of International Economic Relations,* pp. 221–229; John Pincus, *Trade, Aid and Development: The Rich and Poor Nations* (New York:

McGraw-Hill, 1967), pp. 177–185; Finlayson and Zacher, "GATT and Regulation of Trade Barriers," pp. 293–295; Dam, *The GATT*, pp. 225–231; Harry G. Johnson, *Economic Policies Toward Less Developed Countries* (Washington, D.C.: Brookings Institution, 1967), p. 18.

    17. Pincus, *Trade, Aid, and Development*, pp. 233–235; Walter LaFeber, *Inevitable Revolutions: The United States in Central America* (New York: W. W. Norton, 1983), pp. 90–91; Magdoff, *The Age of Imperialism*, pp. 155–157; J. A. C. Brown, "A Brief Survey of Prospects for African Exports of Agricultural Products," in *African Primary Products and International Trade* (Edinburgh: Edinburgh University Press, 1965), pp. 1–6; Spero, *Politics of International Economic Relations*, p. 227; GATT, *International Trade, 1963* (Geneva: GATT, 1964), pp. 111, 120–132.

    18. Kaufman, *Trade and Aid*, pp. 10, 7, 88–91, 97–100, 124–131, 147–151, 163; W. W. Rostow, *Eisenhower, Kennedy, and Foreign Aid* (Austin: University of Texas Press, 1985), pp. 10, 44–49; Pollard and Wells, "1945–1960," p. 362; Aggarwal, *Liberal Protectionism*, pp. 56–72; David B. Yoffie, *Power and Protectionism: Strategies of the Newly Industrializing Countries* (New York: Columbia University Press, 1983), pp. 64–77; Position Papers for Senator Kennedy Prepared by Professor Fred Burke [Africa], 1960; Position Papers on Cuba and Latin America, 1960; Foreign Policy Memorandum, Latin America, August 30, 1960, box 993, Pre-Presidential Papers, John F. Kennedy Library, Boston, Massachusetts (hereafter PPP); *Historical Statistics*, pt. II, pp. 903, 905.

    19. The balance of payments is the total value of U. S. international economic transactions in current and capital accounts. The current account includes merchandise exports and imports, expenditures and receipts for such services as tourism and transportation, income from investments, government grants, military spending, and other remittances. The capital account shows outflows and inflows of financial assets. A deficit occurs when outflows from both accounts result in an excess of debits over credits. A settlement must be made to balance out the accounts, often in the form of payment in gold. For a breakdown of the U.S. payments balance, see Block, *Origins of International Economic Disorder*, chap. 7.

    20. Kaufman, *Trade and Aid*, pp. 176–180; Howard S. Piquet, *The U.S. Balance of Payments and International Monetary Reserves* (Washington, D.C.: American Enterprise Institute for Public Policy Research, 1966), p. 1; Spero, *Politics of International Economic Relations*, p. 44; Block, *Origins of International Economic Disorder*, p. 159.

    21. Kaufman, *Trade and Aid*, pp. 177, 180–189, 192; Seymour E. Harris, "Some Material Ideas on the Dollar Problem and the Competitive Position of the United States," in *Public Policy*, edited by Friedrich and Harris, p. 136; Block, *Origins of International Economic Disorder*, pp. 162–170.

    22. Gary M. Walton and Ross M. Robertson, *History of the American Economy*, 5th ed. (New York: Harcourt, Brace, Jovanovich, 1983), p. 633; Herbert Stein, *Presidential Economics: The Making of Economic Policy from Roosevelt to Reagan and Beyond* (New York: Simon and Schuster, 1985), pp. 86–88; Seymour E. Harris, *Economics of the Kennedy Years and a Look Ahead* (New York: Harper and Row, 1964), p. 26; E. Ray Canterbury, *Economics on a New Frontier*

(Belmont, Calif.: Wadsworth, 1968), pp. 30, 96; *Historical Statistics*, pt. I, p. 228; James N. Giglio, *The Presidency of John F. Kennedy* (Lawrence: University of Kansas Press, 1991), pp. 9, 17, 24–26.

23. *Historical Statistics*, pt. I, p. 900; Sorenson, "Contradictions in U.S. Trade Policy," pp. 185–189.

24. *Historical Statistics*, pt. II, pp. 889, 898–900; Frank W. Tuttle and Joseph M. Perry, *An Economic History of the United States* (Cincinnati: South-Western Publishing, 1970), p. 786; U.S. Senate Committee on Interstate and Foreign Commerce, *Foreign Commerce Study: U.S. Trade and the Common Market*, 86th Cong., 2d sess., 1960, pp. 217–218; Trudy H. Peterson, *Agricultural Exports, Farm Income, and the Eisenhower Administration* (Lincoln: University of Nebraska Press, 1979), pp. 27–28, 114–118; John M. Leddy, "United States Commercial Policy and the Domestic Farm Program," in *Studies in United States Commercial Policy*, edited by William B. Kelly, Jr. (Chapel Hill: University of North Carolina Press, 1963), p. 174.

25. Dallek, *Roosevelt*, pp. 84, 92; Arthur A. Stein, "The Hegemon's Dilemma: Great Britain, the United States, and the International Order," *International Organization* 38 (Spring 1984):380.

26. Pastor, *Congress*, pp. 94, 99–100; John M. Leddy and Janet L. Norwood, "The Escape Clause and Peril Points under the Trade Agreements Program," in *Studies in United States Commercial Policy*, edited by Kelly, pp. 124–146; Sorenson, "Contradictions in U.S. Trade Policy," p. 186; Dam, *GATT*, pp. 260–261; Sidney Ratner, *The Tariff in American History* (New York: D. Van Nostrand, 1972), pp. 64–65; Kaufman, *Trade and Aid*, p. 45.

27. Ibid., p. 29; see also chaps. 7, pp. 43–44, 74–76. See also Pastor, *Congress*, pp. 101–104; Harry C. Hawkins and Janet L. Norwood, "The Legislative Basis of United States Commercial Policy," in *Studies in United States Commercial Policy*, edited by Kelly, pp. 110–114; Leddy and Norwood, "Escape Clause," pp. 138–143; Bauer, de Sola Pool, and Dexter, *American Business*, p. 73.

28. Kennedy to Linda Chapman, November 20, 1959, box 727, PPP; see also Paul Samuelson Oral History, p. 63, and Seymour E. Harris Oral History, pp. 2–3, Council of Economic Advisors Oral History (hereafter CEA Oral History with last name); Myer Rashish Oral History, p. 2 (hereafter Rashish Oral History), all in John F. Kennedy Library, Boston, Massachusetts; Interview, George W. Ball, March 21, 1986, Princeton, New Jersey.

29. Kennedy to Frederick Putnam, February 11, 1954, box 654, PPP; James MacGregor Burns, *John Kennedy: A Political Profile* (New York: Harcourt, Brace and Company, 1960), p. 181; *Congressional Quarterly-Almanac*, roll calls, 5 (1949):50; 7 (1951):260; 9 (1953):210; 10 (1954):296; and 14 (1958):448.

30. Memorandum I, box 993, undated; Memorandum II, box 993, undated; Memorandum, New England Delegation to Sinclair Weeks, February 3, 1958, box 707, PPP.

31. John F. Kennedy, "Let's Fight for New England," August 8, 1952, box 93, PPP. See also Kennedy to President Eisenhower, December 19, 1956, box 681, PPP.

32. Kennedy to Frederick Putnam, February 11, 1954, box 656, PPP. See also John F. Kennedy, "New England: Promise and Problem," July 22, 1953, box 5;

Testimony of Senator John F. Kennedy Before the Senate Committee on Interstate and Foreign Commerce Upon S. 3229, Federal Fisheries Assistance Act, July 17, 1958, box 19, Papers of Theodore C. Sorensen, John F. Kennedy Library, Boston, Massachusetts (hereafter Sorensen Papers); L. J. Hart to Kennedy, June 2, 1952, box 93; JFK for U.S. Senator, *Congressional Record* Report on Kennedy, p. xiv, 1952, box 101, PPP.

33. Kennedy speech, "The Future of Massachusetts," Massachusetts State CIO Convention, October 5, 1952, box 93, PPP.

34. "Reciprocal Trade Agreements," [1952], box 102, PPP.

35. Kennedy to Edgar Brossard, April 15, 1953, box 413, PPP.

36. Kennedy to Charles Kindleberger, April 2, 1958; Kennedy to H. D. Baker, Jr., [November 1957], box 707, PPP; *Congressional Record*, vol. 99, pt. 4, May 7, 1953, A2445.

37. Adjustments to the National Trade Policy, June 22, 1954, *John F. Kennedy: A Compilation of Statements and Speeches Made During His Service in the United States Senate and House of Representatives*, 88th Cong., 2d sess., Senate Doc. No. 79 (Washington, D.C.: U.S. Government Printing Office, 1964), pp. 325, 327, 329 (hereafter *Kennedy Statements*). See also "Should an Old Massachusetts Industry Be Penalized?," *Kennedy Statements*, June 25, 1952, p. 118; *Congressional Record*, vol. 99, pt. 4, May 25, 1953, 5461.

38. Press release, February 26, 1959, box 635, PPP. See also Kennedy to Charles Lewin, March 17, 1955, box 656; Remarks of Senator John F. Kennedy in Introduction of a Bill on Adjustments to the National Trade Policy, June 21, 1954, box 635; Kennedy to Charles Hamilton, June 9, 1958, box 707; Kennedy to President Eisenhower, draft, [1959]; Press release, Office of Senator John F. Kennedy, June 21, 1954, box 635; Kennedy to Walter Reuther, July 19, 1954, box 656; Kennedy to Gertrude Beard, August 16, 1954, box 657, PPP; Kaufman, *Trade and Aid*, pp. 20–22; Leddy and Norwood, "Escape Clause," pp. 124–146. From 1947 to 1962, the Tariff Commission instituted 134 escape clause investigations. It completed 112, in which no injury was found in 71, and protectionism recommended in 41 cases. Very few of the products, however, received protection in the form of the escape clause. Of the 22 not completed, 9 were terminated, 9 withdrawn by the applicant, and 4 were still pending as of 1962.

39. Press release, undated, box 98, PPP; Adjustments to the National Trade Policy, June 22, 1954, *Kennedy Statements*, p. 329; Kennedy to Mrs. Edward Peck, Jr., January 20, 1958, box 708, PPP. See also *Congressional Record*, vol. 99, pt. 5, June 22, 1954, 8628–8629.

40. David E. Koskoff, *Joseph P. Kennedy: A Life and Times* (Englewood Cliffs, N.J.: Prentice-Hall, 1974), pp. 52–53, 172–175.

41. "Should An Old Massachusetts Industry Be Penalized?," June 25, 1952, *Kennedy Statements*, p. 118. See also Trade Adjustment Act of 1957, *Kennedy Statements*, p. 567; Statement of Senator John F. Kennedy of Massachusetts Submitted to the U.S. Tariff Commission, August 31, 1953, box 413; Kennedy to Linda Chapman, November 20, 1959, box 727; Kennedy to Arthur J. Bastarache, September 15, 1958, box 707, PPP.

42. Kennedy to Harry Kimball, August 4, 1958, box 707, PPP. See also Kennedy to Robert Reece, August 13, 1954, box 657, PPP.

43. Kennedy to Arthur Mann, March 26, 1958, box 707, PPP. See also Kennedy to Senator Harry F. Byrd, March 21, 1955, box 657, PPP; Robert E. Baldwin, "Protectionist Pressures in the United States," in *Challenges to a Liberal Economic Order,* edited by Ryan C. Amacher, Gottfried Haberler, and Thomas D. Willett (Washington, D.C.: American Enterprise Institute for Public Policy Research, 1979), p. 233.

44. Kennedy to Charles Hamilton, June 9, 1958; Kennedy to Arthur Mann, March 26, 1958, box 707, PPP; Remarks of Senator John F. Kennedy before the Joint Convention of the Tobacco Association of the United States and the Leaf Tobacco Export Association upon Reciprocal Trade, June 24, 1958, box 901, PPP. See also Kennedy to W. S. Ginn, June 29, 1954, attached to Ginn to Kennedy, June 22, 1954, box 641; Kennedy to George Bell, July 9, 1957, box 676, PPP.

45. Revision and Renewal of International Wheat Agreement, March 5, 1959, *Kennedy Statements,* p. 800; Giglio, *Presidency of JFK,* pp. 14–15, 221–222; Rostow, *Eisenhower,* pp. 57, 61, 64; John F. Kennedy, *The Strategy of Peace,* edited by Allan Nevins (New York: Popular Library, 1961), pp. 73–82, and "Areas of Trial" section; "The Economic Gap," February 19, 1959, *Kennedy Statements,* pp. 788–792; At a Democratic Dinner, San Juan, Puerto Rico, December 15, 1958, *Strategy of Peace,* p. 170; Second Annual Conference of the American Society of African Culture, New York City, June 28, 1959, *Strategy of Peace,* pp. 163–164. For Eisenhower's trade policies in Latin America, see Stephen G. Rabe, *Eisenhower and Latin America: The Foreign Policy of Anticommunism* (Chapel Hill: University of North Carolina Press, 1988), chap. 4.

46. In the Senate, March 25, 1958, *Strategy of Peace,* p. 195; speech, "The Destiny of Europe," September 1956, box 561, PPP.

47. Kennedy to Claus Cosman, August 21, 1958; Kennedy to H. D. Baker, Jr., January 7, 1958; Kennedy to D. W. Ellis, June 9, 1958; box 707; Kennedy to G. H. McCutcheon, October 6, 1959, box 727, PPP; *U.S.-Common Market Hearings,* p. 214.

48. Kennedy to Nicholas Nyary, July 21, 1958, box 707, PPP. See also Kennedy to Paul Douglas, February 4, 1958; Kennedy to George Clark, June 24, 1958; Kennedy to Ernest Henderson, July 14, 1958; Kennedy to Mrs. David Owen, June 29, 1958; Kennedy to Theodore Johnson, June 30, 1958, box 707, PPP.

49. Remarks of Senator John F. Kennedy before the Joint Convention of the Tobacco Association of the United States and the Leaf Tobacco Export Association upon Reciprocal Trade, June 24, 1958, box 901, PPP.

50. *U.S.-Common Market Hearings,* Monroney, pp. 14–15, 87–88, and also David J. Steinberg, Corporation for Economic and Industrial Research, p. 88; Lloyd Neidlinger, U.S. Council of International Chamber of Commerce, p. 5; Emile Benoit, Professor of International Business, p. 51. See also Joint Appearances of Kennedy and Nixon, p. 436; Jim F. Heath, *John F. Kennedy and the Business Community* (Chicago: University of Chicago Press, 1969), p. 2; Memorandum, Economic Growth—Administration Miscalculations, September 2, 1960, box 992; Kennedy to Gertrude Weiss, May 3, 1960, box 748; Economic Speech, October 5, 1960, box 992; Kennedy to Gavitt, March 28, 1960, box 773, PPP.

51. "News and Comment," *Textile World* 110 (August 1960):18–20. See also

Foreign Trade Policy—Briefing Papers, [1960], box 993, PPP; Ithiel de Sola Pool, Robert P. Abelson, Samuel L. Popkin, *Candidates, Issues, Strategies: A Computer Simulation of the 1960 Presidential Election* (Cambridge, Mass.: MIT Press 1964), p. 107; "Washington Outlook," *Textile World* 110 (October 1960):22; "Washington Outlook," *Textile World* 110 (July 1960):24.

    52. Democratic Platform, pp. 9–10, 14–15, July 12, 1960, box 539, PPP; Peter Kenen, Memorandum on United States Foreign Trade Policy, September 19, 1960, box 196, Records of the Democratic National Committee, John F. Kennedy Library, Boston, Massachusetts (hereafter DNC); Foreign Trade Policy—Briefing Paper, undated [1960], box 993, PPP; What Nixon Said, Subject: Trade-Tariffs, [1960], box 256, 432–433, DNC; U.S. Congress, Senate Freedom of Communications Subcommittee of Committee on Interstate and Foreign Commerce, *Part III: The Joint Appearances of Senator John F. Kennedy and Vice-President Richard M. Nixon and Other Campaign Presentations*, 87th Cong., 1st sess. 1961, 435; U.S. Congress, Senate Freedom of Communications Subcommittee of Committee on Interstate and Foreign Commerce, *Part II: The Speeches, Remarks, Press Conferences, and Statements of Vice-President Richard M. Nixon, August 1 through November 7, 1960*, 87th Cong., 1st sess., 1961, 404; Constant Southworth to Archibald Cox, August 30, 1960; Statement on Foreign Trade Policy, September 19, 1960; Craig Mathews to Myer Feldman, September 19, 1960, box 993, PPP; Kennedy to Senator Ernest Hollings, U.S. Congress, August 31, 1960, Senate Freedom of Communications Subcommittee of Committee on Interstate and Foreign Commerce, *Part I: The Speeches, Remarks, Press Conferences, and Statements of Senator John F. Kennedy, August 1 through November 7, 1960*, 87th Cong., 1st sess., 1961, pp. 66–67 (hereafter *Part I-Kennedy Statements, 1960*).

    53. Statement on Foreign Trade Policy, September 19, 1960, box 993, PPP.

2. A New Frontier in Trade, 1960–1962

    1. Louis W. Koenig, *The Chief Executive* (New York: Harcourt, Brace, and World, 1968), pp. 171–176; Kennedy to Dean Rusk, April 12, 1961, attached to Richard Neustadt to George Ball, April 18, 1961, box 5, Papers of Jack N. Behrman, John F. Kennedy Library, Boston, Massachusetts (hereafter Behrman Papers); George Ball to Myer Feldman, May 15, 1961, box 64, Sorensen Papers; George W. Ball, *The Past Has Another Pattern: Memoirs* (New York: W. W. Norton, 1982), pp. 103, 199; Arthur M. Schlesinger, Jr., *A Thousand Days: John F. Kennedy in the White House* (Boston: Houghton Mifflin, 1965), p. 440. For background to Ball's career and ideas, see David L. DiLeo, *George Ball, Vietnam, and the Rethinking of Containment* (Chapel Hill: University of North Carolina Press, 1991), pp. 1–36, esp. p. 35. Don Oberdorfer and Walter Pincus, "Businessmen in Politics-Luther Hodges and J. Edward Day," in *The Kennedy Circle*, edited by Lester Tanzer (Washington, D.C.: Robert B. Luce, 1961), pp. 242–254.

    2. James Tobin Oral History in CEA Oral History, p. 39; Kennedy to Thomas Lamont, June 1, 1960, box 773, PPP.

    3. Special Message to the Congress on Gold and the Balance of Payments Deficit, February 6, 1961, *Public Papers of the Presidents of the United States, John F. Kennedy, 1961* (Washington, D.C.: U.S. Government Printing Office,

1962), p. 57 (hereafter *Public Papers, 1961*); see also Robert Solomon, *The International Monetary System, 1945–1981* (New York: Harper and Row, 1982), p. 39; Schlesinger, *A Thousand Days*, pp. 652–655; Ball, interview with author; Theodore C. Sorensen Oral History, John F. Kennedy Library, Boston Massachusetts (hereafter Sorensen Oral History), pp. 114, 117; U.S. Senate Finance Committee, *Staff Data and Materials on U.S. Trade and the Balance of Payments*, 93d Cong., 2d sess., 1974 (hereafter *Data on Trade and Payments*), p. 1.

4. Walter Heller to the President, September 15, 1961, box 73, CEA, President's Office Files, John F. Kennedy Library, Boston, Massachusetts (hereafter POF); Robert V. Roosa, *The Dollar and World Liquidity* (New York: Random House, 1967), pp. 15–16; Canterbury, *Economics*, pp. 199–202; Prospects and Policies for the 1961 American Economy: A Report to President-Elect Kennedy by Paul A. Samuelson, [January 1961], box 1071, PPP; Calleo, *Imperious Economy*, pp. 9–21.

5. Borden, "Defending Hegemony," pp. 65–69; Block, *Origins of International Economic Disorder*, pp. 177–181; Solomon, *International Monetary System*, pp. 37–49; Eckes, *Search for Solvency*, pp. 245–254; Calleo, *Imperious Economy*, pp. 17–24; Roosa, *Dollar and World Liquidity*; Spero, *Politics of International Economic Relations*, pp. 43–52. Milton Friedman, an economist at the University of Chicago, also addressed the gold-liquidity problem by advocating floating exchange rates, or letting currency seek its own value according to free-market dictums. Proposed in the early 1960s, but not accepted until years later, the plan would eliminate government management of financial markets by ending payments deficits, which would be brought into balance naturally by the free market. See Eckes, *Search for Solvency*, p. 252.

6. Report to the Honorable Task Force on the Balance-of-Payments, December 27, 1960, box 1073, PPP; Peter Jones to the Secretary of Commerce on Hyannisport meeting, November 24, 1961, box 24, White House Staff Files-Myer Feldman (hereafter Feldman Files); Special Message to the Congress on Gold and the Balance of Payments Deficit, February 6, 1961, *Public Papers, 1961*, p. 59; Christopher Layton, *Trans-Atlantic Investments* (Boulogne-Sur-Seine, France: Atlantic Institute, 1966), chap. 1; Mira Wilkins, *The Maturing of Multinational Enterprise: American Business Abroad from 1914 to 1970* (Cambridge, Mass.: Harvard University Press, 1974), p. 334; Canterbury, *Economics*, p. 187; Leslie Stein, *Trade and Structural Change* (London: Croom Helm, 1984), p. 59. See also Richard N. Cooper, *The Economics of Interdependence: Economic Policy in the Atlantic Community* (New York: McGraw-Hill, 1968).

7. Report to the Honorable John F. Kennedy by the Task Force on Foreign Economic Policy, December 31, 1960, box 1073, PPP.

8. Special Message to the Congress on Gold and the Balance of Payments Deficit, February 6, 1961, *Public Papers, 1961*, pp. 57, 58, 60, 62–64. See also the President's News Conference of November 29, 1961, *Public Papers, 1961*, p. 763.

9. *Wall Street Journal*, April 17, 1961:1, 12; Statistical Briefing: U.S. Trade and the Common Market, [1962], box 2, Petersen Files; *Agence Internationale D'Information Pour La Presse-Europe*, January 19, 1961 (hereafter *Agence Presse-Europe*).

10. Jacob Viner, "Economic Foreign Policy on the New Frontier," *Foreign Affairs* 39 (July 1961):560, 565, 575; *Agence Press-Europe*, January 3, 1961.
11. Henry G. Aubrey, *Atlantic Economic Cooperation: The Case of the OECD* (New York: Praeger, 1967), pp. 24–25; Statement by the President Following Ratification of Convention Establishing the Organization for Economic Cooperation and Development, March 23, 1961, *Public Papers, 1961*, p. 212.
12. U.S. Senate Hearings before the Committee on Foreign Relations, *Organization for Economic Cooperation and Development*, 87th Cong., 1st sess., 1961, (hereafter OECD Hearings), O. R. Strackbein, pp. 133–134. See also *Congressional Record*, vol. 107, pt. 4, March 16, 1961, 4170 (the vote was 72–18); OECD Hearings, Fulbright, p. 1; Proposed Position on the OECD, attached to Minutes of Meeting of NAM International Economic Affairs Committee, August 29, 1961, box 23, Committee Minutes, Series V, Records of the National Association of Manufacturers, Hagley Museum and Library, Wilmington, Delaware (hereafter Series IV or V, NAM records); OECD Hearings, Cong. James Davis (D-Ga.), p. 113; O. R. Strackbein, Nation-wide Committee on Import-Export Policy, pp. 133–134; Enoch R. Rust, Glass and Ceramics Workers of North America, pp. 170, 174.
13. Aubrey, *Atlantic Economic Cooperation*, pp. 29–30.
14. Richard Neustadt to George Ball, April 18, 1961, box 5, Behrman Papers; Rowland Burnsten to Myer Feldman, May 22, 1961, box 29, Feldman Files; Register to the White House Staff Files of President John F. Kennedy: Howard C. Petersen, 3–5, John F. Kennedy Library, Boston, Massachusetts; Petersen, interview with author, June 20, 1986, Radnor, Pennsylvania; Exchange of Letters between the President and Howard C. Petersen, November 21, 1962; Petersen, address, "An American Look at the Commercial Policy of the North Atlantic Community," July 6, 1961, Papers of Howard C. Petersen, Radnor, Pennsylvania (hereafter Petersen Papers).
15. Proposals for 1962 United States Foreign Trade and Tariff Legislation from Petersen, [October 23, 1961]; The "Peril Point" Provision (Petersen), October 23, 1961, George Ball to the President, October 23, 1961, box 50, POF. See also Ernest H. Preeg, *Traders and Diplomats: An Analysis of the Kennedy Round Negotiations under the General Agreement on Tariffs and Trade* (Washington, D.C.: Brookings Institution, 1970), p. 44; Pastor, *Congress*, pp. 105–106, 106*n*; Bauer, Pool, and Dexter, *American Business*, p. 74; Schlesinger, *A Thousand Days*, pp. 846–847; Theodore C. Sorensen, *Kennedy* (New York: Harper and Row, 1965), p. 410. Documents support the claims of Preeg and Sorensen that the timing issue was the key point of difference between Ball and Petersen.
16. Harold Macmillan, *Pointing the Way, 1959–1961* (London: Macmillan, 1972), p. 316. See also Robert J. Pfaltzgraff, Jr., *Britain Faces Europe* (Philadelphia: University of Pennsylvania Press, 1969), chap. 3, pp. 88–115; David Nunnerly, *President Kennedy and Britain* (New York: St. Martin's Press, 1972), pp. 167–168; Miriam Camps, *Britain and the European Community, 1955–1963* (Princeton: Princton University Press, 1964), chps. 8–10, pp. 300–301, 338–351, 363–366; Randall Hinshaw, *The European Community and American Trade: A Study in Atlantic Economics and Policy* (New York: Praeger, 1964), pp. 103–104, 106–125; Drew Middleton, *The Supreme Choice: Britain and Europe* (New

York: Knopf, 1963), pp. 103, 104–119, 144–147; Walter Lippmann, *Western Unity and the Common Market* (Boston: Little, Brown, 1962), pp. 14–17; John Pinder, *Britain and the Common Market* (London: Cresset Press, 1961), pp. 81–84. Nearly 25 percent of Commonwealth (mostly farm) exports went to Britain, 95 percent entering duty-free. But once Britain joined the EEC, these exports would be subject to duties, a fact which upset such major exporters as New Zealand and Australia.

17. Alistair Horne, *Harold Macmillan: Volume II, 1957–1986* (New York: Viking Penguin, 1989), p. 317. See also Nunnerly, *Kennedy and Britain*, p. 168; Spaak, *The Continuing Battle*, pp. 436–447, 472–473; Camps, *Britain*, pp. 305–309; Middleton, *Supreme Choice*, pp. 102, 144–147; Hinshaw, *European Community*, p. 101; Charles De Gaulle to Prime Minister Harold Macmillan, August 1, 1961, Charles de Gaulle, *Lettres, Notes, et Carnets, 1961–1963* (Paris: Librairie Plon, 1985), pp. 121–122; Charles de Gaulle, *Memoirs of Hope: Renewal and Endeavor* (New York: Simon and Schuster, 1971), p. 219.

18. David Reynolds, *The Creation of the Anglo-American Alliance, 1937–1941: A Study in Competitive Co-operation* (Chapel Hill: University of North Carolina Press, 1981), pp. 12–13, 85; Nunnerly, *Kennedy and Britain*, pp. 7–8, 11; Pfaltzgraff, *Britain Faces Europe*, p. 74; Camps, *Britain*, pp. 283, 327; Pinder, *Britain and the Common Market*, p. 81; Robert Estabrook interview with Donald Maitland, February 6, 1962, British Foreign Office, box 1, Papers of Robert Estabrook, John F. Kennedy Library, Boston, Massachusetts (hereafter Estabrook Papers); Frank Costigliola, "The Failed Design: Kennedy, de Gaulle, and the Struggle for Europe," *Diplomatic History* 8 (Summer 1984):234. For a view that Britain exercised realpolitik in pursuing the special relationship by hitching itself to America, see Geoffrey Warner, "The Anglo-American Special Relationship," *Diplomatic History* 13 (Fall 1989):479–499.

19. Schlesinger, *A Thousand Days*, p. 845; The President's News Conference, May 17, 1962, *Public Papers of the Presidents of the United States, John F. Kennedy, 1962* (Washington, D.C.: U.S. Government Printing Office, 1963), p. 406 (hereafter *Public Papers, 1962*); The President's News Conference, August 10, 1961, *Public Papers, 1961*, p. 554; The President's News Conference, May 23, 1962, *Public Papers, 1962*, pp. 436–437; Frank Costigliola, "The Pursuit of Atlantic Community: Nuclear Arms, Dollars, and Berlin," in *Kennedy's Quest for Victory*, edited by Paterson, p. 27; Macmillan, *Pointing the Way*, p. 350.

20. Ball, *The Past Has Another Pattern*, pp. 213, 215, 218; George Ball to the President, August 7, 1961, box 170, National Security Files, John F. Kennedy Library, Boston, Massachusetts (hereafter NSF-JFK). See also George W. Ball, *The Discipline of Power: Essentials of a Modern World Structure* (Boston: Little, Brown, 1968), p. 79; Camps, *Britain*, p. 336; George Ball to the President, October 23, 1961, box 170, NSF-JFK; Nunnerly, *Kennedy and Britain*, pp. 172–173; Pfaltzgraff, *Britain Faces Europe*, pp. 118–136; Schlesinger, *A Thousand Days*, pp. 845–846; Joint Statment Following Discussions with Prime Minister Macmillan, April 29, 1962, *Public Papers, 1962*, p. 346; George Ball to the President, August 23, 1961, box 170, NSF-JFK; Costigliola, "The Failed Design," p. 228; Horne, *Macmillan*, pp. 295, 300.

21. George Ball to the President, October 23, 1961, box 50, POF; Ball, *The Past Has Another Pattern*, p. 198; Ball to Ambassadors, July 25, 1962; George Ball to McGeorge Bundy, July 27, 1962, box 170A, NSF-JFK; Petersen, address, "An American Look at the Commercial Policy of the North Atlantic Community," July 6, 1961, Petersen Papers; Howard Petersen to the President, October 23, 1961, box 50, POF; Myer Rashish to Howard Petersen, October 18, 1961, box 1, Petersen Files.

22. Eric Wyndham White, address, "Looking Outward," April 6, 1960, box 8, Behrman Papers; Isaiah Frank, *The European Common Market: An Analysis of Commercial Policy* (New York: Praeger, 1961), pp. 194–196.

23. *Agence Presse-Europe*, May 8, 1961; *U.S.-EEC Hearings*, Ball, p. 138, O. R. Strackbein, pp. 171–172; Harris Oral History, pp. 61–62; "GATT Tariff Negotiations Conference Opens at Geneva," Department of State *Bulletin* 43 (September 19, 1960):453–454; "Issues Facing GATT in the New Trading World," Department of State *Bulletin* 46 (January 1, 1962):4; Curzon and Curzon, "Management," p. 169.

24. Report on Article XXIV: 6 Negotiations with the Common Market, February 8, 1962, box 8, Behrman Papers; Curzon and Curzon, "Management," pp. 169–171, 200*n*.

25. White, "Looking Outward," April 6, 1960, box 8, Behrman Papers. For explanations of the CAP and its effects, see John O. Coppock, *Atlantic Agricultural Unity: Is It Possible?* (New York: McGraw-Hill, 1966), p. 19; Ross B. Talbot and Don F. Hadwiger, *The Policy Process in American Agriculture* (San Francisco: Chandler, 1968), p. 336; Brian E. Hill, *The Common Agricultural Policy: Past, Present, and Future* (London: Methuen, 1984), pp. 18–32; Alex F. McCalla, "Protectionism in International Agricultural Trade, 1850–1968," *Agricultural History* 43 (July 1969):338; Hanns Peter Muth, *French Agriculture and the Political Integration of Western Europe* (Leyden, Holland: A. W. Sijthoff, 1970), p. 15; Johnson, "Mercantilism," pp. 12–13; T. K. Warley, "Western Trade in Agricultural Products," in *International Economic Relations*, edited by Shonfield, p. 308. For debate on the CAP, see *Agence Presse-Europe*, January 18, 1961, March 17, 1961, and January 2, 1962.

26. Robert Estabrook interview with Ambassador Douglas MacArthur II (Belgium), November 28, 1961; Dr. Oscar Zagletz, November 28, 1961, box 1, Estabrook Papers; Interdepartmental Committee of Undersecretaries on Foreign Economic Policy meeting, United States Agricultural Policy, February 19, 1962, box 8, Behrman Papers; Warley, *Western Trade*, pp. 319–322; McCalla, "Protectionism," p. 340; Coppock, *Agricultural Unity*, pp. 22–26; Petersen, *Agricultural Exports*, 1979, pp. 115–118.

27. Special Message to the Congress on Foreign Trade Policy, January 25, 1962, *Public Papers, 1962*, p. 72. See also Warley, "Western Trade," p. 321; Special Message to the Congress on Gold and the Balance of Payments Deficit, February 6, 1961, *Public Papers, 1961*, p. 63; Special Message to the Congress on Agriculture, March 16, 1961, *Public Papers, 1961*, p. 197. For Kennedy's farm program, see Giglio, *Presidency of JFK*, pp. 107–112.

28. Preeg, *Traders*, p. 32; Joint Statement Following Meeting with Dr. Walter Hallstein, President of the European Economic Community, May 16, 1961, *Public*

Papers, 1961, p. 380; Interdepartmental Committee of Under Secretaries on Foreign Economic Policy meeting, February 19, 1962, box 8, Behrman Papers.

29. Orville Freeman to the President, November 27, 1961, box 9, Papers of Orville Freeman, John F. Kennedy Library, Boston, Massachusetts (hereafter Freeman Papers). See also Orville Freeman to the President, October 1961, and December 12, 1961, box 9, Freeman Papers.

30. President Kennedy to Senator Herman Talmadge (D-Ga.), December 15, 1961, box 237, White House Central Files, John F. Kennedy Library, Boston, Massachusetts (hereafter WHCF-JFK); *Agence Presse-Europe,* September 7, 1961; Report on Article XXIV: 6 Negotiations with the Common Market, February 8, 1962, box 8, Behrman Papers; John P. Duncan to Myer Feldman, November 30, 1961, box 24, Feldman Files; Howard Petersen, interview with author; "U.S. Exchanges Tariff Concessions with GATT Contracting Parties," Department of State *Bulletin* 46 (April 2, 1962):564; Orville Freeman Oral History, John F. Kennedy Library, Boston, Massachusetts, p. 23 (hereafter Freeman Oral History); Murphy to Interdepartmental Under Secretaries Committee on Foreign Economic Policy, February 19, 1962, box 8, Behrman Papers; Coppock, *Agricultural Unity,* p. 49.

31. *Wall Street Journal,* December 14, 1961, p. 5.

32. John W. Evans, *The Kennedy Round in American Trade Policy: The Twilight of the GATT?* (Cambridge, Mass.: Harvard University Press, 1971), pp. 153, 161–162; Lawrence B. Krause, *European Economic Integration and the United States* (Washington, D.C.: Brookings Institution, 1968), pp. 209–211; "Issues Facing GATT in the New Trading World," Department of State *Bulletin* 46 (November 27, 1961):4.

33. Curzon and Curzon, "Management," p. 174; Krause, *European Integration,* p. 210; Yeager and Tuerck, *Trade Policy,* p. 269; Pierre Uri, *Partnership for Progress: A Program for Transatlantic Action* (New York: Harper and Row, 1963), p. 16; "U.S. Exchanges Tariff Concessions with GATT Contracting Parties," Department of State *Bulletin* 46 (April 2, 1962):563–564; Howard Petersen, interview with author.

34. Paul Luyten [EEC] to the author, August 10, 1989; Press Release from the White House, March 7, 1962, box 7, Petersen Files; *Agence Presse-Europe,* March 8, 1961; U.S. House Ways and Means Committee, *The Trade Expansion Act of 1962,* 87th Cong., 2d sess., 1962, Exhibit C, 2233–2235 (hereafter *TEA-House*); Preeg, *Traders,* p. 41; Krause, *European Integration,* p. 210; Curzon and Curzon, "Management," p. 175.

35. Special Message to the Congress on the Trade Agreements Concluded at the Geneva Tariff Conference, March 7, 1962, *Public Papers, 1962,* pp. 204, 206–207. See also Howard Petersen to the President, December 20, 1961, box 31, POF; Statement to the President by the Public Advisors to the United States Delegation to the GATT Tariff Conference, March 9, 1962, box 36, Petersen Files.

36. Evans, *Kennedy Round,* p. 139; U.S. Subcommittee on Foreign Economic Policy of the Joint Economic Committee, *Foreign Economic Policy,* 87th Cong., 1st sess., December 4–12, 1961 (hereafter *Foreign Economic Policy Hearings*), Boggs pp. 1–2; Christian A. Herter and William L. Clayton, "A New Look

Foreign Economic Policy in Light of the Cold War and the Extension of the Common Market in Europe," submitted at the *Foreign Economic Policy Hearings,* November 1, 1961, pp. 1–2, 5–6, 8–10.

37. Ball address, "The Threshold of a New Trading World," November 1, 1961, Department of State *Bulletin* 45 (November 20, 1961):832–837. See also Chester Bowles to Diplomatic and Consular Posts, November 2, 1961, box 284–285, NSF-JFK.

For Kennedy's efforts to liberalize East-West trade, the congressional restraints on his policy, and Western Europe's sales to the Soviet bloc, see United States Economic Defense Policy, July 17, 1962, NSC meeting no. 503, box 313; Summary Record of NSC Meeting, July 17, 1962; Revision of U.S. Economic Defense Policy—NSC 5704/5, December 4, 1962, box 286, NSF-JFK; Philip Funigiello, *American-Soviet Trade in the Cold War* (Chapel Hill: University of North Carolina, 1988), chap. 6. Hoping to wean satellites away from Moscow, Kennedy put in the TEA a grant of MFN status to Poland and Yugoslavia, which the Senate rejected.

38. George Ball, "The Less-Developed Countries and the Atlantic Partnership," Department of State *Bulletin* 46 (March 12, 1962):417. See also Special Message to the Congress on Foreign Aid, March 22, 1961, *Public Papers, 1961,* pp. 203–208. For the Alliance for Progress, see Giglio, *Presidency of JFK,* pp. 233–235.

39. Seymour Harris to the President, December 7, 1961, box 24, Feldman Files. See also the President's News Conference of November 8, 1961, *Public Papers, 1961,* pp. 707–708; Hyannisport meeting in Peter Jones to Luther Hodges, November 24, 1961, box 24, Feldman Files; Howard Petersen to George Ball, October 18, 1961, box 1, Petersen Files.

40. Myer Rashish to Howard Petersen, September 8, 1961, box 1, Petersen Files. See also Giglio, *Presidency of JFK,* pp. 38–39, which criticizes Kennedy's legislative style; Sorensen Oral History, p. 111; Lawrence O'Brien, *No Final Victories: A Life in Politics—from John F. Kennedy to Watergate* (Garden City, N.Y.: Doubleday, 1974), pp. 130–131; Lawrence O'Brien to the author, January 10, 1986; Rashish Oral History, p. 15; George Ball, interview with author; Dean Rusk to the author, January 13, 1986.

41. Address in New York City to the National Association of Manufacturers, December 6, 1961; address in Miami at the Opening of the AFL-CIO Convention, December 7, 1961, *Public Papers, 1961,* pp. 775–779, 781–784, 791–792, 795.

42. Annual Message to the Congress on the State of the Union, January 11, 1962, *Public Papers, 1962,* p. 14. See also Summary of New Trade Legislation Sent by the President to the Congress on January 25, 1962, box 2, Petersen Files.

43. Special Message to the Congress on Foreign Trade Policy, January 25, 1962, *Public Papers, 1962,* pp. 74–75; Memorandum for the Vice-President, Subject: The Trade Expansion Act of 1962: A Brief Description and Analysis, January 8, 1962, box 2, Petersen Files. For an overview of the TEA, see also Stanley D. Metzger, *Trade Agreements and the Kennedy Round: An Analysis of the Economic, Legal, and Political Aspects of the Trade Expansion Act of 1962 and the Prospects for the Kennedy Round of Tariff Negotiations* (Fairfax, Va.: Coiner, 1964), chaps. 3–7.

44. Hawkins and Norwood, "Legislative Basis," pp. 119–120; Don D. Hum-

phrey, *The United States and the Common Market: A Background Study* (New York: Praeger, 1964), p. 169; Summary of New Trade Legislation as Sent by the President on January 25, 1962, box 2, Petersen Files; Judith Goldstein, "Ideas, Institutions, and American Trade Policy," *International Organization* (Winter 1988):190, 192.

45. Humphrey, *U.S. and the Common Market,* pp. 173–174; Special Message to the Congress on Foreign Trade Policy, January 25, 1962, *Public Papers, 1962,* p. 75–76; Memorandum to the Vice-President, Subject: The Trade Expansion Act of 1962: A Brief Description and Analysis, January 8, 1962, box 2, Petersen Papers; "President Sends Trade Bill to Congress," *Congressional Quarterly-Weekly Report* 20 (January 26, 1962):98; Hawkins and Norwood, "Legislative Basis," pp. 120–121.

46. Special Message to the Congress on Foreign Trade Policy, January 25, 1962, *Public Papers, 1962,* p. 76. See also Summary of Attached Draft Adjustment Assistance Bill, [May 1961], box 29, Feldman Files; Charles R. Frank, Jr., *Foreign Trade and Domestic Aid* (Washington, D.C.: Brookings Institution, 1977), pp. 40–45; Goldstein, "Ideas," pp. 209, 215. An Adjustment Assistance Advisory Board, chaired by the secretary of commerce, overlooked the program. The Department of Labor was responsible for worker claims while Commerce, the Small Business Administration, and others oversaw firms and management under the program.

47. Joseph Kraft, *The Grand Design: From Common Market to Atlantic Partnership* (New York: Harper and Brothers, 1962), pp. 119–120. See also Special Message to the Congress on Foreign Trade Policy, January 25, 1962, *Public Papers, 1962,* p. 77.

48. Schlesinger, *A Thousand Days,* p. 847.

49. Special Message to the Congress on Foreign Trade Policy, January 25, 1962, *Public Papers, 1962,* p. 77. See also Schlesinger, *A Thousand Days,* p. 847.

50. *American Letter,* no. 2246, September 16, 1961, Petersen Papers. See also C. Wilson Harder to Undersecretary George Ball, November 2, 1961, box 23, Petersen Files; Barrie, "Congress and the Executive," p. 175; *Wall Street Journal,* November 2, 1961, p. 26.

3. The Politics of Protection in Textiles and Lumber

1. "Congress-1961," *Congressional Quarterly-Almanac* 17 (1961):63. See also William S. White, "The Kennedy Era Stage Two: The Coming Battle With Congress," *Harper's* 224 (February 1962):102; John J. Lindsay, "The '62 Legislative Outlook," *The Nation* 194 (January 6, 1962):12–13; Sorensen, *Kennedy,* p. 339; Theodore Sorensen to the President, January 8, 1962, box 50, POF; Henry H. Wilson to Lawrence O'Brien, November 8, 1961, box 3, White House Staff Files-Congressional Liaison Office, Henry Hall Wilson Files, John F. Kennedy Library, Boston, Massachusetts (hereafter Wilson Files).

2. " 'Conservative Coalition' Appeared on 28% of Roll Calls," *Congressional Quarterly-Weekly Report* 19 (November 3, 1961):1796; Giglio, *Presidency of JFK,* p. 37; Sorensen, *Kennedy,* pp. 340, 411; John F. Manley, *The Politics of Finance: The House Committee on Ways and Means* (Boston: Little, Brown,

1970), chap. 4; William S. White, "The Kennedy Era: Stage Two, The Coming Battle With Congress," *Harper's* 224 (February 1962):97, 102; Herbert S. Parmet, *JFK; The Presidency of John F. Kennedy* (New York: Dial Press, 1983), pp. 205–206.

 3. Karl E. Meyer, "Politics of Trade," *New Statesman* 63 (March 23, 1962):405–406; *Congressional Record-Appendix*, vol. 108, reel 11, January 30, 1962, Cong. John Dent, A669; John Dent to Friend, [1962], box Trade-Tariffs-GATT, John H. Dent Collection, Westmoreland County Community College, Youngwood, Pennsylvania (hereafter Dent Collection); Press Release, January 25, 1962; Press Release, April 28, 1962, box 7, RG 69:13, Papers of Prescott S. Bush, Connecticut State Library, Hartford, Connecticut (hereafter Bush Papers). For the chief leader of the societal protectionists, see O. R. Strackbein, *American Enterprise and Foreign Trade* (Washington, D.C.: Public Affairs Press, 1965).

 4. Theodore Sorensen to John F. Shaw, July 13, 1955, box 658, PPP; "News and Comment," *Textile World* 110 (August 1960):17–18, 20; Nelson Lichtenstein, *Political Profiles: The Kennedy Years* (New York: Facts on File, 1976), p. 231; Senator Kennedy to Governor Ernest Hollings, August 31, 1960, *Part I-Kennedy Statements, 1960*, pp. 66–67; Myer Feldman Oral History, John F. Kennedy Library, Boston, Massachusetts (hereafter Feldman Oral History), pt. 3, pp. 134–142; Theodore H. White, *The Making of the President, 1960* (New York: Pocket Books, 1962), pp. 420–422. A revised version of the cotton textile case can be found in Thomas W. Zeiler, "Free Trade Politics and Diplomacy: John F. Kennedy and Textiles," *Diplomatic History* 11 (Spring 1987):127–142.

 5. "The Reciprocal Trade Issue: Background and Analysis," *Congressional Quarterly-Weekly Report* 20 (January 5, 1962):18; *Historical Statistics*, pp. 898, 900; U.S. House Subcommittee on the Impact of Imports and Exports on American Employment of the Committee on Education and Labor, *Impact of Imports and Exports on Employment (Textiles)*, 87th Cong., 1st sess., 1961 (hereafter *Textile Imports-Exports Hearings*), pp. 60, 129, 244, 248, 250; U.S. Congress, Senate Subcommittee of the Committee on Interstate and Foreign Commerce, *Problems of the Domestic Textile Industry*, 87th Cong., 1st sess., 1961 (hereafter *Textile Industry Hearings I*), pp. 25, 302, 305; Survey of Congressional Voting Records: Textiles, undated, box 28, Petersen Files.

 6. *Textile Imports-Exports Hearings*, pp. 129, 60; *Textile Industry Hearings I*, p. 305.

 7. Alexander Trowbridge Oral History, tape 2, Lyndon Johnson Library, Austin, Texas, 22 (hereafter Trowbridge Oral History). See also TEA-House, pt. 5, George Baldanzi, United Textile Workers of America, 2825; pt. 4, Jerome M. Pitofsky, American Association of Apparel and Textile Importers, 2740; Aggarwal, *Liberal Protectionism*, p. 35; "Trade Battle Features Unique Lobby Alliances," *Congressional Quarterly-Weekly Report* 20 (March 9, 1962):406; Henry Wilson to Lawrence O'Brien, [December 1961], box 3, Wilson Files; National Cotton Council resolutions, 1961 and 1962, Records of the National Cotton Council of America, Memphis, Tennessee; Summary of record of meeting of Economic Consultants, October 3, 1961, box 32, Papers of Kermit Gordon, John F. Kennedy Library, Boston, Massachusetts (hereafter Gordon Papers); *Textile*

Imports-Exports Hearings, Dent, 51, Cong. Charles S. Joelson, (D-N.J.), p. 3, Strackbein, p. 115, E. B. Shaw to President John F. Kennedy, December 11, 1961, pp. 205–207, Cleveland M. Bailey (D-W.Va.), 26; U.S. Joint Economic Committee of the Congress, *Hearings before the Foreign Economic Policy Hearings,* 87th Cong., 1st sess., 1961 (hereafter *Foreign Economic Hearings*), Henry Gemmill, "Protectionism Versus Free Trade," p. 506.

8. White, *Making of the President, 1960,* pp. 421, 430–431; Thomas Finney to Peter Jones, March 20, 1962, box 14, Petersen Files; Memorandum for Mr. Albert, June 25, 1962, box 56, Carl Albert Papers, Carl Albert Congressional Research and Studies Center Congressional Archives, University of Oklahoma, Norman, Oklahoma (hereafter Albert Papers); Giglio, *Presidency of JFK,* p. 37; Bauer, Pool, and Dexter, *American Business,* pp. 359, 362; Thomas Blake to the President, January 26, 1962, box 480, WHCF-JFK.

9. Aggarwal, *Liberal Protectionism,* p. 86. See also "1948–1961 Voting Records on Reciprocal Trade," *Congressional Quarterly-Weekly Report* 20 (April 27, 1962):680–681; Memorandum for Secretary Hodges, March 27, 1961, box 94, POF; U.S. House Subcommittee on the Impact of Imports and Exports on American Employment of the Committee on Education and Labor, *Impact of Imports and Exports on Employment (Coal and Residual Fuel Oil),* 87th Cong., 1st sess., 1961, (hereafter *Coal/Oil Hearings*), Dent, p. 2; 30 senators to the President, June 22, 1961; 34 senators to the President, January 23, 1962, box Pastore-General Files-Textiles, John O. Pastore Collection, Phillips Memorial Library Archives, Providence College, Providence, Rhode Island (hereafter Pastore Papers).

10. Pastore, address to ACMI, March 25, 1961, box Pastore-General Files-Textiles, Pastore Papers; *Textile Industry Hearings I,* Pastore, pp. 1–3, J. M. Cheatham, ACMI, p. 10, Robert T. Stevens, J. P. Stevens, p. 95, Seabury Stanton, Northern Textile Association, pp. 64–65; Ernest Hollings, "The Textile Import Problem: The Issue and Solution," February 14, 1961, Feldman Files; "Washington Outlook," *Textile World* 111 (March 1961):24.

11. Lichtenstein, *Political Profiles,* p. 227; Luther Hodges Oral History, John F. Kennedy Library, Boston, Massachusetts (hereafter Hodges Oral History), pp. 78, 87–89; Agenda: Textile Foreign Trade Conference, January 25, 1961; Explanation of Textile Trade Bill, February 10, 1961, box 100, Series I-Annual File, Papers of the National Association of Cotton Manufacturers and the Northern Textile Association, Museum of American Textile History, North Andover, Massachusetts (hereafter NACM-NTA Papers); "U.S. Trade Policy Approaching Major Crisis," *Congressional Quarterly-Weekly Report* 19 (August 4, 1961):1350; The President's News Conference of March 8, 1961, *Public Papers, 1961,* p. 159; Executive Council Statement, *Recent Developments in International Trade Policy,* October 12, 1961, AFL-CIO Press Releases, vol. 6.

12. "Textile Imports," *Congressional Quarterly-Weekly Report* 19 (March 24, 1961):489; "U.S. Trade Policy Approaching Major Crisis," *Congressional Quarterly-Weekly Report,* (August 4, 1961):1348; "OECD," *Congressional Quarterly-Almanac* 17 (1961):67; Sorensen, *Kennedy,* p. 348; House Textile Group to the President, March 23, 1961, box 94, POF; Group I, Survey of House Voting by States, undated, box 31, White House Staff Files-Congressional Liaison Office, Lawrence O'Brien Files, John F. Kennedy Library, Boston, Massachusetts (here-

after O'Brien Files); Ball, *The Past Has Another Pattern,* p. 189; Aggarwal, *Liberal Protectionism,* pp. 50–53.

13. "At Last, Action on Imports and Reaction in the Industry," *Textile World* 111 (June 1961):43–45; President to Carl Vinson, February 26, 1962, box 21, Feldman Files.

14. GATT, *International Trade, 1961* (Geneva: GATT, 1962), p. 21. See also Ball, *The Past Has Another Pattern,* p. 189; Leroy Werhle to Kermit Gordon, November 14, 1961, box 32, Gordon Papers; Trade Expansion Problems of the Less-Developed Countries, Meeting of the Interdepartmental Committee on Foreign Economic Policy, October 25, 1961, box 8, Behrman Papers.

15. Ball, *The Past Has Another Pattern,* p. 187.

16. Leroy Werhle to Kermit Gordon, November 14, 1961, box 32, Gordon Papers; "At Last, Action on Imports and Reaction in the Industry," *Textile World* 111 (June 1961):46; "Sharing Burdens in Textiles" *The Economist* 199 (May 6, 1961):547; Aggarwal, *Liberal Protectionism,* pp. 79, 90; transcript, Conference of Cotton Textile Industry with Ball, June 19, 1961, box Textiles-General, Pastore Papers; "Mr. Ball's Weaving," *The Economist* 199 (May 20, 1961):761; Ball, interview with author; Ball, *The Past Has Another Pattern,* p. 192.

17. Memorandum, June 22, 1961, box 25, Feldman Files. See also J. M. Cheatham for the ACMI and textile groups to the President, June 29, 1961, box 100; Memorandum on Washington meetings, June 19, 1961, box 103, NACM-NTA Papers; Mike Manatos to Lawrence O'Brien, March 2, 1962, box 1, White House Staff Files-Congressional Liaison Office, Mike Manatos Files, John F. Kennedy Library, Boston, Massachusetts (hereafter Manatos Files); Senators to the President, June 22, 1961, box Textiles-General, Pastore Papers.

18. Memorandum for Conference on Textile Matters with Undersecretary Ball, June 19, 1961, box Textiles-General, Pastore Papers.

19. "GATT Not Playing Ball," *The Economist* 200 (July 22, 1961):374; Aggarwal, *Liberal Protectionism,* pp. 80–83; "Cotton in Torment," *The Economist* 200 (July 15, 1961):265–266.

20. Ibid., p. 266. See also UN, *World Economic Survey, 1962–I: The Developing Countries in World Trade,* (New York: United Nations, 1963), p. 69; EEC *Bulletin* 4 (July 1961):47; Hickman Price to Myer Feldman, June 23, 1961, box 25, Feldman Files; Aggarwal, *Liberal Protectionism,* pp. 81–82.

21. Telegram, Hickman Price to Secretary of State Rusk, July 16, 1961, box 25, Feldman Files; "News and Comment," *Textile World* 111 (August 1961):22; "News and Comment," *Textile World,* 111 (November 1961):46; Aggarwal, *Liberal Protectionism,* pp. 83–90; 207–210. Adherents to the Short-Term Arrangement were the U.S., Canada, Great Britain (representing Hong Kong), the EEC, Sweden, Norway, Austria, Spain, Australia, Japan, India, and Pakistan.

22. Robert T. Stevens [J. P. Stevens] and J. Spencer Love [Burlington Industries], July 25, 1961; Statement of the Position of the ACMI on the International Cotton Textile Trade Agreement, August 2, 1961, box 25, Feldman Files; Joint Statement of Congressmen Carl Vinson and W. J. Bryan Dorn, July 27, 1961, box Pastore-General Files-Textiles, Pastore Papers; "News and Comment," *Textile World* 111 (September 1961):20; R. Buford Brandis, *The Making of Textile Trade Policy, 1935–1981* (Washington, D.C.: American Textile Manufacturers Insti-

tute, 1982), pp. 20–21; *Bulletin of the EEC* 4 (September-October 1961):48–49; Lucius Battle to Myer Feldman, December 4, 1961, box 26, Feldman Files; *Bulletin of the EEC* 5 (July-August 1962):21–22; "No General Agreement," *The Economist* 201 (November 4, 1961):485; Aggarwal, *Liberal Protectionism,* p. 92.

23. "News and Comment," *Textile World* 111 (October 1961):20, 22; Sung Jae Koh, *Stages of Industrial Development in Asia: A Comparative History of the Cotton Industry in Japan, India, China, Korea* (Philadelphia: University of Pennsylvania Press, 1966), pp. 254–257; Hunsberger, *Japan and the United States,* pp. 293–294; U.S.-Japan Trade Council, *U.S. Trade With Japan, 1956–1960,* no. 5, August 1961, box 8, Petersen Files; UN, *Yearbook of International Trade Statistics, 1961* (New York: United Nations, 1963), pp. 575, 580; UN, *Economic Bulletin for Asia and the Far East* (Bangkok: United Nations, 1958), 9:15–18; *Impact of Textile Imports-Exports Hearings,* pp. 133, 137; U.S.-Japan Trade Council, *Japan Buys American in All 50 States,* Japanese-American Trade Relations-Pamphlets undated, box 8, Petersen Files; Fact Sheet on Japanese Cotton Textile Imports, attached to Mike Masaoka to Senator Pastore, June 12, 1961, box Pastore-General Files-Textiles, Pastore Papers.

24. The President's News Conference of March 8, 1961, *Public Papers, 1961,* p. 159; U.S.-Japan Trade Council, *Japan Buys American in All 50 States,* undated; "Kennedy on Protectionism: Kennedy Seeks Trade Expansion as Protectionist Pressures Rise," reprint from *New York Times,* February 12, 1961; *U.S. Trade with Japan, 1956–1960,* August 1961, box 8, Petersen Files; Memorandum for the President from W. W. Rostow, Japan and the OECD, March 4, 1961, box 104, POF; "Washington Outlook," *Textile World* 111 (August 1961):22; "News and Comment," *Textile World* (November 1961):40.

25. Joint Statement Following Discussions with Prime Minister Ikeda of Japan, June 22, 1961, p. 471; The President's News Conference of June 28, 1961, *Public Papers, 1961,* p. 480. See also "Unprecedented Prosperity in Japan, Economy Operates at Peak," *Foreign Commerce Weekly* 66 (August 21, 1961):12; "Japan Trade Deficit Increases; Imports from U.S. Up 10 Percent," *Foreign Commerce Weekly* (October 2, 1961):7; *New York Times,* June 22, 1961, p. 41; Summary Minutes of Meeting of Interdepartmental Committee of Under Secretaries on Foreign Economic Policy, May 31, 1962, box 32, Gordon Papers; *Data on Trade and Payments,* p. 17.

26. "News and Comment," *Textile World* 111 (October 1961):20; Hunsberger, *Japan and the United States,* pp. 329–330; President Kennedy to Ben Dorfman [Tariff Commission], November 21, 1961, box 21, Feldman Files; Burris Jackson to Senator Pastore, July 11, 1962, box Pastore-General Files-Textiles; Statement of Senator John O. Pastore, September 6, 1962, box Textiles General, Pastore Papers; "House Approves Cotton Subsidy Bill, 216–182," *Congressional Quarterly-Weekly Report* 21 (December 6, 1963):2111–2112. The commission rejected the fee in September 1962, but Kennedy ordered the USDA to find a solution to the two-price problem, and a subsidy went into effect in 1963.

27. Robert Stevens to Senator Pastore, November 3, 1961, box Textiles-General, Pastore Papers; White, "The Kennedy Era: Stage Two, The Coming Battle With Congress," p. 102; Schlesinger, *A Thousand Days,* p. 848; " 'Effective

Congress' Group," *Congressional Quarterly-Weekly Report* 19 (December 29, 1961):1991.

28. Howard Petersen, interview with author, June 10, 1986, Radnor, Pennsylvania. See also Summary Minutes of Meeting of the Interdepartmental Committee on Foreign Economic Policy, October 4, 1961, box 8, Behrman Papers; Hickman Price to Myer Feldman, June 23, 1961, box 25, Feldman Files.

29. Press release, Geneva, February 9, 1962; Undersecretary of Labor Willard Wirtz, statement to the Cotton Textile Committee, January 31, 1962, box 21, Feldman Files.

30. "Restrictions First," *The Economist* 200 (July 29, 1961):474; Hunsberger, *Japan and the United States,* 331; "Activities of the Community," *Bulletin of the EEC* 4 (December 1961):26–27; Aggarwal, *Liberal Protectionism,* pp. 85–90; "Geneva Formula," *The Economist* 202 (February 17, 1962):642; Hickman Price to Myer Feldman, February 13, 1962 and attached draft letter, Cotton-Cotton Textile Agreement-2/9/62, 4/61–2/62, box 21, Feldman Files. Under the LTA, Denmark and Portugal joined the seventeen nations that had signed the Short-Term Arrangement.

31. "Unkind Cut?," *The Economist* 202 (March 17, 1962):1052–1053; K. Y. Chen, "The Economic Setting," in *The Business Environment in Hong Kong,* edited by David G. Lethbridge (Hong Kong: Oxford University Press, 1980), pp. 26–27, 48; Aggarwal, *Liberal Protectionism,* p. 92.

32. "Should You Back the Trade Expansion Act?," *Textile World* 112 (April 1962):39–40. See also President Kennedy to Carl Vinson, February 26, 1962, box 21, Feldman Files. In addition to the LTA, the equalization fee request, and a national security investigation, Kennedy also planned to boost research, development, and market analysis, granted generous depreciation allowances, authorized Small Business Administration modernization loans for over $6 million, and offered adjustment assistance under the TEA.

33. *TEA-House,* pt. 6, Burris C. Jackson, National Cotton Council to Wilbur Mills, April 9, 1962, 4130; Proposed Resolution of the ACMI for Annual Meeting, March 31, 1962, box 21, Feldman Files.

34. Carl Vinson to Hickman Price, March 16, 1962, box 21, Feldman Files. See also "Administration's Coup on Textiles," *Business Week* no. 1695 (February 24, 1962):34; Telephone Conversation with Senator Pastore, February 9, 1962; Senator John Pastore to Seabury Stanton, February 23, 1962, box Pastore-General Files-Textiles, Pastore Papers; Carl Vinson to Robert T. Stevens, March 24, 1962, attached to Lawrence O'Brien to Vinson, March 28, 1962, box 479, WHCF-JFK; Carl Vinson to Myer Feldman, March 15, 1962, box 55, Petersen Files; Secretary Luther Hodges to Cong. Carl Vinson, March 22, 1962, box 21, Feldman Files.

35. *Textile Industry Hearings II,* William J. Bernhard, American Chamber of Commerce for Trade with Italy, pp. 66–67; *TEA-House,* Pitofsky, American Association of Apparel and Textile Importers, 2736–2737.

36. "Cotton Textile Imports," *Congressional Quarterly-Almanac* 18 (1962):346–348; "Congress, President Present Mixed Record in 1962," *Congressional Quarterly-Weekly Report* 20 (October 19, 1962):1937.

37. Myer Feldman to Senator Jacob Javits (R-N.Y.), October 3, 1962, box 479, WHCF-JFK; Rashish Oral History, pp. 24–25; Carl Vinson to the President,

February 15, 1962, box 14, Petersen Files; Carl Vinson to the President, June 13, 1962, attached to the President to Vinson, June 27, 1962, box 479, WHCF-JFK; The Wool Textile Problem, attached to memorandum from Undersecretary George Ball, March 4, 1963, box 88A, POF; John Pastore to Senator Norris Cotton (R-N.H.), August 27, 1962, box Pastore-General Files-Textiles, Pastore Papers.

38. Henry Wilson to Lawrence O'Brien, July 2, 1962, box 3, Wilson Files. See also Pastor, *Congress*, pp. 114–116; Thomas D. Blake to the President, July 23, 1962, box 480, WHCF-JFK; Henry Wilson to Lawrence O'Brien, July 2, 1962, box 31, O'Brien Files; House and Senate Support for Key Presidential Programs, 87th Cong., 1st Sess., October 1961, box 50, POF. For regional and party voting on the TEA, see Barrie, "Congress," pp. 263–272.

39. United States Senate, 87th Cong., 2d sess., Degree of Republican Opposition on Key Issues, [1962], box 52, POF; House of Representatives, 87th Cong., 2d sess.: Total Support, [1962], box 32, O'Brien Files; Myer Feldman to the President, October 10, 1962, box 29A, POF; Luther Hodges to Myer Feldman, August 6, 1962, attached to Memorandum for the President from Feldman, August 10, 1962, box 26, Feldman Files; Harris Oral History, pp. 60, 63; Hodges Oral History, p. 82; Bauer, Pool, and Dexter, *American Business*, p. 79. House Republicans voted 80–90 against, and Democrats 218–35 in favor, of the TEA. Southern Democrats (SDs) voted 82–23 in favor, while Senate Republicans voted 22–7, Democrats 56–1, and SDs 19–1 for the bill. The House defeated the Mason motion 171–253, with SDs against 37–69. The Senate rejected the Bush amendment 34–45, SDs voting 9–10, and the Curtis 20–63 (SDs 1–19), Dirksen 28–56 (SDs 5–16), and Prouty amendments 21–54 (SDs 1–16).

40. *Congressional Record-Senate*, vol. 108, pt. 6, May 16, 1962, 8534. See also White, *Making of the President, 1960*, pp. 420–421. Softwood lumber includes pine, spruce, fir, and hemlock.

41. Darius Adams and Richard Haynes, "U.S.-Canadian Lumber Trade: The Effect of Restrictions," in *U.S. International Forest Products Trade*, edited by Roger A. Sedjo (Washington, D.C.: Resources for the Future, 1981), p. 103; U.S. Senate Committee on Commerce, *The Impact of Lumber Imports on the United States Softwood Lumber Industry, Part II*, 87th Cong., 2nd sess., 1962, Edwin C. Rettig, Potlach Forests, 463–464 (hereafter *Lumber Hearings-II Lewiston* or *Olympia*); Commodity Research Bureau, *Commodity Yearbook, 1972* (New York: Commodity Research Bureau, 1972), p. 200; Department of Commerce study, *Impact of Imported Canadian Lumber on the United States Lumber Industry*, January 29, 1962, box 9, Petersen Files; UN, *Yearbook of Forest Products Statistics, 1962* (Rome: United Nations, 1962), p. ix, and *Yearbook of Forest Products Statistics, 1963* (Rome: United Nations, 1963), p. vii.

42. "1950–1960 Was a Boom Decade for Lumber," *Timberman* 62 (May 29, 1961):20; U.S. Senate Committee on Commerce, *The Impact of Lumber Imports on the United States Softwood Lumber Industry, Part I*, 87th Cong., 2d sess., 1962, pp. 45–46, and Cong. Clem Miller (D-Calif.), pp. 4–5 (hereafter *Lumber Hearings-I*); "Commerce Dept. Reviews Past Year; Sees Uptrend," *Crow's Lumber Digest* 40 (February 8, 1962):45; "Soaring Sixties Turn Soggy in Housing," *Timberman* 62 (May 29, 1961):17; Commodity Research Bureau, *Commodity Yearbook, 1963* (New York: Commodity Research Bureau, 1963), p. 200, and

Commodity Yearbook, 1972, p. 202; Myer Feldman to the President, July 24, 1962, box 102, POF; *Historical Statistics*, pt. II, 671.

43. Myer Feldman to the President, July 24, 1962, box 102, POF; *Lumber Hearings-I*, Robert Dywer, Lumbermen's Economic Survival Committee, 64; *Lumber Hearings-II Lewiston*, Melvin O'Neal, Idaho First National Bank, 554; James to Senator Wayne B. Morse, February 8, 1962, Papers of Wayne B. Morse (D-Ore.), University of Oregon, Eugene, Oregon (hereafter Morse Papers); Senator Jack Westland to the President, February 22, 1962, box 13, Petersen Files.

44. "Canadian Dollar Marked Down to Speed Recovery," *Foreign Commerce Weekly* 66 (July 17, 1961):5; *Lumber Hearings-I*, State Department, "Imports of Softwood Lumber from Canada," pp. 29–30, G. Griffith Johnson, Asst. Secretary of State for Economic Affairs, pp. 105, 113; "Canada Applies Surcharge to 3 Import Schedules Affecting U.S. Exporters; Lists 650 Items," *International Commerce* 68 (July 9, 1962):6–7; "Loggers in British Columbia Ask for Log Export Boost," *Timberman* 63 (February 1962):54; *Lumber Hearings-I*, Mortimer Doyle, NLMA, p. 38, Joseph Miller, Western Forest Industries Association, pp. 81–83; 'Adams and Haynes, "Lumber Trade," p. 109; Report on Pacific Northwest Log and Lumber Exports to Japan, attached to Richard McArdle to Senator Wayne Morse, February 16, 1962, box 9, Petersen Files; U.S. House Subcommittee on Forests of the Committee on Agriculture, *Serial X: Export of Logs to Japan*, 87th Cong., 1st sess., 1961, Morse, pp. 2–4, 14.

45. *Lumber Hearings-I*, State Department, "Imports of Softwood Lumber from Canada," February 27, 1962, pp. 30, 34, Senator Maurine B. Neuberger (D-Ore.), p. 97; "Wanted: Equal Shipping Rates," *Crow's Lumber Digest* 40 (January 25, 1962):3; *Lumber Hearings-II Olympia*, William G. Reed, Simpson Timber Co. to Clarence D. Martin, Jr., Undersecretary of Commerce for Transportation, January 9, 1962, pp. 301–304, Richard Ford, Washington Public Ports Association, pp. 287–288; *Historical Statistics*, pt. II, p. 757. The freehold delayed transit of lumber cars, giving speculators time to dump lumber at prices below cost or hold out for a higher price. The U.S. Interstate Commerce Commission outlawed the freehold in 1960, though railroads then delayed by a circuitous routing system. Canada dropped the freehold in 1962.

46. Albert Hall, "What's Happening in Forestry," *Report to Private Forestry Enterprise*, 13, no. 5 (March 1, 1962):5; Wayne Morse and eight senators to Secretary Orville Freeman, March 5, 1962, attached to Freeman to Morse, April 17, 1962, box 9, Petersen Files. The USDA supervised the National Forest Service and the 42 forests in the Northwest and Inland Empire. "Controversy . . .: U.S. Lumber Market to be Major Topic at WCLA Meeting," *Crow's Lumber Digest* 40 (March 22, 1962):8; "Readers Reply to Crow Poll on Canadian Lumber Imports," *Crow's Lumber Digest* 40 (May 3, 1962):28, 30.

47. *Lumber Hearings-I*, Mortimer Doyle, NLMA, p. 40, G. Cleveland Edgett, West Coast Lumbermen's Association, p. 13.

48. Frank Welch to Cong. Julia B. Hansen (D-Wash.), May 16, 1962, box 9, Petersen Files; *Congressional Record-House*, vol. 108, pt. 4, March 27, 1962, Pelly, 5189; *Congressional Record-Appendix*, vol. 108, Reel 12, June 13, 1962, Pelly, A4384; *Congressional Record-Appendix*, July 3, 1962, Mundt, A5115.

49. *Lumber Hearings-I*, "Time for Action Near on Timber," *Oregon Journal*,

June 1, 1962, p. 133, "Some Relief for Coast Lumbermen Foreseen," *Seattle Times,* June 3, 1962, pp. 131–132, G. Griffith Johnson, p. 105; Department of Commerce, Preliminary: Trade Relations Between Canada and the United States, February 6, 1962, box 31, Petersen Files; *Data on Trade Payments,* p. 18; *Commodity Yearbook, 1972,* p. 200.

50. *Lumber Hearings-I,* "Seattle's Business: Timber Industry Pledged U.S. Aid," *Seattle Post-Intelligencer,* June 1, 1962, pp. 133–134, G. Griffith Johnson, p. 107; State Department Briefing Memorandum for Meeting with Prime Minister Diefenbaker, [1961] box 113, POF; Raymond Vernon to the Undersecretary, [October 1963], attached to Memorandum for McGeorge Bundy, October 10, 1963, box 19–20, NSF-JFK.

51. Petersen to Senators Morse and Henry M. Jackson (D-Wash.), May 9, 1962, attached to Leonard Weiss to Myer Rashish, May 8, 1962, box 9, Petersen Files. See also Howard Petersen to Senator Dennis Chavez (D-N.M.), May 24, 1962, box 9, Petersen Files; Howard Petersen to Senator Morse, May 24, 1962, Morse Papers.

52. Robert Barrie to Joe Gunterman, April 23, 1962, box 9, Petersen Files; Statement of Policy on the Trade Expansion Act of the American Pulp and Paper Association, attached to Myer Feldman to H. E. Whitaker, March 1, 1962, box 238, WHCF-JFK; *TEA-House,* pt. 5, David J. Winton, Winton Lumber Co., 2814; G. Colbert Thomas to the President, May 14, 1962, attached to Myer Feldman to Thomas, May 28, 1962, box 480, WHCF-JFK; H. D. Gresham to Robert Barrie, March 6, 1962, box 23; *The Lumber Letter,* February 23, 1962, box 9, Petersen Files; *TEA-House,* pt. 4, Mortimer Doyle, NLMA, 2096, Gordon Connor for Birch Club, Northern Hardwood and Pine Association, and Timber Producers Association, 2379–2384, Robert E. Hollowell, Fine Hardwoods Association, 2374, and Byron E. Bryan, for Southern and Atlantic hardwood plywood producers, 2385–2387; *Lumber Hearing-I,* W. Spencer Fox, Southern Pine Industry Committee, pp. 55–56; State Department, "Hardwood Plywood," February 1, 1962, box 31, Petersen Files.

53. *Lumber Hearing-I,* Cong. Miller, p. 3; Albert Hall, "What's Happening in Forestry," Report to Private Forestry Enterprise 13, no. 12 (June 16, 1962):1; *Congressional Record-Senate,* vol. 108, pt. 10, July 19, 1962, Morse, 14103 and pt. 2, February 19, 1962, Morse, 2441; Morse form letter, May 3, 1962, Morse Papers.

54. *Congressional Record-Appendix,* vol. 108, reel 12, June 13, 1962, "U.S. Loggers Seek an Ax for Canadian Imports," A4385. See also *Congressional Record-Appendix,* vol. 108, reel 12, June 13, 1962, Dent, A4385; *Congressional Record-House,* vol. 108, pt. 9, June 28, 1962, Hansen, 12085.

55. *Congressional Record-House,* vol. 108, pt. 10, July 18, 1962, Congress of the United States to President John F. Kennedy, June 12, 1962, 14068; "1948–1961 Voting Records on Reciprocal Trade," *Congressional Quarterly-Weekly Report* 20 (April 27, 1962):680–681; "House Extends Defense Productions, Export Control Acts; Enacts Kennedy Trade Bill After Defeating Substitute," *Congressional Quarterly-Almanac* 18 (1962):618–619.

56. *Congressional Record-Senate,* vol. 108, pt. 6, May 4, 1962, 7806–7807 and pt. 10, July 18, 1962, 13914. See also *Lumber Hearings-I,* Magnuson, p. 108,

Morse, pp. 119–120, E. L. Bartlett (D-Ark.), p. 116, and Frank Church (D-Ida.), p. 16; *Congressional Record-Senate,* vol. 108, pt. 7, June 1, 1962, 9593–9595.

57. White House Statement on a Program of Assistance to the Lumber Industry, July 26, 1962, *Public Papers, 1962,* pp. 580–581; Myer Feldman to the President, July 24, 1962, box 102, POF; "Kennedy Airs Views on Lumber," *Crow's Lumber Digest* 40 (August 9, 1962):10.

58. Press release, Committee for a National Trade Policy, July 27, 1962, box 9, Petersen Files; "WCLA's Reaction to JFK"; "WPA [Western Pine Association]: Immediate Break Needed"; "LESC [Lumbermen's Economic Survival Committee]—Committee to Continue Work," *Crow's Lumber Digest* 40 (August 9, 1962):10–11; U.S. Senate Finance Committee, *The Trade Expansion Act of 1962,* 87th Cong., 2d sess., 1962, pt. 4, Henry Bahr, NLMA, 1767–1768, 1835–1836 (hereafter *TEA-Senate*); *Congressional Record-House,* vol. 108, pt. 15, Hansen, September 24, 1962, 20557–20559; *Congressional Record-Senate,* vol. 108, pt. 11, July 31, 1962, Hansen, 15182 and July 27, 1962, 14903–14904.

59. "Canada-U.S. Talks Set," *Crow's Lumber Digest* 40 (August 23, 1962):18; *Wall Street Journal,* July 27, 1962, p. 5; *New York Times,* August 27, 1962, p. 31.

60. *Lumber Hearings-II Olympia,* "U.S. Mills Hurt By Own Laws," *Tacoma News-Tribune,* January 12, 1962, p. 333; "Editorial," *British Columbia Lumberman* 46 (September 1962):9; *Congressional Record-Appendix,* v. 108, reel 13, August 9, 1962, "Crucial Time for Lumber Aid," *Seattle Times,* A6170; "CLA [Canadian Lumbermen's Association] Sounds Off on Import Crisis," *Crow's Lumber Digest* 40 (August 23, 1962):17; "Industry with Problems on All Sides," *Forest Industries* 89 (July 1962):48; "Market Review," *British Columbia Lumberman* 46 (August 1962):82; "Editorial," *British Columbia Lumberman* (September 1962):7; "More Bellowing," *British Columbia Lumberman* 46 (October 1962):69.

61. "Editorial," *British Columbia Lumberman* 46 (July 1962):8. See also "Lumbermen Fight Back," *Business Week* no. 1722 (September 1, 1962):23.

62. *New York Times* (August 30, 1962):37; "Second Tariff Meeting Finds Each Side in Doubt," *Crow's Lumber Digest* 40 (November 15, 1962):42; Memorandum of Conversation between the President and the Prime Minister at Hyannisport, May 11, 1963, box 5, Feldman Files; David Jones to Dean R. Rust, August 23, 1962, box 945, WHCF-JFK; "The U.S.-Canadian Situation," *Forest Industries* 89 (October 1962):38; "The Cream Puff Barrage," *Crow's Lumber Digest* 40 (November 1, 1962):40; "Tariff Commission Rejects Move to Regulate Imports," *Crow's Limber Digest* 41 (February 21, 1963):33. The TEA's concept of injury required a tariff or quota only if a trade concession was the direct cause of injury. The commission pointed instead to Canada's depreciated dollar, its cheaper shipping and rail rates, and higher U.S. timber prices as responsible for American lumber hardships.

63. "House Extends Defense Productions, Export Control Acts; Enacts Kennedy Trade Bill After Defeating Substitute," *Congressional Quarterly-Almanac,* pp. 618–619, 688, Thomas Kuchel of California was the lone Republican in the bloc; Parmet, *JFK,* p. 206, writes that 44.3 percent of New Frontier legislation for 1962 passed, although he argues that this figure is deceptive.

64. Carroll Kilpatrick, "The Kennedy Style and Congress," *Virginia Quarterly Review* 39 (Winter 1963):1, 6.

65. Bauer, Pool, and Dexter, *American Business*, pp. 77, 362. See also Barrie, "Congress," p. 176; Theodore Hesburgh Oral History, p. 7, John F. Kennedy Library, Boston, Massachusetts.

66. *Commodity Yearbook, 1972,* p. 200; John H. Young, "Study 1. The Traditional Export Industries," in *Trade Liberalization and a Regional Economy: Studies of the Impact of Free Trade on British Columbia,* edited by Ronald A. Shearer, John H. Young, and Gordon R. Munro, in *Regional and Adjustment Aspects of Trade Liberalization,* edited by H. Edward English (Toronto: University of Toronto, 1973), pp. 69–70; Ronald Shearer, "Study 1. The Economy of British Columbia" in *Regional and Adjustment Aspects,* edited by English, pp. 26–27; *Data on Trade and Payments,* p. 18. U.S.-Canada trade balance in chap. 1.

67. Aggarwal, *Liberal Protectionism,* p. 92; *TEA-Senate,* pp. 1002, 1005; "Hong Kong Growth Continues; U.S. Textile Ban Causes Concern," *International Commerce* 68 (July 23, 1962):40; Shik Chun Young, "The GATT's Long-Term Cotton Textile Arrangement and Hong Kong's Cotton Textile Trade," Ph.D. dissertation, Washington State University, 1969, pp. 1, 4, 30, 46–48, 62–69, 121–122, 139, 158, 163, 178.

68. *Bulletin of the EEC* 5 (November 1962):20–21; UN, *World Economic Survey, 1963, I: Trade and Development-Trends, Needs, and Policies* (New York: United Nations, 1964), p. 195; Summary of May 23, 1963 meeting of Interdepartmental Committee of Under Secretaries on Foreign Economic Policy, June 4, 1963, box 8, Behrman Papers; Brandis, *Making of Textile Trade,* pp. 29, 33; Aggarwal, *Liberal Protectionism,* pp. 92–94, 101–102, 111; Brian Toyne et al., *The Global Textile Industry* (London: Allen and Unwin, 1984), appendix 2; Lenway, *Politics of Trade Policy,* p. 95.

69. Chen, "Economic Setting," p. 48; "Washington Outlook," *Textile World* 112 (August 1962):19–20; Aggarwal, *Liberal Protectionism,* pp. 87, 90–94, 112–136; UN, *World Economic Survey, 1969–1970: The Developing Countries in the 1960s-The Problem of Appraising Progress* (New York: United Nations, 1971), p. 152; Brandis, *Making of Textile Trade,* pp. 66–67, chap. 5.

4. Political Trade-Offs in Oil and Tariffs

1. Douglas R. Bohi and Milton Russell, *Limiting Oil Imports: An Economic History and Analysis* (Baltimore: Johns Hopkins University Press, 1978), chaps. 1–3; Gerald D. Nash, *United States Oil Policy, 1890–1964* (Pittsburgh: University of Pittsburgh Press, 1968), pp. 202–206; Edward W. Chester, *United States Oil Policy and Diplomacy: A Twentieth Century Overview* (Westport, Conn.: Greenwood Press 1983), chaps. 1, 3, pp. 140–157; Kaufman, *Trade and Aid,* pp. 89–90. For a history of oil policy, see U.S. Senate Subcommittee on Multinational Corporations of the Committee on Foreign Relations, *Report on Multinational Oil Corporations and U.S. Foreign Policy,* 93d Cong., 2d sess., 1975 (hereafter *Multinational Oil Hearings*). A revised version of the oil case can be found in

Thomas W. Zeiler, "Kennedy, Oil Imports, and the Fair Trade Doctrine," *Business History Review* 64 (Summer 1990):286–310.

2. Kennedy to George Mills, March 19, 1959, box 724, PPP. See also "Oil Could Be Top Topic in Congress," *Petroleum Week* 11 (January 8, 1960):13; "A Look at the Record Shows How the Oil Industry Might Fare," *Oil and Gas Journal* 58 (July 18, 1960):62; Kennedy, "The Economic Problems of New England: A Program for Congressional Action," no. 3, May 25, 1953, box 774; New England Senate Delegation to the President, March 5, 1959, box 724, PPP.

3. The President's News Conference of March 1, 1961, *Public Papers, 1961*, p. 138. See also Briefing Paper from Bill Brubeck and Myer Rashish, Oil Import Situation, 1960, box 993, PPP; White, *Making of the President, 1960*, pp. 420–421; "The Election is Important to Oil," *Petroleum Week* 11 (July 22, 1960):11–13; Justinus Gould to Cong. Wright Patman (D-Tex.), May 16, 1961, box 288, Papers of Tom Steed, Carl Albert Congressional Research and Studies Center, Congressional Archives, University of Oklahoma, Norman, Oklahoma (hereafter Steed Papers); *New York Times*, February 18, 1961, p. 25; Telegram, Senator Robert C. Byrd to the White House, February 17, 1961, box 23, Feldman Files; "Residual Controls: Is the Game Worth the Candle?," *Oil and Gas Journal* 59 (February 27, 1961):56; Bohi, *Oil Imports*, pp. 149–150.

4. "The New Defense Concept Threatens JFK Import Control," *Oil and Gas Journal* 60 (January 8, 1962):29; Study by John M. Kelly, In Support of Proposals to Amend the Oil Import Program (Charts 6 and 7), November 21, 1961, box 23, Feldman Files; Summary Minutes of Meeting of the Interdepartmental Committee of Undersecretaries on Foreign Economic Policy, December 13, 1961, box 32, Gordon Papers; Myer Feldman to the President, December 14, 1961, box 63, POF; U.S. House Hearings before Subcommittee No. 4 of the Select Committee on Small Business, *Small Business Problems Created by Petroleum Imports*, pt. 1, 87th Cong., 1st sess., 1961 (hereafter *Petroleum Hearings-I or II*), Clarence W. Nichols, assistant to the Asst. Secretary of State for Economic Affairs, p. 198.

5. Summary Record of Meeting on World Oil Problems, Department of State, January 15, 1962, box 33, Gordon Papers; George Feldman, "The OECD, the Common Market, and American Foreign Policy," attached to Lawrence O'Brien to Congressman John McCormack, January 10, 1962, box 237, WHCF-JFK; Remarks of Stewart L. Udall to the American Petroleum Institute Meeting, July 27, 1961, box 93, Papers of Stewart L. Udall, Special Collections, University of Arizona (hereafter Udall Papers); "News," *Petroleum Management* 34 (April 1962):1.

6. "The Bright Spots in Oil Abroad," *Oil and Gas Journal* 59 (December 25, 1961):81; *New York Times*, August 31, 1961, p. 39; "Conference Table," *Petroleum Management* 34 (May 1962):12; Stephen G. Rabe, *The Road to OPEC: United States Relations with Venezuela, 1919–1976* (Austin: University of Texas Press, 1982), pp. viii, 109–110, 123–129; Schlesinger, *A Thousand Days*, p. 766; GATT, *International Trade, 1963*, p. 111; *Wall Street Journal*, July 3, 1961, pp. 1, 10; "1960: Bleak Year for Venezuelan Oil," *Petroleum Week* 12 (January 6, 1961):40; William G. Harris, "The Impact of the Petroleum Export Industry on the Pattern of Venezuelan Economic Development," Ph.D. dissertation, University

of Oregon, 1967, p. 1; General Economic Situation [Venezuela], December 5, 1961, box 235–238, NSF-JFK.

7. Arthur Schlesinger, Jr., The Current Crisis in Latin America, Pt. I, 1961, box 121A, POF.

8. Address in New Orleans at the Opening of the New Dockside Terminal, May 4, 1962, *Public Papers, 1962,* p. 360. See also The President's Visit to Venezuela and Colombia, Background Paper, December 1961, box 235–239, NSF-JFK.

9. Rabe, *Road to OPEC,* pp. 97–140; Marvin R. Zahniser and W. Michael Weis, "A Diplomatic Pearl Harbor? Richard Nixon's Goodwill Mission to Latin America in 1958," *Diplomatic History* 13 (Spring 1989):180–183; Romulo Betancourt, *Venezuela: Oil and Politics* (Boston: Houghton Mifflin, 1979), pp. 387–388; Current Political Situation in Venezuela, December 6, 1961, box 235–238, NSF-JFK; Arthur Schlesinger, Jr., The Current Crisis in Latin America, Pt. I, box 121A, POF.

10. Rabe, *Road to OPEC,* pp. 117–120, 158–160; R. K. Pachauri, *The Political Economy of Global Energy* (Baltimore: Johns Hopkins University Press, 1985), pp. 56–58; Franklin Tugwell, *The Politics of Oil in Venezuela* (Stanford: Stanford University Press, 1975), chap. 3; Telegram, American Embassy Caracas to Secretary of State, May 5, 1961, box 192, NSF-JFK; *Multinational Oil Report,* p. 88; Foreign Service Dispatch, Caracas to the Department of State, December 5, 1961, box 24, Feldman Files; Position Paper, The President's Visit to Venezuela and Colombia, Oil Import Program, December 6, 1961, box 235, NSF-JFK; "Looking Ahead in Washington," *Petroleum Week* 12 (March 10, 1961):24; *Petroleum Hearings-I,* A Request for Elimination of Restrictions on the Import of Residual Oil Filed with the Office of Civil and Defense Mobilization by the New England Council, the Oil Users Association, and American Public Power Association, p. 309.

11. Betancourt, *Venezuela,* p. 389; John Kelly to Myer Feldman, October 22, 1961; Myer Feldman to the President, December 14, 1961, box 24; Myer Feldman to the President, December 15, 1961, box 23, Feldman Files; Joint Statement Following Discussions with the President of Venezuela, December 17, 1961, *Public Papers, 1961,* p. 808. See also "Eximbank Increases Loan to Venezuela," *Foreign Commerce Weekly* 66 (September 11, 1961):39; "Charter of Punta del Este" [Alliance for Progress], Department of State *Bulletin* 45 (September 11, 1961):463–464, 467–469; Briefing, The President's Trip to Venezuela and Colombia, December 1961, box 235, NSF-JFK; Remarks Upon Arrival at Maiquetia Airport, Caracas, Venezuela, December 16, 1961, *Public Papers, 1961,* p. 804; John M. Kelly Oral History, John F. Kennedy Library, Boston, Massachusetts, (hereafter Kelly Oral History), p. 21.

12. "Imports Battle Must Be Fought All Over Again," *Oil and Gas Journal* 59 (December 11, 1961):50–51; Stewart Udall to the President, February 2, 1962, box 23, Feldman Files; "Steed Fears U.S. Oil Policy Not Adequate," *Oklahoma City Times,* November 24, 1961, p. 1, Steed Papers; "Watching Washington," *Oil and Gas Journal* 59 (December 11, 1961):51; "1962 Will be a Showdown Year for Kennedy on Oil," *Oil and Gas Journal* 60 (January 8, 1962):3.

13. *Commodity Yearbook, 1963,* pp. 82–83; *Petroleum Hearings-I,* p. 185.

Other coal states were Alabama, Colorado, Illinois, Indiana, Kentucky, Ohio, Pennsylvania, Utah, and West Virginia.

14. "Buying off the Opposition," *Business Week*, no. 1699 (March 24, 1962):32. See also *Coal/Oil Hearing*, G. Don Sullivan, National Coal Association, p. 38; *Petroleum Hearings-II*, C. J. Potter, Rochester and Pittsburgh Coal Company, p. 465; *TEA-House*, pt. 3, Thomas Kennedy, [UMW], 1714; Henry Wilson to Lawrence O'Brien, December 20, 1961, box 3, Wilson Files; Mike Manatos to Lawrence O'Brien, March 14, 1962, box 1, Manatos Files; Joseph Moody to Secretary Stewart Udall, May 3, 1962, box 5, Feldman Files; Thomas Kennedy to President Kennedy, June 28, 1961, box 489, WHCF-JFK; "Fuels Group Rejects End-Use Controls," *Oil and Gas Journal* 60 (September 24, 1962):85–86; The President's Special News Conference with Business Editors and Publishers, September 25, 1962, p. 709 *Public Papers 1962;* Letter to the President of the Senate and to the Speaker of the House Transmitting a Bill to Stimulate Construction of Coal Pipelines, March 20, 1962, pp. 249–250, *Public Papers, 1962.* The industry sought a national fuels study (rejected by Congress) and a slurry to pipe coal into regions where resid enjoyed little competition.

15. *TEA-House*, pt. 3, Thomas Kennedy, UMW, 1714. See also Coal and the Trade Expansion Act, March 30, 1962; Department of State, Energy Policy: Coal, Hydroelectric Power, Natural Gas, and Oil, February 2, 1962, box 31, Petersen Files; *Coal/Oil Hearings*, Harry Gilroy, "U.S. Coal Men Face New Woes in Declining European Market," p. 199; senators Robert C. Byrd and Jennings Randolph (D-W.Va.) to Lawrence O'Brien, June 28, 1961, box 5, Feldman Files; *TEA-Senate*, pt. 2, Douglas, p. 568; Paul H. Douglas, *In the Fullness of Time: The Memoirs of Paul H. Douglas* (New York: Harcourt, Brace, Jovanovich, 1972), pp. 480–481.

16. *New York Times*, December 17, 1961, III, pp. 1, 7; "Independents Plan Fight for Import-Control Legislation," *Oil and Gas Journal* 59 (December 18, 1961):40; Press Release, Texas Independent Producers and Royalty Owners Association (TIPRO) Information Service, March 11, 1962, box 23, Feldman Files; TIPRO Information Service to President James West, April 2, 1962, box 14, Petersen Files; E. A. Smith to Robert Bleiberg, December 8, 1961; Joseph Moody to Cong. Tom Steed, December 1, 1961, box 288, Steed Papers; *TEA-House*, pt. 3, Harold Decker, IPAA, 1724; Memorandum for Meeting with Prime Minister Diefenbaker, [1961], box 113, POF; Chester, *United States Oil Policy*, pp. 138–139. The Brownsville shuffle involved unloading Mexican oil from tankers to trucks once it arrived in America and sending the trucks to Mexico, from which they then returned by crossing the border by land, and thus avoiding customs port houses. Then the oil, now officially in the United States, was reloaded back onto tankers and shipped to U.S. consumers. In short, the oil bypassed American customs at the port of Brownsville, entered the country officially by land, and was therefore not subject to tariffs or quotas under the overland exemption provision.

17. *Commodity Yearbook, 1963*, pp. 245, 247; *Petroleum Hearings-I*, pp. 66, 496; *Petroleum Hearings-II*, p. 540; Bohi, *Oil Imports*, pp. 22–23, 25.

18. For campaign bankrolling from oilmen, see Robert A. Caro, *The Path to Power: The Years of Lyndon Johnson* (New York: Vintage, 1983), p. 663. *Congressional Record-Appendix*, vol. 108, reel 11, January 10, 1962, Cleveland

M. Bailey, pp. A12, A14, and February 7, 1962, Arch A. Moore, A943; *Coal and Residual Imports Hearing,* Dent, p. 139; Legislative Highlights, February 26, 1962, box 50, POF; "Oil Still Leery of Kennedy's Business Views," *Oil and Gas Journal* 60 (May 7, 1962):63; "Steed Group Backing Cut in Imports," *Oil and Gas Journal* 59 (December 4, 1961):102; "Steed Hearing Indicates There is No Long-Range Imports Policy," *Oil and Gas Journal* 59 (November 27, 1961):64–65; *Petroleum Hearings-I,* Steed, pp. 2, 413; Minutes of Meeting, Subcommittee No. 4, House Small Business Committee, July 18, 1961; Record of Meeting between Steed and leaders of the Oklahoma Independent Petroleum Association, December 21, 1961, box 288, Steed Papers, *Congressional Record-House,* vol. 108, pt. 5, April 18, 1962, Steed, 6958 and pt. 11, July 20, 1962, 14385; Steed and Moore to Colleagues, April 12, 1962 and attached bill, box 307, Steed Papers.

19. "Congress Speaks on Domestic Fuels, Oil Imports, and National Security," National Coal Policy Conference, Inc., March 1962, box 30, Petersen Files; *Congressional Record-House,* vol. 108, pt. 8, June 13, 1962, Advertisement from the *New York Times,* April 1, 1962, 10429.

20. John K. Evans to the President, August 28, 1962, box 23, Feldman Files; *Coal/Oil Hearings,* Humble Oil and Refining Co., pp. 128–130; *TEA-Senate,* pt. 2, John H. Lichtblau, Petroleum Institute Foundation, Inc., p. 566; John K. Evans to Myer Feldman, April 30, 1962, box 23, Feldman Files; *Petroleum Hearing-I,* Charles W. Colsen and James S. Couzens, New England Council, pp. 291, 294–295; *TEA-House,* pt. 3, Edward M. Carey, Independent Fuel Oil Marketers of America, 1830; *Commodity Yearbook, 1963,* pp. 247, 245, 248; "Would Unlimited Resid Imports Hurt?," *Oil and Gas Journal* 59 (February 27, 1961):57–58.

21. *Congressional Record-Appendix,* vol. 108, reel 11, March 7, 1962, Keith, A1980; "Protectionism in Oil," *Boston Herald,* December 30, 1961, A1718. See also *Congressional Record-Appendix,* vol. 107, reel 11, September 12, 1961, Dante B. Fascell (D-Fla.), A7167, and Conte, A7542; Mike Manatos to Lawrence O'Brien, November 8, 1961, box 1, Manatos Files.

22. Henry Wilson to Lawrence O'Brien, February 23, 1962, box 14, O'Brien Files; Lawrence O'Brien to the President, March 6, 1962 and attached memorandum from Steed, My Proposed Conference with the President, box 50, POF; Address by Secretary Stewart Udall to the IPAA, April 30, 1962, Udall Papers; "Petty's Oil Letter," in *The Oil Daily,* March 28, 1962, attached to James West to Lindley Beckworth, June 6, 1962, box 14; Questions for Harold Decker, IPAA, on his testimony before the House Ways and Means Committee, [1962], box 10, Petersen Files.

23. *TEA-House,* pt. 2, Udall, p. 804; Howard Petersen to Johnny Mitchell, April 25, 1962, box 599, WHCF; Proposed Exchange of Letters between the President and Cong. Clark Thompson, May 11, 1962, box 23, Feldman Files; Truman Richardson to Ross Porter, March 14, 1962, box 307, Steed Papers; *Congressional Record-Senate,* vol. 108, pt. 9, July 5, 1962, Cleveland Bailey, 12798; Myer Feldman to the President, June 25, 1962, attached to Memorandum for Cong. Clark W. Thompson, box 23, Feldman Files; W. E. Turner to Tom Steed, March 28, 1962, box 307, Steed Papers; "Oil/Gas and the November Election," *World Oil* 154 (August 1, 1962):23.

24. "House Extends Defense Production, Export Control Act; Enacts Kennedy

Trade Bill After Defeating Substitutes," *Congressional Quarterly-Almanac* 18 (1962):618–619.

25. "Oil/Gas and the November Elections," *World Oil* 154 (August 1, 1962):14, 18. See also "Platt's Oilgram" May 4, 1962, attached to Henry Wilson to Myer Rashish, May 10, 1962, box 14, Petersen Files; "Key Oil Decisions Coming Soon," *Oil and Gas Journal* 60 (August 27, 1962):43–44.

26. Pamphlet, "Congress Speaks on Domestic Fuels, Oil Imports, and National Security," March 1962, box 30, Petersen Files. See also *Congressional Record-Senate*, vol. 107, pt. 2, February 20, 1961, Letter from [New England Delegation] to the President, February 7, 1961, 2363; Mike Manatos to O'Brien, April 7, 1962, box 327, O'Brien Files; Senator Harry Byrd to the President, April 12, 1962, box 599, WHCF; *Coal/Oil Hearings, G.* Don Sullivan to Secretary Stewart Udall, p. 9; *Congressional Record-House*, v. 107, pt. 3, March 2, 1961, Byrd, 20801 and 18 Senators to Kennedy, 3137–3138.

27. Coal-oil bloc senators came from Alabama, Alaska, Arkansas, Colorado, Illinois, Indiana, Kansas, Kentucky, Louisiana, Maryland, Missouri, Montana, North Dakota, Nevada, New Mexico, Ohio, Oklahoma, Pennsylvania, Tennessee, Texas, Utah, Virginia, Washington, West Virginia, and Wyoming.

28. Anne H. Morgan, *Robert S. Kerr: The Senate Years* (Norman: University of Oklahoma Press, 1977), p. 221, also pp. 209–210, 242.

29. Ibid., pp. 232–233. See also Rashish Oral History, pp. 28–30; Luther Hodges to the President, Memorandum Reporting the Status of the Trade Expansion Act, August 20, 1962, box 51, POF.

30. Morgan, *Kerr*, pp. 210, 233. The "whales" were veterans Richard B. Russell (D-Ga.), Carl Hayden (D-Ariz.), Allen Ellender (D-La.), and James Eastland (D-Miss.). E. A. Smith to Kerr, March 27, 1962, box 69, Papers of Congressman Page Belcher, Carl Albert Congressional Research and Studies Center Congressional Archives, University of Oklahoma, Norman, Oklahoma, for report by Oilgram News Service of March 25, 1962 that Kerr traded pet projects for the TEA.

31. Robert Kerr to John H. Cosey, May 4, 1955, box 34; Kerr to Cleo C. Ingle, April 13, 1955, box 34; Kerr, "The Reader Writes: Senator Kerr's Amendment," *Christian Science Monitor*, July 26, 1958, box 1; Address to the Midyear 1958 Meeting of the IPAA, April 29, 1958, box 8; Press release, Kerr and Senator A. S. Monroney (D-Okla.), February 28, 1959, box 18; Transcript of Television Show on the Trade Expansion Act of 1962, Washington, D.C., June 14, 1962, box 25, Papers of Senator Robert S. Kerr, Carl Albert Congressional Research and Studies Center, Congressional Archives, University of Oklahoma, Norman, Oklahoma (hereafter Kerr Papers); Press Release, March 28, 1962; Press Release, Kerr and A. S. "Mike" Monroney (D-Okla.), June 20, 1962, box 56, Petersen Files; "Watching Washington," *Oil and Gas Journal* 60 (April 23, 1962):65; "Kerr, Steed on Different Sides on Oil Amendment," *Oklahoman*, April 1, 1962, box 307; Kerr to Thomas Williams, April 16, 1962, box 4; Kerr to J. Howard Edmondson, May 21, 1962, box 4, Kerr Papers; Morgan, *Kerr*, p. 233.

32. Kerr to E. A. Smith, October 8, 1962, Kerr Papers; "What Kerr Says About Changing Import Controls," *Oil and Gas Journal* 60 (July 30, 1962):90; Kelly Oral History, p. 44; Luther Hodges to Myer Feldman, August 2, 1962, box 23,

Feldman Files; Harold Decker to members of IPAA, October 12, 1962 and attached copy from the *Congressional Record,* Russell Long (D-La.), box 11, Kerr Papers. Rumors circulated that Kerr locked a signed document of the deal in his safe; no written accord was found in the Kerr or Kennedy papers. Kerr said that a speech by Udall to the IPAA in September 1962 was the only "positive assurance" of a revised plan that he received from the administration. Long later said that he, senators Frank Carlson (R-Kan.), Ralph Yarborough (D-Tex.), Ellender, and Kerr (all "whales") got Kennedy's pledge that imports would be limited and independents would get a greater share of the U.S. market.

33. Kelly Oral History, pp. 43–46; Statement by Senator Robert S. Kerr on Trade Bill-Compensation for Import Damage, October 9, 1962, box 25; Statement by Senator Robert S. Kerr on Trade, October 9, 1962, box 11, Kerr Papers; "Other Major Developments Related to 1962 Trade Act," *Congressional Quarterly-Almanac* 18 (1962):289; "Senate Passes Trade Bill After Rejecting Escape Clause, Farm Import Restriction, Shorter Duration; Ratifies Treaty," *Congressional Quarterly-Almanac* 18 (1962):688, Homer E. Capehart (R-Ind.) and Wallace F. Bennett (R-Ut.) opposed the TEA.

34. A Report to the President by the Petroleum Study Committee, OEP, September 4, 1962, box 23, Feldman Files; The President's News Conference of September 26, 1962, *Public Papers, 1962,* p. 715; Proclamation 3509, November 30, 1962, box 23, Feldman Files; Bohi, *Oil Imports,* p. 107; *New York Times,* pp. 1, 29; Kelly Oral History, p. 42; Myer Feldman to Harold Decker, December 19, 1962, box 13, Petersen Files; Kerr to E. A. Smith, October 8, 1962, box 4; Remarks of Senator Robert Kerr to the IPAA Annual Meeting, Dallas, Texas, October 29, 1962, box 11; "Kerr's Magic Sways Oilmen," *Oklahoman,* November 4, 1962, box 11; Statement by Harold Decker, IPAA, November 30, 1962, box 25, Kerr Papers.

35. Report by the United States Delegation to the United States-Canadian Discussions of Petroleum Policies and Programs, December 13–14, 1962, box 104, POF; Bohi, *Oil Imports,* pp. 107, 132–134; Rabe, *Road to OPEC,* p. 198.

36. Airgram, USAID-Caracas to the Department of State, September 21, 1962, box WH-23, Arthur S. Schlesinger Papers, John F. Kennedy Library, Boston, Massachusetts (hereafter Schlesinger Papers); "Venezuela Survives Buffeting of 2 Revolts, Exchange Reform," *International Commerce* 68 (July 2, 1962):33; "Venezuela Business Prospers Despite Revolts and Currency Reform: Outlook Optimistic," *International Commerce* 68 (August 27, 1962):47; "Oil Output, Exchange Reform Brighten Venezuelan Outlook," *International Commerce* 68 (October 29, 1962):68; Robert J. Alexander, *Romulo Betancourt and the Transformation of Venezuela* (New Brunswick, N.J.: Rutgers University Press, 1982), pp. 554–557; Telegrams, Ambassador C. Allan Stewart, Caracas, to the Secretary of State, July 2, 1962 and December 18, 1962; CIA Reference Biographic Register of Juan Pablo Pérez Alfonzo; Memorandum, Visit to the United States of Dr. Juan Pablo Pérez Alfonzo, April 1962, box 192, NSF-JFK.

37. Report of Myer Feldman on Discussions with President Betancourt on the United States Oil Import Program, Caracas, attachment 1, December 29–30, 1962, box 104, POF; Betancourt, *Venezuela,* pp. 390–391.

38. Ibid., p. 391; Report by Myer Feldman on Discussions with President

Betancourt on the United States Oil Import Program, Caracas, attachments 1 and 2, December 29–30, 1962, box 104, POF; White House Situation Room to General Godfrey McHugh for the President, December 23, 1962, box 192, NSF-JFK.

39. Betancourt, *Venezuela*, p. 390; telegram, Ambassador C. Allan Stewart, American Embassy, Caracas to the Secretary of State, January 2, 1963, box 24, Feldman Files; Joint Statement with the Venezuelan President, February 20, 1963, *Public Papers of the Presidents of the United States, John F. Kennedy, 1963* (Washington, D.C.: U.S. Government Printing Office, 1964), p. 188 (hereafter *Public Papers, 1963*).

40. Magin A. Valdez, "The Petroleum Policies of the Venezuelan Government," Ph.D. dissertation, New York University, 1971, pp. 6–7; Shaffer, *The Oil Import Program*, p. 95; Bohi, *Oil Imports*, p. 146; *Commodity Yearbook, 1971*, p. 254.

41. American Carpet Institute, *Basic Facts about the Carpet and Rug Industry* (New York: American Carpet Institute, 1960), p. 8, (1965), p. 12, The Carpet and Rug Institute Library, Dalton, Georgia (hereafter Carpet and Rug Institute); *Congressional Record-Appendix*, vol. 107, reel 10, June 1, 1961, Stratton, A3944; Leddy and Norwood, "Escape Clause," p. 172; Resolution [ACMI Board of Directors] Supporting Tariff Commission Carpet Industry Finding, August 3, 1961, box 100, NACM-NTA Papers.

42. "The Glass Industry, 1960: A Review," *Glass Industry* 42 (February 1961):67; White, *Making of the President, 1960*, pp. 420–421.

43. "The Glass Industry, 1960: A Review," *Glass Industry* 42 (February 1961):69–70; "The Tariff Situation," *Glass Industry*, 42 (August 1961):432.

44. "The Tariff Situation," *Glass Industry* 42 (August 1961):431; U.S. House Subcommittee on the Impact of Imports on American Employment of the Committee on Education and Labor, *Impact of Imports and Exports on Employment (Glass, Pottery, Toys), pt. 3*, 87th Cong., 1st sess., 1961, (hereafter *Glass Import Hearings*), Donald J. Sherbondy, Pittsburgh Plate Glass Company, p. 36.

45. President's Statement, TPC draft package for the President, June 27, 1961, box 26, Feldman Files; "The Tariff Situation," *Glass Industry* 42 (August 1961):430; Domestic Sheet Glass Industry Production and Shipments, undated, box 10, Petersen Files; "U.S. Trade Policy Approaching Major Crisis," *Congressional Quarterly-Weekly Report* 19 (August 4, 1961):1349.

46. *Glass Import Hearings*, Oh.-Pa.-W.Va.-Ind. Glass Workers Protective League to President John F. Kennedy, April 22, 1961, pp. 119–120. See also "The Tariff Situation," *Glass Industry* 42 (August 1961):432, the congressmen were Ed Edmondson (D-Okla.), William Bray (R-Ind.), Overton Brooks (D-La.), James Trimble (D-Ark.), Dent, and Bailey.

47. *Congressional Record-House*, vol. 107, pt. 2, February 20, 1961, Dent, 2456. See also *Congressional Record-House.*, vol. 107, pt. 3, March 13, 1961, Dent, 3801–3804; John Dent to [a] Friend, [1962], box Trade-Tariffs-GATT, Dent Collection.

48. *Glass Import Hearings*, Jennings Randolph to John Dent, July 11, 1961, and telegram, Sen. Robert C. Byrd to the President, p. 3; Cong. Overton Brooks to the Executive Office of the President, May 27, 1961, attached to Lawrence O'Brien to Brooks, June 8, 1961; Sen. J. W. Fulbright to the President, May 25,

1961, attached to O'Brien to Fulbright, May 29, 1961; Sen. Estes Kefauver to the President, June 13, 1961, attached to O'Brien to Cong. James G. Fulton (R-Pa.), May 29, 1961, box 945, WHCF-JFK; Oklahoma House and Senate Delegation to the President, January 15, 1962, box 25, Kerr Papers. Seven firms operated fourteen sheet glass plants—four in West Virginia, two each in Oklahoma and Pennsylvnia, and one in Arkansas, Illinois, Indiana, Louisiana, Ohio, and Tennessee.

49. Lucius Battle to Myer Feldman, December 4, 1961, box 26, Feldman Files.

50. H. D. Gresham to Robert Barrie on G. P. MacNichol, Libbey-Owens-Ford, March 6, 1962, box 23, Petersen Files; statement, Manufacturers of Flat Glass Products, [1962], HR 11970, Record Group 46, U.S. Senate Committee on Finance Records, National Archives, Washington, D.C. (hereafter Senate Finance Records); John Dent to the President, December 15, 1961, box 478, WHCF-JFK.

51. Press Release, White House, March 19, 1962 and attached, President Kennedy to Ben Dorfman, March 19, 1962, box 20, Petersen Files; Myer Feldman to Cong. Samuel Stratton, June 25, 1962, box 13, Petersen Files; Sorensen Oral History, p. 113.

52. *TEA-House*, pt. 4, Robinson F. Barker, Pittsburgh Plate Glass Company, 2268, and Mildred Homko, Oh.-Pa.-W.Va.-Ind. Glass Workers Protective League, 2330; Petersen to the President, March 28, 1962, box 23, Petersen Files; "Sheet Glass and the Tariff," *Glass Industry* 43 (March 1962):240–242.

53. State Department Report on American Opinion, March-April 1962; box 14, Petersen Files. See also *Congressional Record-Appendix*, vol. 108, reel 11, April 4, 1962, Capehart, A2614; Mike Manatos to Lawrence O'Brien, March 20, 1962, box 1, Manatos Files; *Congressional Record-Senate*, vol. 108, pt. 9, July 5, 1962, Bailey, 12798.

54. Sen. Harry Byrd to President Lyndon Johnson, January 21, 1964, box 12, White House Central Files, Lyndon B. Johnson Library, Austin, Texas (hereafter WHCF-LBJ); "Buying of the Opposition," *Business Week*, no. 1699 (March 24, 1962):32; Comments on Administration's Trade Bill, April 17, 1962, attached to Peter Jones to Myer Feldman, April 17, 1962, box 26, Feldman Files; House Extends Defense Production, Export Control Act; Enacts Kennedy Trade Bill After Defeating Substitutes," *Congressional Quarterly-Almanac* 18 (1962):618–619, 688.

55. *New York Times*, pp. 1, 14. See also *New York Times*, March 31, 1962, p. 4 and April 13, 1962, p. 16; *Glass Import Hearings*, Rene Lambert, Permanent Representative for the Belgian Sheet Glass Industry in the U.S. and Canada, pp. 29–30.

56. "Tariff Reprisals," *Chemical and Engineering News* 40 (June 11, 1962):7; "A Wary Eye on the EEC," *Chemical Week* 90 (June 16, 1962):39.

57. Carpet and Rug Institute Industry Review, (1968):9, (1970):16, and (1978–1979):16; UN, *Yearbook of International Trade Statistics, 1966* (New York: United Nations, 1968), pp. 87–88, 863, and *1970–1971* (New York: United Nations, 1973), pp. 53, 796, 798.

58. The President's News Conference of June 14, 1962, *Public Papers, 1962*, p. 496. See also The President's News Conference of March 29, 1962, *Public Papers, 1962*, p. 277.

59. Myer Feldman to John H. Randolph, August 27, 1962, box 945, WHCF-JFK.

60. John Meagher and Harald Malmgren, "A Historical View of Congress' Impact on Trade Legislation and Negotiation," in *Congress and U.S. Trade Policy,* edited by LTV Corporation (Dallas: LTV Corporation, 1983), pp. 39–40. For Kennedy's pragmatism, see Parmet, *JFK,* p. 355 and John L. Paper, *The Promise and the Performance: The Leadership of John F. Kennedy* (New York: Crown, 1975), p. 270.

61. David S. Painter, *Oil and the American Century: The Political Economy of U.S. Foreign Oil Policy, 1941–1954* (Baltimore: Johns Hopkins University Press, 1986), pp. 206–207.

62. Lowi, "American Business and Public Policy," p. 685.

63. Rabe, *Road to OPEC,* p. 116. For two of the class conflict critics, see Magdoff, *Age of Imperialism* and Williams, *Tragedy.* See also Harris, "Petroleum Export Industry," pp. 12, 77, 93, 102.

64. *Commodity Yearbook, 1971,* pp. 93, 253; Bohi, *Oil Imports,* p. 23.

65. Rusk to the American Embassy Caracas, December 20, 1962, box 192, NSF-JFK; Rabe, *Road to OPEC,* p. 194.

66. *Historical Statistics,* pt. II, p. 884; *Yearbook of Trade Statistics, 1970–1971,* p. 796.

5. Kennedy Drives for Exports

1. Kaufman, *Trade and Aid,* pp. 20–22; Bauer, Pool, and Dexter, *American Business,* pp. 40, 375–387, 447; Functions to be Performed by Petersen and Staff, attached to Petersen-O'Brien Meeting Agenda, undated; Henry Wilson to Lawrence O'Brien, December 21, 1961, box 24, Feldman Files.

2. See John Hight to Frank Ellis, September 25, 1961, box 27, Gordon Papers; "Trade Battle Features Unique Lobby Alliances," *Congressional Quarterly-Weekly Report* 20 (March 9, 1962):403–404; Peter Davies to Howard Petersen, January 30, 1962, box 15; Rachel Bell to John Hight, February 6, 1962; Proposed CNTP Program of Operation in 1962, undated, box 17, Petersen Files. A different view is in G. William Domhoff, "Who Made American Foreign Policy, 1945–1962?," in *Corporations and the Cold War,* edited by Horowitz.

3. Seymour Harris to Arthur Schlesinger, December 13, 1961, box WH-11, Schlesinger Papers; "Why Small Firms Should Enter the Export Field," *Commercial and Financial Chronicle* 195 (February 15, 1962):40.

4. Address to the National Association of Manufacturers, December 6, 1961, *Public Papers, 1961,* p. 780. See also CBS Reports, "Breaking the Trade Barrier," May 24, 1962, box 480, WHCF-JFK.

5. Address in New Orleans at the Opening of the New Dockside Terminal, May 4, 1962, *Public Papers, 1962,* p. 359. See also Summary Record of Meeting of Economic Consultants, October 3, 1961; W. W. Rostow to Kermit Gordon, June 15, 1962, box 32, Gordon Papers.

6. CBS Report, "Breaking the Trade Barrier," May 24, 1962, box 480, WHCF-JFK.

7. Statement by the President Upon Establishing Awards for Significant Contri-

butions to the Export Expansion Program, December 5, 1961, *Public Papers, 1961*, p. 770.

8. Hodges Oral History, p. 65; Jack N. Behrman to author, March 20, 1986; Memorandum of Agreement between the Department of State and the Department of Commerce on International Commercial Activities, November 13, 1961; Jack Behrman to Secretary Hodges, Franklin Roosevelt, Jr., and Peter Jones, January 2, 1964; Memorandum on Commercial Services Program, Behrman to Hodges and Roosevelt, October 1, 1963, box 4, Behrman Papers; Statement by the President Concerning Export Credit Facilities, October 27, 1961, *Public Papers, 1961*, pp. 685–686; *Historical Statistics*, pt. II, p. 898.

9. David R. Andrews to Myer Feldman, May 14, 1962, box 480, WHCF-JFK; Summary Record of Meeting of Economic Consultants, October 3, 1961, box 32, Gordon Papers; *New York Times*, April 10, 1962, p. 39 and May 3, 1962, p. 43; Luther Hodges to the President, September 19, 1963, box 8, Behrman Papers. Apathy was not limited to the 1960s; see William H. Becker, *The Dynamics of Business-Government Relations: Industry and Exports, 1893–1921* (Chicago: University of Chicago Press, 1982), pp. 9, 41–42.

10. Peter L. Bernstein, "American Shoppers and the Common Market," *The Nation* 194 (January 27, 1962):79; George H. Gallup, *The Gallup Poll: Public Opinion, 1935–1971* (New York: Random House, 1972), pp. 1746, 1750, 1761, polls taken December 17, 1961, January 10, 1962, and April 8, 1962; J. Robert Schaetzel, "The United States and the Common Market," Department of State *Bulletin* 47 (September 3, 1962):351.

11. *TEA-House*, pt. 1, Luther Hodges, p. 65; Kennedy statement (inside cover), *Foreign Commerce Weekly* 68 (June 18, 1962); *Historical Statistics*, pt. II, pp. 884, 887; "International Markets," *Dun's Review and Modern Industry* 79 (April 1962):105–106; Foreign Trade Fact Sheet-States, undated, box 22, Feldman Files; Sen. Prescott Bush to Secretary of Commerce Luther Hodges, March 8, 1962, attached to Press Release, March 11, 1962, box 7, RG 69:13, Bush Papers; Ben G. Seligman, "Tariffs, the Kennedy Administration, and American Politics," *Commentary* 33 (March 1962):187–188.

12. *TEA-House*, pt. 2, Freeman, pp. 839, 837–840. See also Foreign Trade Fact Sheet-States, undated, box 22, Feldman Files; Raymond A. Ioanes, "Trends and Structure of U.S. Agricultural Trade," in *U.S. Trade Policy*, edited by Iowa State, pp. 96, 100; Arthur B. Mackie, "Patterns of World Agricultural Trade," in *U.S. Trade Policy*, edited by Iowa State; U.S. Department of Agriculture, *U.S. Agriculture and the Balance-of-Payments, 1960–1967* (Washington, D.C.: U.S. Government Printing Office, 1968), pp. 3, 12.

13. Ross B. Talbot, *The Chicken War: An International Trade Conflict Between the United States and the European Economic Community, 1961–1964* (Ames: Iowa State University Press, 1978), pp. ix-xi, 3–4, 33–37, 64–66.

14. Ibid., pp. 53–55, 71, 159–164; C. E. Clegg to the President, June 2, 1962; Statement by Gov. S. Ernest Vandiver [Ga.]; Gov. Ross Barnett [Miss.] to the President, [May-June 1962], box 24, Feldman Files.

15. Hodges Oral History, p. 85; Summary of Major Points, House Ways and Means Executive Hearings on HR 9900, 6th Executive Session, May 1, 1962, box 8, Petersen Files; Memorandum on the Impact of the Common Market Proposals

on U.S. Poultry, [May-June 1962], box 24, Feldman Files; Talbot, *Chicken War,* pp. 55–56, 162–163.

16. Orville Freeman to the President, July 10, 1962, box 9, Freeman Papers; Myer Feldman to the President, June 4, 1962, box 24, Feldman Files; Warley, "Western Trade," p. 381.

17. Draft Letter, President John F. Kennedy to Chancellor Adenauer, June 8, 1962, box 24, Feldman Files.

18. William Brubeck to Myer Feldman, August 10, 1962, box 24, Feldman Files.

19. Chancellor Adenauer to the President, June 18, 1962; draft letter to Governors Vandiver, Tawes, and Barnet, [1962], box 24, Feldman Files.

20. Talbot, *Chicken War,* pp. 73–122; Draft Report of the European Trip of Secretary of Agriculture Orville Freeman, November 23, 1962, box 24, Feldman Files; Report to the President on Agricultural Trade Problems with the EEC, February 14, 1963, box 24, Feldman Files; Sorensen, *Kennedy,* p. 412; Toasts of the President and President Lubke at a Luncheon at the Villa Hammerschmidt, June 24, 1963, *Public Papers, 1963,* p. 504; Diary of Orville Freeman, July 12, 1963, John F. Kennedy Library, Boston, Massachusetts (hereafter Freeman Diary); *Agence Presse-Europe,* September 2, 1963.

21. Talbot, *Chicken War,* pp. 135, 140–141.

22. *TEA-House,* pt. 5, Charles B. Shuman, Farm Bureau, 3210–3227; Farm Bureau Policies for 1962, Resolution on National Issues, December 14, 1961, box 4, Petersen Papers; "Shuman Discusses Trade Legislation During Visit with Kennedy at the White House," *American Farm Bureau Newsletter* 40 (October 30, 1961):173; Herschel Newsom to Myer Feldman, January 17, 1962, box 478, WHCF-JFK; Purpose of Amendments to H.R. 11970 Suggested by the National Grange, attached to Sen. Harry Byrd to Herschel Newsom, August 24, 1962, Senate Finance Records; Address, John M. Eklund of the National Farmers Union, February 17, 1962, box 6, Papers of the National Farmers Union, Western Historical Archives, University of Colorado, Boulder, Colorado (hereafter NFU Papers); *TEA-House,* pt. 5, Tobacco Institute, 2905–2905 and U.S. National Fruit Export Council, 3137–3163.

23. U.S. Congress, Subcommittee on the Impact of Imports and Exports on American Employment of the Committee on Education and Labor, pt. 8, *Impact of Imports and Exports on Employment (Agricultural Products, Chemical, Oil, Machinery, Motion Pictures, Transportation, and Other Industries),* 87th Cong., 1st sess., 1961 (hereafter *Agricultural* or *Chemical Import Hearings*), National Milk Producers Federation, 3133–3134, National Cheese Institute, 2–3, California State Board of Agriculture, 214–215, California Olive Industry, 868–876, California Fig Institute, 249–250, Imperial Valley (Calif.) tomato growers, 222–223, California Strawberry Advisory Board, 884, Ohio Greenhouse Co-operative Association, 253, Western Growers Association, 179–213; Memorandum, Fruit, undated, Fruit and Almond Growers; H. B. McCormack [lemons] to Howard Petersen, February 2, 1962, box 7, Petersen Files; *TEA-House,* pt. 3, American Almond Producers, 1640–1647; pt. 4, American National Cattlemen's Association, 2572–2582; Cherry Growers and Industries Foundation, 2626–2655; pt. 5, National Board of Fur Farm Organizations, 2952–2954, Association of Pacific

Fisheries, 3380–3381; pt.6, National Cotton Council, 4130; *TEA-Senate*, pt. 2, National Potato Council, 656; pt. 4, Pineapple Growers Association of Hawaii, 1958; pt. 5, Texas Sheep and Goat Raisers Association, 1394–1395.

24. *Agricultural Import Hearings*, Western Growers Association to California Congressional Delegation, October 11, 1961, p. 207. See also senators Jacob Javits and Kenneth Keating to Sen. Harry Byrd, July 31, 1962, box 29, Senate Finance Records; State Department memorandum, Strawberries, February 1, 1962, box 7, Petersen Files; *TEA-House*, pt. 2, Ullman, 865; Senator Clair Engle to Senator Harry Byrd, July 12, 1962, Senate Finance Records; Luther Hodges to the President, Memorandum Reporting the Status of the Trade Expansion Act, August 20, 1962, box 50, POF.

25. Robert W. Rudd, "Can Exports Solve the Farm Problem?," *World Trade: What are the Issues?*, no. 6, March 1962, box 15, Petersen Files; *Wall Street Journal*, January 24, 1962, p. 12; Lauren K. Soth, "Farm Policy, Foreign Policy, and Farm Opinion," in *Agricultural Policy, Politics, and the Public Interest*, edited by Charles M. Hardin in *The Annals of the American Academy of Political and Social Science* (Philadelphia: American Academy of Political and Social Science, 1960), pp. 104–108; 1962 Policy Statements of the National Farmers Union, March 21, 1962, box 6, NFU Papers; James Patton to Cong. Carl Albert, June 21, 1962, box 55, Albert Papers; Ross B. Talbot, "Effect of Domestic Political Groups and Forces in U.S. Trade Policy," in *U.S. Trade Policy*, edited by Iowa State, p. 148.

26. Charles Taft to David Bell, February 12, 1962, box 14, Petersen Files; TEA and Agriculture: The Sense of Congress, undated, box 16, White House Staff Files-Christian A. Herter (hereafter Herter Files); White, *Making of the President, 1960*, pp. 420–421; Parmet, *JFK*, p. 62.

27. Address by George Harrison, May 17, 1962, AFL-CIO Press Release 7 (1962):4. See also *TEA-House*, pt. 2, Secretary of Labor Arthur Goldberg, 685–695; Eva E. Jacobs and Ronald E. Kutscher, "Domestic Employment Attributable to U.S. Exports, 1960," *Monthly Labor Review* 85 (July 1962):771.

28. *Congressional Record-Senate*, vol. 108, pt. 4, Gore, March 20, 1962, 4557.

29. Statement by the AFL-CIO Executive Council on International Trade, AFL-CIO Press Releases 7 (August 16, 1962):30. See also AFL-CIO Detailed Recommendations to [Democratic] Platform Committee, July 8, 1960, box 61, AFL-CIO Office of the President, George Meany Memorial Archives, Silver Spring, Maryland.

30. Meany, "The Balance of Payments Issue: A Front for Domestic Reaction," AFL-CIO Press Release 6 (1961); President George Meany to AFL-CIO Economic and Legislative Conference, AFL-CIO Press Releases 7 (January 22, 1962).

31. Address, George Harrison, AFL-CIO Press Releases 7 (May 22, 1962):2–4. See also CBS Reports, "Breaking the Trade Barrier," May 24, 1962, box 480, WHCF-JFK.

32. Joseph A. Loftus, "Is Labor Turning Protectionist?," *The Nation* 192 (March 11, 1962):211–214; AFL-CIO [Annual Convention] Proceedings 1 (1961):264–280; *TEA-House*, pt. 4, Sidney Zagri, Teamsters, 2210–2216, and

James B. Carey, International Union of Electrical, Radio, and Machine Workers, 2392–2395.

33. *TEA-House*, pt. 2, Meany, 1152, also 1210. See also Rashish Oral History, p. 23.

34. *TEA-House*, pt. 2, Meany, 1210. See also Solomon Barkin, "Labor's Position on Tariff Reduction," reprint from *Industrial Relations* (May 1962), attached to Senator Harry Byrd to Barkin, August 18, 1962, Senate Finance Records.

35. Bauer, Pool, and Dexter, *American Business*, pp. 148–149; Eldridge Haynes to Peter Davies, January 8, 1962, box 15, Petersen Files; "Being Right When It Hurts" [Roper poll], *Life* 52 (April 27, 1962):4; *New York Times*, June 27, 1962, p. 11; *Congressional Record-House*, vol. 108, pt. 5, April 18, 1962, Congressman Francis P. Bolton (D-Oh.), 6994; "Push for Free Trade," *Business Week* (December 9, 1961):26; Heath, *Kennedy and Business*, p. 89.

36. "The Export Market: A Plum for Those Who Reach," *Crow's Lumber Digest* 40 (November 1, 1962):25–26, 30; "European Trip Plans Set for WCLA Delegates," *Crow's Lumber Digest* 41 (March 7, 1963):18; Address Before the Conference on Trade Policy, May 17, 1962, *Public Papers, 1962*, p. 411; Remarks and Question and Answer Period at the American Bankers Association Symposium on Economic Growth, February 25, 1963, *Public Papers, 1963*, p. 217.

37. Robert A. Dahl, *Pluralist Democracy in the United States: Conflict and Consensus* (Chicago: Rand-McNally, 1967), pp. 414–415; Ronald J. Hrebner and Ruth K. Scott, *Interest Group Politics in America* (Englewood Cliffs, N.J.: Prentice-Hall, 1982), p. 199; Subcommittee on International Trade Policy, 1961–1962, attached to Kenneth Campbell to Howard Petersen, October 4, 1961; Export Luncheon Group, attached to Kenneth Campbell, October 30, 1961 and November 21, 1961, box 3, Petersen Files; *TEA-House*, pt. 3, A. B. Sparboe, Pillsbury Co. and U.S. Chamber of Commerce, 2062–2065; Press Release, News Service of the U.S. Chamber of Commerce, February 24, 1962, box 11, Petersen Files; U.S. Chamber of Commerce, *The Impact of the Common Market on the American Economy* (Washington, D.C.: U.S. Chamber of Commerce, 1962); *New York Times*, May 3, 1962, pp. 1, 3 and May 4, 1962, p. 32; William Ruder to Myer Feldman, February 23, 1962, box 478, WHCF-JFK.

38. Hrebner and Scott, *Interest Group*, p. 199; Reciprocal Trade Agreements Position Paper, undated, box 855.2, Vada Horsch Papers, National Association of Manufacturers Collection, Hagley Museum and Library, Wilmington, Delaware (hereafter Horsch Papers); NAM, *Industry Believes, 1962: Policies on Current Problems as Adopted by the Board* (New York: NAM, April 1962), p. 17; Minutes of Meeting of the Economic Advisory Committee, September 19, 1961; Minutes of the NAM Unemployment Compensation Subcommittee, [May-September 1962], Series IV, NAM records; National Industrial Council Release, "Senate Committee Reports Foreign Trade Bill," September 17, 1962, Series I Government-Legislation, National Association of Manufacturers Records, Hagley Museum and Library, Wilmington, Delaware (hereafter Series I, NAM Records); *TEA-Senate*, pt. 3, R. T. Compton, NAM, 1630.

39. Address in New York City to the National Association of Manufacturers, December 6, 1961, *Public Papers, 1961*, p. 773. For corporate liberalism, see

Allen J. Matusow, *The Unraveling of America: A History of Liberalism in the 1960s* (New York: Harper and Row, 1984), pp. 32–36; Bruce Miroff, *Pragmatic Illusions: The Presidential Politics of John F. Kennedy* (New York: David McKay, 1976), pp. 187–192; Wolfe, *America's Impasse*, pp. 33–35.

40. For the view that the Kennedy-business relationship was confrontational, see Sorensen, *Kennedy*, pp. 440, 459–469; Schlesinger, *A Thousand Days*, pp. 631–634; Heath, *Kennedy and Business*, 8; Giglio, *Presidency of JFK*, pp. 129–140. See also Memorandum on International Chamber of Commerce, attached to Emilio Collado to Peter Davies, February 15, 1962, box 15, Petersen Files.

41. *TEA-House*, pt. 2, The Recent Record of U.S. Foreign Trade Exports and Imports-Overall Major Categories, Fact Sheet, 1184; pt. 3, Harvey Williams, U.S. Council of the International Chamber of Commerce, 1394–1405; pt. 4, Hugh Hyde, Johnston International Publishing Corporation, 2703; pt. 5, Theodore Houser, CED, 3129; "Another Exciting and Turbulent Year Ahead," *Commercial and Financial Chronicle* 195 (February 8, 1962):6; Some U.S. Corporations Supporting the U.S. Foreign Trade Program, undated, box 45, Papers of James M. Landis, John F. Kennedy Library, Boston, Massachusetts; Carl Levin to Edward Flynn, Western Committee for Trade Expansion [Paul Hoffman, Crown Zellerbach, Lockheed, oil companies], February 5, 1962, box 15, Petersen Files; James W. Lindeen, "Interest-Group Attitudes Toward Reciprocal Trade Legislation," *Public Opinion Quarterly* 34 (Spring 1970):112; Krasner, "U.S. Commercial and Monetary Policy," p. 78.

42. Gene E. Bradley, *Building the American-European Market: Planning for the 1970s* (Homewood, Ill.: Dow Jones-Irwin, 1967), p. 205; Katzenstein, "International Relations," pp. 25–28; Ronald Steel, ed., *U.S. Foreign Trade Policy* (New York: H. W. Wilson, 1962), p. 5; *Wall Street Journal*, January 26, 1962, p. 2; *Congressional Record-Appendix*, reel 11, February 15, 1962, Robert H. Michel (R-Ill.) for Caterpillar, A1080; Peter Davies to Howard Petersen, May 1, 1962, box 3; Louis Krauthoff to Carl Levin, January 23, 1962, box 17, Petersen Files; "Should We Have Freer Trade," *Steel* 150 (May 28, 1962):74–77.

43. The Effect of the President's Trade Expansion Bill of 1962 on the Electronics Industry, [1962]; CNTP, Background Information, The Electronics Industry and U.S. Trade Policy, [1962], Peter Davies to Myer Rashish, May 25, 1962; Hickman Price to Peter Jones, December 27, 1961, box 7, Petersen Files.

44. "Ahead: Import-Export Shift," *Chemical Week* 88 (April 15, 1961):39. See also Conrad Berenson, *The Chemical Industry: Viewpoints and Perspectives* (New York: John Wiley and Sons, 1963), p. 1; *TEA-House*, pt. 6, 3640; "C&EN Reviews and Previews the Chemical World: 1961 and 1962," *Chemical and Engineering News* 40 (January 1, 1962):9–27.

45. Graham D. Taylor and Patricia E. Sudnik, *Dupont and the International Chemical Industry* (Boston: Twayne, 1984), pp. 112–113; "Europe's Chemical Industry," *Chemical and Engineering News* 38 (October 3, 1960):104–113; *New York Times*, February 26, 1962, p. 38; "Positioning to Tariff Bill Showdown," *Chemical Week* 90 (May 12, 1962):21; "Backing for Both Sides," *Chemical Week* 90 (February 17, 1962):40; *TEA-Senate*, pt. 2, 605; "Candidates Told by Chemical Men to Start Talking," *Oil, Paint, and Drug Reporter* 178 (October 10,

1960):45; "Washington Talks it Over," *Oil, Paint, and Drug Reporter* 179 (January 30, 1961):9.

46. "Coming: Credit Aid for Exporters," *Chemical Week* 88 (May 13, 1961):31–33; "Chemical Men Nagged by JFK Power Grab," *Oil, Paint and Drug Reporter* 181 (June 11, 1962):5, 36; "Viewpoint-Depreciation: Key to Survival," *Chemical Week* 88 (March 25, 1961):5; "Washington Newsletter," *Chemical Week* 88 (May 20, 1961):28; "Ideas on Taxes and Trade," *Oil, Paint, and Drug Reporter* 181 (May 7, 1962):31; "Chemical Subsidiaries Abroad Not in For as Big a Tax Wallop as Was First Anticipated," *Oil, Paint, and Drug Reporter* 181 (July 23, 1962):7; "Coming: New Crimp on Foreign Investment," *Chemical Week* 88 (February 18, 1961):35; "Americans Headed for Europe," *Chemical and Engineering News* 38 (January 4, 1960):71; "U.S. Companies Make More Overseas," *Chemical and Engineering News* 40 (October 8, 1962):25; Heath, *Kennedy and Business*, p. 40; "Viewpoint-European Appraisal Needed," *Chemical Week* 89 (August 12, 1961):5; "Totaling Foreign Investment Tab," *Chemical Week* 87 (September 10, 1960):30; "Chemical Barometers for 1961 Pointing to Serious Pressures: Costs, Competition, Capacity," *Oil, Paint, and Drug Reporter* 178 (September 19, 1960):5, 64; "Selling Chemicals Abroad," *Oil, Paint, and Drug Reporter* 180 (August 21, 1961):9.

47. "Viewpont-Tariffs: Reason Plus Self Interest," *Chemical Week* 87 (January 9, 1960):7. See also Memorandum for Undersecretary [Treasury] Robert Roosa to Jack Behrman, May 27, 1963, box 1, Behrman Papers; "Chemicals Have Big Stake in Tariff Cut Plans," *Chemical and Engineering News* 38 (July 18, 1960):32–36; B. L. Lemke to U.S. Tariff Commission, February 10, 1961, attached to Myer Feldman to Lemke, March 2, 1961, box 945, WHCF-JFK.

48. "European-American Trade Harmony," *Chemical and Engineering News* 39 (October 9, 1961):7; "Dumping?—Charges Fly Both Ways," *Chemical Week* 89 (November 11, 1961):21; "As Others See Us," *Chemical Week* 90 (February 3, 1962):5; "Washington Newsletter," *Chemical Week* 90 (March 10, 1962):35; "Britain Objects to U.S. Tariff Policy," *Chemical and Engineering News* 39 (November 6, 1961):66.

49. "Washington Talks it Over," *Oil, Paint, and Drug Reporter* 180 (October 18, 1961):9.

50. "Edging Into Free Trade," *Chemical Week* 90 (January 27, 1962):21; "Washington Concentrates," *Chemical and Engineering News* 40 (March 12, 1962):19; "Kennedy Tells Trade Program and Chemical Executives Get Big Surprise on Peril Point," *Oil, Paint, and Drug Reporter* 181 (January 29, 1962):5; "Tariff Bill Concessions Shake Up," *Chemical Week* 89 (December 23, 1961):15.

51. "Washington Talks it Over," *Oil, Paint, and Drug Reporter* 181 (January 15, 1962):34; "Taking Sides on New Tariff Bill," *Chemical Week* 90 (February 10, 1962):22; *TEA-House*, pt. 6, John T. Powers, Pfizer International, 4105; "Kennedy Stampedes Foes of Trade Bill," *New York Herald Tribune*, April 3, 1962, box 102, POF; *Chemical Import Hearings*, Lewis LLoyd, Dow Chemical, p. 705; "Edging Into Free Trade," *Chemical Week* 90 (January 27, 1962):21; Dan J. Forrestal, *The Story of Monsanto: Faith, Hope, and $5000: The Trials and Triumphs of the First 75 Years* (New York: Simon and Schuster, 1977), pp. 66,

172–173; "Monsanto Hits Kennedy's Plans for Reducing Tariffs," *Oil, Paint, and Drug Reporter* 181 (February 19, 1962):5.

52. Taylor and Sudnik, *Dupont,* pp. 193–194; "Viewpoint—No Selling Without Buying," *Chemical Week* 88 (February 11, 1961):5; "Tariffs and the Chemical Industry: Past and Present," *Commercial and Financial Chronicle* 196 (September 20, 1962):39; Crawford Greenewalt to Senator Harry Byrd, August 2, 1962, box 29, Senate Finance Records; "Washington Talks it Over," *Oil, Paint, and Drug Reporter* 178 (September 19, 1960):9. Eisenhower had not permitted chemical leaders to attend the Dillon Round, but Kennedy agreed to let twelve spokesmen sit in on Washington strategy meetings.

53. Quoted in Carl Spitzer, "ECM: Deterrent to War, Challenge to Americans," *Wyandotte Chief* (Winter Quarter, 1962), box 22, Petersen Files. See also "JFKs Tariff Plan is Chilling Notion to Chemical Men," *Oil, Paint, and Drug Reporter* 180 (December 11, 1961):50; "Organic Chemical Producers Rallied to Go All-Out in Fight Against Sweeping Tariff Cuts," *Oil, Paint, and Drug Reporter* 180 (November 20, 1961):3; *TEA-House,* pt. 6, Helen Booth, DCAT, to Congressman Wilbur Mills, March 22, 1962, 4104, 4107, and Kenneth Egeler, DCAT, 3534–3543; "Tariff Fight Gets Down to Essentials," *Chemical Week* 90 (March 17, 1962):40; *TEA-House,* pt. 4, Semple, 2603. The 800–member Drug, Chemical, and Allied Trade group, and the 23–producer Dry Color Manufacturers Association, joined SOCMA in opposing the TEA.

54. *TEA-House,* pt. 4, Semple, 2605–2606.

55. HR 11970: Background Files and Publications, undated, box 30; The Effect of the President's Trade Expansion Bill of 1962 on the Chemical Industry, undated, attached to Robert Semple to Howard Petersen, February 19, 1962; Peter Jones to Myer Rashish, February 14, 1962, box 3; Peter Jones to Luther Hodges, March 21, 1962, box 5, Petersen Files; "Chemical Industry: 'Healthy Giant'?," *Chemical Week* 90 (April 14, 1962):22; "Administration Plugs for Tariff Cuts," *Chemical and Engineering News* 40 (March 12, 1962):22; Howard Petersen, interview with author.

56. Rashish Oral History, p. 24. See also Confidential Briefing Concerning the Effect of the President's Trade Expansion Bill on the American Chemical Industry, undated; Howard Petersen to the President, March 28, 1962, box 5, Petersen Files; Myer Rashish to Kenneth O'Donnell, April 6, 1962, box 102, POF; Sorensen Oral History, pp. 111–112; "HR 9900's Final Shape Seen Not Very Likely to Conform to Chemical Industry's Views," *Oil, Paint, and Drug Reporter* 181 (April 16, 1962):5; Henry Wilson to Myer Feldman, December 20, 1961, box 3, Wilson Files; John Hull to the President, April 11, 1962, attached to Feldman to Hull, April 13, 1962, box 479, WHCF; "Slow March to Freer Trade," *Chemical Week* 90 (May 12, 1962):5; "Chemical People Shift Tactics in Battle Against Trade Bill to Concentrate on Safeguards," *Oil, Paint, and Drug Reporter* 181 (August 6, 1962):3, 59.

57. *TEA-House,* pt. 5, Gerstacker and Mills, 3327–3328; David Bell to Cong. Sidney Yates, May 25, 1962, box 13, Petersen Files; *New York Times,* November 26, 1962, III:1; "Make the Best of the New Trade Bill," *Chemical Week* 91 (September 29, 1962):5.

58. *Wall Street Journal,* March 23, 1962, p. 1.

59. [Twenty-two congressmen] to the President, August 22, 1961 box 29, Sorensen Papers; White, *Making of the President, 1960,* p. 421; *Congressional Record-Senate,* vol. 108, pt. 5, April 16, 1962, Senator Frank Carlson (R-Kan.), 6639–6640.

60. President Kennedy to Nate White, December 26, 1961, box 238, WHCF-JFK. For a sampling of the vast literature on the Grand Design, see Van der Beugel, *From Marshall Aid,* Harold van B. Cleveland, *The Atlantic Idea and Its European Rivals* (New York: McGraw-Hill, 1966); William C. Cromwell, "The United States," in *Political Problems of Atlantic Partnership: National Perspectives* (Bruges, Belgium: College of Europe, 1968); Grosser, *Western Alliance,* pp. 200–202; Hinshaw, *European Community;* Uwe Kitzinger, *The Challenge of the Common Market* (Oxford: Basil Blackwell, 1962); Kraft, *Grand Design;* Frank Munk, *The Atlantic Dilemma: Partnership or Community* (Dobbs Ferry, N.Y.: Oceana Publications, 1964); Uri, *Partnership;* Wilcox and Haviland, eds., *Atlantic Community.* For the administration's view, see Ball, *The Past Has Another Pattern,* pp. 208–222; George McGhee, "The President's Trade Program—Key to the Grand Design," Department of State *Bulletin* 46 (January 19, 1962); Rashish Oral History, p. 16.

61. Address Before the Conference on Trade Policy, May 17, 1962, *Public Papers, 1962,* pp. 409–410. See also Address at Independence Hall, Philadelphia, July 4, 1962, *Public Papers, 1962,* p. 538.

62. Address in New Orleans at the Opening of the New Dockside Terminal, May 4, 1962, *Public Papers, 1962,* p. 361. See also Ball, *The Past Has Another Pattern,* p. 209.

63. Christian A. Herter, *Toward an Atlantic Community* (New York: Harper and Row, 1963), p. 47; Robert Estabrook interviews with Walter Hallstein, November 29, 1961, Robert Marjolin, November 28, 1961, and Hugo de Grood, October 26, 1961, box 1, Estabrook Papers; Brombergers, *Jean Monnet,* pp. 225–226.

64. *TEA-House,* pt. 2, Gilpatric, 755. See also Special Message to the Congress on Foreign Trade Policy, January 25, 1962, *Public Papers, 1962,* p. 71. See also Beloff, *Unity of Europe,* pp. 112–117; Kraft, *Grand Design,* p. 119; McGeorge Bundy, Remarks to the Economic Club of Chicago, December 6, 1961, box WH-20, Schlesinger Papers; Roger Hilsman to the Secretary of State, April 4, 1962, box 14, Petersen Files; Address at Independence Hall, Philadelphia, July 4, 1962, *Public Papers, 1962,* p. 539.

65. Javits in *Congressional Record-Senate,* vol. 108, pt. 1, January 15, 1962, Clifford P. Case (R-N.J.), p. 171. See also J. W. Fulbright, "A Concert of Free Nations," in *Atlantic Community,* edited by Wilcox and Haviland, pp. 276–277; Hartke-Memorandum no. 12, August 1, 1962, box 14, Petersen Files; *Congressional Record-House,* vol. 108, pt. 9, 87th Cong., 2d sess., June 28, 1962, Lindsay, 12016 and Moorehead, 12051. See also Congressman Henry Reuss (D-Wis.) to the President, November 2, 1961, box 29, Sorensen Papers.

66. Pastor, *Congress,* pp. 112–113.

67. Henry Reuss Oral History, John F. Kennedy Library, Boston, Massachusetts, p. 62.

68. Jack Behrman to author; *TEA-Senate,* pt. 1, Ball, 2252; Summary of Major

Points Raised in House Ways and Means Executive Hearings on HR 9900, April 17, 1962, box 8, Petersen Files; Wilbur Mills to the President, May 17, 1962, box 50, POF; Press release, December 10, 1962, box 14, Herter Files; Ball, interview with author; Ball, *The Past Has Another Pattern*, pp. 198–200.

69. Pastor, *Congress*, p. 115; Henry Reuss, *The Critical Decade: An Economic Policy for America and the Free World* (New York: McGraw-Hill, 1964), pp. 42–46; Luther Hodges to the President, Memorandum Reporting the Status of the Trade Expansion Act, [August 1962], box 51, POF; Howard Petersen to Cong. Henry Reuss, May 29, 1962, box 69, Sorensen Papers.

70. *Congressional Record-Senate*, vol. 108, pt. 15, McCarthy, September 19, 1962, 19872. See also Brief Summary of Amendments to HR 11970, Introduced on September 17–18, 1962, attached to Summary of Senate Amendments to HR 11970, undated, box 29, Finance Committee Records; Senator Prescott Bush remarks, August 2, 1962, box 7, RG 69: 13, Bush Papers; Howard Petersen to Senator Harry Byrd, August 20, 1962, box 50, POF; Pastor, *Congress*, pp. 115–116, 197; Myer Feldman to author, October 4, 1988.

71. Lowi, "Public Philosophy," pp. 15–17; McCormick, "Drift or Mastery?," pp. 321–328; Hogan, *Marshall Plan*, pp. 2–3.

72. Special Message to the Congress on Foreign Trade Policy, January 25, 1962, *Public Papers, 1962*, p. 70.

73. Remarks Upon Signing the Trade Expansion Act, October 11, 1962, *Public Papers, 1962*, p. 760.

74. Remarks Upon Signing the Trade Expansion Act, October 11, 1962, *Public Papers, 1962*, p. 759.

6. Round One to Europe, 1963–1964

1. Excerpts of d'Estaing speech, attached to Rene Larré to Howard Petersen, April 2, 1962, box 23, Petersen Files. See also Preeg, *Traders*, pp. 53–54; Evans, *Kennedy Round*, pp. 163, 183–185; *Bulletin of the EEC* 6 (December 1962):11; Roy H. Ginsberg, "The European Community and the United States of America," in *Institutions and Policies of the European Community*, edited by Juliet Lodge (New York: St. Martin's Press, 1983), p. 172; Stanley Hoffmann, "Discord in Community: The North Atlantic Area as a Partial International System," in *Atlantic Community*, edited by Wilcox and Haviland, pp. 18–19; Costigliola, "Pursuit of Atlantic Community," p. 30.

2. Horne, *Macmillan*, p. 445; De Gaulle, *Memoirs*, p. 171. See also Calleo and Rowland, *America and the World*, p. 81; Nora Beloff, *The General Says No: Britain's Exclusion from Europe* (Harmondsworth, Great Britain: Penguin, 1963), pp. 152–163; D. C. Watt, "The American Impact on Europe," *Political Quarterly* 34 (October-December 1963):327–328; Costigliola, "Pursuit of Atlantic Community," p. 50; Richard J. Barnet, *The Roots of War: The Men and Institutions Behind U.S. Foreign Policy* (New York: Atheneum, 1972), p. 149; Walter Hallstein, *Europe in the Making* (New York: W. W. Norton, 1972), p. 269. See also Robert Kleiman, *Atlantic Crisis: American Confronts a Resurgent Europe* (New York: W. W. Norton, 1964).

3. Beloff, *General Says No*, pp. 38, 153; [U.S. Ambassador to France] Charles

Bohlen to the Secretary of State, January 23, 1963; Article from *Agra-Quotidien*, February 7, 1963, Brubeck to McGeorge Bundy, March 22, 1963; Bohlen to Secretary of State, February 25, 1963, box 72, NSF-JFK.

4. Van der Beugel, *Marshall Aid*, pp. 402–407; Arthur Schlesinger to Undersecretary George Ball, February 12, 1963, box WH-9, Eldon Griffith, position paper, "The Rebellion in Europe," undated, Common Market, box WH-4, Schlesinger Papers; Costigliola, "Pursuit of Atlantic Community," p. 33; Borden, "Defending Hegemony" p. 64; Stanley Hoffmann, *Gulliver's Troubles, or the Setting of American Foreign Policy* (New York: McGraw-Hill, 1968), pp. 164–165, 396; C. D. Jackson, Overseas Report, June 25, 1962, box 127, POF; Stanley Hoffman, "De Gaulle, Europe, and the Atlantic Alliance," *International Organization* 18 (Winter 1964):1–17; Thomas Hughes to Secretary of State, De Gaulle's Foreign Policy in 1964, April 20, 1964, box 169, National Security Files, Lyndon B. Johnson Library, Austin, Texas (hereafter NSF-LBJ); Grosser, *Western Alliance*, p. 202; Robert Estabrook conversation with Herman Van Roijen, June 7, 1962, box 1, Estabrook Papers.

5. Bromberger and Bromberger, *Jean Monnet*, p. 241; Horne, *Macmillan*, pp. 448–449; Spaak, *Continuing Battle*, p. 478; "How the Five Took It," *The Economist* 206 (January 19, 1963):201. See also Amitai Etzioni, "U.S. and Europe, Limited," *Columbia University Forum* 6 (Winter 1963):5–6; John Pinder, *Europe Against De Gaulle* (New York: Praeger, 1963), p. 2; Paul-Henri Spaak, "Hold Fast," *Foreign Affairs* 41 (July 1963):620; Undersecretary Ball to the President, March 1, 1963, box 117, POF. For a critique of de Gaulle's policies, see Bromberger and Bromberger, *Jean Monnet*, chaps. 14, 15.

6. Memorandum for the Files from Orville Freeman, March 1, 1963, Freeman Diary. See also Edward R. Murrow to the President, February 4, 1963 and February 6, 1963, box 91, POF; USIA, Reaction to the European Situation, February 6, 1963, box WH-4; USIA, Attitudes Toward the Common Market in Western Europe, August 1963, WH-9, Schlesinger Papers; John Tuthill to the Secretary of State, February 28, 1963, box 116, POF; *Wall Street Journal*, February 15, 1963, p. 14; U.S. Ambassador to Italy G. Frederick Reinhardt to the Secretary of State, February 6, 1963; William N. Fraleigh to the Secretary of State, February 18, 1963, box 120a; George Ball to the President, March 1, 1963, box 9–10, NSF-JFK; "Can De Gaulle Shape Europe to His Mold," *Business Week* no. 1743 (January 26, 1963):82; *Congressional Record-House*, vol. 109, pt. 2, February 18, 1963, John Dent, 2493; George Ball to Ambassador Charles Bohlen, September 25, 1963, box 116a, POF; Annual Message to the Congress on the State of the Union, January 14, 1963, p. 15; The President's News Conference, January 24, 1963, p. 98 and February 7, 1963, p. 149; Address in the Assembly Hall at the Paulskirche in Frankfurt, June 25, 1963, *Public Papers, 1963*, p. 519; John F. Kennedy to a Friend [MacMillan], [1963], box 127, POF.

7. Proposed Douglas-Reuss Statement on Introduction of Trade Expansion Act Amendment, January 24, 1963, attached to Henry S. Reuss to Howard Shuman, January 24, 1963, Papers of Senator Paul H. Douglas, Chicago Historical Society, Chicago, Illinois; Reuss Oral History, pp. 52–56; *Congressional Record-House*, vol. 109, pt. 1, January 28, 1963, Reuss, 1156, and Javits, 1417–1418; Douglas, *Fullness of Time*, pp. 482–485.

8. C. Douglas Dillon to the President, May 9, 1962, roll 7, Records of the Department of Commerce, John F. Kennedy Library, Boston, Massachusetts. See also James Tobin on the Galbraith Proposals, August 11, 1963, box 29, Sorensen Papers; Piquet, *Balance-of-Payments,* p. 11; Dean Acheson Oral History, John F. Kennedy Library, Boston, Massachusetts, pp. 31–32; Allen J. Matusow, "Kennedy, the World Economy, and the Decline of America," in *John F. Kennedy: Person, Policy, Presidency,* edited by J. Richard Snyder (Wilmington, Del.: Scholarly Resources, 1988), pp. 114–115; Luther Hodges to the President, March 1963, box 72A, POF; Special Message to the Congress on the Balance of Payments, July 18, 1963, *Public Papers, 1963,* pp. 575–577; Carl Kaysen to the President, May 4, 1963, box 64, POF.

9. Address and Question and Answer Period at the Economic Club of New York, December 14, 1962, *Public Papers, 1962,* pp. 881–882.

10. William Roth, "The Johnson Trade Policy," Department of State *Bulletin* 54 (May 30, 1966):857. See also W. Michael Blumenthal, "The Kennedy Round," Department of State *Bulletin* 53 (April 26, 1965):628; J. Robert Schaetzel, "The United States and the Common Market," Department of State *Bulletin* 47 (September 3, 1962):325; Borden, "Defending Hegemony," p. 70.

11. Components of a Strategy for the Kennedy Round, December 10, 1963, attached to George Ball to Christian Herter, December 10, 1963, box 7, Herter Files; Lawrence A. Fox, Report on the Trade Executive Task Force, February 21 and 25, 1963, box 8, Behrman Papers.

12. Components of a Strategy for the Kennedy Round, December 10, 1963, attached to George Ball to Christian Herter, December 10, 1963, box 7; Minutes of May 8, 1963 Meeting of the Trade Expansion Act Advisory Committee, box 10, Herter Files; Curzon and Curzon, "Management," p. 256; U.S. Mission (Geneva) to Department of State, February 1, 1963; Memorandum of Conversation with Japanese Ambassador Morio Aoki, [January-February 1963], box 16; Christian Herter to the President, April 29, 1963, box 10, Herter Files. For the LDCs, see chap. 7.

13. *Bulletin of the EEC* 7 (March 1963):16; UN, *Economic Survey of Europe, 1962, pt. 1, The European Economy in 1962* (New York: United Nations, 1963), chap. II, p. 39; EEC Commission, 8th General Report on the Activities of the Community, April 1, 1964–March 31, 1965, (Brussels, June 1965):270; U.S. Mission, Geneva to Secretary of State, May 18, 1963, box 11, Herter Files; Sicco Mansholt, press conference, April 10, 1963, box 441.2 (103), ER: Pt. 1, U.S.-EEC Files, Delegation of the Commission of the European Community, Washington, D.C. (hereafter EC Delegation Files).

14. "Study of 181 Items Exported to EEC Reveals Little Ground for U.S. Complacency," *International Commerce* 69 (February 25, 1963):2–7. George M. Taber, *Patterns and Prospects of Common Market Trade* (London: Peter Owen, 1974), p. 91; Country Committee I-EEC, attached to Bernard Norwood to Christian Herter, October 27, 1964, box 12, Herter Files; Ingo Walter, *The European Common Market: Growth and Patterns of Trade and Production* (New York: Praeger, 1967), p. 15.

15. Preeg, *Traders,* p. 55; Components of a Strategy for the Kennedy Round, December 10, 1963, attached to George Ball to Christian Herter, December 10,

1963, box 7, Herter Files; "France and the Kennedy Round," *The Economist* 207 (April 13, 1963):169; European reactions to the U.S. Trade Expansion Act, Canadian Embassy Confidential Paper, attached to Harold Cleveland to Myer Rashish, December 19, 1962, box 23, Petersen Files; European reactions to the U.S. Trade Expansion Act, Canadian Embassy Confidential Paper, attached to Harold Cleveland to Myer Rashish, December 19, 1962, box 23, Petersen Files; *Bulletin of the EEC* 8 (July 1963):6; Christian Herter to the President, June 19, 1963, box 1; Components of a Strategy for the Kennedy Round, December 10, 1963, attached to George Ball to Christian Herter, December 10, 1963, box 7, Herter Files.

16. Ludwig Erhard, *The Economics of Success* (London: Thames and Hudson, 1963), pp. 305, 402–403; Paul Luyten to author, August 10, 1989. See also Vaughan, *Twentieth-Century Europe*, pp. 138–139; F. Roy Willis, *France, Germany, and the New Europe, 1945–1967*, rev. ed. (London: Oxford University Press, 1968), pp. 327–328; Costigliola, "Pursuit of Atlantic Community," p. 35; Hallstein, *Europe in the Making*, chaps. 4–5.

17. Components of a Strategy for the Kennedy Round, December 10, 1963, attached to George Ball to Christian Herter, December 10, 1963; Background paper, French Attitudes Toward the Kennedy Round, March 11, 1964, box 7; Irwin Hedges notes of Herter-Erhard meeting, June 15, 1964, box 8; STR office, Brussels to Secretary of State, April 19, 1963, box 7; Christian Herter to the President, June 19, 1963, box 1, Herter Files; Bromberger and Bromberger, *Jean Monnet*, pp. 244–254.

18. Preeg, *Traders*, pp. 54–55; Evans, *Kennedy Round*, pp. 164–165, 186–192; Christian Herter to the President, May 1, 1963, box 10; Christian Herter to C. Douglas Dillon, March 20, 1963, box 8; American Embassy, Bonn to Secretary of State, April 18, 1963; Geneva to Secretary of State, April 24 and 25, 1963, box 7, Herter Files.

19. Christian Herter to C. Douglas Dillon, March 20, 1963, box 8, Herter Files.

20. "The Common Market and Its Impact on Trade," *Commercial and Financial Chronicle* 195 (May 3, 1963):11; *Agence Press-Europe*, May 14, 1963; Report, Analysis of Dutiable Imports of Industrialized Countries with Respect to Linear Negotiating Approach, [May 1963]; Department of Commerce, Some Implications of Linear Tariff Cutting for the United States, [April-May 1963], box 8, Behrman Papers; Telegram to State Department, May 4, 1963, box 11, Herter Files.

21. STR, Geneva to State Department, May 20, 1963, box 11, Herter Files. See also Evans, *Kennedy Round*, pp. 192–195; Preeg, *Traders*, pp. 66–67; *Agence Presse-Europe*, August 2, 1963; GATT, *Basic Instruments and Selected Documents*, 12th supp., 21st sess., 1963 (Geneva: GATT, June 1964), pp. 47–49 (hereafter *BISD* with volumes and dates); Herter, Resume of Meeting on Tariff Disputes, June 3, 1963, box 10, Herter Files; Administrative History of the Department of State, vol. I, chap. 9, International Economic Relations Overview and Section A, Lyndon B. Johnson Library, Austin, Texas (hereafter State Department History); Metzger, *Trade Agreements*, pp. 106–110; President's News Conference, May 22, 1963, *Public Papers, 1963*, p. 420.

22. Herter, *Toward an Atlantic Community,* p. 33; Report of the Task Force on Non-Tariff Barriers, undated, box 12, Behrman Papers; "Lashing Out on Tariffs," *Chemical Week* 92 (March 30, 1963):22; "Mills Seek Curbs on Steel 'Dumping,' " *Iron Age* 190 (October 4, 1962):420; "Steel Gets Support on Dumping," *Iron Age* 191 (May 16, 1963):57; "No Dumping Allowed," *Fortune* 67 (May 1963):87, 92; State Department History. NTBs included a host of devices, many of them deceptive, which restricted trade. Among them were the ASP, antidumping laws, the Buy American Act, strict sanitation requirements, packaging rules, and quotas.

23. *Congressional Record-House,* vol. 110, pt. 9, May 21, 1964, Thomas Curtis, 11684; McCalla, "Protectionism," p. 341; Warley, "Western Trade," p. 377; Sherwood O. Berg, "How Farm Programs Affect Trade," in *Farm Prosperity-Imports and Exports,* edited by National Farm Institute (Ames: Iowa State University Press, 1965), p. 34; Shonfield, "Economic Relations," pp. 32–33; Irwin Hedges to Christian Herter, August 1, 1963, box 9, Herter Files; Warley, "Western Trade," p. 295; Wallace E. Ogg, "Farm Policy and Trade," in *Farm Prosperity,* edited by National Farm Institute, pp. 9–11; Thomas B. Curtis and John Robert Vastine, Jr., *The Kennedy Round and the Future of American Trade* (New York: Praeger, 1971), p. 27; Address by Irwin Hedges, STR, Agriculture to the National Farm Institute, February 11, 1965, box 9, Herter Files.

24. U.S. Congress, House Subcommittee on Poultry of the Committee on Agriculture, *Poultry Exports,* 88th Cong., 1st sess., 1963, Freeman, pp. 6–9 (hereafter *Poultry Hearings*); Freeman Diary, November 24, 1962.

25. Report to the President on Agricultural Trade Problems with the EEC by Secretary of Agriculture Orville Freeman, February 4, 1963; Draft Report on the European Trip of Secretary of Agriculture Orville Freeman, November 23, 1962, box 24, Feldman Files.

26. Freeman Oral History, p. 24. See also Orville Freeman to the President, January 14, 1963, Agriculture-1/63–4/63; Orville Freeman to the President, November 12, 1963, Agriculture-9/63–11/63, box 69, POF; USDA, *U.S. Agriculture,* p. 3; Freeman Diary, November 24, 1962, January 11, 1963, and February 4, 1963.

27. Freeman Diary, November 24, 1962 and November 12, 1963; W. Michael Blumenthal, address, "The World Economic Situation and Outlook," Department of State *Bulletin* 47 (December 3, 1962):843–844. See also *Wall Street Journal,* January 23, 1963, p. 2.

28. Address and Question and Answer Period at the Economic Club of New York, December 14, 1962, *Public Papers, 1962,* p. 881. See also Borden, "Defending Hegemony," p. 79.

29. Special Message to the Congress on Agriculture, January 31, 1963, *Public Papers, 1963,* p. 118.

30. "Europe's Farm Problem-Bad News for U.S.," *U.S. News and World Report 55* (July 22, 1963):68–69; *Agence Presse-Europe* May 22, 1963 and May 14, 1963; GATT, *BISD,* 11th Supp., 20th sess. (Geneva, March 1963), 237 and 13th Supp., 22d sess. (Geneva, July 1965), pp. 133–134; Edward L. Morse, *Foreign Policy and Interdependence in Gaullist France* (Princeton: Princeton University Press, 1973), pp. 77–82; Paul Luyten to the author.

31. Sicco Mansholt, "European View," in *Farm Prosperity*, edited by National Farm Institute, pp. 46–47; Warley, "Western Trade," pp. 383–384; Evans, *Kennedy Round*, pp. 209–211.

32. "Pawn to King 5," *The Economist* 207 (May 18, 1963):639; *Agence Presse-Europe*, May 10, 1963, and May 22, 1963; Memorandum of conversation on September 30, 1963 with Kurt Birrenbach, Committee on the Bundestag, October 2, 1963, box 11, Herter Files; Preeg, *Traders*, pp. 72–73.

33. Karin Kock, *International Trade Policy and the GATT, 1947–1967* (Stockholm: Almquist and Widsell, 1969), pp. 177–179; Warley, "Western Trade," pp. 383–384; State Department History; Components of a Strategy for the Kennedy Round, December 10, 1963, attached to George Ball to Christian Herter, December 10, 1963; W. Michael Blumenthal to Christian Herter, July 11, 1963, box 7, Herter Files; "Partners-In-Law," *The Economist* 207 (June 22, 1963):1229; Freeman Diary, July 12, 1963.

34. *Congressional Record-House*, vol. 109, pt. 1, January 17, 1963, E. Y. Berry (R-S.D.), p. 579.

35. *Congressional Record-House*, January 10, 1963, Durward G. Hall (R-Mo.), pp. 105–106; Giglio, *Presidency of JFK*, pp. 107–112. See also William Gossett to Christian Herter, December 18, 1962, box 9, Herter Files; *Poultry Hearings*, Cong. Charles B. Hoeven (R-Ia.), p. 19; Borden, "Defending Hegemony," p. 73; Dale E. Hathaway, "Farm Policy at a Crossroads," *Challenge* 12 (December 1963):3–6; President's News Conference, May 22, 1963, *Public Papers, 1963*, p. 423; Freeman Diary, June 8, 1962.

36. AFL-CIO Executive Council on Trade Adjustment Assistance, August 13, 1963, roll 9, Records of the AFL-CIO, John F. Kennedy Library, Boston, Massachusetts; *New York Times*, November 20, 1963, p. 25; Christian Herter to 108 Congressmen, September 13, 1963, box 8, Herter Files; P. Loring Reed to Senator Leverett Saltonstall (R-Mass.), February 26, 1963, and attached Record of the Administration's Commitments on Wool Textiles Import Limitations, February 1963, box Pastore-General-Textiles; Myer Feldman to Senator Pastore, September 25, 1963, box Textiles-General, Pastore Papers; 11 New England Congressmen to the President, August 21, 1963, box 8; Undersecretary Ball to the President, March 4, 1963, box 88A, POF; William Roth to Charles Murphy, September 9, 1963, box 5, Herter Files; President's News Conference, February 21, 1963, *Public Papers, 1962*, p. 207.

37. Mills in Hickman Price to Christian Herter, May 9, 1963, box 11, Herter Files. See also *Congressional Record-House*, vol. 109, pt. 9, Javits, June 25, 1963, 11546; *Congressional Record-Senate*, vol. 109, pt. 8, June 11, 1963, Stuart Symington (D-Mo.), 10614; *Wall Street Journal* (May 21, 1963), p. 20; Memorandum of Telephone Conversation between the White House and the Congressional Negotiating Team, June 11, 1963, box 8, Herter Files.

38. Curtis and Vastine, *Kennedy Round*, pp. 10–11; *International Trade Reporter's Survey and Analysis*, October 25, 1963, box 9, Behrman Papers; Administrative History of the Special Representative for Trade Negotiations, vol. 1, The Kennedy Round, Lyndon B. Johnson Library, Austin, Texas (hereafter STR History). Other escape clause exceptions included lead, zinc, watch movements, stainless steel flatware, clinical thermometers, safety pins, and cotton typewriter

316 *Notes to pp. 175–180*

ribbon cloth. The congressional delegation included congressmen Cecil King (D-La.) and Thomas Curtis (R-Mo.), and senators Herman Talmadge (D-Ga.) and John Williams (R-Del.).

39. Ambassador John Tuthill to Ambassador Blumenthal, September 6, 1963, box 16, Herter Files; M. H. Fisher, "What Chance of Lower Tariffs?," *World Today* 19 (May 1963):209, 212; "Is Kennedy in Political Trouble at Home?," *U.S. News and World Report* 55 (July 8, 1963):38–40.

40. Freeman Diary, October 20, 1962; Freeman Oral History, p. 24; Borden, "Defending Hegemony," p. 80.

41. Address before a Joint Session of the Congress, November 27, 1963, *Public Papers of the Presidents: Lyndon B. Johnson, 1963–1964, Vol. I,* (Washington, D.C.: U.S. Government Printing Office, 1965), p. 9 (hereafter *Public Papers, 1963–1964–I*).

42. Caro, *Path to Power,* pp. 241–243, 306–307.

43. Radio address in Galveston, Texas, July 9, 1948, Statements of Lyndon B. Johnson, (hereafter LBJ Statements). See also Edward R. Fried Oral History, tape 1, p. 24; W. DeVier Pierson Oral History, tape 1, p. 5, Lyndon B. Johnson Library, Austin, Texas (hereafter Fried or Peirson Oral History); Radio address, July 5, 1948, box 7; Johnson Speech at Farmers Home Administration meeting in Dallas, October 9, 1952, box 11, LBJ Statements. *Congressional Quarterly-Almanac* 1 (1945):308, 4 (1948):223, 5 (1949):431, 7 (1951):234, 11 (1955):123, and 14 (1958):448.

44. Johnson to Richard Claghorn, May 21, 1953, box 246, Legislative Files. See also G.W. Siegel to Senator Johnson on conversation between Johnson, Herbert Hoover, Jr., and Robert Anderson, March 28, 1955, box 260, Senate Legislative Files, Lyndon B. Johnson Library, Austin, Texas (hereafter Legislative Files); Johnson Address to the Lions Club, November 28, 1953, box 4, LBJ Statements; Johnson to Harley Walker, June 10, 1952, box 236; Johnson to Louis Miller, April 25, 1953; Johnson to Albert Krohn, April 29, 1953, box 246; Johnson to Walter Goeppinger, December 16, 1960; Johnson to Lamar Fleming Jr., May 26, 1960, box 755, Legislative Files.

45. Johnson to March Oliver, May 31, 1951, box 236, Legislative Files. See also Harald B. Malmgren, "An Historical View," p. 52.

46. Johnson to Robert G. Payne, March 28, 1955, box 260, Legislative Files.

47. Statement on the floor of the Senate, March 12, 1958, box 592, Senate Subject Files, Lyndon B. Johnson Library, Austin, Texas. For the importance of the oil industry to Johnson, see Caro, *Path to Power,* p. 663.

48. Johnson to E. I. Thompson, September 17, 1949, box 217, Legislative Files. See also Johnson to Enos Burt, March 18, 1955; Remarks, [1955]; Memorandum, undated, box 260, Legislative Files.

49. Johnson to B. H. Freeland, April 11, 1955, Legislative Files; Statement, March 8, 1957, box 20, LBJ Statements; Johnson to James Branch, July 27, 1960, box 756, Legislative Files.

50. "Washington Outlook," *Business Week* no. 1602 (May 14, 1960):39; Johnson to Evan Nance, February 10, 1959, box 656, Legislative Files; Myer Feldman to the author.

51. Block, *Origins of International Economic Disorder,* pp. 181–191; Burton

I. Kaufman, "Foreign Aid and the Balance of Payments Problem: Vietnam and Johnson's Foreign Economic Policy," in *The Johnson Years, Volume Two: Vietnam, the Environment, and Science* (Lawrence: University of Kansas Press, 1987), pp. 85–86; Presidential Statement No. 3 on Economic Issues: Strengthening Our Balance of Payments, October 26, 1964, *Public Papers of the Presidents of the United States: Lyndon B. Johnson, 1963–1964, Vol. II* (Washington D.C.: U.S. Government Printing Office, 1965), pp. 1460–1461 (hereafter *Public Papers, 1963–1964–II*).

52. Executive Order 11132, 12 December 1963, box 130, WHCF-LBJ; Remarks to the Cabinet Committee on Export Expansion, April 7, 1964, *Public Papers, 1963–1964–I*, p. 445; *Historical Statistics*, pt. II, p. 864; Press Release, December 31, 1963, attached to telegram, December 19, 1963, box 156, WHCF-LBJ; Memorandum, Wool Group Meeting, February 7, 1964, box 133, NACM-NTA Papers; Memorandum from 54 Senators and 115 Representatives, [February 1964], box Pastore-General Files (Textiles), Pastore Papers; Statement by the President on the Textile Industry, October 26, 1964, *Public Papers, 1963–1964–II*, pp. 1448–1449.

53. Administrative History of the Department of Agriculture, vol. 1, chap. 3, International Trade, box 1, Lyndon B. Johnson Library, Austin, Texas (hereafter USDA History); "Cut Off at the Joint," *The Economist* 210 (March 7, 1964):893; U.S. Congress, Senate Committee on Finance, *Meat Imports, Pt. 1*, 88th Cong., 2d sess., 1964, pp. 1–3, 49, 77; C. W. MacMillan to the President, May 27, 1964, box 7; Special Program for Beef, May 15, 1964; Dorothy Jacobson to the President, April 22, 1964; Orville Freeman to Myer Feldman, June 10, 1964, box 1, WHCF-LBJ; Remarks to the National Farm Editors Association, May 12, 1964, *Public Papers, 1963–1964–I*, pp. 687–688; Orville Freeman to E. F. King, June 30, 1964, box 8, WHCF-LBJ.

54. *Congressional Record-House*, vol. 110, pt. 7, April 28, 1964, 9334–9385, and April 29, 1964, 9458–9503; William Roth to Christian Herter, May 4, 1964, box 8, Herter Files; "Tariff Ups and Downs," *The Economist* 213 (November 7, 1964):588; Acting Commerce Secretary to the President, [1964], box 14, Herter Files; *Congressional Record-Senate*, vol. 110, pt. 17, September 25, 1964, Javits, 22896–22897. Containers and microscopes got quotas.

55. Remarks to the Members of the Public Advisory Committee on Trade Negotiations, April 21, 1964, *Public Papers, 1963–1964–I*, p. 506. See also Excerpts [from President's speech and letters], [April 1963–1964], box 10, Herter Files; "Insiders Take the Stand," *International Commerce* 69 (December 23, 1963):19; Preeg, *Traders*, p. 84; Curtis and Vastine, *Kennedy Round*, pp. 10–13; STR History; Lyndon B. Johnson, *The Vantage Point: Perspectives of the Presidency, 1963–1969* (New York: Holt, Rinehart, and Winston, 1971), p. 311; Annual Message to the Congress on the State of the Union, January 8, 1964, p. 117; President's News Conference at the LBJ Ranch, December 27, 1963, p. 90; Joint Statement Following Discussions with Chancellor Erhard, December 29, 1963, p. 99; President's News Conference, April 11, 1964, p. 459; Presidential Policy Statement Paper No. 4: Farm Policy, *Public Papers-II, 1963–1964*, p. 1569.

56. "Grand Design Frayed," *The Economist* 210 (March 14, 1964):971–972;

"Germany's Erhard Talks About Trade, Tariffs, The U.S. Dollar," *U.S. News and World Report* 56 (June 8, 1964):63–64; Evans, *Kennedy Round,* pp. 199–200; W. Michael Blumenthal to Christian Herter, January 31, 1964, box 7; Memorandum of Conversation, State Department, April 10, 1964, box 15; Talking Points-Visit of EEC Commissioners, March 4, 1964, box 8, Herter Files; State Department History; *Agence Presse-Europe,* May 8, 1964 and December 20, 1963.

57. Lois Pattison de Menil, *Who Speaks for Europe? The Vision of Charles de Gaulle* (London: Weidenfeld and Nicolson, 1977), pp. 123–131; Charles Bohlen to the Secretary of State, November 27, 1963; Bohlen to the President, March 11, 1964, box 169, NSF-LBJ; George Ball to Christian Herter, November 21, 1963, box 10; *Agence Presse-Europe,* December 19 and 20, 1963; Visit of Chancellor Erhard of Germany, November 25–27, 1963; Memorandum of Conversation between George Ball and Ludwig Erhard, December 29, 1963, box 8 Herter Files; "Crossing the Bar," *The Economist* 209 (December 21, 1963):1252–1253; *Bulletin of the EEC* 9 (July 1964):12–13; "Kennedy Round," *The Economist* 210 (June 13, 1964):1220; *Wall Street Journal* (January 7, 1964):1; Ambassador Hervé Alphand address, February 24, 1964, box 169, NSF-LBJ.

58. *International Trade Reporter's Survey and Analysis,* no. 893, May 8, 1964, box 9, Behrman Papers. See also Joseph Hajda to Christian Herter, October 5, 1964, box 9, Herter Files; President's News Conference, July 24, 1964, p. 887; Remarks at the State Capitol in Des Moines, October 7, 1964, p. 1229, both in *Public Papers-I, 1963–1964;* USDA History; "FB Calls U.S. Trade Negotiating Plan a 'Blueprint for Defeat,' " *American Farm Bureau News* (June 8, 1964):89; *Congressional Record-Senate,* vol. 110. pt. 3, March 3, 1964, Morse, 4224, pt. 8, May 8, 1964, Carlson, 10443, and pt. 13, July 31, 1964, Resolution, 17489; Congressional Letter on French Fruit, April 24, 1964, box 8, Herter Files.

59. STR History; Orville Freeman to the President, December 27, 1963; Orville Freeman to McGeorge Bundy, February 14, 1964; Freeman Diary, November 16, 1963; Christian Herter to Orville Freeman and George Ball, February 6, 1964, box 5, Herter Files; *Agence Presse-Europe,* April 3, 1964.

60. "Up to its Neck," *The Economist* 213 (October 31, 1964):522. See also International Grains Agreement, February 11, 1964, attached to Schnittker to Herter, February 11, 1964, box 5; Erhard-Herter discussions, June 13, 1964; Suggested Talking Points for Ball-Erhard Discussions, November 10, 1964, box 8, Herter Files; STR History; Christian Herter to Vice-President Jean Rey, December 16, 1964, box 9, Herter Files; *Agence Presse-Europe,* November 11, 1964; State Department Memorandum of Conversation, November 3, 1964, box 15, Herter Files.

61. Curtis and Vastine, *Kennedy Round,* pp. 32–33; Orville Freeman to the President, November 16, 1964, box 9, Herter Papers; Preeg, *Traders,* pp. 83ff.

62. McGeorge Bundy to the President, November 9, 1964, box 52, National Security Council History of the Kennedy Round, Lyndon B. Johnson Library, Austin, Texas (hereafter NSC Kennedy Round History); State Department History; Herter-Robertson Talks on the Kennedy Round, Briefing Paper, September 24–25, 1964, box 14, Herter Files; Evans, *Kennedy Round,* p. 223; Preeg, *Traders,* p. 88; Curtis and Vastine, *Kennedy Round,* p. 88; "Dealing the First Hand," *The Economist* (November 21, 1964):897.

63. *Agence Presse-Europe*, November 12 and 16, 1964; Preeg, *Traders*, p. 85; Curzon and Curzon, "Management," p. 182; "Dealing the First Hand," *The Economist* 213 (November 21, 1964):897; "Kennedy Round Gets Down to Business," *Business Week* no. 1838 (November 21, 1964):30; EEC Commission, 8th General Report on the Activities of the Community, April 1, 1964–March 31, 1965 (Brussels, June, 1965), p. 274; Curtis and Vastine, *Kennedy Round*, pp. 88–89.

64. Costigliola, "Pursuit of Atlantic Community," p. 55.

65. Werner J. Feld, *The European Community in World Affairs: Economic Power and Political Influence* (New York: Alfred, 1976), p. 186.

66. Krause, *European Integration*, pp. 74, 102; Irving B. Kravis, "The U.S. Trade Position and the Common Market," in *Problems in the Modern Economy*, edited by Belassa, pp. 90–92.

67. Presidential Statement No. 8 on Economic Issues: Expanding World Trade, October 28, 1964, *Public Papers, 1963–1964–II*, p. 1518; The Kennedy Round and Trade Policy Problems, 1965–1969, [1964], box 15, Herter Files.

68. Rusk in *Wall Street Journal*, (November 27, 1964):6. See also "Kennedy Round Talks Get Down to Business," *Business Week* no. 1838 (November 21, 1964):30.

69. Task Force Report on Foreign Economic Policy, November 25, 1964, box 1, Task Force Reports, Lyndon B. Johnson Library, Austin, Texas.

7. The Third World Revolt

1. Steve Chan, *International Relations in Perspective: The Pursuit of Security, Welfare, and Justice* (New York: Macmillan, 1984), p. 243. See also The President's News Conference at the Foreign Ministry in Bonn, June 24, 1963, *Public Papers, 1963*, p. 508; The President's News Conference, January 24, 1963, p. 97 and February 14, 1963, p. 175; Special Message to the Congress on Free World Defense and Assistance Programs, April 2, 1963, p. 302, *Public Papers, 1963;* President's Trip to San Jose Meeting of the Presidents, Communique and World Reaction, March 19, 1963, box 235–238, NSF-JFK.

2. The President's News Conference at the Foreign Ministry in Bonn, June 24, 1963, *Public Papers, 1963*, p. 508.

3. Report of Task Force IV: Less-Developed Countries, February 18, 1963, box 12, Behrman Papers.

4. John Tuthill to the Secretary of State, January 27, 1963, box 309–310, NSF-JFK.

5. Finlayson and Zacher, "GATT," pp. 581–582; STR telegram (Geneva) to the Secretary of State, May 17, 1963, box 11, Herter Files; A. S. Friedberg, *The United Nations Conference on Trade and Development of 1964: The Theory of the Peripheral Economy at the Centre of International Political Discussions* (Rotterdam: Rotterdam University Press, 1970), pp. 13–14.

6. *BISD*, March 1963, 11th supp., 20th sess., pp. 169–205; STR [Geneva] to the Secretary of State, May 8, 1963 and May 17, 1963, box 11, Herter Files; *Bulletin of the EEC* 8 (July 1963):11. On French policy, see J. Barron Boyd, Jr., "France and the Third World: The African Connection," in *Third World Policies*

of *Industrialized Nations*, edited by Phillip Taylor and Gregory A. Raymond (Westport, Conn.: Greenwood Press, 1982), pp. 56–58.

7. A. Glenn Mower, Jr. *The European Community and Latin America: A Case Study in Global Role Expansion* (Westport, Conn.: Greenwood Press, 1982), pp. 39–40; Pincus, *Trade, Aid and Development*, p. 182; Feld, *European Community*, pp. 113, 131; *Agence Press-Europe*, February 14, 1961 and March 1, 1961; "Negotiating on New Treaty to Continue Close Ties of 16 New African Nations with EEC," *International Commerce* 68 (July 30, 1962):13; Common Market Preferences on Tropical Products, 1961, box 2, NSF-JFK; "Outward Bound," *The Economist* 205 (October 27, 1962):332; "The Outsiders," *The Economist* 206 (March 2, 1963):780.

8. Feld, *European Community*, pp. 108–111; *Agence Press-Europe*, January 6, 1961 and November 15, 1961.

9. The President's News Conference, July 23, 1962, *Public Papers, 1962*, p. 571; Henry Tasca to G. Mennan Williams, March 9, 1961; Some Suggested Principles Regarding Trade and Economic Relationship with Western Europe, Africa, and the U.S., [1961], box 2, NSF-JFK; Krause, *European Integration*, p. 189; Significance of EEC-African Association Agreement, September 13, 1963, box 3, NSF-JFK; Reappraisal of Current Economic Relations Between the United States and Europe: A Summary of the Bowie-Vernon Paper, June 5, 1962, box 33, Gordon Papers; President's Visit to de Gaulle, [May-June 1961], box 116a, POF; Measures for the Expansion of Trade of Developing Countries as a Means of Furthering Their Economic Development, report by the [GATT] Drafting Group, May 21, 1963, box 11; GATT Press Release, Discussions at First Meeting of Action Committee, September 13, 1963, box 12, Herter Files.

10. Report of the Interdepartmental Committee on Foreign Economic Policy, Export Opportunities for the Manufactured Exports of Less-Developed Countries, June 4, 1963, box 8, Behrman Papers.

11. GATT, *International Trade, 1963*, p. 110, *1964* (Geneva: GATT, 1965), p. 37, and *1968*, p. 237; Pincus, *Trade, Aid, and Development*, p. 178; Hal B. Lary, *Imports of Manufactures from Less Developed Countries* (New York: National Bureau of Economic Research, 1968), pp. 1–3; David Morawetz, *Twenty-Five Years of Economic Development, 1950 to 1975* (Baltimore: Johns Hopkins University Press, 1977), p. 26.

12. Report of the Interdepartmental Committee on Foreign Economic Policy, Export Opportunities for the Manufactured Exports of Less-Developed Countries, June 4, 1963, box 8, Behrman Papers.

13. Ibid.

14. OECD Ministerial Meeting, Bellagio Conference, November 19–20, 1963, box 13, Herter Files; Remarks to the Cabinet Committee on Export Expansion, April 7, 1964, *Public Papers, 1963–1964–I*, p. 445; State Department History.

15. Friedberg, *United Nations*, pp. 8–15, 88–89; Spero, *Politics of International Economic Relations*, pp. 230–233; Branislav Gosovic, *UNCTAD: Conflict and Compromise* (Leiden, Holland: A. W. Sijthoff, 1972), chap. 1. The inclusion of organizations let non-UN members West Germany and Switzerland take part.

16. Raul Prebisch, "Toward a New Trade Policy for Development," in UN, *Proceeding of the United Nations Conference on Trade and Development*, March

23–June 16, 1964 (New York: United Nations, 1964), vol. II, p. 7 (hereafter *UNCTAD Proceedings* with volume and pages).

17. Spero, *Politics of International Economic Relations*, p. 232; Blake and Walters, *The Politics of Global Economic Relations* (Englewood Cliffs, N.J.: Prentice-Hall, 1976), pp. 34–36; Pincus, *Trade, Aid, and Development*, pp. 77–82; "The Geneva Marathon Starts," *The Economist* 210 (March 21, 1964):1123; Prebisch statement, March 24, 1964, *UNCTAD Proceedings*, vol. II, pp. 74–77; UNCTAD strategy paper, February 24, 1964, attached to George Ball to McGeorge Bundy, March 3, 1964, box 293, NSF-LBJ.

18. CIA special report, UNCTAD, March 20, 1964, box 293, NSF-LBJ; Douglas Evans, *The Politics of Trade: The Evolution of the Superbloc* (New York: John Wiley and Sons, 1974), p. 4; Interdepartmental Committee on Foreign Economic Policy Report, United States Interests and Objectives at the UNCTAD, May 2, 1963 and Export Opportunities for the Manufactured Exports of Less-Developed Countries, June 4, 1963, box 8, Behrman Papers.

19. CIA special report, UNCTAD, March 20, 1964, box 293, NSF-LBJ; Report on the Summit Conference of Independent African States, Resolutions, June 20, 1963, box 3, NSF-JFK; "Untidy UNCTAD," *The Economist* 211 (April 4, 1964):32; Interdepartmental Committee on Foreign Economic Policy, United States Interests and Objectives at the UNCTAD, May 2, 1963, box 8, Behrman Papers; Annex I, Attitudes of Latin American Countries Toward Issues to be Raised at the United Nations Conference on Trade and Development, February 3, 1964, box 293, NSF-JFK.

20. CIA special report, UNCTAD, March 20, 1964, box 293, NSF-LBJ; *UNCTAD Proceedings*, vol. IV, p. 44; "Overall Latin America Trend is Upward for Imports and Exports," *International Commerce* 69 (November 14, 1963):7; "Far East Gains and Gains," *International Commerce* 71 (January 18, 1965):31; "A Changing Market in Changing Africa," *International Commerce* 70 (October 19, 1964):17–18; Committee for Economic Development, *Trade Policy Toward Low Income Countries* (New York: CED, 1967), pp. 37–38; GATT, *International Trade, 1964*, pp. 142–144, 154–158, 160–161; GATT, *International Trade, 1965* (Geneva: GATT, 1966), pp. 203, 216, 225, 238; GATT, *International Trade, 1967* (Geneva: GATT, 1968), p. 4; GATT, *International Trade, 1968* (Geneva: GATT, 1969), p. 237; Pincus, *Trade, Aid, and Development*, pp. 180, 243, 62.

21. Interdepartmental Committee on Foreign Economic Policy Report, United States Interests and Objectives at the UNCTAD, May 2, 1963, box 8, Behrman Papers; EEC Commission, 8th General Report of the Activities of the Community, April 1, 1964–March 31, 1965 (June 1965):291; *Agence Presse-Europe*, March 19, 1964; Pincus, *Trade, Aid, and Development*, pp. 82–83; CIA special report, UNCTAD, March 20, 1964, box 293, NSF-LBJ; Memorandum, France's Foreign Aid Program, April 10, 1964, box 169, NSF-LBJ; "Geneva Stereotype," *The Economist* 210 (March 28, 1964):1287; Department of State, Memorandum of Conversation between Herter and West German Minister of the Economy Kurt Schmuecker, April 8, 1964, box 15, Herter Files; "The Non-Kennedy Round," *The Economist* 210 (January 25, 1964):324–325.

22. Department of State, Memorandum of Conversation between George Ball

and Permanent Secretary of the British Board of Trade Sir Richard Powell, April 21, 1964, box 15, Herter Files; Statement by Edward Heath, *UNCTAD Proceedings,* vol. II, pp. 392–394.

23. George Ball to McGeorge Bundy, March 3, 1964, box 293, NSF-LBJ. See also Bundy to Ball, October 20, 1963, box 7, Herter Files; Bundy to Ball, November 9, 1963, box 309–310, NSF-JFK.

24. Components of a Strategy for the Kennedy Round, December 10, 1963, attached to George Ball to Christian Herter, December 10, 1963, box 7, Herter Files. See also UNCTAD strategy paper, February 24, 1964, attached to George Ball to McGeorge Bundy, March 3, 1964, box 293, NSF-LBJ.

25. Ball, *The Past Has Another Pattern,* pp. 193–194; Department of State, Memorandum of Conversation between George Ball and EEC Commission Vice-President Jean Rey, March 5, 1964, box 15, Herter Files.

26. Position paper, Preferences for Less-Developed Countries in the Markets of Developed Countries, March 23, 1964, box 16, Herter Files; Ronald I. Meltzer, "The Politics of Policy Reversal: The U.S. Response to Granting Trade Preferences to Developing Countries and Linkages Between International Organizations and National Policy Making," *International Organization* 30 (Autumn 1976):654–655.

27. Ball, *The Past Has Another Pattern,* p. 194.

28. George Ball to the President, March 30, 1964, box 293, NSF-LBJ. See also Ball speech, March 24, 1964, *UNCTAD Proceedings,* vol. II, pp. 394–399; Bernard Norwood to William Roth, March 23, 1964, box 12, Herter Files.

29. Ball, *The Past Has Another Pattern,* p. 194; Message to the UN Conference on Trade and Development, March 25, 1964, *Public Papers, 1963–1964–I,* p. 418.

30. Ball, *The Past Has Another Pattern,* p. 195; Department of State, Memorandum of Conversation with UNCTAD President Abdel Moneim El Kaissouni, July 7, 1964, box 15, Herter Files; *New York Times* May 27, 1964, p. 50. For debate over and results of UNCTAD, see *UNCTAD Proceedings;* Freidberg, *United Nations;* Kamal M. Hagras, *The United Nations Conference on Trade and Development: A Case Study in UN Diplomacy* (New York: Praeger, 1975).

31. Background paper, Visit of British Prime Minister Douglas-Home, UNCTAD, February 5, 1964, box 210–212, NSF-LBJ; Position paper, Preferences for Less-Developed Countries in the Markets of Developed Countries, March 23, 1964, box 16, Herter Files; Harry G. Johnson, "U.S. Trade Policies Toward Less Developed Countries," in *American Foreign Economic Policy,* edited by Cohen, pp. 389–391; Reginald H. Green, "UNCTAD and After: Anatomy of a Failure," *Journal of Modern African Studies* 5 (September 1967):244–248.

32. State Department, Memorandum of Conversation between the Permanent Secretary of the British Board of Trade Sir Richard Powell, Anthony Solomon, Thomas Mann, and Phillip Trezise, November 8, 1965, box 15, Herter Files; Meltzer, "Politics of Policy Reversal," pp. 657–658.

33. State Department History. See also Meltzer, "Politics of Policy Reversal," p. 658; Annex 2, September 18, 1965, State Department History.

34. Meltzer, "Politics of Policy Reversal," pp. 658–659; Trade Preferences for Less-Developed Countries, State Department History.

35. George Ball to Christian Herter, John Connor, and Willard Wirtz, August 12, 1966, Annex 4, State Department History; Dean Rusk to the President, February 22, 1967, box 1, NSF Name File-Francis Bator, Lyndon B. Johnson Library, Austin, Texas (hereafter NSF Name File-Bator); Annex 4, George Ball to Christian Herter, John Connor, and Willard Wirtz, August 12, 1966; Chronology, State Department History; W. W. Rostow to the President, January 27, 1967, box 12, NSF-LBJ. U.S. Subcommittee on Foreign Economic Policy of the Joint Committee of Congress, *The Future of U.S. Foreign Trade Policy*, 90th Cong., 1st sess., 1967 (hereafter *Future of Foreign Trade Hearings*), p. 89, and *Report*, p. 13; W. W. Rostow to the President, April 4, 1967; What We Can Say on Trade Preferences, box 3, Office Files of the White House Aides-George Christian, Lyndon B. Johnson Library, Austin, Texas; Latin American Reactions to the Summit, undated, box 12, NSF-LBJ; Johnson, *Vantage Point*, p. 350.

36. *Wall Street Journal* March 28, 1968, p. 12. See also Senator Jacob Javits, *Future of U.S. Foreign Trade Policy-Report*, pp. 20–21; *New York Times,* June 30, 1967, p. 47; "Lining Up for Battle," *The Economist* 223 (May 27, 1967):934; *New York Times,* February 20, 1968, p. 66 and March 4, 1968, p. 51; "Modest Progress on Preferences," *The Economist* 226 (March 30, 1968):65.

37. Spero, *Politics of International Economic Relations,* pp. 237–239; Rolf J. Langhammer and Andre Sapir, *Economic Impact of Generalized Tariff Preferences* (London: Gower, 1987), p. 69.

38. GATT, *International Trade, 1968,* pp. 2, 196, 237, 245, 250, 258, 265; UN, *World Economic Survey 1969–1970: The Developing Countries in the 1960s-The Problem of Appraising Progress* (New York: United Nations, 1971), p. 138.

39. Internal problems included political instability, unreliable currencies, lack of a secure investment climate, inordinate population growth, inadequate social institutions, and cultural factors. See Charles W. Kegley, Jr. and Eugene R. Wittkopf, *World Politics: Trends and Transformation* (New York: St. Martin's Press, 1981), pp. 73–90; Gilpin, *The Political Economy,* pp. 278–279.

40. "GATT Ministers Open Kennedy Round of Trade Negotiations," Department of State *Bulletin* 50 (June 1, 1964):880; State Department History; Evans, *Kennedy Round,* pp. 246–248; Kock, *International Trade,* pp. 244–245; Finalyson and Zacher, "GATT," pp. 582–583.

41. *BISD,* 13th supp., 23d sess., pp. 69–71; Memorandum, The Kennedy Round and Trade Policy Problems, 1965–1969, 1964, box 15, Herter Files; State Department History; Evans, *Kennedy Round,* p. 250.

42. *BISD,* 14th supp., 23d sess. (Geneva, July 1966):66–78.

43. State Department History; Aggarwal, *Liberal Protectionism,* pp. 102–103; Curtis and Vastine, *Kennedy Round,* p. 171; Preeg, *Traders,* p. 108.

44. The Kennedy Round and Trade Policy Problems, 1965–1969, 1964, box 15; Christian Herter to Myer Feldman, September 25, 1963, box 9, Herter Files. See also Benjamin H. Reed to McGeorge Bundy, December 19, 1963, box 13, WHCF-JFK; Revision of United States Policy for Bilateral Cotton Textile Arrangements, March 16, 1965, box 40, Confidential File, Lyndon B. Johnson Library, Austin, Texas (hereafter Confidential File).

45. *BISD*, 14th supp., 23d sess., pp. 78–81. See also President's Cabinet Textile Advisory Committee Meeting, August 24, 1965 and April 7, 1966, box 40, Confidential Files.

46. Preeg, *Traders*, p. 108; Evans, *Kennedy Round*, pp. 230–232.

47. Review of United States Policy for Bilateral Cotton Textile Agreements, March 16, 1965; President's Cabinet Textile Advisory Committee Meeting, August 24, 1965 and President's Cabinet Textile Advisory Committee Meeting, April 7, 1966, box 40, Confidential Files; Current Textile Import Situation, April 8, 1967, box 24, WHCF-LBJ.

48. Francis Bator to the President, February 2, 1966 and November 3, 1966, box 1, NSF Name File-Bator.

49. Francis Bator to the President, March 15, 1967, box 1, NSF Name File-Bator. See also Curtis and Vastine, *Kennedy Round*, p. 175; Aggarwal, *Liberal Protectionism*, pp. 104–106.

50. Aggarwal, *Liberal Protectionism*, pp. 107–113; Curtis and Vastine, *Kennedy Round*, pp. 174–175; Conference with Senator Pastore from William F. Sullivan, January 18, 1967, box 147, NACM-NTA Papers; DeVier Pierson to the President, April 8, 1967, box 24, WHCF-LBJ. Under the agreement, there would not be any one-shot quota raises. Also, Hong Kong had agreed to comprehensive controls, and Mexico, the largest textile exporter not under the LTA, had joined the agreement.

51. "The Kennedy Round is a Rich Man's Deal," *The Economist* 223 (May 20, 1967):813; Preeg, *Traders*, pp. 227, 230–232. See also Evans, *Kennedy Round*, pp. 250–253; Curtis and Vastine, *Kennedy Round*, p. 224; Kock, *International Trade*, p. 246.

52. Curtis and Vastine, *Kennedy Round*, pp. 221–224; Evans, *Kennedy Round*, p. 253; Preeg, *Traders*, p. 269; State Department History.

53. Bela Belassa, *The Newly Industrializing Countries in the World Economy* (New York: Pergamon Press, 1981), p. 110.

54. Phillip Darby, *Three Faces of Imperialism: British and American Approaches to Asia and Africa, 1870–1970* (New Haven: Yale University Press, 1987), pp. 200, 208.

8. The American Retreat, 1965–1968

1. State Department History; Curtis and Vastine, *Kennedy Round*, p. 90; Preeg, *Traders*, pp. 89–90, 93; Christian Herter, "The Kennedy Round: Progress Report," Department of State *Bulletin* 53 (July 5, 1965):33–34; William Roth to Senator Jacob Javits, July 13, 1965, box 5, Herter Files.

2. Department of State, Memorandum of Conversation between Christian Herter, President Walter Hallstein, and John Tuthill, February 1, 1965, box 16, Herter Files. See also Charles Bohlen to the Secretary of State, April 1, 1965, box 171, NSF-LBJ; Orville Freeman to the President, February 1, 1965, box 2, WHCF-LBJ.

3. Kenneth Auchincloss to STR Christian Herter, April 7, 1965, box 5, Herter Files.

4. Hubert Humphrey to Christian Herter on conversation between Humphrey

and Sicco Mansholt, March 4, 1965, attached to William Roth to Hubert Humphrey, March 8, 1965, box 14, Herter Files.

5. Department of State History; Christian Herter to the President, January 19, 1965, box 52, NSC Kennedy Round History; *Congressional Record-Senate,* vol. 111, pt. 3, February 25, 1965, Senator Herman Talmadge, 3557–3558; W. Michael Blumenthal to Christian Herter, December 15, 1964, box 7, Herter Files.

6. State Department History; Curtis and Vastine, *Kennedy Round,* pp. 51–53.

7. USDA History; Irwin R. Hedges, "Kennedy Round Agricultural Negotiations and the World Grains Agreement," *Journal of Farm Economics* 49 (December 1967):1333–1335; Preeg, *Traders,* pp. 94, 151–155; Curtis and Vastine, *Kennedy Round,* pp. 53–58. Exporters were the U.S., the EEC, Canada, Argentina, and Australia, while importers were the EEC, Norway, Britain, Denmark, Switzerland, and Japan.

8. Charles Bohlen to the Secretary of State, February 2, 1965, box 170; Charles Bohlen to the Secretary of State, April 28, 1965 and June 16, 1965, box 171, NSF-LBJ; Paul Luyten to author.

9. Charles Bohlen to the Secretary of State, April 1, 1965, box 171, NSF-LBJ.

10. Preeg, *Traders,* pp. 111–112; State Department History; Memorandum of Conversation between Christian Herter, Belgian Foreign Minister Paul-Henri Spaak, and Belgian Ambassador to the United States Louis Scheyven, October 22, 1965, box 10, Herter Files; John Newhouse, *Collision in Brussels: The Common Market Crisis of 30 June 1965* (London: Faber and Faber, 1967), pp. 45, 67–68, 123–124; Memorandum of Conversation with Emile Noel, EEC Commission and Thomas W. Fina, U.S. ambassador's office to the European Community, July 1, 1965, box 1, NSF Name File-Bator; *Agence Presse-Europe,* July 1, 1965; Bromberger and Bromberger, *Jean Monnet,* chap. 17; Spaak, *The Continuing Battle,* pp. 481–486.

11. Blumenthal in McGeorge Bundy to the President, August 17, 1965, attached to Francis Bator to the President, August 17, 1965, box 91, Confidential Files. See also State Department History; Preeg, *Traders,* pp. 114–115; John Schnittker Oral History, tape 1, p. 18, Lyndon B. Johnson Library, Austin, Texas (hereafter Schnittker Oral History).

12. Preeg, *Traders,* p. 115; Herschel Newsom to Harry McPherson, September 16, 1965, box 2, WHCF-LBJ; William Roth, Discussions with Congressional Advisors, August 17, 1965, box 91, Confidential Files; State Department History; Christian Herter to the President, September 13, 1965, box 5, Herter Files. The U.S. withheld $350 million on meat and dairy products pending action by a special sector group.

13. "Tariffs: 'Ghastly Problem,' " *Newsweek* 66 (September 20, 1965):80; *Congressional Record-House,* vol. 111, pt. 15, August 16, 1965, William Bray (R-Ind.), 20498; Preeg, *Traders,* p. 117, quoting Andre Naef, *Tribune de Geneve.*

14. Newhouse, *Collision,* pp. 149–157; "The Goal in Sight," *The Economist* 219 (May 14, 1966):696–698; Preeg, *Traders,* pp. 124–125; *Agence Presse-Europe,* April 1, 1966; Bromberger and Bromberger, *Jean Monnet,* chap. 18.

15. State Department History; Orville Freeman to the President, August 1, 1966, box 5, Herter Files.

16. National Fruit Export Council, adopted September 20, 1966, box 4,

WHCF-LBJ. See also Schnittker Oral History, tape 2, p. 36; State Department, Memorandum of Conversation, February 27, 1965, box 15; State Department, Memorandum of Conversation between the STR and fruit growers, September 20, 1966, box 5, Herter Files; Curtis and Vastine, *Kennedy Round,* p. 30.

17. *Congressional Record-Senate,* vol. 112, pt. 14, August 4, 1966, Sparkman, 18328. See also 12 Senators of Agriculture Committee to the President, October 3, 1966, box 5, Herter Files.

18. Francis Bator to the President, August 4, 1966, box 76, Aides Files-Bill Moyers, Lyndon B. Johnson Library, Austin Texas; Christian Herter to the President, January 27, 1966, box 441.2 (103) ER:Pt. 1, EC Delegation Files; William Roth to the President, August 2, 1966, box 52, NSC Kennedy Round History; James Patton to Christian Herter, October 5, 1966; Reuben Johnson to Tony Dechant, October 14, 1966, box 2, NFU Papers.

19. Christian Herter to Senator Russell Long, December 9, 1966, box 4, Herter Files. See also "Kennedy Crunch," *The Economist* 221 (October 22, 1966):374.

20. Christian Herter to Dean Acheson, May 10, 1966, box 16, Papers of Dean Acheson, Manuscripts and Archives, Sterling Memorial Library, Yale University (hereafter Acheson Papers).

21. Curtis and Vastine, *Kennedy Round,* pp. 186–208; Christian Herter to the President, October 11, 1966, box 52, NSC Kennedy Round History; W. Michael Blumenthal to William Roth, June 1, 1965, box 7, Herter Files. See also Administrative History of the Department of Commerce, box 2, Lyndon B. Johnson Library, Austin, Texas (hereafter Commerce Department History); The U.S.-Canadian Automotive Products Trade Agreement, attached to Matt Nimetz to Joe Califano, April 3, 1968; Lyndon Johnson to Speaker John McCormack, March 31, 1965, box 156, WHCF-LBJ. The U.S.-Canadian agreement rationalized the auto market, and helped America retain a large, but shrinking, auto trade surplus. In fact, U.S. subsidiaries on the Canadian side were able to increase their exports across the border, as well as raise their production levels to the point where they surpassed U.S. domestic automakers' outputs by 1967. See also Preeg, *Traders,* pp. 97–102; Memorandum of Conversation between the STR and Reynolds, Alcoa, and Kaiser [aluminum companies], January 14, 1965, box 10, Herter Files.

22. Curtis and Vastine, *Kennedy Round,* pp. 127–131, 136–141; Preeg, *Traders,* p. 103; State Department History; Country Committee I (EEC) to Trade Staff Committee, August 26, 1964, box 12; State Department, Memorandum of Conversation between ECSC leaders and the State Department, October 8, 1964, box 10, Herter Files. For a survey of steel and trade, see Kent Jones, *Politics vs. Economics in World Steel Trade* (London: Allen and Unwin, 1986), pp. 25–28.

23. J. Robert Schaetzel to Dean Acheson, December 5, 1966, box 28, Acheson Papers. See also Janice Wickstead Jadlow, "Trade Liberalization in the Chemical Industry: The Impact on the United States," Ph.D. dissertation, Oklahoma State University, 1977, p. 13; *Agence Presse-Europe,* May 25, 1966 and June 17, 1966; Curtis and Vastine, *Kennedy Round,* pp. 117–118.

24. Francis Bator to the President, February 21, 1967, box 52, NSC Kennedy Round History. See also Preeg, *Traders,* pp. 108–110; Curtis and Vastine, *Kennedy Round,* pp. 101–102.

25. Preeg, *Traders,* pp. 171–172.

26. William Roth to the President, February 15, 1967, box 52, NSC Kennedy Round History. See also "Chemical Men Make a Case for a Tough Stand on ASP," *Chemical Week* 99 (September 17, 1966):40; Henry Wilson letters in 1967 to congressional delegations, box 14, WHCF-LBJ; Letters on Behalf of the Benzenoid Chemical Industry, undated, box 22, Aides Files-DeVier Pierson, Lydon B. Johnson Library, Austin, Texas (hereafter Pierson Files). Preeg, *Traders,* p. 128; Pastor, *Congress,* pp. 120–121; *Congressional Record-Senate,* vol. 113, pt. 2, February 3, 1967, Russell Long, 2435.

27. Curtis and Vastine, *Kennedy Round,* pp. 118–119; Francis Bator to the President, February 21, 1967, box 52, NSC Kennedy Round History.

28. Problems Ahead in Europe and attached Summary Notes of 569th NSC Meeting, May 3, 1967, box 2, NSC Meeting File, Lyndon B. Johnson Library, Austin, Texas. See also Grosser, *Western Alliance,* pp. 209–226, 237–243; Background paper, UK Policy Toward the EEC, Visit of Foreign Secretary George Brown, October 10, 1966, box 215–216, NSF-LBJ; Hoffmann, *Gulliver's Troubles,* p. 290; Kurt Birrenbach to Dean Acheson, February 2, 1965, box 3, Acheson Papers.

29. Summary Notes of 569th NSC Meeting, May 3, 1967, box 2, NSC Meeting File. See also Feld, *European Community,* p. 186; EEC Commission, *10th General Report on the Activities of the Community,* April 1, 1966–March 31, 1967 (Brussels: EEC, June 1967), p. 303; UN, *European Economy from the 1950s to the 1970s,* p. 6; Secretary of State Dean Rusk to the President, February 11, 1967, box 1, NSF Name File; Francis Bator to the President, June 16, 1966, box 1, NSF Name File.

30. Block, *Origins of International Economic Disorder,* pp. 181–183; Spero, *Politics of International Economic Relations,* p. 38; Administrative History of the Council of Economic Advisors, box 1, chp. IV, Lyndon B. Johnson Library, Austin, Texas (hereafter CEA History); Statement by the President Outlining a Program of Action to Deal with the Balance of Payments Problem, January 1, 1968, *Public Papers of the Presidents of the United States: Lyndon B. Johnson, 1968–1969* (Washington, D.C.: U.S. Government Printing Office, 1970), pp. 8–9 (hereafter *Public Papers, 1968–1969*).

31. Block, *The Origins,* 184–193; Solomon, *International Monetary System,* chap. 8.

32. U.S. House Subcommittee on Foreign Economic Policy of the Committee on Foreign Affairs, *The Foreign Policy Aspects of the Kennedy Round,* 89th Cong., 2d sess., 1966, Farbstein, p. 1 (hereafter cited as *Aspects of the Kennedy Round Hearing*). See also "The Johnson Trade Policy," Department of State *Bulletin* 54 (May 30, 1966):857–858; Administration's Record on Escape Clause Actions, [October 12, 1967], box 22, Pierson Files.

33. Preeg, *Traders,* pp. 159–160; *New York Times,* January 20, 1967, p. 16.

34. J. Robert Schaetzel to Dean Acheson, December 5, 1966, box 28, Acheson Papers.

35. Grosser, *Western Alliance,* p. 232; *Aspects of the Kennedy Round Hearings,* Ball, pp. 6–7, Herter, p. 66; *Congressional Record-House,* vol. 113, pt. 1, January 19, 1967, Curtis, 1052; Preeg, *Traders,* p. 161.

36. Francis Bator to the President, April 18, 1967; The Kennedy Round Crisis, [April-June 1967], box 52, NSC Kennedy Round History. The Command Group included Bator, Undersecretary Eugene Rostow and Assistant Secretary Anthony Solomon of the Department of State, Acting Secretary of Commerce Alexander Trowbridge, USDA Undersecretary John Schnittker, and John Rehm of the STR office. See also Preeg, *Traders,* pp. 131–133, 142, 164–168; *Agence Presse-Europe,* January 3, January 9, and January 13, 1967; Curtis and Vastine, *Kennedy Round,* pp. 91–92.

37. State Department History; Francis Bator to the President, May 1, 1967, box 52, NSC Kennedy Round History; Curtis and Vastine, *Kennedy Round,* pp. 190–191, 200–201. There were substantial cuts in the pulp and paper sector but disappointing results in the aluminum. Both sectors were of secondary importance, but of interest to America.

38. Curtis and Vastine, *Kennedy Round,* pp. 129, 142–143.

39. Preeg, *Traders,* pp. 180–192; Francis Bator to the President, May 1, 1967; The Kennedy Round Crisis, [May-June 1967], box 52, NSC Kennedy Round History.

40. The Kennedy Round Crisis, [April-June 1967], NSC Kennedy Round History; Preeg, *Traders,* p. 194; Curtis and Vastine, *Kennedy Round,* [[/ 101, 120–121; Jadlow, "Trade Liberalization," pp. 18–21.

41. Preeg, *Traders,* p. 150; Evans, *Kennedy Round,* pp. 291–292; Curtis and Vastine, *Kennedy Round,* p. 47; 18 Senators to the President, April 19, 1967, box 4, WHCF-LBJ; Kennedy Round Crisis, [April-June 1967], box 52, NSC Kennedy Round History.

42. James Patton to Tony Dechant, April 11, 1967, box 3, NFU Papers. See also USDA History.

43. J. Robert Schaetzel to Dean Acheson, April 2, 1967, box 28, Acheson Papers; Francis Bator to the President, April 28, 1967, box 52, NSC Kennedy Round History; Schnittker Oral History, tape 2, p. 35.

44. Roger Tubby [Brussels] to the State Department, April 26, 1967; Alexander Trowbridge, Memorandum for the File, April 21, 1967, box 52, NSC Kennedy Round History; Preeg, *Traders,* pp. 154–155; USDA History; Kennedy Round Crisis, [April-June 1967], box 52, NSC Kennedy Round History; Curtis and Vastine, *Kennedy Round,* pp. 57–58; Conversation between W. Michael Blumenthal and French GATT delegate Henri Corson April 21, 1966, box 10, Herter Files.

45. USDA History; Curtis and Vastine, *Kennedy Round,* pp. 30, 58–61; Evans, *Kennedy Round,* p. 271; Hedges, "World Grains," p. 1335; State Department History.

46. Francis Bator to the President, May 10, 1967, box 52, NSC Kennedy Round History.

47. Kennedy Round Crisis, [April-June 1967], box 52, NSC Kennedy Round History; Preeg, *Traders,* chap. 12. The EEC was unhappy because U.S. withdrawals relating to Japan had unbalanced the whole Kennedy Round, supposedly to America's favor. This assessment was an exaggeration, but the STR restored some concessions. Another hitch was Japan's resistance to the food aid commitment, a position taken by Tokyo because the country lacked adequate supplies of grain

for its own consumption. Japan was allowed to substitute other forms of aid for grains.

48. Curzon and Curzon, "Management," p. 176; Harald Malmgren, *International Economic Peacekeeping in Phase II* (New York: Atlantic Council of the United States, Quadrangle Books, 1972), p. 16; *La Metropole,* Belgium, réaction de la presse après la conclusion du Kennedy-round, May 16, 1967, EC Delegation Files. See also "Kennedy Round Agreements Signed at Geneva," Department of State *Bulletin* 57 (July 24, 1967):96–100; President Lyndon Johnson, STR William Roth, Secretary of Commerce Alexander Trowbridge, "The Kennedy Round: Proud Chapter in the History of International Commerce," Department of State *Bulletin* 57 (July 31, 1967):123–130; Special Message to the Congress Transmitting the Multilateral Trade Agreement Concluding the Kennedy Round of Trade Negotiations, November 27, 1967, *Public Papers of the Presidents of the United States: Lyndon B. Johnson, 1967* (Washington, D.C.: U.S. Government Printing Office, 1968), pp. 1072–1074 (hereafter *Public Papers, 1967*); Preeg, *Traders,* pp. 202–203.

49. Ibid., pp. 12, 214, 237, 260; Evans, *Kennedy Round,* pp. 281–282, 294–296; Curtis and Vastine, *Kennedy Round,* p. 227.

50. Alexander Trowbridge, Memorandum for the File, April 21, 1967, box 52, NSC Kennedy Round History; Preeg, *Traders,* pp. 184–188, 257–260.

51. Preeg, *Traders,* pp. 201, 245–247, 257; *Future of Foreign Trade Policy,* Roth, p. 44.

52. Schnittker Oral History, tape 2, p. 34. See also Preeg, *Traders,* pp. 251, 258; Evans, *Kennedy Round,* p. 392; Feld, *European Community,* pp. 187–189.

53. John C. Obert to Lloyd Hackler, July 21, 1967, box 5, WHCF-LBJ.

54. Schnittker Oral History, tape 2, p. 34; USDA History; "The Kennedy Round: Proud Chapter in the History of International Commerce," Department of State *Bulletin* 57 (July 31, 1967):132–134.

55. USDA History; George Baldanzi to the President, August 1, 1967, box 4, WHCF-LBJ; Strackbein in Preeg, *Traders,* p. 197. See also Curtis and Vastine, *Kennedy Round,* pp. 60–61; "Wheat Trade Convention Could Restrain U.S. Exports," *American Farm Bureau Newsletter* 47 (January 22, 1968):15; "Foreign Trade and U.S. Agriculture," *American Farm Bureau Newsletter* 46 (August 7, 1967):26.

56. *Wall Street Journal,* May 24, 1967, p. 1.

57. Senator Vance Hartke to Tony Dechant, November 28, 1967, box 3, NFU Papers. See also Congressional Briefing on the Kennedy Round, May 16, 1967, box 52, NSC Kennedy Round History; *Congressional Record-Senate,* vol. 113, pt. 17, August 14, 1967, Langen, 22484 and pt. 10, May 16, 1967, E. Y. Berry (R-S.D.), 12817; pt. 10, May 17, 1967, Dent, 13112; Commerce Department History; Pierson Oral History, tape 1, pp. 6–7.

58. Henry Fowler to Senator Russell Long, October 18, 1967, box 155, WHCF-LBJ.

59. Francis Bator to the President, March 16, 1967, box 1, NSF Name File-Bator; Francis Bator to the President, May 15, 1967, box 52, NSC Kennedy Round History.

60. Remarks to the Delegates to the 1967 Consumer Assembly, November 2,

1967, *Public Papers, 1967,* pp. 984–985. See also Trowbridge Oral History, tape 2, p. 21.

61. Special Message to the Congress: "Greater Prosperity Through Expanded World Trade," *Public Papers, 1968–1969,* pp. 648–665; Frank, *Foreign Trade,* pp. 55–57; John Hoving to William Roth, June 27, 1967, box 130; DeVier Pierson to the President, December 5, 1967; Barefoot Sanders to Joe Califano, March 28, 1968, box 155, WHCF-LBJ; Memorandum from Henry Wilson, Trade Legislation for 1967, box 16, Aides Files-Henry Wilson, Lyndon B. Johnson Library, Austin, Texas; U.S. House Ways and Means Committee, *Foreign Trade and Tariff Proposals, Pt. II,* 90th Cong., 2d sess., 1968, 5629–5641; William Roth to the President, June 7, 1968; Harry McPherson to the President, August 28, 1968, box 1; DeVier Pierson to the President, July 11, 1968, box 155, WHCF-LBJ; Pastor, *Congress,* pp. 121–122; "Trade Expansion, Protectionist Moves Both Blocked," *Congressional Quarterly-Almanac* 24 (1968):729–733.

62. Trowbridge Oral History, tape 2, p. 4; Fried Oral History, pp. 4–9; Calleo, *Imperious Economy,* pp. 56–58; Harald Malmgren, *Trade Wars or Trade Negotiations: Non-Tariff Barriers and Economic Peacekeeping* (Washington, D.C.: Atlantic Council of the United States, 1970), pp. 4–5, 9; Block, *The Origins,* pp. 193–198; Statement by the President Outlining a Program of Action to Deal with the Balance of Payments Problem, January 1, 1968, pp. 8–12; Letter to the President of the Senate and to the Speaker of the House urging Actions to Increase American Exports, March 20, 1968, *Public Papers, 1968–1969–I,* pp. 417–418; *Historical Statistics,* pt. II, p. 887; Eugene Braderman to Anthony Solomon, July 10, 1968, box 7, Aides Files-E. Ernest Goldstein, Lyndon B. Johnson Library, Austin, Texas; AFL-CIO Resolution on International Trade, October 1969; Elizabeth Jager to Andrew Biemiller, May 2, 1969, box 20, AFL-CIO Department of Legislation, Meany Archives; Solomon, *International Monetary System,* pp. 186–187; Shonfield, "International Economic Relations," chap. 3; Spero, *Politics of International Economic Relations,* pp. 53–55.

63. J. Robert Schaetzel to Alice and Dean Acheson, November 17, 1967, box 28, Acheson Papers; Talking Points with EEC Commission President Jean Rey, February 7, 1968, box 45–57, NSF-LBJ; Curtis and Vastine, *Kennedy Round,* p. 232; *New York Times,* April 13, 1968, p. 36.

64. Curtis and Vastine, *Kennedy Round,* p. 231.

65. William Diebold, Jr., *The United States and the Industrial World: American Foreign Economic Policy in the 1970s* (New York: Praeger, 1972), p. 39.

66. Eric Wyndham White, "Stimulating Worldwide Trade," in *Building the American-European Market,* edited by Bradley, p. 198; Remarks Upon Signing the Kennedy Round Trade Negotiations Proclamation, December 16, 1967, *Public Papers, 1967–II,* p. 1148; "The One That Didn't Get Away," *The Economist* 223 (May 20, 1967):767; State Department History; Preeg, *Traders,* pp. 196, 197ff.

67. Spero, *Politics of International Economic Relations,* p. 38.

68. Warley, "Western Trade," p. 387. See also Preeg, *Traders,* p. 262.

69. Isaiah Frank, "The Economic Constraints," in *America and the World: From the Truman Doctrine to Vietnam,* edited by Robert E. Osgood et al. (Baltimore: Johns Hopkins University Press, 1970), p. 249.

9. American Trading Power in the 1960s and Beyond

1. Matusow, "Kennedy," p. 122.

2. Annual Message to the Congress: The Economic Report of the President, January 16, 1969, *Public Papers, 1968–1969*, pp. 1320–1321. See also U.S. Senate Finance Committee, *The Trade Reform Act of 1973*, 93d, Cong., 2d sess., 1974, pt. 1, pp. 117–119 (hereafter *Trade Reform Act Hearings*); Calleo, *Imperious Economy*, pp. 60–68; Matusow, "Kennedy," pp. 118–119; "Trade Policy, Quotas," *Congressional Quarterly-Alamanac* 25 (1969):1005–1006; "Foreign Trade Bill Dies in Senate at End of Session," *Congressional Quarterly-Alamanac* 26 (1970):1051; Ball, *The Past Has Another Pattern*, p. 450.

3. *Trade Reform Act Hearings*, pt. 1, Long, pp. 1–2.

4. J. Robert Schaetzel, summary of off the record speech before the Mid-Atlantic Group, September 21, 1971, box 28, Acheson Papers.

5. Shonfield, "International Economic Relations," p. 109; Krasner, "Commercial Policy," p. 83; Pastor, *Congress*, p. 339; Goldstein, "A Re-examination," p. 421.

6. GATT, *International Trade, 1976/77* (Geneva: GATT, 1977), p. 75; U.S. Department of Commerce, *International Economic Indicators* (Washington, D.C.: U.S. Government Printing Office, November 1974), pp. 56–57; Richard Rosecrance, *The Rise of the Trading State: Commerce and Conquest in the Modern World* (New York: Basic Books, 1986), pp. 118–121; Council on International Economic Policy, *Annual Report* pp. 7, 37; Taber, *Patterns and Prospects*, pp. 97–98; U.S. Department of Commerce, *International Economic Indicators and Competitive Trends 5* (Washington, D.C.: U.S. Government Printing Office, March 1979), p. 46; GATT, *International Trade, 1973/74* (Geneva: GATT, 1974), pp. 76, 90.

7. Spero, *Politics of International Economic Relations*, pp. 237–239; GATT, *International Trade, 1971* (Geneva: GATT, 1972), p. 142; GATT, *International Trade, 1977* (Geneva: GATT, 1977), p. 104; GATT, *International Trade, 1980–81* (Geneva: GATT, 1981), pp. 133–137; Morawetz, *Twenty-Five Years*, pp. 67–68.

8. Calleo, *Imperious Economy*, p. 17. For a positive assessment, see Preeg, *Traders*, p. 261, and references in the previous chapter.

9. Shonfield, "International Economic Relations," pp. 30–31, 94; Benjamin Cohen, "The Industrial World," in *American Foreign Economic Policy*, edited by Cohen, p. 188; Calleo, *Imperious Economy*, p. 17; Krasner, "The Tokyo Round," p. 497; Lundestad, *American "Empire"*, p. 89.

10. Feld, *European Community in World Affairs*, pp. 187–189; Ginsberg, "European Community and the United States," pp. 174, 179; Talbot, *Chicken War*, pp. 135, 140–142; Spero, *Politics of International Economic Relations*, p. 105.

11. Warley, "Western Trade," p. 388. See also Calleo, *Imperious Economy*, p. 16; Spero, *Politics of International Economic Relations*, p. 105.

12. Shonfield, "International Economic Relations," pp. 26–39.

13. OECD, *Historical Statistics of Foreign Trade, 1965–1980* (Paris: OECD, 1982), p. 10; *International Economic Indicators* (November 1974), pp. 56, 72;

Shonfield, "International Economic Relations," p. 42; Curzon and Curzon, "Management," p. 256; Blake and Walters, *Politics of Global Economic Relations,* p. 17; *Historical Statistics,* pt. II, p. 903; Feld, *European Community in World Affairs,* p. 186; U.S. Department of Commerce, *Statistical Abstract of the United States, 1976* (Washington, D.C.: U.S. Government Printing Office, 1976), p. 826.

14. *International Economic Indicators* (November 1974), p. 72; Spero, *Politics of International Economic Relations,* pp. 38–39.

15. Shonfield, "International Economic Relations," p. 26.

16. Krasner, "Commercial Policy," pp. 56–57, 58–59. See also Kennedy, *Rise and Fall of the Great Powers,* pp. 421–436.

17. Kraft, *Grand Design,* p. 120. See also Calleo, *Beyond American Hegemony,* p. 143.

18. U.S. Joint Economic Committee, Subcommittee on Foreign Economic Policy, *A Foreign Economic Policy for the 1970s,* 91st Cong., 1st sess., 1969, pt. 1, Bator, p. 110.

BIBLIOGRAPHY

Archival Sources
John F. Kennedy Library, Boston, Massachusetts

Dean Acheson Oral History
AFL-CIO Records
Jack N. Behrman Papers
Council of Economic Advisers Oral History
  Paul Samuelson
  James Tobin
Democratic National Committee Records, 1952–1963
Department of Commerce Records
Robert Estabrook Papers
Myer Feldman Oral History
Orville Freeman Diary
Orville Freeman Oral History
Orville Freeman Papers
Kermit Gordon Papers
Seymour E. Harris Oral History
Theodore Hesburgh Oral History
Luther Hodges Oral History
John M. Kelly Oral History
James M. Landis Papers
National Security Files
Pre-Presidential Papers
President's Office Files
Myer Rashish Oral History
Register to the White House Staff Files
Henry Reuss Oral History
Arthur M. Schlesinger, Jr. Papers
Theodore C. Sorensen Oral History
Theodore C. Sorensen Papers

Bibliography

whiteouse Central Files
White House Staff Files-Congressional Liaison Office
  Henry Hall Wilson Files
  Mike Manatos Files
  Lawrence F. O'Brien Files
White House Staff Files-Myer Feldman
White House Staff Files-Christian A. Herter
White House Staff Files-Howard C. Petersen

Lyndon B. Johnson Library, Austin, Texas

Administrative History of the Department of Agriculture
Administrative History of the Department of Commerce
Administrative History of the Council of Economic Advisers
Administrative History of the Department of State Administrative History of the
  Special Representative for Trade Negotiations
Aides Files-George Christian
Aides Files-James Gaither
Aides Files-E. Ernest Goldstein
Aides Files-Bill Moyers
Aides Files-DeVier Pierson
Aides Files-Henry Wilson
Confidential Files
Edward R. Fried Oral History
National Security Council History of the Kennedy Round
National Security Council Meetings File
National Security Files
National Security Files Name File—Francis Bator
W. DeVier Pierson Oral History
John Schnittker Oral History
Senate Legislative Files
Senate Subject Files
Statements of Lyndon B. Johnson
Task Force Report on Foreign Economic Policy
Alexander Trowbridge Oral History
White House Central Files

Other Collections

Dean Acheson Papers, Manuscripts and Archives, Sterling Memorial Library, Yale
  University, New Haven, Connecticut.
AFL-CIO Department of Legislation Papers, George Meany Memorial Archives,
  Silver Spring, Maryland.
AFL-CIO Office of the President Papers, George Meany Memorial Archives, Silver
  Spring, Maryland.
Carl Albert Papers, Carl Albert Congressional Research and Studies Center
  Congressional Archives, University of Oklahoma, Norman, Oklahoma.

Page Belcher Papers, Carl Albert Congressional Research and Studies Center Congressional Archives, University of Oklahoma, Norman, Oklahoma.

Prescott S. Bush Papers, Connecticut State Historical Library, Hartford, Connecticut.

Carpet and Rug Institute Documents, Carpet and Rug Institute, Dalton, Georgia.

John H. Dent Collection, Westmoreland County Community College, Youngwood, Pennsylvania.

Paul H. Douglas Papers, Chicago Historical Society, Chicago, Illinois.

Vada Horsch Papers, National Association of Manufacturers Records, Hagley Museum and Library, Wilmington, Delaware.

Robert S. Kerr Papers, Carl Albert Congressional Research and Studies Center Congressional Archives, University of Oklahoma, Norman, Oklahoma.

Wayne B. Morse Papers, University of Oregon, Eugene, Oregon.

National Association of Cotton Manufacturers and the Northern Textile Association Papers, Museum of American Textile History, North Andover, Massachusetts.

National Association of Manufacturers, Series I Government-Legislation, National Association of Manufacturers Records, Hagley Museum and Library, Wilmington, Delaware.

National Association of Manufacturers Series IV and V, Committee Minutes, National Association of Manufacturers Records, Hagley Museum and Library, Wilmington, Delaware.

National Cotton Council of America Records, Memphis, Tennessee.

National Farmers Union Papers, Western Historical Archives, University of Colorado, Boulder, Colorado.

John O. Pastore Papers, Phillips Memorial Library Archives, Providence College, Providence, Rhode Island.

Howard C. Petersen Papers, personal possession, Radnor, Pennsylvania.

Tom Steed Papers, Carl Albert Congressional Research and Studies Center Congressional Archives, University of Oklahoma, Norman, Oklahoma.

Stewart L. Udall Papers, Special Collections, University of Arizona, Tucson, Arizona.

United States-European Economic Community Files, ER: Pt. 1, Delegation of the Commission of the European Community, Washington, D.C.

United States Senate, Committee on Finance Records, HR 11970, Record Group 46, National Archives, Washington, D.C.

Interviews

George W. Ball, Princeton, New Jersey, March 21, 1986.
Howard C. Petersen, Radnor, Pennsylvania, June 20, 1986.

Correspondence

Jack N. Behrman to author, March 20, 1986.
Myer Feldman to author, October 4, 1988.

Orville Freeman to author, September 20, 1988.
Paul Luyten to author, August 10, 1989.
Lawrence O'Brien to author, January 10, 1986.
Dean Rusk to author, January 13, 1986.

Government Documents, Reports, and Statements

Bulletins of the European Economic Community (1962–1967).
Department of State *Bulletin*, vols. 43–59 (1960–1968).
European Economic Community Commission. *General Reports on the Activities of the Community.* Brussels: EEC, 1962–1969.
Foreign Relations of the United States, 1955–57, vol. IV. Washington, D.C.: U.S. Government Printing Office, 1986.
General Agreement on Tariffs and Trade. *Basic Instruments and Selected Documents*, 11th–16th supps. Geneva: GATT, March 1963–April 1969.
Public Papers of the Presidents of the United States: John F. Kennedy, 1961–1963. Washington, D.C.: U.S. Government Printing Office, 1962–1964.
Public Papers of the Presidents of the United States: Lyndon B. Johnson, 1963–1968. Washington, D.C.: U.S. Government Printing Office, 1965–1970.
United Nations. *Proceedings of the United Nations Committee on Trade and Development, March 23–June 16, 1964*, vols. I–VIII. New York: United Nations, 1964.
Vital Speeches of the Day. New York: The City News Publishing Co., 1945.

Congressional Hearings, Reports, and Publications

Congressional Quarterly-Weekly Report, vols. 19–20 (1961–1962).
Congressional Quarterly-Almanac, vols. 5–26 (1949–1970).
Congressional Record, vols. 99–114 (1953–1968).
U.S. Congress. House Committee on Ways and Means. *Foreign Trade and Tariff Proposals*, 90th Cong., 2d sess., 1968.
U.S. Congress. House Committee on Ways and Means. *Trade Expansion Act of 1962*, 87th Cong., 2d sess., 1962.
U.S. Congress. House General Subcommittee on Labor of the Committee on Education and Labor. *Impact of Imports on American Industry and Employment*, 90th Cong., 1st sess., 1967.
U.S. Congress. House Subcommittee on Foreign Economic Policy of the Committee on Foreign Affairs. *The Foreign Policy Aspects of the Kennedy Round.* 89th Cong., 2d sess., 1966.
U.S. Congress. House Subcommittee on Forests of the Committee on Agriculture. *Serial X: Export of Logs to Japan*, 87th Cong., 1st sess., 1961.
U.S. Congress. House Subcommittee on the Impact of Imports and Exports on American Employment of the Committee on Education and Labor. *Pt. 1– Impact of Imports and Exports on Employment: Coal and Residual Fuel*, 87th Cong., 1st sess., 1961.
U.S. Congress. House Subcommittee on the Impact of Imports and Exports on

American Employment of the Committee on Education and Labor. *Pt. 3– Impact of Imports and Exports on Employment: Glass, Pottery, Toys,* 87th Cong., 1st sess., 1961.

U.S. Congress. House Subcommittee on the Impact of Imports and Exports on American Employment of the Committee on Education and Labor. *Pt. 4– Impact of Imports and Exports on Employment: Textiles,* 87th Cong., 1st sess., 1961.

U.S. Congress. House Subcommittee on the Impact of Imports and Exports on American Employment of the Committee on Education and Labor. *Pt. 8– Impact of Imports and Exports on Employment: Agricultural Products, Chemical, Oil, Machinery, Motion Pictures, Transportation, and Other Industries,* 87th Cong., 1st sess., 1961.

U.S. Congress. House Subcommittee No. 4 of the Select Committee on Small Business. *Small Business Problems Created by Petroleum Imports,* 87th Cong., 1st sess., 1961.

U.S. Congress. House Subcommittee on Poultry of the Committee on Agriculture. *Poultry Exports,* 88th Cong., 1st sess., 1963.

U.S. Congress. Joint Economic Committee. Subcommittee on Foreign Economic Policy. *Foreign Economic Policy,* 87th Cong., 1st sess., 1961.

U.S. Congress. Joint Economic Committee. Subcommittee on Foreign Economic Policy. *Foreign Economic Policy,* 87th Cong., 1st sess., November 1, 1961. Christian A. Herter and William L. Clayton, "A New Look at Foreign Economic Policy in Light of the Cold War and the Extension of the Common Market in Europe."

U.S. Congress. Joint Economic Committee. Subcommittee on Foreign Economic Policy. *A Foreign Economic Policy for the 1970s,* 91st Cong., 1st sess., 1969.

U.S. Congress. Joint Economic Committee. Subcommittee on Foreign Economic Policy. *The Future of U.S. Foreign Trade Policy,* 90th Cong., 1st sess., 1967.

U.S. Congress. Senate Committee on Commerce. *Impact of Lumber Imports on the United States Softwood Lumber Industry, Pts. I and II,* 87th Cong., 2d sess., 1962.

U.S. Congress. Senate Committee on Finance. *Import Quotas Legislation,* 90th Cong., 1st sess., 1967.

U.S. Congress. Senate Committee on Finance. *Meat Imports,* 88th Cong., 2d sess., 1964.

U.S. Congress. Senate Committee on Finance. *Trade Expansion Act of 1962,* 87th Cong., 2d sess., 1962.

U.S. Congress. Senate Committee on Finance. *The Trade Reform Act of 1973,* 93d Cong., 2d sess., 1974.

U.S. Congress. Senate Committee on Foreign Relations. *Organization for Economic Cooperation and Development,* 87th Cong., 1st sess., 1961.

U.S. Congress. Senate Committee on Interstate and Foreign Commerce. *Foreign Commerce Study: U.S. Trade and the Common Market,* 86th Cong., 2d sess., 1960.

U.S. Congress. Senate Committee on Interstate and Foreign Commerce. *Problems of the Domestic Textile Industry, First Supplementary Report,* 87th Cong., 1st sess., 1961.

U.S. Congress. Senate Freedom of Communications Subcommittee of Committee on Interstate and Foreign Commerce. *Part I: The Speeches, Remarks, Press Conferences, and Statements of Senator John F. Kennedy, August 1, through November 7, 1960,* 87th Cong., 1st sess., 1961.

U.S. Congress. Senate Freedom of Communications Subcommittee of Committee on Interstate and Foreign Commerce. *Part II: The Speeches, Remarks, Press Conferences, and Statements of Vice-President Richard M. Nixon, August 1, through November 7, 1960,* 87th Cong., 1st sess., 1961.

U.S. Congress. Senate Freedom of Communications Subcommittee of Committee on Interstate and Foreign Commerce. *Part III: The Joint Appearances of Senator John F. Kennedy and Vice-President Richard M. Nixon and Other 1960 Campaign Presentations,* 87th Cong., 1st sess., 1961.

U.S. Congress. Senate Subcommittee of the Committee on Interstate and Foreign Commerce. *Problems of the Domestic Textile Industry,* 87th Cong., 1st sess., 1961.

U.S. Congress. Senate Subcommittee of the Committee on Interstate and Foreign Commerce. *Study of the Domestic Textile Industry,* 87th Cong., 2d sess., 1962.

U.S. Library of Congress, Legislative Reference Service. Senate Document 79. *John F. Kennedy: A Compilation of Statements and Speeches Made During His Service in the United States Senate and House of Representatives.* 88th Cong., 2d sess. Washington, D.C., 1964.

Statistics

American Carpet Institute. *Basic Facts about the Carpet and Rug Industry.* New York: American Carpet Institute, 1960–1968.

Commodity Research Bureau. *Commodity Yearbook, 1963, 1972.* New York: Commodity Research Bureau, 1963, 1972.

Council on International Economic Policy. *Annual Report and International Economic Report to the President.* Washington, D.C.: CIEP, 1973.

General Agreement on Tariffs and Trade. *International Trade, 1961–1981.* Geneva: GATT, 1962–1981.

Mitchell, B. R. *European Historical Statistics, 1750–1970.* New York: Columbia University Press, 1978.

Organization for Economic Cooperation and Development. *Historical Statistics of Foreign Trade, 1965–1980.* Paris: OECD, 1982.

UN Economic Commission for the Far East and Asia. *Economic Bulletin for Asia and the Far East, 1958.* Bangkok: United Nations, 1958.

UN Economic Commission for Europe. *Economic Survey of Europe,1962, pt. 1: The European Economy in 1962.* Geneva: United Nations, 1964.

UN Economic Commission for Europe. *Economic Survey of Europe in 1971, pt. 1: The European Economy from the 1950s to the 1970s.* Geneva: United Nations, 1972.

UN Department of Economic and Social Affairs. *World Economic Survey, 1962–*

I: The Developing Countries in World Trade. New York: United Nations, 1963.

UN Department of Economic and Social Affairs. *World Economic Survey, 1963– I: Trade and Development—Trends, Needs, and Policies.* New York: United Nations, 1964.

UN Department of Economic and Social Affairs. *World Economic Survey, 1969– 1970: The Developing Countries in the 1960s—The Problem of Appraising Progress.* New York: United Nations, 1963.

UN Department of Economic and Social Affairs. *Yearbook of International Trade Statistics, 1960, 1966, 1970–1971.* New York: United Nations, 1962, 1968, 1973.

UN Food and Agricultural Organization. *Yearbook of Forest Products Statistics, 1962, 1963.* Rome: United Nations, 1962, 1963.

U.S. Congress. Senate Committee on Finance. *Executive Branch Study No. 4. Effects of Regional Trade Groups on U.S. Foreign Trade: The EC and EFTA Experiences,* 93d Cong., 1st sess., 1973.

U.S. Department of Agriculture. *U.S. Agriculture and the Balance-of-Payments.* Washington, D.C.: U.S. Government Printing Office, 1968.

U.S. Department of Commerce. *Historical Statistics of the United States: Colonial Times to 1970.* Washington, D.C.: U.S. Government Printing Office, 1975.

U.S. Department of Commerce. *International Economic Indicators, 2d pilot issue and vol. 10.* Washington, D.C.: U.S. Government Printing Office, November 1974 and December 1984.

U.S. Department of Commerce. *Statistical Abstract of the United States, 1976, 1978, 1979, 1982–1983, 1987, 1988.* Washington, D.C.: U.S. Government Printing Office, 1976–1988.

U.S. Senate. Committee on Finance. *Staff Data and Materials on U.S. Trade Data and the Balance of Payments,* 93d Cong., 2d sess., 1974.

Newspapers and Periodicals

AFL-CIO Press Releases
Agence Internationale D'Information Pour La Presse (European Community)
American Farm Bureau Newsletter
British Columbia Lumberman
Business Week Challenge
Chemical and Engineering News
Chemical Week
Commentary
Commercial and Financial Chronicle
Crow's Lumber Digest
Dun's Review and Modern Industry
The Economist
Foreign Commerce Weekly
Forest Industries

Fortune
Glass Industry
Harper's
International Commerce
Iron Age
Life
Monthly Labor Review
The Nation
National Petroleum News
New Statesman
Newsweek
New York Times
Oil and Gas Journal
Oil, Paint, and Drug Reporter
Petroleum Management
Petroleum Week
Saturday Evening Post
Steel
Textile World
Timberman
Time
U.S. News and World Report
Wall Street Journal
What's Happening in Forestry
World Oil

Secondary Sources

Articles

Becker, William H. "American Manufacturers and Foreign Markets, 1870–1900: Business Historians and the 'New Economic Determinists.' " *Business History Review* 47 (Fall 1973):466–481.

Costigliola, Frank. "The Failed Design: Kennedy, De Gaulle, and the Struggle for Europe." *Diplomatic History* 8 (Summer 1984):227–251.

Etzioni, Amitai. "U.S. and Europe, Limited." *Columbia University Forum* 6 (Winter 1963):4–9.

Fisher, M. H. "What Chance of Lower Tariffs?" *World Today* 19 (May 1963):208–212.

Gaddis, John L. "The Emerging Post-Revisionist Synthesis on the Origins of the Cold War." *Diplomatic History* 7 (Summer 1983):171–190.

Galambos, Louis. "Technology, Political Economy, and Professionalization: Central Themes of the Organizational Synthesis." *Business History Review* 57 (Winter 1983):471–493.

Goldstein, Judith L. "Ideas, Institutions, and American Trade Policy." *International Organization* 42 (Winter 1988):179–217.

Goldstein, Judith L. "The Political Economy of Trade: Institutions of Protection." *American Political Science Review* 80 (March 1986):161–184.

Green, Reginald H. "UNCTAD and After: Anatomy of a Failure." *Journal of Modern African Studies* 5 (September 1967):243–267.

Hedges, Irwin R. "Kennedy Round Agricultural Negotiations and the World Grains Agreement." *Journal of Farm Economics* 49 (December 1967):1332–1344.

Hoffmann, Stanley. "De Gaulle, Europe, and the Atlantic Alliance." *International Organization* 18 (Winter 1964):1–28.

Hogan, Michael J. "Corporatism: A Positive Appraisal." *Diplomatic History* 10 (Fall 1986):363–372.

Holsti, Kal J. "Politics in Command: Foreign Trade as National Security Policy." *International Organization* 40 (Summer 1986):643–671.

Johnson, Harry G. "Mercantilism: Past, Present, and Future." *Journal of World Trade Law* 8 (January-February 1974):1–16.

Katzenstein, Peter J. "International Relations and Domestic Structures: Foreign Economic Policies of Advanced Industrial States." *International Organization* 30 (Winter 1976):1–40.

Kilpatrick, Carroll. "The Kennedy Style and Congress." *Virginia Quarterly Review* 39 (Winter 1963):1–11.

Krasner, Stephen D. "The Tokyo Round: Particularistic Interests and Prospects for Stability in the Global Trading System." *International Studies Quarterly* 23 (December 1979):491–531.

Lindeen, James W. "Interest Group Attitudes Toward Reciprocal Trade Legislation." *Public Opinion Quarterly* 34 (Spring 1970):108–112.

Lowi, Theodore J. "American Business and Public Policy: Case Studies and Political Theory." *World Politics* 16 (July 1964):677–693.

Lowi, Theodore J. "The Public Philosophy: Interest-Group Liberalism." *American Political Science Review* 61 (March 1967):5–25.

McCalla, Alex F. "Protectionism in International Agricultural Trade, 1850–1968." *Agricultural History* 43 (July 1969):329–343.

McCormick, Thomas J. "Drift or Mastery? A Corporatist Synthesis for American Diplomatic History." *Reviews in American History* 10 (December 1982):318–330.

McCormick, Thomas. "World Systems." *Journal of American History* 77 (June 1990):125–132.

Meltzer, Ronald I. "The Politics of Policy Reversal: The U.S. Response to Granting Trade Preferences to Developing Countries and Linkages Between International Organizations and National Policy Making." *International Organization* 30 (Autumn 1976):649–668.

Ninkovich, Frank. "Ideology, the Open Door, and Foreign Policy." *Diplomatic History* 6 (Spring 1982):185–208.

Pelz, Stephen E. "A Taxonomy for American Diplomatic History." *Journal of Interdisciplinary History* 19 (Autumn 1988):259–276.

Reich, Robert B. "Beyond Free Trade." *Foreign Affairs* 61 (Spring 1983):773–804.

Spaak, Paul-Henri. "Hold Fast." *Foreign Affairs* 41 (July 1963):611–620.

Stein, Arthur A. "The Hegemon's Dilemma: Great Britain, the United States, and the International Order." *International Organization* 38 (Spring 1984):355–386.

Stewart, Gordon T. " 'A Special Contiguous Country Economic Regime': An Overview of America's Canadian Policy." *Diplomatic History* 6 (Fall 1982):339–357.

Strange, Susan. "The Persistent Myth of Lost Hegemony." *International Organization* 41 (Autumn 1987):551–574.

Strange, Susan. "Protectionism and World Politics." *International Organization* 39 (Spring 1985):233–259.

Viner, Jacob. "Economic Foreign Policy on the New Frontier." *Foreign Affairs* 39 (July 1961):560–577.

Warner, Geoffrey. "The Anglo-American Special Relationship." *Diplomatic History* 13 (Fall 1989):479–499.

Watt, D. C. "The American Impact on Europe." *The Political Quarterly* 34 (October-December 1963):327–338.

Zahniser, Marvin R., and Weiss, W. Michael. "A Diplomatic Pearl Harbor? Richard Nixon's Goodwill Mission to Latin America in 1958." *Diplomatic History* 13 (Spring 1989):163–190.

Zeiler, Thomas W. "Free-Trade Politics and Diplomacy: John F. Kennedy and Textiles." *Diplomatic History* 11 (Spring 1987):127–142.

Zeiler, Thomas W. "Kennedy, Oil Imports, and the Fair Trade Doctrine." *Business History Review* 64 (Summer 1990):286–310.

Zimmerman, William. "Issue Area and Foreign Policy Process: A Research Note in Search of a General Theory." *American Political Science Review* 67 (December 1973):1204–1212.

Books

Adams, Darius, and Richard Haynes. "U.S.-Canadian Lumber Trade: The Effect of Restrictions." In *U.S. International Forest Products Trade,* edited by Roger A. Sedjo. Washington, D.C.: Resources for the Future, 1981.

Aggarwal, Vinod K. *Liberal Protectionism: The International Politics of Organized Textile Trade.* Berkeley: University of California Press, 1985.

Alexander, Robert J. *Romulo Betancourt and the Transformation of Venezuela.* New Brunswick, N.J.: Rutgers University Press, 1982.

Allen, Robert Loring, and Ingo Walter. *The Formation of United States Trade Policy: Retrospect and Prospect.* New York: Bulletin of New York University Graduate School of Business Administration, 1971.

Ambrose, Stephen A. *Rise to Globalism: American Foreign Policy Since 1938.* 5th rev. ed. New York: Penguin, 1988.

Amin, Samir. *Unequal Development: An Essay on the Social Formation of Peripheral Capitalism.* New York: Monthly Review Press, 1976.

Aubrey, Henry G. *Atlantic Economic Cooperation: The Case of the OECD.* New York: Praeger, 1967.

Bailey, Thomas A. *A Diplomatic History of the American People.* 8th ed. New York: Meredith Corporation, 1969.

Baldwin, Robert E. *The Political Economy of U.S. Import Policy.* Cambridge, Mass.: MIT Press, 1985.

Baldwin, Robert E. "Protectionist Pressures in the United States." In *Challenges to a Liberal International Economic Order,* edited by Ryan C. Amacher, Gottfried Haberler, and Thomas D. Willett. Washington, D.C.: American Enterprise Isntitute for Public Policy Research, 1979.

Ball, George W. *The Discipline of Power: Essentials of a Modern World Structure.* Boston: Little, Brown, 1968.

Ball, George W. *The Past Has Another Pattern: Memoirs.* New York: W. W. Norton, 1982.

Barnet, Richard J. *The Roots of War: The Men and Institutions Behind U.S. Foreign Policy.* New York: Atheneum, 1972.

Bauer, Raymond A., Ithiel de Sola Pool, and Anthony L. Dexter. *American Business and Public Policy: The Politics of Foreign Trade.* New York: Aldine, 1972.

Becker, William H. *The Dynamics of Business-Government Relations: Industry and Exports, 1893–1921.* Chicago: University of Chicago Press, 1982.

Becker, William H., and Samuel F. Wells, Jr. *Economics and World Power: An Assessment of American Diplomacy Since 1789.* New York: Columbia University Press, 1984.

Belassa, Bela. "Competitiveness of American Manufacturing in World Markets." In Bela Belassa, *Problems in the Modern Economy: Changing Patterns in Foreign Trade and Payments.* New York: W. W. Norton, 1964.

Belassa, Bela. *The Newly Industrializing Countries in the World Economy.* New York: Pergamon Press, 1981.

Beloff, Max. *The United States and the Unity of Europe.* Washington, D.C.: Brookings Institution, 1963.

Beloff, Nora. *The General Says No: Britain's Exclusion from Europe.* Harmondsworth, Great Britain: Penguin, 1963.

Benoit, Emile. *Europe at Sixes and Sevens: The Common Market, the Free Trade Association, and the United States.* New York: Columbia University Press, 1961.

Berensen, Conrad. *The Chemical Industry: Viewpoints and Perspectives.* New York: John Wiley and Sons, 1963.

Berg, Sherwood O. "How Farm Programs Affect Trade." In *Farm Prosperity— Imports and Exports,* edited by the National Farm Institute. Ames: Iowa State University Press, 1965.

Betancourt, Romulo. *Venezuela: Oil and Politics.* Boston: Houghton Mifflin, 1979.

Beugel, Ernst van der. *From Marshall Aid to Atlantic Partnership: European Integration as a Concerns of American Foreign Policy.* Amsterdam, Holland: Elsevier, 1966.

Blake, David H., and Robert S. Walters. *The Politics of Global Economic Relations.* Englewood Cliffs, N.J.: Prentice-Hall, 1976.

Block, Fred L. *The Origins of International Economic Disorder: A Study of United States International Monetary Policy from World War II to the Present.* Berkeley: University of California Press, 1977.

Bohi, Douglas R., and Milton Russell. *Limiting Oil Imports: An Economic History and Analysis.* Baltimore: Johns Hopkins University Press, 1978.

Bolling, Richard, and John Bowles. *America's Competitive Edge: How to Get Our Country Moving Again.* New York: McGraw-Hill, 1982.

Borden, William S. "Defending Hegemony: American Foreign Economic Policy." In *Kennedy's Quest for Victory: American Foreign Policy, 1961–1963*, edited by Thomas G. Paterson. New York: Oxford University Press, 1989.

Borden, William S. *The Pacific Alliance: United States Foreign Economic Policy and Japanese Trade Recovery, 1947–1955.* Madison: University of Wisconsin Press, 1984.

Boyd, J. Barron, Jr. "France and the Third World: The African Connection." In *Third World Policies of Industrialized Nations*, edited by Phillip Taylor and Gregory A. Raymond. Westport, Conn.: Greenwood Press, 1982.

Bradley, Gene E. *Building the American-European Market: Planning for the 1970s.* Homewood, Ill.: Dow Jones-Irwin, 1967.

Brandis, R. Buford. *The Making of Textile Trade Policy, 1935–1981.* Washington, D.C.: AMerican Textile Manufacturers Institute, 1982.

Bromberger, Merry, and Serge Bromberger. *Jean Monnet and the United States of Europe.* New York: Coward-McCann, 1969.

Brown, J. A. C. "A Brief Survey of Prospects for African Exports of Agricultural Products." In *African Primary Products and International Trade*, edited by I. G. Stewart and H. W. Ord. Edinburgh: University of Edinburgh Press, 1965.

Brown, William A., Jr. *The United States and the Restoration of World Trade.* Washington, D.C.: Brookings Institution, 1950.

Burns, James MacGregor. *John Kennedy: A Political Profile.* New York: Harcourt, Brace, 1960.

Burns, Richard Dean, "Overviews: Diplomatic Surveys, Themes, and Theories." In *Guide to American Foreign Relations Since 1700*, edited by Richard Dean Burns. Santa Barbara, Calif.: ABC-Clio, 1983.

Calleo, David P. *The Atlantic Fantasy: The U.S., NATO, and Europe.* Baltimore: Johns Hopkins University Press, 1970.

Calleo, David P. *Beyond American Hegemony.* New York: Twentieth Century Fund, 1987.

Calleo, David P. *The Imperious Economy.* Cambridge, Mass.: Harvard University Press, 1982.

Calleo, David P., and Benjamin M. Rowland. *America and the World Political Economy: Atlantic Dreams and National Realities.* Bloomington: Indiana University Press, 1973.

Camps, Miriam. *Britain and the European Community, 1955–1963.* Princeton: Princeton University Press, 1964.

Canterbury, E. Ray. *Economics on the New Frontier.* Belmont, Calif.: Wadsworth, 1968.

Caro, Robert A. *The Path to Power: The Years of Lyndon Johnson.* New York: Vintage Books, 1983.

Chan, Steve. *International Relations in Perspective: The Pursuit of Security, Welfare, and Justice.* New York: Macmillan, 1984.
Chase-Dunn, Christopher. *Structures of the World-Economy.* Cambridge: Basil Blackwell, 1989.
Chen, K. Y. "The Economic Setting." In *The Business Environment in Hong Kong,* edited by David G. Lethbridge. Hong Kong: Oxford University Press, 1980.
Chester, Edward W. *United States Oil Policy and Diplomacy: A Twentieth Century Overview.* Westport, Conn.: Greenwood Press, 1983.
Cleveland, Harold Van B. *The Atlantic Idea and its European Rivals.* New York: McGraw-Hill, 1966.
Cohen, Benjamin J. "The Industrial World." In *American Foreign Economic Policy: Essays and Comments,* edited by Benjamin J. Cohen. New York: Harper and Row, 1968.
Cohen, Benjamin J. *The Question of Imperialism: The Political Economy of Dominance and Dependence.* New York: Basic Books, 1973.
Cohen, Stephen D. *The Making of United States International Economic Policy: Principles, Problems, and Proposals for Reform.* 2d ed. New York: Praeger, 1981.
Combs, Jerald A. *The History of American Foreign Policy.* New York: Knopf, 1986.
Cooper, Richard N. *The Economics of Interdependence: Economic Policy in the Atlantic Community.* New York: McGraw-Hill, 1968.
Cooper, Richard N. "Trade Policy as Foreign Policy." In *U.S. Trade Policies in a Changing World Economy,* edited by Robert M. Stern. Cambridge, Mass.: MIT Press, 1987.
Coppock, John O. *Atlantic Agricultural Unity: Is It Possible?* New York: McGraw-Hill, 1966.
Corbet, Hugh, ed. *Trade Strategy and the Asian-Pacific Region.* Toronto: University of Toronto Press, 1970.
Costigliola, Frank. "The Pursuit of Atlantic Community: Nuclear Arms, Dollars, and Berlin." In *Kennedy's Quest for Victory: American Foreign Policy, 1961–1963,* edited by Thomas G. Paterson. New York: Oxford University Press, 1989.
Coughlin, Cletus C., K. Alec Chrystal, and Geoffrey E. Wood. "Protectionist Trade Policies: A Survey of Theory, Evidence, and Rationale." In *International Political Economy: Perspectives on Global Power and Wealth,* 2d ed., edited by Jeffry A. Frieden and David A. Lake. New York: St. Martin's Press, 1991.
Cromwell, William C. "The United States." In *Political Problems of Atlantic Partnership: National Perspectives,* edited by William C. Cromwell. Bruges, Belgium: College of Europe, 1968.
Cumings, Bruce. *The Origins of the Korean War, Vol. II: The Roaring of the Cataract, 1947–1950.* Princeton: Princeton University Press, 1990.
Curtis, Thomas B., and John R. Vastine, Jr. *The Kennedy Round and the Future of American Trade.* New York: Praeger, 1971.
Curzon, Gerard. *Multilateral Commercial Diplomacy: The General Agreement on*

Tariffs and Trade and Its Impact on National Commercial Policies and Techniques. New York: Praeger, 1965.

Curzon, Gerard, and Victoria Curzon. "The Management of Trade Relations in the GATT." In *International Economic Relations of the Western World, 1959–1971, Vol. 1: Politics of Trade,* edited by Andrew Shonfield. London: Oxford University Press, 1976.

Dahl, Robert A. *Pluralist Democracy in the United States: Conflict and Consent.* Chicago: Rand McNally, 1967.

Dallek, Robert. *Franklin D. Roosevelt and American Foreign Policy, 1932–1945.* New York: Oxford University Press, 1981.

Dam, Kenneth W. *The GATT: Law and International Economic Organization.* Chicago: University of Chicago Press, 1970.

Darby, Phillip. *Three Faces of Imperialism: British and American Approaches to Asia and Africa, 1870–1970.* New Haven: Yale University Press, 1987.

De Gaulle, Charles. *Lettres, Notes, and Carnet, 1961–1963.* Paris: Librairie Plon, 1986.

De Gaulle, Charles. *Memoirs of Hope: Renewal and Endeavor.* New York: Simon and Schuster, 1971.

De Menil, Lois Pattison. *Who Speaks for Europe? The Vision of Charles de Gaulle.* London: Weidenfeld and Nicolson, 1977.

DePorte, A. W. *Europe Between the Superpowers: The Enduring Balance.* New Haven: Yale University Press, 1979.

De Sola Pool, Ithiel, Robert P. Abelson, and Samuel L. Popkin. *Candidates, Issues, Strategies: A Computer Simulation of the 1960 Presidential Election.* Cambridge, Mass.: MIT Press, 1964.

Destler, I. M. *American Trade Politics: System Under Stress.* New York: Twentieth Century Fund, 1986.

Diebold, William, Jr. "The Process of European Integration." In *The Common Market: Progress and Controversy,* edited by Lawrence B. Krause. Englewood Cliffs, N.J.: Prentice-Hall, 1964.

Diebold, William, Jr. *The United States and the Industrial World: American Foreign Economic Policy in the 1970s.* New York: Praeger, 1972.

DiLeo, David L. *George Ball, Vietnam, and the Rethinking of Containment.* Chapel Hill: University of North Carolina Press, 1991.

Domhoff, G. William. "'Who Made American Foreign Policy?'" In *Corporations and the Cold War,* edited by David Horowitz. New York: Monthly Review Press, 1969.

Dougherty, James E., and Robert L. Pfaltzgraff, Jr. *Contending Theories of International Relations: A Comprehensive Survey.* 2d ed. New York: Harper and Row, 1981.

Douglas, Paul H. *In the Fullness of Time: The Memoirs of Paul H. Douglas.* New York: Harcourt, Brace, Jovanovich, 1972.

Eckes, Alfred E., Jr. *The Search for Solvency: Bretton Woods and the International Monetary System, 1941–1971.* Austin: University of Texas Press, 1975.

Emmanuel, Arghiri. *Unequal Exchange: A Study of the Imperialism of Trade.* New York: Montly Review Press, 1972.

Erhard, Ludwig. *The Economics of Success.* London: Thames and Hudson, 1963.

Evans, Douglas. *The Politics of Trade: The Evolution of a Superbloc.* New York: John Wiley and Sons, 1974.

Evans, John W. *The Kennedy Round in American Trade Policy: The Twilight of the GATT?* Cambridge, Mass.: Harvard University Press, 1971.

Feld, Werner J. *The European Community in World Affairs: Economic Power and Political Influence.* New York: Alfred, 1976.

Finlayson, Jock A., and Mark W. Zacher. "The GATT and the Regulation of Trade Barriers: Regime Dynamics and Functions." In *International Regimes,* edited by Stephen D. Krasner. Ithaca, N.Y.: Cornell University Press, 1983.

Forbes, D. K. *The Geography of Underdevelopment: A Critical Survey.* Baltimore: Johns Hopkins University Press, 1984.

Forrestal, Dan J. *The Story of Monsanto: Faith, Hope and $5000: The Trials and Triumphs of the First 75 Years.* New York: Simon and Schuster, 1977.

Frank, Charles, Jr. *Foreign Trade and Domestic Aid.* Washington, D.C.: Brookings Institution, 1977.

Frank, Isaiah. "The Economic Constraints." In *America and the World: From the Truman Doctrine to Vietnam,* edited by Robert E. Osgood et al. Baltimore: Johns Hopkins University Press, 1970.

Frank, Isaiah. *The European Common Market: An Analysis of Commercial Policy.* New York: Praeger, 1961.

Freidberg, A. S. *The United Nations Conference on Trade and Development: The Theory of the Peripheral Economy at the Centre of International Political Discussion.* Rotterdam, Holland: Rotterdam University Press, 1970.

Frieden, Jeffry A., and David A. Lake. "Introduction: International Politics and International Economics." In *International Political Economy: Perspectives on Global Power and Wealth,* 2d ed., edited by Jeffry A. Frieden and David A. Lake. New York: St. Martin's Press, 1991.

Fulbright, J. W. "A Concert of Free Nations." In *The Atlantic Community: Progress and Prospect,* edited by Francis O. Wilcox and H. Field Haviland, Jr. New York: Praeger, 1964.

Funigiello, Philip. *American-Soviet Trade in the Cold War.* Chapel Hill: University of North Carolina Press, 1988.

Gallup, George H. *The Gallup Poll: Public Opinion, 1935–1971.* Vol. 3. New York: Random House, 1972.

Gardner, Lloyd C., Walter LaFeber, and Thomas J. McCormick. *Creation of the American Empire: U.S. Diplomatic History.* Chicago: Rand-McNally, 1973.

Gardner, Richard N. *Sterling-Dollar Diplomacy: The Origins and the Prospects of Our International Economic Order.* 2d ed. New York: McGraw-Hill, 1969.

Giglio, James N. *The Presidency of John F. Kennedy.* Lawrence: University of Kansas Press, 1991.

Gilpin, Robert. *The Political Economy of International Relations.* Princeton: Princeton University Press, 1987.

Ginsburg, Roy H. "The European Community and the United States of America." In *Institutions and Policies of the European Community,* edited by Juliet Lodge. New York: St. Martin's Press, 1983.

Goldstein, Walter. "U.S. Economic Penetration of Western Europe." In *Testing*

Theories of Economic Imperialism, edited by Steven J. Rosen and James R. Kurth. Lexington, Mass.: D. C. Heath, 1974.

Gosovic, Branislav. *UNCTAD: Conflict and Compromise.* Leiden, Holland: A. W. Sijthoff, 1972.

Gowa, Joanne. "Public Goods and Political Institutions: Trade and Monetary Processes in the United States." In *The State and American Foreign Economic Policy,* edited by G. John Ikenberry, David A. Lake, and Michael Mastanduno. Ithaca, N.Y.: Cornell University Press, 1988.

Granatstein, J.L. "When Push Came to Shove: Canada and the United States." In *Kennedy's Quest for Victory: American Foreign Policy, 1961–1963,* edited by Thomas G. Paterson. New York: Oxford University Press, 1989.

Grant, Roderick. "The European Common Market and U.S. Trade." In *Public Policy. Vol. 11: International Economic Problems,* edited by Carl J. Friedrich and Seymour E. Harris. Cambridge, Mass.: Harvard University Graduate School of Public Administration, 1961.

Gray, H. Peter. *International Trade, Investment, and Payments.* Boston: Houghton Mifflin, 1979.

Green, Robert T., and James M. Lutz. *The United States and World Trade: Changing Patterns and Dimensions.* New York: Praeger, 1978.

Grosser, Alfred. *The Western Alliance: European-American Relations Since 1945.* New York: Continuum, 1980.

Hagras, Kamal M. *The United Nations Conference on Trade and Development: A Case Study in UN Diplomacy.* New York: Praeger, 1975.

Hallstein, Walter. *Europe in the Making.* New York: W. W. Norton, 1972.

Harris, Seymour E. *Economics of the Kennedy Years and a Look Ahead.* New York: Harper and Row, 1964.

Harris, Seymour E. "Some Material Ideas on the Dollar Problem and the Competitive Position of the United States." In *Public Policy. Vol. 11: International Economic Problems,* edited by Carl J. Friedrich and Seymour E. Harris. Cambridge, Mass.: Harvard University Graduate School of Public Administration, 1961.

Hawkins, Harry C., and Janet L. Norwood. "The Legislative Basis of United States Commercial Policy." In *Studies in United States Commercial Policy,* edited by William B. Kelly, Jr. Chapel Hill: University of North Carolina Press, 1963.

Heath, Jim F. *John F. Kennedy and the Business Community.* Chicago: University of Chicago Press, 1969.

Herter, Christian A. *Toward an Atlantic Community.* New York: Harper and Row, 1963.

Hill, Brian E. *The Common Agricultural Policy: Past, Present, and Future.* London: Methuen, 1984.

Hinshaw, Randall. *The European Economic Community and American Trade: A Study in Atlantic Economics and Policy.* New York: Praeger, 1964.

Ho, Alfred K. *Japan's Trade Liberalization in the 1960s.* White Plains, N.Y.: International Arts and Sciences Press, 1973.

Hoffmann, Stanley. "Discord in Community: The North Atlantic Area as a Partial

International System." In *The Atlantic Community: Progress and Prospect,* edited by Francis O. Wilcox and H. Field Haviland, Jr. New York: Praeger, 1964.

Hoffmann, Stanley. *Gulliver's Troubles, or the Setting of American Foreign Policy.* New York: McGraw-Hill, 1968.

Hogan, Michael J. *The Marshall Plan: American, Britain, and the Reconstruction of Western Europe, 1947–1952.* Cambridge: Cambridge University Press, 1987.

Horne, Alistair. *Harold Macmillan: Volume II, 1957–1986.* New York: Penguin, 1989.

Horowitz, David, ed. *Corporations and the Cold War.* New York: Monthly Review Press, 1969.

Hrebner, Ronald J., and Ruth K. Scott. *Interest Group Politics in America.* Englewood Cliffs, N.J.: Prentice-Hall, 1982.

Humphrey, Don D. *The United States and the Common Market: A Background Study.* New York: Praeger, 1964.

Hunsberger, Warren S. *Japan and the United States in World Trade.* New York: Harper and Row, 1964.

Ikenberry, G. John, David A. Lake, and Michael Mastanduno. "Introduction: Approaches to Explaining Foreign Economic Policy." In *The State and American Foreign Economic Policy,* edited by G. John Ikenberry, David A. Lake, and Michael Mastanduno. Ithaca, N.Y.: Cornell University Press, 1988.

Ioanes, Raymond A. "Trends and Structure of U.S. Agricultural Trade." In *U.S. Trade Policy and Agricultural Exports,* edited by Iowa State University Center for Agricultural and Rural Development. Ames: Iowa State University Press, 1973.

Johnson, Harry G. *Canada in a Changing World Economy.* Toronto: University of Toronto Press, 1962.

Johnson, Harry G. *Economic Policies Toward Less-Developed Countries.* Washington, D.C.: Brookings Institution, 1967.

Johnson, Harry G. "U.S. Trade Policies Toward Less-Developed Countries." In *American Foreign Economic Policy: Essays and Comments,* edited by Benjamin J. Cohen. New York: Harper and Row, 1968.

Johnson, Lyndon B. *The Vantage Point: Perspectives of the Presidency, 1963– 1969.* New York: Holt, Rinehart, and Winston, 1971.

Jones, Kent. *Politics vs Economics in World Steel Trade.* London: Allen and Unwin, 1986.

Katzenstein, Peter J. "Introduction: Domestic and International Forces and Strategies of Foreign Economic Policy." In *Between Power and Plenty: Foreign Economic Policies of Advanced Industrial States.* Madison: University of Wisconsin Press, 1978.

Kaufman, Burton I. "Foreign Aid and the Balance of Payments Problem: Vietnam and Johnson's Foreign Economic Policy." In *The Johnson Years—Vol. Two: Vietnam, The Environment, and Science,* edited by Robert A. Divine. Lawrence: University of Kansas Press, 1987.

Kaufman, Burton I. *Trade and Aid: Eisenhower's Foreign Economic Policy, 1953–1961.* Baltimore: Johns Hopkins University Press, 1982.

Kegley, Charles W., and Eugene R. Wittkopf, Jr. *World Politics: Trends and Transformation.* New York: St. Martin's Press, 1981.

Kennedy, John F. *The Strategy of Peace,* edited by Allan Nevins. New York: Popular Library, 1961.

Kennedy, Paul. *The Rise and Fall of the Great Powers: Economic Change and Military Conflict from 1500 to 2000.* New York: Random House, 1987.

Keohane, Robert O. *After Hegemony: Cooperation and Discord in the World Political Economy.* Princeton: Princeton University Press, 1984.

Kitzinger, Uwe. *The Challenge of the Common Market.* 4th ed. Oxford: Oxford University Press, 1962.

Kleiman, Robert. *Atlantic Crisis: American Confronts a Resurgent Europe.* New York: W. W. Norton, 1964.

Knoke, David. "Power Structures." In *The Handbook of Political Behavior,* vol. 3, edited by Samuel L. Long. New York: Plenum Press, 1981.

Kock, Karin. *International Trade Policy and the GATT, 1947–1967.* Stockholm: Almquist and Widsell, 1969.

Koenig, Louis W. *The Chief Executive.* New York: Harcourt, Brace, and World, 1968.

Koh, Sung Jae. *Stages of Industrial Development in Asia: A Comparative History of the Cotton Industry in Japan, India, China, and Korea.* Philadelphia: University of Pennsylvania Press, 1966.

Kolko, Gabriel. *The Roots of American Foreign Policy: An Analysis of Power and Purpose.* Boston: Beacon Press, 1969.

Koskoff, David E. *Joseph P. Kennedy: A Life and Times.* Englewood Cliffs, N.J.: Prentice-Hall, 1974.

Kraft, Joseph. *The Grand Design: From Common Market to Atlantic Partnership.* New York: Harper and Brothers, 1962.

Krasner, Stephen D., ed. *International Regimes.* Ithaca, N.Y.: Cornell University Press, 1983.

Krasner, Stephen D. "State Power and the Structure of International Trade." In *International Political Economy: Perspectives on Global Power and Wealth,* 2d ed., edited by Jeffry A. Frieden and David A. Lake. New York: St. Martin's Press, 1991.

Krasner, Stephen D. "U.S. Commercial and Monetary Policy: Unraveling the Paradox of External Strength and Internal Weakness." In *Between Power and Plenty: Foreign Economic Policies of Advanced Industrial States,* edited by Peter J. Katzenstein. Madison: University of Wisconsin Press, 1978.

Krause, Lawrence B. *European Economic Integration and the United States.* Washington, D.C.: Brookings Institution, 1968.

Kravis, Irving B. "The U.S. Trade Position and the Common Market." In *Problems in the Modern Economy: Changing Patterns in Foreign Trade and Payments.* New York: W. W. Norton, 1964.

LaFeber, Walter. *America, Russia, and the Cold War: 1945–1980.* 5th ed. New York: John Wiley and Sons, 1985.

LaFeber, Walter. *Inevitable Revolutions: The United States in Central America.* New York: W. W. Norton, 1983.

Lake, David A. *Power, Protection, and Free Trade: International Sources of U.S. Commercial Strategy, 1887–1939.* Ithaca, N.Y.: Cornell University Press, 1988.

Langhammer, Rolf J., and Andre Sapir. *Economic Impact of Generalized Tariff Preferences.* London: Gower, 1987.

Lary, Hal B. *Imports of Manufactures from Less Developed Countries.* New York: National Bureau of Economic Research, 1968.

Layton, Christopher. *Trans-Atlantic Investments.* Boulogne-Sur-Seine, France: Atlantic Institute, 1966.

Leddy, John M. "United States Commercial Policy and the Domestic Farm Program." In *Studies in United States Commercial Policy,* edited by William B. Kelly, Jr. Chapel Hill: University of North Carolina Press, 1963.

Leddy, John M., and Janet L. Norwood. "The Escape Clause and Peril Points Under the Trade Agreements Program." In *Studies in United States Commercial Policy,* edited by William B. Kelly, Jr. Chapel Hill: University of North Carolina Press, 1963.

Lenway, Stefanie Ann. *The Politics of U.S. International Trade: Protection, Expansion, and Escape.* Marshfield, Mass.: Pitman, 1985.

Lichtenstein, Nelson, ed. *Political Profiles: The Kennedy Years.* New York: Facts on File, 1976.

Lippmann, Walter. *Western Unity and the Common Market.* Boston: Little, Brown, 1962.

Lipson, Charles. "The Transformation of Trade: The Sources and Effects of Regime Change." In *International Regimes,* edited by Stephen D. Krasner. Ithaca, N.Y.: Cornell University Press, 1983.

Lowi, Theodore J. *The End of Liberalism: Ideology, Policy and the Crisis of Public Authority.* New York: W. W. Norton, 1969.

Lundestad, Geir. *The American "Empire".* Oslo: Norwegian University Press, 1990.

McCormick, Thomas J. *America's Half Century: United States Foreign Policy in the Cold War.* Baltimore: Johns Hopkins University Press, 1989.

McGowan, Pat, and Charles W. Kegley, Jr., eds. *Foreign Policy and the Modern World-System.* Beverly Hills: Sage, 1983.

Mackie, Arthur B. "Patterns of World Agricultural Trade." In *U.S. Trade Policy and Agricultural Exports,* edited by Iowa State University Center for Agricultural and Rural Development. Ames: Iowa State University Press, 1973.

Macmillan, Harold. *Pointing the Way, 1959–1961.* London: Macmillan, 1972.

Magdoff, Harry. *The Age of Imperialism: The Economics of U.S. Foreign Policy.* New York: Modern Reader, 1969.

Magee, Stephen P., and Leslie Young. "Endogenous Protection in the United States, 1900–1984." In *U.S. Trade Policies in a Changing World Economy,* edited by Robert M. Stern. Cambridge, Mass.: MIT Press, 1987.

Maier, Charles. "The Politics of Productivity: Foundations of American International Economic Policy After World War II." In *Between Power and Plenty: Foreign Economic Policies of Advanced Industrial States,* edited by Peter J. Katzenstein. Madison: University of Wisconsin Press, 1978.

Malmgren, Harald. *International Economic Peacekeeping in Phase II.* New York: Atlantic Council of the United States, Quadrangle Books, 1972.

Malmgren, Harald. *Trade Wars or Trade Negotiations: Non-Tariff Barriers and Economic Peacekeeping.* Washington, D.C.: Atlantic Council of the United States, 1970.

Malmgren, Harald B. "The United States." In *Economic Foreign Policies of Industrial States,* edited by Wilfrid Kohl. Lexington, Mass.: D. C. Heath, 1977.

Mandel, Ernest. *Europe Versus America: Contradictions of Imperialism.* New York: New Left Books, 1970.

Manley, John F. *The Politics of Finance: The House Committee on Ways and Means.* Boston: Little, Brown, 1970.

Mansholt, Sicco. "European View." In *Farm Prosperity-Imports and Exports,* edited by National Farm Institute. Ames: Iowa State University Press, 1965.

Martin, Edwin M. "New Trends in United States Economic Foreign Policy." In *Whither American Foreign Policy,* edited by James C. Charlesworth. The Annals of the American Academy of Political and Social Science. Philadelphia: American Academy of Political and Social Science, 1960.

Matusow, Allen J. "Kennedy, the World Economy, and the Decline of America." In *John F. Kennedy: Person, Policy, Presidency,* edited by J. Richard Snyder. Wilmington, Del.: Scholarly Resources, 1988.

Matusow, Allen J. *The Unraveling of America: A History of Liberalism in the 1960s.* New York: Harper and Row, 1984.

Meagher, John, and Malmgren, Harald. "A Historical View of Congress' Impact on Trade Legislation and Negotiation." In *Congress and U.S. Trade Policy,* edited by LTV Corporation. Dallas: LTV, 1983.

Metzger, Stanley D. *Trade Agreements and the Kennedy Round: An Analysis of the Economic, Legal, and Political Aspects of the Trade Expansion Act of 1962 and the Prospects for the Kennedy Round of Tariff Negotiations.* Fairfax, Va.: Coiner, 1964.

Meyer, F. V. *International Trade Policy.* London: Croom Helm, 1978.

Middleton, Drew. *The Supreme Choice: Britain and Europe.* New York: Knopf, 1963.

Mills, C. Wright. *The Power Elite.* New York: Oxford University Press, 1959.

Miroff, Bruce. *Pragmatic Illusions: The Presidential Politics of John F. Kennedy.* New York: David McKay, 1976.

Morawetz, David. *Twenty-Five Years of Economic Development, 1950 to 1975.* Baltimore: Johns Hopkins University Press, 1977.

Morgan, Anne H. *Robert S. Kerr: The Senate Years.* Norman: University of Oklahoma Press, 1977.

Morse, Edward L. *Foreign Policy and Interdependence in Gaullist France.* Princeton: Princeton University Press, 1973.

Mower, A. Glenn, Jr. *The European Community and Latin America: A Case Study in Global Role Expansion.* Westport, Conn.: Greenwood Press, 1982.

Munk, Frank. *Atlantic Dilemma: Partnership or Community.* Dobbs Ferry, N.Y.: Oceana, 1964.

Muth, Hanns Peter. *French Agriculture and the Political Integration of Western Europe.* Leyden, Holland: A. W. Sijthoff, 1970.

Myrdal, Gunnar. *Rich Lands and Poor: The Road to World Prosperity.* New York: Harper and Row, 1957.

Nash, Gerald D. *United States Oil Policy, 1890–1964.* Pittsburgh: University of Pittsburgh Press, 1968.

Newhouse, John. *Collision in Brussels: The Common Market Crisis of 30 June 1965.* London: Faber and Faber, 1967.

Nunnerly, David. *President Kennedy and Britain.* New York: St. Martin's Press, 1972.

Nye, Joseph, Jr. *Bound to Lead: The Changing Nature of American Power.* New York: Basic Books, 1990.

Oberdorfer, Don, and Walter Pincus. "Businessmen in Politics-Luther Hodges and J. Edward Day." In *The Kennedy Circle,* edited by Lester Tanzer. Washington, D.C.: Robert B. Luce, 1961.

O'Brien, Lawrence F. *No Final Victories: A Life in Politics—From John F. Kennedy to Watergate.* Garden City, N.Y.: Doubleday, 1974.

Ogg, Wallace E. "Farm Policy and Trade." In *Farm Prosperity—Imports and Exports,* edited by National Farm Institute. Ames: Iowa State University Press, 1965.

Pachauri, R. K. *The Political Economy of Global Energy.* Baltimore: Johns Hopkins University Press, 1985.

Painter, David S. *Oil and the American Century: The Political Economy of U.S. Foreign Oil Policy, 1941–1954.* Baltimore: Johns Hopkins University Press, 1986.

Paper, John L. *The Promise and the Performance: The Leadership of John F. Kennedy.* New York: Crown, 1975.

Parmet, Herbert S. *JFK: The Presidency of John F. Kennedy.* New York: Dial Press, 1983.

Pastor, Robert A. *Congress and the Politics of U.S. Foreign Economic Policy.* Berkeley: University of California Press, 1980.

Peterson, Trudy Huskamp. *Agricultural Exports, Farm Income, and the Eisenhower Administration.* Lincoln: University of Nebraska Press, 1979.

Pfaltzgraff, Robert L., Jr. *Britain Faces Europe.* Philadelphia: University of Pennsylvania Press, 1969.

Pincus, John. *Trade, Aid, and Development: The Rich and Poor Nations.* New York: McGraw-Hill, 1967.

Pinder, John. *Britain and the Common Market.* London: Cresset Press, 1961.

Pinder, John. *Europe Against De Gaulle.* New York: Praeger, 1963.

Piquet, Howard S. *The U.S. Balance of Payments and International Monetary Reserves.* Washington, D.C.: American Enterprise Institute for Public Policy Research, 1960.

Pollard, Robert A., and Samuel F. Wells, Jr. "1945–1960: The Era of American Hegemony." In *Economics and World Power: An Assessment of American Diplomacy Since 1789*, edited by William H. Becker and Samuel F. Wells, Jr. New York: Columbia University Press, 1984.

Pollard, Robert A. *Economic Security and the Origins of the Cold War, 1945–1950*. New York: Columbia University Press, 1985.

Postan, M. M. *An Economic History of Western Europe, 1945–1964*. London: Methuen, 1967.

Prebisch, Raul. *The Economic Development of Latin America and Its Principal Problems*. New York: United Nations, 1950.

Preeg, Ernest H. *Traders and Diplomats: An Analysis of the Kennedy Round of Negotiations Under the General Agreement on Tariffs and Trade*. Washington, D.C.: Brookings Institution, 1970.

Rabe, Stephen G. *Eisenhower and Latin America: The Foreign Policy of Anticommunism*. Chapel Hill: University of North Carolina Press, 1988.

Rabe, Stephen G. *The Road to OPEC: United States Relations with Venezuela, 1919–1976*. Austin: University of Texas Press, 1982.

Ratner, Sidney. *The Tariff in American History*. New York: D. Van Nostrand, 1972.

Ray, Edward John. "Changing Patterns of Protectionism: The Fall in Tariffs and the Rise in Non-Tariff Barriers." In *International Political Economy: Perspectives on Global Power and Wealth*, 2d ed., edited by Jeffry A. Frieden and David A. Lake. New York: St. Martin's Press, 1991.

Ray, James Lee. "The 'World-System' and the Global Political System: A Crucial Relationship?" In *Foreign Policy and the Modern World-System*, edited by Pat McGowan and Charles W. Kegley, Jr. Beverly Hills: Sage, 1983.

Reuss, Henry. *The Critical Decade: An Economic Policy for America and the Free World*. New York: McGraw-Hill, 1964.

Reynolds, David. *The Creation of the Anglo-American Alliance, 1937–1941: A Study in Competitive Co-Operation*. Chapel Hill: University of North Carolina Press, 1981.

Rogowski, Ronald. *Commerce and Coalitions: How Trade Affects Domestic Political Alignments*. Princeton: Princeton University Press, 1989.

Roosa, Robert V. *The Dollar and World Liquidity*. New York: Random House, 1967.

Rosecrance, Richard. *America's Economic Resurgence: A Bold New Strategy*. New York: Harper and Row, 1990.

Rosecrance, Richard. *The Rise of the Trading State: Commerce and Conquest in the Modern World*. New York: Basic Books, 1986.

Rostow, W. W. *Eisenhower, Kennedy, and Foreign Aid*. Austin: University of Texas Press, 1985.

Ruggie, John G. "International Regimes, Transactions, and Change: Enbedded Liberalism in the Postwar Economic Order." In *International Regimes*, edited by Stephen D. Krasner. Ithaca, N.Y.: Cornell University Press, 1983.

Salisbury, Robert H. "Why No Corporatism in America?" In *Trends Toward Corporatist Intermediation*, edited by Philippe C. Schmitter and Gerhard Lehmbruch. London: Sage, 1979.

Schattsschneider, E. E. *Politics, Pressures, and the Tariff: A Study of Free Enterprise in Pressure Politics, as Shown in the 1929–1930 Revision of the Tariff.* Hamden, Conn.: Archon Books, 1963.

Schlesinger, Arthur M., Jr. *A Thousand Days: John F. Kennedy in the White House.* Boston: Houghton Mifflin, 1965.

Schlesinger, James R. *The Political Economy of National Security: A Study of the Economic Aspects of the Contemporary Power Struggle.* New York: Praeger, 1960.

Schmitter, Philippe C. "Still the Century of Corporatism?" In *The New Corporatism,* edited by Frederick Pike. South Bend, Ind.: University of Notre Dame Press, 1974.

Shaffer, Edward H. *The Oil Import Program of the United States: An Evaluation.* New York: Praeger, 1968.

Sharp, Mitchell. "Canada's Independence and U.S. Domination." In *U.S.-Canadian Economic Relations: Next Step?,* edited by Edward R. Fried and Philip H. Trezise. Washington, D.C.: Brookings Institution, 1984.

Shearer, Ronald A. "Study 1. The Economy of British Columbia." In *Trade Liberalization and a Regional Economy: Studies of the Impact of Free Trade on British Columbia,* edited by Ronald A. Shearer, John H. Young, and Gordon R. Munro. *Regional and Adjustment Aspects of Trade Liberalization,* edited by Edward English. Toronto: University of Toronto Press, 1973.

Shonfield, Andrew. "International Economic Relations of the Western World: An Overall View." In *International Economic Relations of the Western World, 1959–1971. Vol. 1: Politics of Trade.* London: Oxford University Press, 1976.

Shutt, Harry. *The Myth of Free Trade: Patterns of Protectionism Since 1945.* Oxford: Basil Blackwell, 1985.

Snyder, Richard C., H. W. Bruck, and Burton Sapin. *Foreign Policy Decision-Making: An Approach to the Study of International Politics.* Glencoe, Ill.: Free Press of Glencoe, 1962.

Solomon, Robert. *The International Monetary System, 1945–1981.* New York: Harper and Row, 1982.

Sorensen, Theodore C. *Kennedy.* New York: Harper and Row, 1965.

Sorensen, Vernon L. "Contradictions in U.S. Trade Policy." In *U.S. Trade Policy and Agricultural Exports,* edited by Iowa State University Center for Agricultural and Rural Development. Ames: Iowa State University Press, 1973.

Soth, Lauren K. "Farm Policy, Foreign Policy, and Farm Opinion." In *Agricultural Policy, Politics, and the Public Interest,* edited by Charles M. Hardin. Annals of the American Academy of Political and Social Science. Philadelphia: American Academy of Political and Social Science, 1960.

Spaak, Paul-Henri. *The Continuing Battle: Memoirs of a European, 1936–1966.* London: Weidenfeld and Nicolson, 1971.

Spanier, John. *American Foreign Policy Since World War II.* 9th ed. New York: Holt, Rinehart, and Winston, 1983.

Spero, Joan Endelman. *The Politics of International Economic Relations.* 3d ed. New York: St. Martin's Press, 1985.

Steel, Ronald. *U.S. Foreign Trade Policy.* New York: H. W. Wilson, 1962.

Stein, Herbert. *Presidential Economics: The Making of Economic Policy From Roosevelt to Reagan and Beyond.* New York: Simon and Schuster, 1985.

Stein, Leslie. *Trade and Structural Change.* London: Croom Helm, 1984.

Strackbein, O. R. *American Enterprise and Foreign Trade.* Washington, D.C.: Public Affairs Press, 1965.

Szymanski, Albert. *The Logic of Imperialism.* New York: Praeger, 1981.

Taber, George M. *Patterns and Prospects of Common Market Trade.* London: Peter Owen, 1974.

Talbot, Ross B. *The Chicken War: An International Trade Conflict Between the United States and the European Economic Community, 1961–1964.* Ames: Iowa State University Press, 1978.

Talbot, Ross B. "Effect of Domestic Political Groups and Forces in U.S. Trade Policy." In *U.S. Trade Policy and Agricultural Exports,* edited by Iowa State University Center for Agricultural and Rural Development. Ames: Iowa State University Press, 1973.

Talbot, Ross B., and Hadwiger, Don F. *The Policy Process in American Agriculture.* San Francisco: Chandler, 1968.

Taylor, Graham D., and Patricia E. Sudnik. *DuPont and the International Chemical Industry.* Boston: Twayne, 1984.

Thompson, William R. "The World-Economy, the Long Cycle, and the Question of World-System Time." In *Foreign Policy and the Modern World-System,* edited by Pat McGowan and Charles W. Kegley, Jr. Beverly Hills: Sage, 1983.

Toyne, Brian, Jeffrey S. Arpan, Andy Barnett, et al. *The Global Textile Industry.* London: Allen and Unwin, 1984.

Truman, Harry S. *Memoirs: Years of Trial and Hope.* Vol. 2. Garden City, N.Y.: Doubleday, 1956.

Tugwell, Franklin. *The Politics of Oil in Venezuela.* Stanford: Stanford University Press, 1975.

Tuttle, Frank W., and Joseph M. Perry. *An Economic History of the United States.* Cincinnati: South-Western, 1970.

Uri, Pierre. *Partnership for Progress: A Program for Transatlantic Action.* New York: Harper and Row, 1963.

Vaughan, Richard. *Twentieth-Century Europe: Paths to Unity.* London: Croom Helm, 1979.

Walker, Stephen G., and Pat McGowan. "U.S. Foreign Economic Policy Formation: Neo-Marxist and Neopluralist Perspectives." In *America in a Changing World Political Economy,* edited by William P. Avery and David P. Rapkin. New York: Longman, 1982.

Wallerstein, Immanuel. *The Capitalist World Economy.* New York: Cambridge University Press, 1978.

Wallerstein, Immanuel. *Modern World System II.* New York: Academic Press, 1974–1980.

Wallerstein, Immanuel. *The Politics of the World-Economy: The States, the Movements, and the Civilizations.* Cambridge: Cambridge University Press, 1984.

Walter, Ingo. *The European Common Market: Growth and Patterns of Trade and Production.* New York: Praeger, 1967.

Walton, Gary M., and Ross M. Robertson. *History of the American Economy.* 5th ed. New York: Harcourt, Brace, Jovanovich, 1983.

Warley, T. K. "Western Trade in Agricultural Products." In *International Economic Relations of the Western World, 1959–1971. Vol. 1: Politics of Trade.* London: Oxford University Press, 1976.

Wasserman, Max J., Charles W. Hultman, and Russell F. Moore. *The Common Market and American Business.* New York: Simmons-Boardman, 1964.

White, Eric Wyndham. "Stimulating Worldwide Trade." In *Building the American-European Market: Planning for the 1970s,* edited by Gene E. Bradley. Homewood, Ill.: Dow Jones-Irwin, 1967.

White, Theodore H. *The Making of the President, 1960.* New York: Pocket Books, 1962.

Wilcox, Clair. *A Charter for World Trade.* New York: Macmillan, 1949.

Wilkins, Mira. *The Maturing of Multinational Enterprise: American Business Abroad from 1914 to 1970.* Cambridge, Mass.: Harvard University Press, 1974.

Wilkinson, B. W. *Canada's International Trade: An Analysis of Recent Trends and Patterns.* Quebec: Canadian Trade Committee, Private Planning Association of Canada, February 1968.

Williams, William A. *The Tragedy of American Diplomacy.* Rev. ed. New York: Dell, 1972.

Willis, Roy F. *France, Germany, and the New Europe, 1945–1967.* Rev. ed. London: Oxford University Press, 1968.

Wolfe, Alan. *America's Impasse: The Rise and Fall of the Politics of Growth.* New York: Pantheon, 1981.

Wolfers, Arnold. "Integration in the West: The Conflict of Perspectives." In *The Atlantic Community: Progress and Prospect,* edited by Francis O. Wilcox and H. Field Haviland, Jr. New York: Praeger, 1964.

Wonnacott, Paul. *The United States and Canada: The Quest for Free Trade: An Examination of Selected Issues.* Washington, D.C.: Institute for International Economics, March 1987.

Woods, Randall Bennett. *A Changing of the Guard: Anglo-American Relations, 1941–1946.* Chapel Hill: University of North Carolina Press, 1990.

Yeager, Leland B., and David G. Tuerck. *Trade Policy and the Price System.* Scranton, Pa.: International Textbook, 1966.

Yoffie, David B. *Power and Protectionism: Strategies of the Newly Industrializing Countries.* New York: Columbia University Press, 1983.

Young, John H. "Study 3. The Tradition Export Industries." In *Trade Liberalization and a Regional Economy: Studies of the Impact of Free Trade on British Columbia,* edited by Ronald A. Shearer, John H. Young, and Gordon R. Munro. In *Regional and Adjustment Aspects of Trade Liberalization,* edited by Edward English. Toronto: University of Toronto Press, 1973.

Dissertations and Other Published Sources

Barrie, Robert W. "Congress and the Executive: The Making of U.S. Foreign Trade Policy." Ph.D. dissertation, University of Minnesota, 1968.

Chamber of Commerce of the United States. *The Impact of the Common Market on the American Economy.* Washington, D.C.: U.S. Chamber of Commerce, 1962.

Committee for Economic Development. *A New Trade Policy for the United States.* Washington, D.C.: CED, 1962.

Goldstein, Judith L. "A Re-examination of American Trade Policy: An Inquiry into the Causes of Protectionism." Ph.D. dissertation, UCLA, 1983.

Harris, William George. "The Impact of the Petroleum Export Industry on the Pattern of Venezuelan Economic Development." Ph.D. dissertation, University of Oregon, 1967.

Jadlow, Janice Wickstead. "Trade Liberalization in the Chemical Industry: The Impact on the United States." Ph.D. dissertation, Oklahoma State University, 1977.

National Association of Manufacturers. *Industry Believes, 1962: Policies on Current Problems as Adopted by the Board.* New York: NAM, 1962.

Valdez, Magin A. "The Petroleum Policies of the Venezuelan Government." Ph.D. dissertation, New York University, 1971.

Young, Shik Chun. "The GATT's Long-Term Cotton Textile Arrangement and Hong Kong's Cotton Textile Trade." Ph.D. dissertation, Washington State University, 1969.

INDEX

Access guarantees, *see* International
Grains Agreement
Acheson, Dean, 225
Adenauer, Konrad, 28, 70; on EEC,
160; on poultry trade, 137; signs
Franco-German treaty, 161
Adjustment assistance: farmers' view
of, 139; embraced by Kennedy, 39;
and labor's view of, 141, 143, 174,
250; under TEA, 69, 282*n*46
AFL-CIO, 66–67; on adjustment assistance petitions, 174; on GSP, 205;
on TEA, 141–142
Agricultural Adjustment Act (Section
22), 35; to aid lumber industry, 92
Agriculture: at Kennedy Round, 170–
173, 234–236, 237–239, 244–245
Agriculture, EEC: and British, 57; and
EFTA, 61; and internal organization, 167, 172, 182, 221–223; offers tabled at Kennedy Round, 223–
224; *see also* Common Agricultural
Policy
Agriculture, U.S.: domestic problems,
34, 61; exports, 134–135, 238–
239; exports and payments deficit,
61–62; on IGA, 234; imports, 35;
view of Kennedy Round, 174, 182–
184, 238–240; view of TEA, 139–
140, 249
Aid, foreign, 2–3, 206; in food, 220,
235, 237

Albert, Carl, 77, 121
Alliance for Progress, 65, 106, 205
Alliance, Western, 2, 6, 229, 254–255;
and Congress, 152–154; and
Kennedy Round, 231; and U.S.
trade policy, 45–46, 65, 242,
258
Alphand, Hervé, 182
Aluminum, 218, 225, 328*n*37
Amalgamated Clothing Workers of
America, 79
American Cotton Manufacturers Insti-
tute (ACMI), 76, 80, 86, 98
American Farm Bureau: on chickens,
136; on Kennedy Round, 184, 224,
239; on TEA, 139–140
American selling price (ASP), 147; and
découpage, 227–228; at Dillon
Round, 149; industry reaction to at
Kennedy Round, 239; as Kennedy
Round issue, 169, 175, 182, 185,
226–228, 233–234; retained by
Congress, 237, 241; retained by
Kennedy, 151
Anti-Dumping Code, 236; *see also*
Dumping
Area Redevelopment Act, 39, 42; for
lumber industry, 90
Associated Overseas Countries
(AOCs), 161, 193–194, 200, 208,
212–213, 257; *see also* Third
World

IGA, 220, 235; at Kennedy Round,
164–165; and lumber, 30, 100; and
oil trade, 104, 107, 115–118, 128,
252; and textiles, 81; and trade surplus, 253; and trade with U.S., 100,
129, 258; *see also* British Columbia;
Lumber; Oil
Capehart, Homer, 123
Carpet: tariff hike, 119
Chamber of Commerce, U.S.: on TEA,
144–145, 157; on GSP, 205
Chan, Steve, 191
Chase-Dunn, Christopher, 9, 262*n*3
Chemicals: and congressmen on TEA,
151–152; industry conditions, 147;
industry on glass and carpet tariff
hike, 124; and industry opinions on
TEA, 149–150, 157, 249, 308*n*53;
makers against Kennedy, 148; talks
at Kennedy Round, 218, 226–228,
233–234, 236; trade at Dillon
Round, 64, 148–149; trade history,
147–148; *see also* American selling
price
Chicken: exports and CAP, 135–138,
157; war, 137–139, 224, 252
China, People's Republic of, 83
Civil rights, 77, 99, 176
Class conflict theory, 4, 14; criticized,
249–251, 255, 258; and external
inputs, 6–8, 254; *see also* Neocorporatism
Clayton, William, 64–65, 131
Coal, 104; and Congress, 110, 118,
126; industry conditions, 108–109;
states, 295*n*13
Cold war, *see* Defense
Command Group, Kennedy Round,
see Bator, Francis
Commercial services, 133
Committee for Economic Develop-
ment, 145
Committee for a National Trade Policy
(CNTP): on lumber, 96; promotes
exports, 131–132, 145–146, 157,
249
Common Agricultural Policy (CAP):

and chicken war, 135–138; created,
25–26, 60; at Dillon Round, 61–
63; effect on U.S. exports, 138–139,
256; at Kennedy Round, 164, 170–
173, 182, 224, 234, 238, 257; in
1964 election, 176; and West Germany, 167; *see also* Agriculture
Common Market, *see* European Economic Community
Commonwealth, United Kingdom, 53,
56, 58, 68, 198, 278*n*16
Comparative advantage, 5; in agriculture, 62; of America, 10, 243, 255;
in chemicals, 151; statist view of,
8–9
Congress: influence of 13–15; and
protectionism, 35–36; *see also*
Trade Expansion Act; Kennedy
Round
Connor, John, 210
Conte, Silvio, 111
Cooley, Harold, 136
Costigliola, Frank, 186
Cotton textiles: influence of, 76–78;
and imports in 1950s, 35, 75; indus-
try conditions, 75–76; and Kennedy
Round exceptions, 184–185; and
seven-point program, 79, 87, 98,
252, 287*n*32; and Third World at
Kennedy Round, 208–212; *see also*
Long-Term Cotton Textile Arrange-
ment; Short-Term Cotton Textile
Arrangement
Cumings, Bruce, 4, 262*n*5
Currency convertibility, European 24,
32–33, 51
Curtis, Thomas, 87, 316*n*38; on Ken-
nedy Round, 175, 231, 242

Dahl, Robert, 144
Daley, Richard, 176
Darby, Phillip, 215
Découpage, *see* American selling price
Defense: and balance-of-payments, 33,
187; and Europe, 28, 188; as ratio-
nale for TEA, 71, 152–154, 250;
spending, 1; and trade, 9, 23, 64–

Kennedy, John F. (*Continued*)
U.S. trade, 93; and commitment to textile industry, 75, 88–89; and Congress, 73–74; criticizes Eisenhower policies, 32–34; as Democratic party nominee, 43–45; discusses chickens, 137–138; on Europe and EEC, 41–42; explains tariff hike, 125; and fair trade, 126–129; and foreign policy in 1961, 70–71; goals and expectations of, 246–247, 252–259; and Grand Design, 153–154; and individual level of analysis, 248–249 and investment policy, 148; on Japan, 83; and Kerr, 113–115; as a liberal trader, 38–44; links trade to foreign policy, 132–133; misjudges de Gaulle, 161; and missile gap, 47–48; on 1958 RTA, 42–43; and 1964 election, 176; and political dealings, 84, 98–99, 102, 125–126; on potential glass tariff hike and foreign affairs, 120; presents TEA, 66–67; promotes exports, 131–133; protectionist views of 37–38; and relations with business, 145; on STR and foreign policy, 163; supports New Deal, 38, 44, 248; tables tariff offers, 175; on the Third World, 41–42, 112, 191, 215; and view of farm trade, 61–63; visits Venezuela, 107

Kennedy, Joseph, 39–40

Kennedy, Paul, 259

Kennedy Round, 18; and American power, 242–245; applauded, 236; and balance-of-payments deficit of U.S., 244; and Congress, 174–175, 231; congressional delegation to, 175, 316n38; in "crisis" period, 232–235; domestic reaction to, 239–241, 253; and EEC crisis, 166–167; and lumber duty, 100; named in president's honor, 158–159; and results for core, 236–239, 242, 328n47; and results for Third World, 212–213; and results for U.S., 236–239, 243–245; scope of, 163; and sector talks, 168, 232–234; and Third World, 207–213; and UNCTAD, 201, 206; and U.S. strategy, 163–166, 187; U.S. pessimism about, 231; and U.S. warning list of withdrawals, 231–232

Kerr, Robert: and glass, 121; and Johnson, 178; on oil, 113–116, 126, 298n32

Keynesianism, *see* Productionism

Khrushchev, Nikita, 215; *see also* Soviet Union

Kilpatrick, Carroll, 99

Kindleberger, Charles, 38

Korea, 80

Kraft, Joseph, 70–71, 260

Krasner, Stephen, 145, 259

Labor: and TEA, 140–143, 249–250; turns protectionist, 241

Lamont, Thomas, 48

Lane, Thomas, 111

Langen, Odin, 240

Latin America, 53, 62, 106, 254; and AOCs, 193–194; and Kennedy Round, 244; and TEA, 68; and trade preferences, 204–205

Less-developed countries (LDCs), *see* Third World

Linear tariff reduction, 63–64, 67, 149; at Kennedy Round, 184

Lindeen, James, 145

Lindsay, John, 154

Long, Russell: on base closings, 125–126; criticizes U.S. trade policy of 1960s, 247; on Kennedy Round, 224–225, 231; on oil, 298n32; on quotas, 240

Long-Term Cotton Textile Arrangement (LTA): created, 84–85; renewed at Kennedy Round, 208–213, 215, 218, 225, 324n50; results of, 100–101, 253; as viewed by textile industry, 239

Lowi, Theodore, 127